CANAANITE MYTHS
AND LEGENDS

THE TABLET *UGARITICA V* No. 7 (see page 138)
(by kind permission of Mons. Claude Schaeffer-Forrer)

CANAANITE MYTHS AND LEGENDS

BY

J. C. L. GIBSON
Reader in Hebrew and Semitic Languages
New College, Edinburgh

Originally edited by G. R. Driver, F.B.A., and published in the
series Old Testament Studies under the auspices of the
Society for Old Testament Study

T. & T. CLARK LTD.
38 GEORGE STREET: EDINBURGH

PREFACE TO FIRST EDITION

THIS edition of Canaanite myths and legends from Ugarit (now Râs-aš-Šamrah) on the Syrian coast is based on lectures delivered over the last ten years and is now published in the hope of making these interesting but difficult texts accessible in convenient form to students of the Old Testament and the Semitic languages, of mythology and religion.

No one can occupy himself with these texts without acknowledging his debt to the distinguished pioneers without whom his work could not have even been begun: these are Dr. C. F. A. Schaeffer, who was in charge of the excavations which so successfully recovered the tablets containing them from the soil in which they had lain hidden for some 3500 years; Mons. C. Virolleaud, whose admirably prompt and accurate copies made them available for study, and Prof. E. Dhorme and Prof. H. Bauer, who shared with him the honour of finding the key to the decipherment of the new dialect or language in which these texts were written. That much of their early work has been left behind and that other scholars, notably Prof. H. L. Ginsberg, Dr. T. H. Gaster and Dr. C. H. Gordon, to whom all students of these texts are also greatly indebted, have taken over the task of interpretation, does not detract from the honour of the pioneers. Wherever possible the debt owed to all these and other workers in this field is indicated in the notes and in the glossary.

Much labour of great value has already been expended on these texts; but much work still remains to be done on them, and I hope that the present edition may stimulate others to take up the study of them.

קנאת סופרים תרבה חכמה

The bibliography is not intended to be exhaustive; in fact, it contains the titles almost exclusively of books and articles which have been of any use in the preparation of the present work. The glossary will be found to contain a certain number of alternative words, readings and interpretations; these are added because finality has not yet been reached on innumerable points of interpretation and the decision in these cases may still be left to the reader. In conclusion, my thanks are due to the Old Testament Society and the Trustees of the Pusey and Ellerton Fund at Oxford for generous contributions towards the cost of publication. I wish also to acknowledge my debt to the compositors, who have set up this complicated piece of printing, and the readers, who seem to have checked both printing and references, with a care which is characteristic of all work done by the University Press.

Magdalen College, Oxford   G. R. DRIVER
31 *March*, 1955

PREFACE TO SECOND EDITION

SIR GODFREY DRIVER intended to produce a second edition of *Canaanite Myths and Legends* after retiring from his Chair at Oxford, but the pressure of his commitments with the New English Bible and as time passed his own failing health prevented him from carrying the project beyond a preliminary stage. He asked me some years ago to undertake the task for him, generously conveying to me his annotated copy of the first edition along with several folders of other notes which he had gathered, including contributions received from a number of correspondents. We planned the broad outlines of the revision together and agreed upon most of the changes in format that are incorporated in it, notably (1) the adoption of Mlle. Herdner's system of enumerating the tables, (2) the inclusion in the main body of the work of only the longer and better preserved texts from the first edition, with the smaller and more fragmentary texts being relegated to an Appendix, (3) the inclusion in this Appendix of some of the more important texts discovered or published since the appearance of the first edition, (4) the setting out of the main tablets as far as possible in poetic parallelism, (5) the printing in full of the titles in the Bibliography, and (6) the shortening of the entries in the Glossary and their rearrangement in a more conventional sequence. It was left to me, however, to work out the details, using Sir Godfrey's notes and correspondence as a basis but giving due weight to new studies of the subject which appeared too late to be considered by him. Sir Godfrey consented to read and criticize portions of the revision as I completed them and in the event saw before his death in 1975 initial drafts of around two-thirds of it. Needless to say, I benefited immensely from the many shrewd and searching comments he made upon these; but I alone am answerable for the revision as it is now presented to the public, and its defects should therefore be laid at my door and not his. I hope that it will be judged to repay the confidence he showed in me.

On two matters of some importance Sir Godfrey and I failed to reach accord. I could not share his firm opinions on certain features of Ugaritic grammar and had to ask that the section entitled 'Observations on Philology and Grammar' be omitted from this edition; the most I felt I could attempt (apart from a short Note on Phonology) was to give guidance in the footnotes on possible alternative solutions (including of course Sir Godfrey's) to some of the more troublesome problems. He on the other hand disapproved of the attention I pay in the Introduction and footnotes to listing and sometimes commenting more fully on parallels between the Ugaritic texts and the Hebrew Bible. His scepticism about the propriety of such comparisons is well known and has often been shown to be justified; but since a large number, perhaps the majority, of those who work in the Ugaritic field are also students of the Bible, comparisons will inevitably continue to be made, and it seemed to me wiser to recognize this and, as far as space permitted, to close with the issues involved rather than to play safe by ignoring them. Sir Godfrey and I had several arguments over these two matters and I wish to place on record my deep appreciation of his magnanimity in insisting that I as editor should have the final decision.

One small improvement I would have liked to introduce was in Ugaritic transliterations to substitute for the symbols $\check{z}$ and $\underset{\sim}{z}$ of the first edition appropriate adaptations of the phonetically more accurate symbols $\underline{d}$ and $\underline{t}$, but for typographical reasons this was not possible.

On several occasions I consulted other scholars about problems connected with the revision and I wish to thank those who gave me of their valuable time, particularly Professors John Gray of Aberdeen and Édouard Lipiński of Louvain, and Dr. Wilfred Watson, formerly Research Fellow of Edinburgh University. I am grateful to Mr. William Johnstone of Aberdeen University for letting me see copies of two articles by him which are not yet in print. Of Sir Godfrey's many correspondents I should like especially to mention Professor John Emerton of Cambridge. Finally I am indebted to the senior class in Hebrew and Old Testament Studies at Edinburgh during the academic session 1975–1976, who were subjected to large sections of this edition in draft form and from whose reactions I drew many helpful insights; and to Mr. Kenneth Aitken, a member of that class, who also assisted me with the checking of references.

New College, Edinburgh   J. C. L. GIBSON
September, 1976

CONTENTS

PREFACE TO FIRST EDITION   v
PREFACE TO SECOND EDITION   vii
CONCORDANCE OF TABLETS   xi
SELECT BIBLIOGRAPHY   xiii

INTRODUCTION

A. THE DISCOVERY OF THE TABLETS   1
B. ANALYSIS AND INTERPRETATION OF THE TEXTS   2
    1. Baal and Yam   2
    2. The Palace of Baal   8
    3. Baal and Mot   14
    4. Keret   19
    5. Aqhat   23
    6. Shachar and Shalim and the Gracious Gods   28
    7. Nikkal and the Kotharat   30
    8. The Texts in the Appendix (Brief Notes)   31

TRANSLITERATION AND TRANSLATION OF THE TEXTS

    1. Baal and Yam   37
    2. The Palace of Baal   46
    3. Baal and Mot   68
    4. Keret   82
    5. Aqhat   103
    6. Shachar and Shalim and the Gracious Gods   123
    7. Nikkal and the Kotharat   128
    8. Appendix: Fragmentary and Recently Published Texts
       (Transliteration Only)   130

NOTE ON THE PHONOLOGY OF UGARITIC   140
GLOSSARY   141
BIBLICAL AND OTHER REFERENCES   161
ADDENDA   165
TABLE OF UGARITIC SIGNS   168

CONCORDANCE OF TABLETS

THE table below lists all the Ugaritic tablets and fragments identified as mythological in content. It gives in parallel columns (1) the page numbers of the texts in the order in which they appear in this edition; (2) the sigla employed to identify the tablets by Mlle. Herdner in the official edition (*CTA*); (3) Mons. Virolleaud's sigla in the primary editions (including Professor Eissfeldt's additions to his system); and (4) Dr. Gordon's sigla in the widely used *Ugaritic Textbook* (previously *Handbook* and *Manual*). In this edition Mlle. Herdner's sigla are used as far as they reach; texts published subsequently are referred to by their numbers in the relevant volumes of *PRU* and *Ugaritica* (thus *PRU* II no. 3; *Ugaritica* V no. 3) and in the case of a single tablet separately issued (RS 22.225) by its archaeological campaign number.

THE MAIN TABLETS

Page	Herdner	Virolleaud/Eissfeldt	Gordon
39	1 iv	VI AB iv	'nt pl. X iv
37, 40	2 iii,i,iv	III AB,C,B,A	129,137,68
46	3	V AB	'nt
55	4	II AB	51
68	5	I* AB	67
74	6	I AB	62obv.+49+62rev.
82	14	I K	Krt
90	15	III K	128
94	16	II K	125,126,127
103	17	II D	2 Aqht
110	18	III D	3 Aqht
113	19	I D	1 Aqht
123	23	SS	52
128	24	NK	77

THE TEXTS IN THE APPENDIX

Page	Herdner	Virolleaud/Eissfeldt	Gordon
130	1 ii,iii,v	VI AB ii,iii,v	'nt pls. IX,X ii, iii, v
131	7 I,II	V AB var.A,B	130,131
132	8	II AB var.	51 fragment

Page	Herdner	Virolleaud/Eissfeldt	Gordon
132	10	IV AB	76
133	11	IV AB III*	132
134	12	BH	75
135	20	IV D then I Rp	121 (4 Aqht)
135	21	II Rp	122
136	22	III Rp	123,124
136	—	*PRU* II no. 3 (VI MF)	1003
137	—	RS 22.225	—
		Ugaritica V	
137	—	no. 1 (RS 24.258)	601
137	—	no. 2 (RS 24.252)	602
138	—	no. 3 (RS 24.245)	603
138	—	no. 4 (RS 24.293)	604
138	—	no. 7 (RS 24.244)	607

MYTHOLOGICAL FRAGMENTS NOT INCLUDED

—	9	I MF	133
—	13	6	6
—	25	III MF	136
—	26	II MF	135
—	27	8	8
—	28	—	—
—	—	*PRU* II no. 1 (IV MF)	1001
—	—	no. 2 (V MF)	1002
—	—	*PRU* V no. 1	2001
—	—	no. 2	2002
—	—	no. 3	2003
		Ugaritica V	
—	—	no. 5 (RS 24.257)	605
—	—	no. 6 (RS 24.272)	606
—	—	no. 8 (RS 24.251)	608

Note:—For the sigla used in a recent edition of the texts by Dietrich, Loretz and Sanmartin (1976) see Addenda.

SELECT BIBLIOGRAPHY

The following abbreviations are used:

ANET = J. B. Pritchard (ed.), *Ancient Near Eastern Texts relating to the Old Testament* (Princeton 1950) [2nd edit. (1955)].—*BASOR* = *Bulletin of the American Schools of Oriental Research.*—*CRAIBL* = *Comptes rendus de l'Académie des Inscriptions et Belles Lettres.*—*CTA* = Andrée Herdner, *Corpus des tablettes en cunéiformes alphabétiques découvertes à Ras Shamra-Ugarit de 1929 à 1939* (Paris 1963).—*IEJ* = *Israel Exploration Journal.*—*JANES* = *The Journal of the Ancient Near Eastern Society of Columbia University.*—*JAOS* = *Journal of the American Oriental Society.*—*JBL* = *Journal of Biblical Literatures.*—*JNES* = *Journal of Near Eastern Studies.*—*JNWSL* = *Journal of Northwest Semitic Languages.*—*JSS* = *Journal of Semitic Studies.*—*MIO* = *Mitteilungen des Instituts für Orientforschung.*—*MRS* = *Mission de Ras Shamra* (Paris 1936ff.).—*PRU* = *Le Palais royal d'Ugarit* (Paris 1955ff.).—*RHR* = *Revue de l'histoire des religions.*—*UF* = *Ugarit-Forschungen.*—*VT* = *Vetus Testamentum.*—*ZAW* = *Zeitschrift für die alttestamentliche Wissenschaft.*

1. Official Publications of Texts (usually with photographic plates):

Andrée Herdner, *CTA* (= *MRS* X) (Paris 1963)
[*Note*: For some corrections see W. J. Horwitz, 'Discrepancies in an important publication of Ugarit', *UF* 4 (1972), 47–52]
J. Nougayrol, E. Laroche, Ch. Virolleaud, C. F. A. Schaeffer, *Ugaritica V: Nouveaux textes accadiens, hourrites et ugaritiques des archives et bibliothèques privées d'Ugarit* (= *MRS* XVI) (Paris 1968) [handcopies only]
Ch. Virolleaud, *La légende phénicienne de Danel, texte cunéiforme alphabétique* (= *MRS* I) (Paris 1936)
—— *La légende de Kéret roi des Sidoniens d'après une tablette de Ras Shamra* (= *MRS* II) (Paris 1936)
—— *La déesse Anat: Poème de Ras Shamra, publié, traduit et commenté* (= *MRS* IV) (Paris 1938)
—— *PRU* II, *Textes alphabétiques des archives est, ouest et centrales* (= *MRS* VII) (Paris 1957)
—— *PRU* V, *Textes alphabétiques des archives sud, sud-ouest et du petit-palais* (= *MRS* XI) (Paris 1965)

2. Primary editions (by Ch. Virolleaud unless otherwise stated; usually with handcopies):

(a) The Main Tablets:

1 iv in *La déesse Anat* (Paris 1938), 91–100

2 iii in *Syria* 24 (1944–1945), 1–12
2 i in C. H. Gordon, *Ugaritic Handbook* (Rome 1947), 167–168
2 iv in *Syria* 16 (1935), 29–45
3 A in *Syria* 17 (1936), 335–345
3 B in *Syria* 18 (1937), 85–102
3 C in *Syria* 18 (1937), 256–270
3 D, E, F in *La déesse Anat* (Paris 1938), 43–90
4 in *Syria* 13 (1932), 113–163
5 in *Syria* 15 (1934), 305–356
6 (main portion) in *Syria* 12 (1931), 193–244
6 (small fragment) in *Syria* 15 (1934), 226–243
14 in *La légende de Kéret* (Paris 1936)
15 in *Syria* 23 (1942–1943), 137–172
16 in *Syria* 22 (1941), 105–136, 197–217; 23 (1942–1943), 1–20
17–19 in *La légende phénicienne de Danel* (Paris 1936)
23 in *Syria* 14 (1933), 128–151
24 in *Syria* 17 (1936), 209–228

(b) The Texts in the Appendix and the Fragments not included:

1 ii, iii, v (see above)
7 in *Syria* 24 (1944–1945), 12–14
8 in *Syria* 13 (1932), 158–159
9 in *Syria* 24 (1944–1945), 17–19
10 in *Syria* 17 (1936), 150–173
11 in *Syria* 24 (1944–1945), 14–17
12 in *Syria* 16 (1935), 247–266
13 in *Syria* 10 (1929), pl. LXVI [cuneiform text only]
20–22 in *Syria* 22 (1941), 1–30 (see also for **20** *La légende phénicienne de Danel*, 228–230)
25 in *Syria* 24 (1944–1945), 22–23
26 in *Syria* 24 (1944–1945), 21–22
27 in *Syria* 10 (1929), pl. LXVII [cuneiform text only]
28 in *CTA*, p. 107
PRU II nos. 1–3, ibid., pp. 3–12 [plate of no. 1]
PRU V nos. 1–3, ibid., pp. 3–6
RS 22.225 in *CRAIBL*, 1960, 180–186 [plate]
Ugaritica V (Paris 1968) nos. 1–8, ibid., pp. 545–580
[*Note*: for some corrections see L. R. Fisher, 'New readings for the Ugaritic texts in Ugaritica V', *UF* 3 (1971), 356]

3. Other Editions of the Main Texts:

H. Bauer, *Die alphabetischen Keilschrifttexte von Ras Schamra* (Berlin 1936)
U. Cassuto, *Ha-Elah 'Anat* = *The Goddess Anath: Canaanite Epics of the Patriarchal Age* [in Hebrew] (Jerusalem 1951). Engl. transl. (Jerusalem 1971) [plates]
M. Dietrich and others (1976): see Addenda

P. Fronzaroli, *Leggenda di Aqhat: Testo ugaritico* (Florence 1955)

H. L. Ginsberg, *Kitvey Ugarit = The Ugaritic Texts* [in Hebrew] (Jerusalem 1936)

—— *The Legend of King Keret: A Canaanite Epic of the Bronze Age* (New Haven 1946)

C. H. Gordon, *Ugaritic Textbook: Texts in Transliteration, Cuneiform Selections, Glossary, Grammar* (Rome 1965) with *Supplement* (1967) [earlier editions were entitled *Handbook* (1947) and *Manual* (1955)]

J. Gray, *The KRT Text in the Literature of Ras Shamra: A Social Myth of Ancient Canaan*, 2nd edit. (Leiden 1964)

W. Hermann, *Yariḫ und Nikkal und der Preis der Kuṭarāt-Göttinnen* (Berlin 1968)

R. Largement, *La naissance de l'aurore: Poème mythologique de Ras Shamra-Ugarit* (Gembloux-Louvain 1949)

J. A. Montgomery and Z. S. Harris, *The Ras Shamra Mythological Texts* (Philadelphia 1935)

Z. Rin and Sh. Rin, *Aliloth ha-Elim = Acts of the Gods: The Ugarit Epic Poetry* [in Hebrew] (Jerusalem 1968)

P. Xella, *Il mito di šḥr e šlm: Saggio sulla mitologia ugaritica* (Rome 1973)

4. Translations and Major Textual Studies:

J. Aistleitner, *Mythologische und kultische Texte aus Ras Schamra* (Budapest 1959)

A. Caquot, M. Sznycer, and Andrée Herdner, *Textes Ougaritiques*, I, *Mythes et légendes* (Paris 1974)

R. Dussaud, *Les découvertes de Ras Shamra (Ugarit) et l'Ancien Testament*, 2e éd. (Paris 1941)

T. H. Gaster, *Thespis: Ritual, Myth and Drama in the Ancient Near East*, 2nd edit. (New York 1961)

H. L. Ginsberg, 'Ugaritic myths, epics and legends' in *ANET*, 129–155

C. H. Gordon, *Ugaritic Literature* (Rome 1949)

—— *Ugarit and Minoan Crete* (New York 1966), 40–143

J. Gray, *The Legacy of Canaan: The Ras Shamra Texts and their Relevance to the Old Testament*, 2nd edit. (Leiden 1965)

F. F. Hvidberg, *Graad og later = Weeping and Laughter in the Old Testament: A Study of Canaanite-Israelite Religion* (Copenhagen 1938). Engl. transl. and revision by F. Løkkegaard (Leiden 1962)

A. Jirku, *Kanaanäische Mythen und Epen aus Ras Schamra-Ugarit* (Gütersloh 1962)

J. C. de Moor, *The Seasonal Pattern in the Ugaritic Myth of Ba'lu according to the Version of Ilumilku* (Kevelaer/Neukirchen-Vluyn 1971)

J. Obermann, *Ugaritic Mythology: A Study of its Leading Motifs* (New Haven 1948)

P. J. van Zijl, *Baal: A Study of Texts in connexion with Baal in the Ugaritic Epics* (Kevelaer/Neukirchen-Vluyn 1972)

5. Studies on Specific Texts:

(a) Baal and Yam:

T. H. Gaster, 'The battle of the Rain and the Sea: An ancient Semitic nature-myth', *Iraq* 4 (1937), 21–32

H. L. Ginsberg, 'The victory of the Land-god over the Sea-god', *J. Pal. Or. Soc.* 15 (1935), 327–333

J. A. Montgomery, 'The conflict of Baal and the Waters', *JAOS* 55 (1935), 268–277

J. Obermann, 'How Baal destroyed a rival: A mythological incantation scene', *JAOS* 67 (1947), 195–208

A. van Selms, 'Yammu's dethronement by Ba'al', *UF* 2 (1970), 251–268

(b) The Palace of Baal:

J. Aistleitner, 'Die Anat-Texte aus Ras Schamra', *ZAW* 57 (1939), 193–211

W. F. Albright, 'Anath and the Dragon', *BASOR* 84 (1941), 14–17

—— 'The furniture of El in Canaanite mythology', *BASOR* 91 (1943), 39–44; 93 (1944), 23–25

J. Barr, 'Ugaritic and Hebrew ŠBM?', *JSS* 18 (1973), 17–39

G. A. Barton, 'The second liturgical poem from Ras Shamra', *JAOS* 55 (1935), 49–58

U. Cassuto, 'Il palazzo di Baal nella tavola II AB di Ras Shamra', *Orientalia* 7 (1938), 265–290; see also *JBL* 61 (1942), 51–56

F. E. Diest, 'A note on šḥrrt in the Ugaritic text 51 viii 22', *JNWSL* 1 (1971), 68–70

R. Dussaud, 'Les combats sanglants de 'Anat et le pouvoir universel de El', *RHR* 118 (1938), 133–169

O. Eissfeldt, 'Ugaritisches', *Z. deutsch. morg. Ges.* 98 (1944), 84–100

T. L. Fenton, 'Passages in Ugaritic discourse: Restorations and observations', *UF* 1 (1969), 199–200

T. H. Gaster 'Baal is risen: An ancient Hebrew passion-play from Ras Shamra-Ugarit', *Iraq* 6 (1939), 109–143

—— 'The furniture of El in Canaanite mythology', *BASOR* 93 (1944), 20–23

—— 'A king without a castle: Baal's appeal to Asherat', *BASOR* 101 (1946), 21–30

H. L. Ginsberg, 'Did Anath fight the Dragon?', *BASOR* 84 (1941), 12–14

—— 'Baal's two messengers', *BASOR* 95 (1944), 25–30

A. Goetze, 'Peace on earth', *BASOR* 93 (1944), 17–20

Andrée Herdner, 'Remarques sur *La déesse 'Anat*', *Rev. ét. sém.*, 1942–1945, 33–49

J. Hoftijzer, 'Two notes on the Ba'al cyclus', *UF* 4 (1972), 155–158

E. Lipiński, 'Banquet en l'honneur de Baal', *UF* 2 (1970), 75–88

—— 'Envoi d'un messager (V AB, F 7–11)', *Syria* 50

(1973), 35–37 [see also sect. (e)]

S. E. Loewenstamm, 'The muzzling of the Tannin in Ugaritic mythology', *IEJ* 9 (1959), 260–261

—— 'Anat's victory over the Tunnanu', *JSS* 20 (1975), 22–27

J. A. Montgomery, 'Notes on the mythological epic texts from Ras Shamra', *JAOS* 53 (1933), 97–123, 283–284; 54 (1934), 60–66

J. C. de Moor, 'Der *mdl* Baals im Ugaritischen', *ZAW* 78 (1966), 69–71

A. van Selms, 'A guest-room for Ilu and its furniture: An interpretation of *CTA* 4 i 30–44', *UF* 7 (1975), 469–476

(c) Baal and Mot:

W. F. Albright, 'The North-Canaanite epic of 'Al'eyân-Ba'al and Mot', *J. Pal. Or. Soc.* 12 (1932), 185–208

G. A. Barton, 'A North Syrian poem of the conquest of death', *JAOS* 52 (1932), 221–231

M. Cassuto, 'Baal and Mot in the Ugaritic texts', *IEJ* 12 (1962), 77–86

M. Dijkstra, 'Ba'lu and his antagonists: Some remarks on *CTA* 6 v 1–6', *JANES* 6 (1974), 59–68

J. A. Emerton, 'A difficult part of Mot's message to Baal in the Ugaritic texts (*CTA* 5 i 4–6)', *Austral. J. Bibl. Arch.* 2 (1972), 50–71

T. H. Gaster, 'The combat of Death and the Most High', *J. Royal As. Soc.*, 1932, 587–596; 1936, 225–235

H. L. Ginsberg, 'The rebellion and death of Ba'lu', *Orientalia* 5 (1936), 161–198

V. and I. R. Jacobs, 'The myth of Môt and Aleyan Ba'al', *Harvard Th. Rev.* 38 (1945), 77–109

S. E. Loewenstamm, 'The Ugaritic fertility myth: The result of a mistranslation', *IEJ* 12 (1962), 87–88

—— 'The killing of Mot in Ugaritic myth', *Orientalia* 41 (1972), 378–382

J. A. Montgomery (see under (b) above)

W. Schmidt, 'Baals Tod und Auferstehung', *Z. für Rel.-und Geiteswiss.* 15 (1963), 1–13

A. van Selms 'A systematic approach to *CTA* 5 i 1–8', *UF* 7 (1975), 477–482

P. L. Watson, 'The death of Death in the Ugaritic texts', *JAOS* 92 (1972), 60–64

(d) Keret:

J. Aistleitner, 'Die Keret Legende', *Theologia* 5 (1938), 1–8

M. C. Astour, 'A North Mesopotamian locale of the Keret epic', *UF* 5 (1973), 29–39

K. H. Bernhardt, 'Anmerkungen zur Interpretations des KRT-Textes aus Ras Schamra-Ugarit', *Wiss. Z. der Ernst Moritz Arndt-Univ. Griefswald, Ges. und Sprachw. Reihe* 5 (1955–1956), 101–121

J. A. Emerton, 'The meaning of the root *mzl* in Ugaritic', *JSS* 14 (1969), 22–33

I. Engnell, 'The text II K from Ras Shamra: A preliminary investigation', *Religion och Bibel*, 1944, 1–20

F. C. Fensham, 'Remarks on certain difficult passages in Keret', *JNWSL* 1 (1971), 11–22; 2 (1972), 37–52; 3 (1974), 26–34; 4 (1975), 11–21 [continuing]

R. Follet, 'Le Poème de Krt, mythe social?', *Biblica* 37 (1956), 341–348

T. H. Gaster, 'The Canaanite epic of Keret', *Jew. Qu. Rev.*, 1947, 285–293

H. Gottlieb, 'Ligklagen over Krt, II K, I-II', *Dansk teol. tidsskr.* 32 (1969), 88–105

J. C. Greenfield, 'Some glosses on the Keret epic', *Eretz Isr.* 9 (1969), 60–65

M. Lichtenstein, 'A note on the text of I Keret', *JANES* 2 (1970), 94–100

E. Lipiński, 'Le Bannissement de Yaṣṣib (II Keret vi 57–58)', *Syria* 50 (1973), 38–39

A. A. Merrill, 'The house of Keret: A study of the Keret Legend', *Svensk Exeg. Årsb.* 33 (1968), 5–17

D. Pardee, 'A note on the root *'tq* in *CTA* 16 i 2, 5', *UF* 5 (1973), 229–234

J. Pedersen, 'Die Krt Legende', *Berytus* 6 (1941), 63–105

G. A. Saliba, 'A cure for King Keret', *JAOS* 92 (1972), 107–110

H. Sauren, G. Kestemont, 'Keret roi de Ḥubur', *UF* 3 (1971), 181–221

J. F. A. Sawyer, J. Strange, 'Notes on the Keret text', *IEJ* 14 (1964), 96–98

W. G. E. Watson, 'A suppliant surprised (*CTA* 16 i 41–53)', *JANES* 8 (forthcoming)

(e) Aqhat:

W. F. Albright, 'The traditional home of the Syrian Daniel', *BASOR* 130 (1953), 26–27

J. Blau, S. E. Loewenstamm, 'Ugaritic *ṣly* "to curse" ' [in Hebrew], *Leshonenu* 35 (1970), 7–10

U. Cassuto, 'Daniel e le spighe: Un episodia della tavola I D di Ras Shamra', *Orientalia* 8 (1939), 238–243

—— 'Daniel et son fils dans la tablette II D de Ras Shamra', *R. ét. juives* 105 (1940), 125–131

M. Dijkstra, J. C. de Moor 'Problematic passages in the legend of Aqhâtu', *UF* 7 (1975), 171–215

H. H. P. Dressler, 'Is the bow of Aqhat a symbol of virility?', *UF* 7 (1975), 217–220

H. L. Ginsberg, 'The North-Canaanite myth of Anath and Aqhat', *BASOR* 97 (1945), 3–10; 98 (1945), 15–23

J. Gray, 'The Goren at the gate: Justice and the royal office in the Ugaritic text Aqht', *Pal. Expl. Qu.* 85 (1953), 118–123

L. E. Good, 'Two notes on Aqhat', *JBL* 77 (1958), 72–74

A. Herdner, 'La légende cananéenne d'Aqhat d'après les travaux récents', *Syria* 26 (1949), 1–16

W. Hermann, 'Das Todegeschick als Problem im Altisrael', *MIO* 16 (1972), 14–32

D. R. Hillers, 'The bow of Aqhat: The meaning of a mythological theme' in *Orient and Occident* (Gordon Festschrift) (Kevelaer/Neukirchen-Vluyn 1973), 71–80

J. Hoftijzer, 'A note on G 1083; *ištr* and related matters', *UF* 3 (1971), 361–364

E. Lipiński, 'SKN et SGN', *UF* 5 (1973), 191–206

J. A. Montgomery, 'The Danel text', *JAOS* 56 (1936), 440–445

J. C. de Moor, 'A note on *CTA* **19** (I Aqht) i 39–42', *UF* 6 (1974), 495–496

H.-P. Müller, 'Magisch-mantische Weisheit und die Gestalt Daniels', *UF* 1 (1969), 79–94

J. Obermann, *How Daniel was Blessed with a Son: An Incubation Scene in Ugaritic* (New Haven 1946)

S. Spiegel, 'Noah, Daniel and Job' in *Louis Ginzberg Jubilee Vol.*, Engl. sect. (New York 1955), 305–355

M. Tsevat, 'Traces of Hittite at the beginning of the Ugaritic epic of Aqhat', *UF* 3 (1971), 351–352

(f) **Shachar and Shalim and the Gracious Gods:**

W. F. Albright, 'The myth of the gracious gods', *J. Pal. Or. Soc.* 14 (1934), 133–140

J. Finkel, 'An interpretation of a Ugaritic viticultural poem', *Joshua Starr Memorial Vol.* (New York 1953), 29–58

T. H. Gaster, 'A Canaanite ritual drama: The Spring festival at Ugarit', *JAOS* 66 (1946), 49–76

H. L. Ginsberg, 'Notes on the birth of the gracious and beautiful gods', *J. Royal As. Soc.*, 1935, 45–72

G. Komoróczy, 'Zum mythologischen und literaturgeschichtlichen Hintergrund der ugaritischen Dichtung SS', *UF* 3 (1971), 75–80

H. Kosmala, 'Mot and the vine', *An. Swed. Th. Inst.* 3 (1964), 147–151

M. R. Lehmann, 'A new interpretation of the term ŠDMWT', *VT* 3 (1953), 361–371

J. A. Montgomery, 'The Ugaritic fantasia of the gracious and beautiful gods', *JAOS* 62 (1942), 49–51

J. C. de Moor, *New Year with Canaanites and Israelites* (Kampen 1972), II, 17ff.

D. T. Tsumura, 'A Ugaritic god *Mt-w-šr* and his two weapons', *UF* 6 (1974), 407–413

(g) **Nikkal and the Kotharat:**

J. Aistleitner, 'Die Nikkal-Hymne aus Ras Schamra', *Z. deutsch. morg. Ges.* 93 (1939), 52–59

T. H. Gaster, 'The Graces in Semitic folklore: A wedding song from Ras Shamra', *J. Royal As. Soc.*, 1938, 37–56

H. L. Ginsberg, 'A Hurrian myth in Semitic dress', *Orientalia* 8 (1939), 317–327

A. Goetze, 'The Nikkal poem from Ras Shamra', *JBL* 60 (1941), 353–374

Andrée Herdner, 'Ḫirḫibi et les noces de Yariḫ et de Nikkal dans la mythologie d'Ugarit', *Semitica* 2 (1949), 17–20

M. Lichtenstein, 'Psalm 68:7 revisited', *JANES* 4 (1972), 97–112

F. Løkkegaard, 'The Canaanite divine wetnurses', *Studia theologica* 10 (1956), 53–64

B. Margulis, 'The Kôšarôt/*ktrt*: Patroness-saints of women', *JANES* 4 (1972), 52–61 (with reply to Lichtenstein pp. 113–117)

M. Tsevat, 'The Ugaritic goddess Nikkal wịb', *JNES* 12 (1952), 61–62

J. W. Welch, 'Chiasmus in Ugaritic', *UF* 6 (1974), 421–436

(h) **The texts in the Appendix and texts not included:**

M. C. Astour, 'Un texte d'Ugarit récemment découvert et ses rapports avec l'origine des cultes bachiques grecs', *RHR* 164 (1963), 1–15 [RS 22.225]

——— 'Two Ugaritic serpent charms', *JNES* 27 (1968), 13–36 [*Ugaritica* V nos. 7, 8]

J. Blau, J. C. Greenfield, 'Ugaritic glosses', *BASOR* 200 (1970), 11–17 [*Ugaritica* V texts]

H. Cazelles, 'L'Hymne ugaritique à Anat', *Syria* 33 (1956), 49–57 [*CTA* **13**]

A. Caquot, 'Les Rephaim ougaritiques', *Syria* 37 (1960), 75–90 [*CTA* **20–22**]

——— 'Nouveaux documents ougaritiques', *Syria* 46 (1969), 241–265 [*Ugaritica* V texts]

R. Dussaud, 'Le vrai nom de Baʿal', *RHR* 113 (1936), 5–20 [*CTA* **12**]

F. C. Fensham, 'Some remarks on the first three mythological texts of Ugaritica V', *UF* 3 (1971), 21–24

——— 'The first Ugaritic text in Ugaritica V and the Old Testament', *VT* 22 (1972), 296–303

L. R. Fisher, F. B. Knutson, 'An enthronement ritual at Ugarit', *JNES* 28 (1969), 157–167 [*Ugaritica* V no. 3]

T. H. Gaster, 'An Egyptological text from Ras Shamra', *Egyptian Religion* 3 (1935), 95–110 [*CTA* **13**]

——— 'The harrowing of Baal: A poem from Ras Shamra', *Acta Or.* 16 (1937), 41–48 [*CTA* **12**]

——— 'Baal is risen' etc. (see sect. (b) above) [*CTA* **10**]

——— 'Sharper than a serpent's tooth: A Canaanite charm against snakebite', *JANES* 7 (1975), 33–51 [*Ugaritica* V no. 7]

H. L. Ginsberg, 'Baʿlu and his brethren', *J. Pal. Or. Soc.* 16 (1936), 138–149 [*CTA* **12**]

——— 'Baʿal and ʿAnat', *Orientalia* 7 (1938), 1–11 [*CTA* **10**]

J. Gray, 'The Rephaim', *Pal. Expl. Qu.* 84 (1949), 127–139 [*CTA* **20–22**]

——— 'The hunting of Baʿal: Fratricide and atonement in the mythology of Ras Shamra', *JNES* 10 (1951), 146–155 [*CTA* **12**]

——— 'Baʿal's atonement', *UF* 3 (1971), 61–70 [*CTA* **12**]

W. Johnstone, 'Lexical and comparative philological contributions of the mythological texts of the 24th campaign at Ras Shamra to Ugaritic', *Ugaritica* VII (forthcoming) [*Ugaritica* V texts]

—— 'The Sun and the Serpent: The interpretation of Ugaritic Text RS 24.244', *Glasgow Un. Or. Soc. Transactions* (forthcoming) [*Ugaritica* V no. 7]

A. S. Kapelrud, 'Baal and the devourers', *Ugaritica* VI (1969), 319–332 [*CTA* **12**]

E. Lipiński, 'Les conceptions et couches merveilleuses de 'Anath', *Syria* 42 (1965), 45–73 [RS 22.225; *CTA* **10, 11**]

—— 'Épiphanie de Baal-Haddu', *UF* 3 (1971), 81–92 [*Ugaritica* V no. 3]

—— 'La légende sacrée de la conjuration des morsures de serpents', *UF* 6 (1974), 169–174 [*Ugaritica* V no. 7]

F. Løkkegaard, 'The house of Ba'al', *Acta Or.* 22 (1955), 10–27 [*CTA* **12**]

S. E. Loewenstamm, 'Eine lehrhafte ugaritische Trinkburleske', *UF* 1 (1969), 71–77 [*Ugaritica* V no. 1]

—— 'mṣd', *UF* 3 (1971), 357–359 [*Ugaritica* V no. 1]

B. Margulis, 'A new Ugaritic farce (RS 24.258)', *UF* 2 (1970), 131–138 [*Ugaritica* V no. 1]

—— 'A Ugaritic psalm (RS 24.252)', *JBL* 89 (1970), 292–304 [*Ugaritica* V no. 2]

J. A. Montgomery, 'A myth of Spring', *JAOS* 56 (1936), 226–231 [*CTA* **12**]

J. C. de Moor, 'Studies in the new alphabetic texts from Ras Shamra', *UF* 1 (1969), 167–188; 2 (1970), 303–327 [*Ugaritica* V texts]

—— 'B. Margulis on RS 24.258', *UF* 2 (1970), 247–250 [*Ugaritica* V no. 1]

S. B. Parker, 'The feast of Rāpi'u', *UF* 2 (1970), 243–249 [*Ugaritica* V no. 2]

M. H. Pope, 'A divine banquet at Ugarit', *Studies in Honor of W. F. Stinespring* (Durham N.C. 1972), 170–203 [*Ugaritica* V no. 1]

M. H. Pope, J. H. Tigay, 'A description of Baal', *UF* 3 (1971), 117–130 [*Ugaritica* V no. 3]

A. F. Rainey, 'The Ugaritic texts in Ugaritica 5' *JAOS* 94 (1974), 184–194

H. P. Rüger, 'Zu RS 24.258', *UF* 1 (1969), 203–206 [*Ugaritica* V no. 1]

Ch. Virolleaud, 'Les Rephaïm', *Rev. ét. sém.*, 1940, 77–83 [*CTA* **20–22**]

—— 'Le Père des dieux dans la mythologie d'Ugarit', *RHR* 163 (1963), 144–146 [*Ugaritica* V no. 1]

6. Reference Works:

J. Aistleitner, *Untersuchungen zur Grammatik des Ugaritischen* (Berlin 1954)

—— *Wörterbuch der ugaritischen Sprache* (Berlin 1963)

M. Dietrich, O. Loretz, *Konkordanz der ugaritischen Textzählungen* (Kevelaer/Neukirchen-Vluyn 1972)

P. Fronzaroli, *La fonetica ugaritica* (Rome 1955)

F. Gröndahl, *Die Personennamen der Texte aus Ugarit* (Rome 1967)

S. Moscati (ed.), *An Introduction to the Comparative Grammar of the Semitic Languages* (Wiesbaden 1964)

R. E. Whitaker, *A Concordance of the Ugaritic Literature* (Harvard 1972)

7. General Studies on Language and Poetic Style:

[*Note:* For studies on particular lexical items and grammatical features see the appropriate sections of the *Keilschriftbibliographie* in the periodical *Orientalia*.]

K. Aartun, *Die Partikeln des Ugaritischen* (Kevelaer/Neukirchen-Vluyn 1974)

A. F. Campbell, 'Homer and Ugaritic Literature', *Abr-Naharaim* 5 (1964–1965), 29–56

J. Cantineau, 'La langue de Ras Shamra', *Syria* 13 (1932), 164–179; 21 (1940), 38–61; *Semitica* 3 (1950), 21–34

P. C. Craigie, 'The poetry of Ugarit and Israel', *Tyndale Bull.* 22 (1971), 3–31

F. M. Cross, 'Prose and poetry in the mythic and epic texts from Ugarit', *Harv. Th. Rev.* 67 (1974), 1–15

M. Dahood, 'Ugaritic lexicography', *Mélanges Eugène Tisserant*, I (Vatican City 1964), 81–104

—— *Ugaritic-Hebrew Philology* (Rome 1965)

—— 'Ugaritic-Hebrew syntax and style', *UF* 1 (1969), 15–36

L. Delekat, 'Zum ugaritischen Verbum', *UF* 4 (1972), 11–26

G. R. Driver, 'Ugaritic and Hebrew problems', *Arch. Or.* 17 (1949), 153–157

—— 'Ugaritic problems', *Studia Semitica . . . Ioanni Bakoš Dicata* (Bratislava 1965), 95—110

—— 'Ugaritic and Hebrew Words', *Ugaritica* VI (1969), 181–186

J. J. Duggan (ed.), *Oral Literature: Seven Essays* (Edinburgh/London 1975)

J. A. Emerton, 'Ugaritic notes', *J. Th. St.* NS 16 (1965), 438–443

G. Garbini, *Il semitico di nord-ovest* (Naples 1960)

—— *Le lingue semitiche* (Naples 1972)

I. J. Gelb, *A Study of Writing*, rev. edit. (Chicago 1963)

S. Gevirtz, *Patterns in the Early Poetry of Israel* (Chicago 1963)

S. A. Goetze, 'The tenses of Ugaritic', *JAOS* 58 (1938), 266–309

C. H. Gordon, 'Homer and Bible: The origin and character of East Mediterranean literature', *Hebr. Un. Coll. Ann.* 26 (1955), 43–108

G. B. Gray, *The Forms of Hebrew Poetry* (1915), repr. with prolegomenon by D. N. Freedman (New York 1972)

E. Hammershaimb, *Das Verbum im Dialekt von Ras*

Schamra (Copenhagen 1941)

Z. S. Harris, *Development of the Canaanite Dialects* (New Haven 1939)

W. J. Horwitz, 'Some possible results of rudimentary scribal training', *UF* 6 (1974), 75–83

M. Liverani, 'L'epica ugaritica nel suo contesto storico e letterario', *Atti del convegno sul tema La poesia epica* (Rome 1970), 859–869

A. B. Lord, *The Singer of Tales* (Harvard 1960)

D. Marcus, 'Studies in Ugaritic grammar', *JANES* 1/2 (1969), 55–61; 3/2 (1970–1971), 102–111

B. Margalit, 'Introduction to Ugaritic prosody', *UF* 7 (1975), 289–313

J. C. de Moor, 'Frustula ugaritica', *JNES* 24 (1965), 355–364

—— in P. Fronzaroli (ed.), *Studies on Semitic Lexicography* (Florence 1973), 61–102

S. Moscati, *Il sistema consonantico delle lingue semitiche* (Rome 1954)

G. del Olmo Lete, 'Notes on Ugaritic semantics', *UF* 7 (1975), 89–102

D. G. Pardee, 'The prepositions in Ugaritic', *UF* 7 (1975), 329–378

S. B. Parker, 'Parallelism and prosody in Ugaritic narrative verse', *UF* 6 (1974), 283–294

A. F. Rainey, 'The scribe at Ugarit: His position and influence', *Israel Ac. of Sciences and Humanities* III, no. 4 (Jerusalem 1968)

—— 'Observations on Ugaritic grammar', *UF* 3 (1971), 151–172

M. E. J. Richardson, 'Ugaritic spelling errors', *Tyndale Bull.* 24 (1973), 3–20

S. Segert, 'Ugaritisch und Aramäisch', *Studia Semitica . . . Ioanni Bakoš Dicata* (Bratislava 1965), 215–226

J. M. Solá-Solé, *L'Infinitif sémitique* (Paris 1961)

E. Ullendorff, 'Ugaritic Marginalia', *Orientalia* 20 (1951), 270–274; *JSS* 7 (1962), 339–351; *Israel Or. St.* 2 (1972), 463–469

—— 'Ugaritic studies within their Semitic and Eastern Mediterranean setting', *Bull. John Rylands Libr.* 46 (1963), 236–249

P. Walcot, 'The comparative study of Ugaritic and Greek literatures', *UF* 1 (1969), 111–118; 2 (1970), 273–275; 4 (1972), 129–132

W. A. Ward, 'Comparative studies in Egyptian and Ugaritic', *JNES* 20 (1961), 31–40

W. Whallon, *Formula, Character and Context: Studies in Homeric, Old English and Old Testament Poetry* (Harvard 1969)

Izz-al-Din al-Yasin, *The Lexical Relation between Ugaritic and Arabic* (New York 1952)

8. Archaeology and History of Ugarit:

Margaret S. Drower, *Ugarit* (Cambridge Anc. Hist. monograph, 1968)

J. Gray, *The Canaanites* (*Ancient Peoples and Places*) (London 1964)

—— 'Ugarit' in D. W. Thomas (ed.), *Archaeology and Old Testament Study* (Oxford 1967), 145–167

M. Liverani, *Storia di Ugarit nell'età degli archivi politici* (Rome 1962)

A. R. Millard, 'Canaanites' in D. J. Wiseman (ed.), *Peoples of Old Testament Times* (Oxford 1973), 29–52

A. F. Rainey, *The Social Structure of Ugarit* [in Hebrew] (Jerusalem 1967)

C. F. A. Schaeffer, *The Cuneiform Texts of Ras Shamra-Ugarit* (Oxford 1939)

—— (ed.), *Ugaritica* I, II, VI (=*MRS* III, V, XVII) (Paris 1939, 1949, 1969)

A. van Selms, *Marriage and Family life in Ugaritic Literature* (London 1954)

9. Religion and Mythology of Ugarit:

M. C. Astour, *Hellenosemitica: An Ethnic and Cultural Study in West Semitic Impact on Mycenaean Greece* (Leiden 1967)

—— 'La triade de déesses de fertilité à Ugarit et en Grèce', *Ugaritica* VI (1969), 9–23

K. A. Bernhardt, 'Asherah in Ugarit und im Alten Testament', *MIO* 13 (1967), 163–174

A. Caquot, 'Le dieu 'Athtar et les textes de Ras Shamra', *Syria* 35 (1958), 46–60

—— 'La divinité solaire ougaritique', *Syria* 36 (1959), 90–101

R. J. Clifford, *The Cosmic Mountain in Canaan and the Old Testament* (Harvard 1972)

M. Dahood, 'Ancient Semitic divinities in Syria and Palestine' in S. Moscati (ed.), *Le antiche divinità semitiche* (Rome 1958), 65–94

O. Eissfeldt, *Baal Zaphon, Zeus Kasios und der Durchzug der Israeliten durchs Meer* (Halle 1932)

—— *El im ugaritischen Pantheon* (Berlin 1951)

—— *Sanchuniathon von Beirut und Ilimilku von Ugarit* (Halle 1952)

J. Fortenrose, 'Dagon and El', *Oriens* 10 (1957) 277–279

H. Gese, M. Höfner, K. Rudolph, *Die Religionen Altsyriens, Altarabiens und der Mandäer* (Stuttgart 1970)

J. C. L. Gibson, 'Myth, legend and folklore in the Ugaritic Keret and Aqhat texts', *VT Suppl.* 28 (1975), 60–68

C. H. Gordon, 'Canaanite mythology' in S. N. Kramer (ed.), *Mythologies of the Ancient World* (New York 1961), 181–218

J. Gray, 'The desert god 'Attr in the literature and religion of Canaan', *JNES* 8 (1949), 72–83

—— 'Social aspects of Canaanite religion', *VT Suppl.* 15 (1966), 170–192

—— *Near Eastern Mythology* (London 1969)

—— 'Sacral kingship in Ugarit', *Ugaritica* VI (1969), 289–302

W. Hermann, 'Astart', *MIO* 15 (1969), 6–55

A. Jirku, *Der Mythus der Kanaanäer* (Bonn 1966)

—— 'šnm (Schunama) der Sohn des Gottes 'Il', *ZAW* 82 (1970), 278–279

—— 'Neue Götter und Dämonen aus Ugarit', *Archiv. Or.* 41 (1973), 97–103

A. S. Kapelrud, *Baal in the Ras Shamra Texts* (Copenhagen 1952)

—— *The Violent Goddesses: Anat in the Ras Shamra Texts* (Oslo 1969)

G. S. Kirk, *Myth: Its Meaning and Functions in Ancient and other Cultures* (Cambridge 1970)

R. Labat, A. Caquot, M. Sznycer, M. Vieyra, *Les religions du Proche-Orient asiatique* (Paris 1970)

R. de Langhe, 'Myth, ritual and kingship in the Ras Shamra tablets', in S. H. Hooke (ed.), *Myth, Ritual and Kingship* (Oxford 1958), 122–148

E. Lipiński, 'El's abode: Mythological traditions relating to Mount Hermon and to the mountains of Armenia', *Orientalia Lovaniensia Periodica* 2 (1971), 13–69

—— 'The goddess Atirat in ancient Arabia, in Babylon and in Ugarit', ibid. 3 (1972), 101–119

F. Løkkegaard, 'A plea for El the Bull and other Ugaritic miscellanies' in *Studia Orientalia J. Pedersen Dicata* (Copenhagen 1953), 219–235

J. C. de Moor, 'The Semitic pantheon of Ugarit', *UF* 2 (1970), 187–228

M. J. Mulder, 'Hat man in Ugarit die Sonnenwende begangen?' *UF* 4 (1972), 79–96

U. Oldenburg, *The Conflict between El and Baal in Canaanite Religion* (Leiden 1965)

S. B. Parker, 'The Ugaritic deity Rāpi'u', *UF* 4 (1972), 97–104

R. Patai, 'The goddess Asherah', *JNES* 24 (1965), 37–52

M. H. Pope, *El in the Ugaritic Texts* (Leiden 1955)

H. Ringgren, *Religions of the Ancient Near East*, Engl. transl. (London 1973)

C. F. A. Schaeffer, 'El, Elat et Asherat' in *Hommages à A. Dupont-Sommer* (Paris 1971), 137–149

10. Relations with the Old Testament:

[*Note:* With a few exceptions commentaries on and studies of particular biblical books that make extensive use of Ugaritic material are not included.]

W. F. Albright, *Archaeology and the Religion of Israel*, 2nd edit. (Baltimore 1946)

—— *Yahweh and the Gods of Canaan* (New York 1968)

J. Barr, *Comparative Philology and the Text of the Old Testament* (Oxford 1968)

—— 'Philology and exegesis: Some general remarks with illustrations from Job 3' in C. Brekelmans (ed.), *Questions disputées d'Ancien Testament* (Gembloux 1974), 39–61

W. Baumgartner, 'Ras Schamra und das Alte Testament', *Theol. Rundschau* 12 (1940), 163–188; 13 (1941), 1–20, 85–102, 157–183

L. Bronner, *The Stories of Elijah and Elisha as Polemics against Baal Worship* (Leiden 1968)

U. Cassuto, *A Commentary on the Book of Genesis*, Engl. transl. (Jerusalem 1961ff.)

—— *Biblical and Oriental Studies*, 2 vols. (Jerusalem 1973, 1975; Engl. transl. of Hebrew and Italian articles)

F. M. Cross, *Canaanite Myth and Hebrew Epic: Essays in the History of the Religion of Israel* (Harvard 1973)

M. Dahood, 'Hebrew-Ugaritic lexicography I–XII', *Biblica* 44 (1963), 289–303 and successive vols. (finishing 1974)

—— *Psalms*, 3 vols. (*Anchor Bible*) (New York 1966–1970)

—— 'Northwest Semitic texts and the textual criticism of the Hebrew Bible' in C. Brekelmans (ed.), *op. cit.*, 11–37

G. R. Driver, Review of M. Dahood, *Proverbs and Northwest Semitic Philology* (Rome 1963) in *JSS* 10 (1965), 112–117 (with reply by Dahood in *Biblica* 49 (1968), 89–90)

O. Eissfeldt, *Kleine Schriften*, 4 vols. (Tübingen, 1962–1968)

J. A. Emerton, 'The origin of the Son of Man imagery', *J. Th. St. NS* 9 (1958), 225–242

I. Engnell, *Studies in Divine Kingship in the Ancient Near East* (Uppsala 1943)

L. R. Fisher, 'Creation at Ugarit and in the Old Testament', *VT* 15 (1965), 313–324

—— (ed.), *Ras Shamra Parallels*, I, II (Rome 1972, 1975) (to be continued)

T. H. Gaster, *Myth, Legend and Custom in the Old Testament* (New York/London 1969)

C. H. Gordon, *Before the Bible: The Common Background of Greek and Hebrew Civilisation* (London 1962)

J. Gray, 'The Day of Yahweh in cultic experience and eschatological prospect', *Svensk Exeg. Årsb.* 39 (1974), 5–37

N. C. Habel, *Yahweh versus Baal: A Conflict of Religious Cultures* (New York 1964)

J. W. Jack, *The Ras Shamra Tablets: Their Bearing on the Old Testament* (Edinburgh 1935)

E. Jacob, *Ras Shamra-Ugarit et l'Ancien Testament* (Neuchâtel/Paris 1960)

O. Kaiser, *Die mythologische Bedeutung des Meeres in Ugarit, Aegypten und Israel* (Berlin 1959)

A. S. Kapelrud, *The Ras Shamra Discoveries and the Old Testament*, Engl. transl. (Oxford 1965)

R. de Langhe, *Les textes de Ras Shamra-Ugarit et leur rapports avec le milieu biblique de l'Ancien Testament* (Gembloux/Paris 1945)

E. Lipiński, *La royauté de Yahvé dans la poesie et le culte de l'Ancien Israël* (Brussels 1965)

S. E. Loewenstamm, 'Ugarit and the Bible' (review of Fisher, *Parallels* I), *Biblica* 56 (1975), 103–119

P. D. Miller, *The Divine Warrior in Early Israel* (Harvard 1973)

J. C. de Moor, *New Year with Canaanites and Israelites* (Kampen 1972)

J. C. de Moor, P. van der Lugt, 'The spectre of pan-Ugaritism' (review of Fisher, *Parallels* I), *Biblioth. Orient.* 31 (1974), 3–26

R. J. Moroder, 'Ugaritic and modern translation of the Psalter', *UF* 6 (1974), 249–264

D. Nielsen, *Ras Šamra Mythologie und biblische Theologie* (Leipzig 1936)

J. T. Patton, *Canaanite Parallels in the Book of Psalms* (Baltimore 1944)

C. F. Pfeiffer, *Ras Shamra and the Bible* (Grand Rapids 1962)

R. Rendtorff, 'El, Baal und Jahweh', *ZAW* 78 (1966), 277–292

S. and Sh. Rin, 'Ugaritic-Old Testament affinities', *Bibl. Zeitschr.* NF 7 (1963), 22–33; 11 (1967), 174–192

G. Sauer, 'Die Ugaristik und die Psalmenforschung', *UF* 6 (1974), 401–406

W. Schmidt, *Königtum Gottes in Ugarit und Israel*, 2nd edit. (Berlin 1966)

S. Segert, 'The Ugaritic texts and the textual criticism of the Hebrew Bible' in *Near Eastern Studies in Honor of W. F. Albright* (Baltimore 1971), 413–420

N. J. Tromp, *Primitive Conceptions of Death and the Nether World in the Old Testament* (Rome 1969)

Mary K. Wakeman, *God's Battle with the Monster: A Study in Biblical Imagery* (Leiden 1973)

T. Worden, 'The literary influence of the Ugaritic fertility myth on the Old Testament', *VT* 3 (1953), 273–297

11. Bibliography:

P. C. Craigie (ed.), 'Newsletter for Ugaritic studies', occasional publication since 1972 by the Dept. of Religious Studies, University of Calgary, Alberta

M. Dietrich, O. Loretz, P.-R. Borger, J. Sanmartin, *Ugarit Bibliographie* 1928–1966, 4 vols. (Kevelaer/Neukirchen-Vluyn 1973) (to be continued)

H. Hospers, *A Basic Bibliography for the Study of the Semitic Languages*, I (Leiden 1973)

For continuing bibliography the *Keilschriftbibliographie* appearing annually in the periodical *Orientalia* should be consulted.

The *Elenchus Bibliographicus Biblicus* and the *Zeitschriftenschau* appearing annually in the periodicals *Biblica* and *ZAW* respectively are useful for studies bearing on the Bible.

INTRODUCTION

A. THE DISCOVERY OF THE TABLETS

An Arab peasant, working on his land in the spring of 1928, struck a slab of stone with his plough and, raising it, found traces of an ancient tomb with a number of potsherds and some small undamaged vessels. The *Service des Antiquités en Syrie et au Liban*, as soon as they heard of the discovery, sent out an expedition under Mons. Ch. Virolleaud to explore the site. It turned out to be a necropolis and yielded little that seemed promising; but the archaeologists had in the meantime had their attention drawn by local tradition to a neighbouring mound which was clearly artificial and to which they then directed their efforts. This was the now famous mound of *Ras-ashSham-rah*,[1] which concealed the ancient city of Ugarit, known from Babylonian, Hittite, and Egyptian records.

Excavations were carried out under Mons. C. F. A. Schaeffer in eleven campaigns between 1929 and 1939 and were continued after the Second World War. From the start a remarkable civilization, to which the label Canaanite may loosely but not inappropriately be applied,[2] was brought to light. Thousands of tablets have been unearthed, chiefly in and around the library attached to the temple of Baal and the chamber of the palace used for storing the royal archives[3] but also in other buildings in the city. These tablets are extremely varied in content and include not only the poetic mythological texts which are the subject of the present study but other religious texts like lists of gods and offerings, lexical and scholastic texts, lists of countries and towns, corporations and persons, 'hippiatric' texts, commercial and administrative documents, and official and private letters; and they are written in the Akkadian, Hurrian and Sumerian, as well as the Ugaritic languages. All apparently were discovered in a level which was dated archaeologically between the sixteenth or fifteenth and the twelfth centuries B.C. Objects bearing the names of the Egyptian kings Thutmos IV (*ca.* 1425–1417 B.C.) and Amenophis III (*ca.* 1417–1379 B.C.) found alongside the tablets reduce the period to which they may be assigned; such a date, too, agrees well enough with the fact that certain letters of Niqmad, king of Ugarit, who is named in the colophons of several of the literary tablets, are addressed to the Hittite king Shuppiluliumash (*ca.* 1380–1336 B.C.). The literary texts must therefore like the other documents have been written down between *ca.* 1400 and 1350 B.C., though it should be emphasized that the legends and myths themselves are not necessarily contemporary with the tablets but not improbably go back in some form or other to a much remoter antiquity.

The Ugaritic language, in which the poems and some of the non-literary texts are composed, was entirely new and the greatest credit is due to all responsible for the speedy decipherment of its writing system. Tablets were sent to Mons. Virolleaud in Paris, and he at once recognized that, although they were inscribed with wedge-shaped, i.e. cuneiform, signs, these were not identical with those of the Sumerian or Akkadian or of any other cuneiform script;

---

[1] Meaning 'headland of fennel'; it lies on the Syrian coast between two branches of a river called the *Nahr-alFidd* about 12 km. to the north of *Lâdhiqîyah* (the ancient *Laodicea ad mare*) and about 800 m. from the sea.

[2] Following the general usage in the Bible where the term denotes all the pre- and non-Israelite inhabitants of the Levant without distinction of race.

In extra-biblical sources there is only a territory Canaan, which included the Palestinian and Phoenician coasts but did not apparently reach as far north as Ugarit.

[3] The temple-library was uncovered in the second campaign (1930) and the chamber containing the royal archives was discovered in the course of the tenth and eleventh campaigns (1938–1939).

and he was soon able to establish that there were probably only 26 or 27 signs.[1] Early in 1930 Mons. Virolleaud published the first texts, thus enabling other scholars to work on them. The German Prof. Bauer immediately and correctly guessed, since the words were conveniently separated from one another by a small vertical sign, that the language was Semitic, and was able to identify 17 signs and 9 words by May or June; by December he had raised the number of signs which he could read to 23. Meanwhile the French Prof. Dhorme had also found the key to the decipherment of the script and independently identified some half a dozen signs and two or three words. At the same time Mons. Virolleaud, aided by the large number of well-copied texts which he was able to use, announced in December that he too had achieved a complete decipherment of the writing independently of Prof. Bauer (except for a single letter which he had taken from him) and the identification of a dozen words. Thus the Ugaritic script was made out (except for the exact values of two uncertain signs) and a number of words were identified in the new language in the course of a single year. This language was found to be closely akin to the classical Hebrew of the Bible and to other extant first millennium dialects of the North-west or Syrian Semitic family like Phoenician and Aramaic, though being older by several centuries than any of these it represents an earlier stage in the development of the group.[2]

The tablets here edited and translated are of great importance for the study of literature and religion in an area of the ancient world which chiefly through the avenue of the Hebrew Bible exercised a deep influence on the rise of European civilization. They are enabling scholarship for the first time to arrive at a positive appraisal of the higher levels of Canaanite culture, which is so remorselessly attacked in the Bible but which can now be seen to have contributed more to its composition (and thus indirectly to the thought and poetic imagery of the West) than was previously supposed.[3]

B. ANALYSIS AND INTERPRETATION OF THE TEXTS

1. BAAL AND YAM

The tablets

The story of the conflict between Baal and Yam is chiefly preserved on the large fragment *CTA* **2**, discovered in 1931. This fragment contains the lower portion of a first column with on the reverse the upper portion of a final column, to which Mlle. Herdner assigns the number iv since the unusually long lines make it unlikely that the tablet could have had the normal six columns. A smaller fragment dealing with this conflict, from one side of which the writing had disappeared, was discovered in the same year although not published till much

---

[1] Compared with the many hundreds of syllabic signs in the Mesopotamian systems. There are in fact 30 signs, of which one is not employed in the literary texts. The script is more accurately described as simplified syllabic or alphabeto-syllabic than as alphabetic in the European sense (Gelb), since each sign ideally represents a consonant plus a vowel; see my remarks in *Archivum Linguisticum* 17 (1969), 155ff. The fact that Ugaritic has three signs for the weak consonant ['] depending on whether it has in its vicinity the vowel [a], [i], or [u] is one of the strongest pieces of evidence in favour of this re-definition. The Ugaritic script was probably adapted for scribes used to writing on soft clay from an already existing native Canaanite linear script, an ancestor or precursor of the later Phoenician 'alphabet'.

[2] It is unfortunate that the term Canaanite has become firmly established to denote the Hebrew-Phoenician sub-division of this family as distinguished from the Aramaic sub-division, since such a distinction holds good only for the first millennium B.C. In this more technical sense of the term it is misleading to call Ugaritic a 'Canaanite' dialect, for it contains several features that in the first millennium survive only in Aramaic.

[3] Mention might also be made here of attempts by C. H. Gordon and others to trace contacts between the Ugaritic texts and the Bible on the one hand and Mycenaean and Homeric Greek culture on the other; so far the links they have found are general more often than they are specific, but the field is a new and exciting one.

later. This has equally long lines and is generally associated with the same tablet as the
larger fragment, either as part of a col. iii (so
Herdner) or as the upper part of col. i (so most
other commentators). Neither of these arrangements allows, however, for a satisfactory
development of the narrative, and the fragment
probably belongs to a preceding tablet (Ginsberg). To the information derived from these
three partial columns may be added an episode
concerning Yam which is contained in col. iv
of the extremely ill-preserved tablet *CTA* **1,**
also discovered in 1931, though again publication was delayed because of the poor condition
of the text. This tablet, as Mlle. Herdner's
enumeration implies, is usually placed first in
the long cycle of Baal myths drawn up or
edited by the scribe Elimelek and contained in
CTA **1–6**[1]; but there is evidence, particularly
in some links in vocabulary between its col. v
and an episode related in *CTA* **6** ii 5ff., that
the tablet may not be a member of the series
but a digest or synopsis of it (Caquot and
Sznycer). This hypothesis is provisionally
accepted here and used to justify the extraction
of **1** iv from its present position and the inser-
tion of it between the two fragments **2** iii and
2 i/iv. The resulting order (**2** iii **1** iv **2** i **2** iv)
gives what is as our knowledge stands at the
moment probably the most meaningful sequence
of events for the opening of Elimelek's cycle.
The rest of the cycle (*CTA* **3–6**), where the

text is in a healthier state and the story flows
with fewer fits and starts, is set out in the next
two sections, and the remainder of *CTA* **1** in
the Appendix.

Contents

2

Col. iii   [*Beginning lost*]

Ll. 1–12. Kothar-and-Khasis,[2] the craftsman
of the gods, proceeds to the abode of the
supreme god El at the confluence of the rivers
and the two oceans and does obeisance before
him. El instructs him to build a palace for
prince Yam (the deified Sea), who is also called
judge[3] Nahar (or river), and to do it quickly,
lest it seems (for the text is damaged) he take
hostile action.

Ll. 12–18. On hearing this, the god Athtar,
who is described as possessing the kingship,
takes a torch and carries it down, possibly (for
the text is again damaged) intending to go to
Yam's abode beneath the sea to do mischief
there. He is, however, confronted by the sun-
goddess Shapash,[4] who informs him that El has
decided to bestow the royal power on Yam-
Nahar and that opposition on his part is useless;
he must accept his exclusion from the kingship.

Ll. 18–22. Athtar complains bitterly that,
unlike other gods, he has neither palace nor
court (which are essential to the maintenance of
royal rank) and can only now fear defeat and

---

[1] Several other texts written by different scribes
were linked with this cycle by Virolleaud and are
thus designated AB (for *ảliyn b'l*) along with the
Elimelek tablets (the numbers I, I*, II etc. refer to
the order of discovery); but the long colophon at the
end of *CTA* **6**, which mentions both the high priest
and the king of Ugarit, implies that the latter were
accorded an official status which should not lightly
be extended to the former. The texts in question are
either badly damaged (*CTA* **10**) or very small (*CTA*
7, 8 and **11**) and are given in the Appendix.

[2] He is called *Chousōr* (=*ktr*) in the Greek
account of Phoenician religion derived from Sanchuniathon and equated with Hephaistus. His home
was in Memphis (*ḥkpt*), the city of Ptah his Egyptian
counterpart, with whom evidently he was already
identified at Ugarit. He is also associated with a
place called *kptr*, usually identified with the biblical
Caphtor and thought to be Crete but in the Ugaritic
references more likely to be another name for the

area of Memphis. His double name means 'skilful and
clever' or the like; on his other personal name Heyan,
which links him with Ea, the Mesopotamian deity
who was the patron of craftsmen, see p. 10 note 5.

[3] In parallelism with 'prince' the term 'judge'
may perhaps be more accurately translated 'ruler'
(cp. the biblical major 'Judges'); there is no necessary
reflection of the widespread myth that the trial of the
souls of the dead before admission to the nether-
world takes place on the bank of the world-encircling
river or ocean (though cp. **5** i 21–22).

[4] More accurately Shapshu (a variant of Hebrew
šemeš). Like the name of the sun in Arabic the sun-
deity at Ugarit is feminine. She seems to act as a
messenger or plenipotentiary of El, a role naturally
devolved upon her because in ancient thinking the
sun journeyed daily over the earth; in this role she
intervenes decisively in the action of the plot on not
a few occasions.

death at Yam's hands; yet Yam is to have a palace and El is to honour him. Why should be, Athtar, not be king?

Ll. 22–24. Shapash replies that he has no wife like the other gods (meaning probably that he is too young and therefore unfit to rule).

[*End lost*]

I

Col. iv   [*Beginning lost*]

Ll. 1–8. As El sits in his banqueting hall he is addressed by other deities (one of whom is Athirat[1] his consort, here given her alternative name Elat meaning 'the goddess') who complain that his son Yam is being put to shame for a reason that is not clear (for the text is damaged) but that concerns his palace; they threaten that unless he receives redress he will wreak destruction on the land.

Ll. 9–20. El gives them curdled milk to drink (a mark apparently of esteem) and summons his son; he declares that his name has hitherto been Yaw[2] and invites Elat and her companions to proclaim a new name for him more fitting to his royal dignity.[3] They reply that this task is El's alone, whereupon El proclaims Yam's new name to be 'darling of El'.

Ll. 21–27. He informs Yam, however, that in

order to secure his power he will have to drive his rival Baal (who is, it seems, responsible for Yam's discomfiture) from his throne and from the seat of his dominion,[4] and warns him that unless he takes certain precautions (an account of which is unfortunately not preserved) he will be worsted by him.

Ll. 28–32. El then holds a feast to celebrate the naming ceremony just completed.

[*End lost*]

2

Col. i   [*Beginning lost*]

Ll. 1–10. Kothar-and-Khasis (now arrived under the sea) tells Yam-Nahar that he has risen presumptuously to his present position and that Baal (whom he clearly supports, though he has been instructed to build a palace for Yam) cannot stand idly by. He threatens Yam's destruction by a magic weapon (which as the sequel in the next column shows he himself provides), invoking also to assist in this task the god Horon[5] and the goddess Athtart-name-of-Baal;[6] so shall Yam fall from his high estate.

Ll. 11–19. Yam-Nahar thereupon sends an embassy to El who is sitting in plenary session with the gods. The envoys, who are encouraged to hope that the jubilation of their master's

---

[1] Athirat, though called the 'creatress' (cp. **23**) or 'mistress' of the gods, is at Ugarit especially associated with the sea, her full name being *ảtrt ym*, meaning 'she who treads the sea'. Contrary to the generally accepted opinion she probably does not appear in the Bible, where the term *'ašērāh* 'sacred pole, tree' means simply and more exactly '(holy) place' or 'shrine' (Lipiński).

[2] I.e. his personal name as opposed to the generic title Yam or 'sea'. The name Yaw can only be the same as Greek *Ieuō*, who is in the account of Eusebius based on Sanchuniathon (*Praep. Evang.* i 9, 21) an ancient deity of Beirut and is equated with Poseidon (i 10, 35). It is in spite of some opinions to the contrary probably fortuitous and not significant that a shortened form of the name Yahweh, god of Israel, is also *Yāw* (*Yô*).

[3] The ceremony described in this column may be compared with that of conferring a regnal or throne-name. This custom whereby a king took a new name on his accession was widespread in the ancient Near East; for example, the Assyrian kings Tiglathpileser III and Shalmaneser V took other names on occupy-

ing the Babylonian throne (*ANET*, p. 272) and the Hebrew kings Eliakim and Mattaniah changed theirs at their accession (2 Kgs. xxiii 34   xxiv 17).

[4] This kind of language is conventional and need not be interpreted to mean that Baal was already king, soon to be replaced by Yam; as far as we can tell, Athtar was king at the start of the cycle and had just been demoted in favour of Yam.

[5] Apparently a chthonic deity and therefore associated with the malevolent power of the underworld and death (though he plays a positive role in the difficult text *Ugaritica* V no. 7; see Appendix).

[6] The Ugar.*'ttrt-šm-b'l*=Phoen.*'štrt-šm-b'l* (Eshmunazar inscr. *l.* 18). 'Athtart (Astarte)-name-of-Baal' is a title designed to describe her as a manifestation of Baal, whose consort she in fact is; a similar idea underlies the Punic *tnt-pn-b'l*, 'Tanith-face-of-Baal'. In the Ugaritic texts she figures like Anat, though much less prominently, as a goddess of war and of the chase. There is a reference to her beauty in **14** 146, but no other hint of her fertility role, so well-known from the Bible, where she appears under the falsified name Ashtoreth.

enemies will soon cease, are bidden to proceed without delay to the mount of Lel,[1] where the assembly of the gods meets, and after doing homage to demand the surrender of Baal son of Dagon[2] and his henchmen, in spite of the gods' reverence for his person, in order that he Yam-Nahar may succeed to his possessions.

Ll. 19–29. The envoys start on their journey and arrive at the mount of Lel as the gods are sitting down to a banquet and Baal is standing beside El. The gods on perceiving them have buried their heads in their laps, but Baal angrily asks them why they do so and bids them lift up their heads; if they are afraid to answer the challenge of the envoys, he himself is not.

Ll. 30–48. These enter the assembly, do obeisance to El, and rising with tongues that appear like flaming swords, deliver the message word for word as they have been instructed. El (forestalling Baal) answers that Baal is the slave of Yam-Nahar and will bring him tribute like the other gods, whereupon Baal, losing his temper, makes to attack the envoys with fearsome weapons. The goddesses Anat[3] and Athtart seize his arms to hold him back, reminding him that the person of a messenger is inviolable. Baal, here called Hadad[4] and still angry, contents himself with addressing the

envoys by word of mouth.

[*End lost*]

Col. iv [*Beginning lost*]

Ll. 1–7. Baal has already joined battle with Yam-Nahar and is in despair because of the power of his adversary and of the fierce sea-creatures that move around him. Addressing Kothar-and-Khasis, he counsels their submission before the strength of them both should fall to the ground. Even as he speaks he sinks helpless beneath Yam's throne.

Ll. 7–27. Kothar-and-Khasis, urging him to rise, tells Baal that he has repeatedly promised him victory whereby he will win a kingdom that shall have no end; and he fetches down two divine clubs or maces for his assistance. He gives them two magic names and, perhaps because Baal is too weak to wield them, bids the first leap from his hands like a hunting eagle or falcon and strike Yam-Nahar on the back. When Yam-Nahar remains unbowed, he bids the second strike him on the forehead.[5] Yam-Nahar then collapses in a heap and Baal drags him out and, laying him down, delivers the coup-de-grâce.

Ll. 28–40. Thereupon Athtart, who had (with Anat?) apparently accompanied Baal,

---

[1] Meaning probably 'night'. This mount of assembly is doubtless the same as El's mountainous abode at the confluence of the rivers (see at **3** E 13ff.).

[2] With two exceptions (**24** 14, *Ugar.* V no. 7 *l.* 15) Dagon appears in the mythological texts only in this title, although he figures in lists of deities and in offering tablets and if the archaeologists are to be believed, in fact had a temple in the city. Perhaps as Rapiu (in the title of Daniel in the Aqhat story) was a form of Baal he was only a form of El (Cassuto). This hypothesis would nicely explain both why El had no temple at Ugarit and why Baal occasionally refers to El as father (**17** i 24; cp. **17** vi 29); or to put it another way, the temple accredited by the archaeologists to Dagon is really El's and Baal's relationship to El is the same as that of other gods. On the other hand Baal's addressing El as father (or speaking of himself as his son; **3** E 2 etc.) may be no more than conventional; and certainly Dagon is distinguished from El on the god-lists, which is not the case with Baal and Rapiu. The whole question has still to be resolved, but meanwhile it would be most unwise to build upon Baal's apparently belonging to a different family any theory of a quarrel for supremacy between El and Baal or of a replacement of the former by the latter

(Kapelrud, Pope, Oldenburg etc.). In the Baal myths El is remote but his supremacy is never questioned and his approval or assent is an essential ingredient in legitimatizing claims to the kingship of the gods, which should therefore properly be thought of in terms of viceregency.

[3] This is the first appearance on the scene of Baal's sister, an awesome goddess who plays so prominent a double role in fighting and fertility in the mythological texts and who, if the reference in **3** D 35ff. is taken at its face value, also took part in the defeat of Yam, perhaps as is suggested below in a portion of the text that is now lost. She represents in a few important episodes (notably **3** B and **17** vi–**18** iv) the menacing or erratic aspect of deity, operating as a kind of Ugaritic counterpart of the biblical 'wrath of God'; and by way of contrast and in spite of her title 'virgin' she seems to figure along with Athirat as a mother of the gods in the theogonic text **23**.

[4] Hadad (Akk. *Adad*) is the personal name of Baal, which is a title meaning 'lord'; it apparently means 'thunderer'.

[5] The picture behind this scene is doubtless of the wind and lightning whipping up storms at sea.

rebukes Baal[1] for being slow to press home his advantage and calls upon him to scatter[2] his rival, which he does, twice crying out that now Yam is dead, he Baal shall be king (thus guaranteeing that the heat of spring will not be delayed). The goddess too utters this shout of triumph.

[*End lost*]

Interpretation

Elimelek's purpose in forming his cycle was to bring a measure of order into the corpus of myths about the god Baal that had been handed down, probably over many generations and in several variant forms, among the professional singers who were attached to his temple.[3] It is likely that the cycle was recited during a festival in the autumn[4] at which the pilgrims celebrated the successful conclusion of the agricultural year just past and looked forward in prayer and expectation to the coming of the early rains when the ploughing and sowing for another year's crops could begin. Baal as the deity of rain and wind was the god on whose providence the whole process in their eyes chiefly depended. He was not the head of the gods, a position reserved for El, the creator of the world and of mankind. But he was the deity who impinged most closely on their everyday lives, whether as farmers dependent on the soil (it was this aspect of their existence that decided the date of the festival) or—and this aspect is often forgotten by interpreters—as fishermen and traders dependent on the sea (for Ugarit is situated on the coast). It was Baal who kept at bay the unruly waters of chaos that surrounded their universe, regulating the flow of rain and dew from the heavens above and setting bounds to the sea beneath, and it was Baal who each year brought the dangerous dry season of summer to an end when he arrived in the thunderclaps and downpours of autumn. The hopes and fears thus centred on this one deity were, as was customary in the religious imagination of ancient peoples, projected back into a primaeval past in the form of stories which related how once upon a time their god had defeated his enemies among the other gods (the alien forces of nature just referred to in deified dress) and won their reluctant assent to his superior might, and how he had then been recognized by the father of the gods as his vice-regent who would rule as king over his creation. As the stories were retold each year at the festival the confidence of the pilgrims was kindled anew

---

[1] Interestingly using the title 'the Name', an example of a religious fastidiousness usually thought in biblical circles to be a mark of advanced theological awareness and therefore of late development (Lev. xxiv 11).

[2] For biblical allusions to the motif of scattering the primaeval monster's dismembered corpse see Ps. lxxiv 14 (Leviathan) Ezek. xxix 5 (*tnn*); cp. also Exod. xxxii 20. A similar fate befalls Mot in **6** ii 30ff.

[3] Elimelek's role in the preservation of Ugaritic mythology (he is also responsible for the Keret and Aqhat tablets) may be usefully compared with that of the Yahwist or J-writer in the Pentateuch who arranged and turned into prose the ancient oral poetic epics of the Hebrew people, or with that of Sanchuniathon of Beirut who wrote a definitive account of Phoenician religion, drawing doubtless on poetic originals (Eissfeldt), though one should not press such comparisons too far. Sanchuniathon's work has perished except for extracts from a Greek translation of it which were made rather free use of in Eusebius' *Praeparatio Evangelica* (4 cent. A.D.). Until the Ugaritic tablets were discovered these extracts were apart from the biased evidence of the Hebrew Bible and some pickings from Phoenician inscriptions our only source of knowledge of Canaanite religious belief. Their value used to be doubted because of Eusebius' frequent equations with Greek mythology, but the Ugaritic finds show that they were less contaminated in transmission than was suspected.

[4] As was the *Enuma Elish* at the New Year festival in Babylon. This is the most that can be safely deduced concerning the *Sitz im Leben* of Elimelek's cycle; the frequently expressed view that it was (along with a similar ceremony in Israel) enacted in cultic drama goes beyond the evidence of the texts themselves and is based upon a theory of the ritual origin of myth that is widely held in biblical and Semitic circles but is rather discredited elsewhere (Kirk). From comparison with the epic tales of other races (see the studies of Lord, Bowra, Whallon, Duggan) most of the Ugaritic myths and legends should in fact be classified as oral 'formulaic' literature, the creations of generations of popular or official singers and not librettos drawn up by priests for cultic performances. Elimelek's written versions would perhaps be those approved for use in the training of the singers and should not therefore be regarded as having been meant to stifle creativity or supply a canonical text that had to be slavishly followed.

that his royal power, which had in that distant era been so resoundingly vindicated, would be again revealed and prove sufficient for their present needs.

The four columns here assembled are all that survive from the story of the first of Baal's exploits as recorded by Elimelek, his battle with Yam, also called Nahar, whose names mean 'sea' and 'river'. As the cycle opens a deity called Athtar[1] holds the position of king, but he is peremptorily thrust aside as the two main antagonists face up to each other. At first El favours Yam, but when Baal emerges victorious he is compelled to promote him (though this necessary ending to the narrative is, as it happens, not preserved). There are two later references within the cycle to the defeat of Yam, in 3 D 34ff., where the goddess Anat claims to have slain not only Yam-Nahar but a 'dragon' (*tnn*) or 'serpent' (*btn*), and in 5 i 1ff., where the god Mot speaks of Baal's victory over Leviathan (*ltn*); but it is not clear whether these are attendant monsters of Yam,[2] whose destruction could therefore have been related in the long gap between 2 i and iv or (Gaster) in a missing tablet between *CTA* 2 and 3, or whether they are, as in many references in the Bible (see below), alternative names of one and the same enemy and derived therefore from variant versions of the myth which were in circulation at Ugarit. That there were such variants is shown by the scattered allusions to a primaeval battle in fragmentary texts not written by Elimelek (*CTA* 9 and *PRU* II nos. 1 and 3). Be that as it may, there is no doubt that Yam-Nahar was the chief Ugaritic counterpart of the Babylonian Tiamat, defeated by Marduk (*ANET* pp. 66ff.)[3] and (from a more adjacent

cultural milieu) of the biblical monster defeated by Yahweh, who is variously called Yam (Ps. lxxiv 13 Job iii 8(?) vii 12 xxvi 12), Rahab (Ps. lxxxix 11 Job ix 13 xxvi 12 Isa. li 9), Leviathan (Ps. lxxiv 14 Job iii 8 xl 25ff. Isa. xxvii 1[4]) or simply 'dragon' (*tannîn* Ps. lxxiv 13 Job vii 12 Isa. xxvii 1[4] li 9) or 'serpent' (*nāḥāš* Job xxvi 13 Isa. xxvii 1[4]; *bāšān* Ps. lxviii 23); cp. also the references to 'rivers' (*n'hārôt*) in parallelism with 'sea' in passages like Ps. lxvi 6 lxxiv 15 xciii 3–4 Hab. iii 8. In the Babylonian myth it is related how Marduk after the death of the monster created the firmament out of its carcase, and in several of the biblical passages there are some rather less directly mythological allusions to Yahweh's creative acts (e.g. Ps. lxxiv 15–17 lxxxix 12ff. Job xxvi 7ff.; cp. also Ps. civ 24–26 Gen. i 21). Since at Ugarit El and not Baal (see *CTA* 23) was the creator god it is not surprising to find that specific references to creation are absent from the Ugaritic version. Evidently to the people of Ugarit the sustaining of the seasons and the guaranteeing of the world's order were more important properties of deity than the original creation of things, and it was therefore the god who embodied those active properties and not the venerable and remoter creator-father El who in their mythology slew the monster of old and overcame the forces of chaos.

An interesting peculiarity of the Ugaritic myth has already been noted, namely that being sea-farers the people of Ugarit would naturally discern evidence of Yam's power in the tides that lashed their coast in winter and that put sailing in that season virtually out of the question.[5] By defeating him Baal makes it

---

[1] Cp. 6 i 53ff. where this deity makes another bid for royal power. On his identity see p. 19.

[2] Cp. the allusions to 'helpers' of Rahab in Job ix 13; cp. also Ezek. xxx 8 and 2 iv 4.

[3] Also of the Sumerian Asag, the Vedic Vitra and Kaliya, the Egyptian Apophis and Seth, the Hittite Hahhimas, the Hurrian Kumarbi and Ullikummi, the Greek Typhon etc. For an analysis of the similarities between these various monster stories and the motifs they hold in common see Miss Wakeman's penetrating study.

[4] These allusions occur in an apocalyptic rather than a primaeval context; in this regard the apocalyptic movement involved a kind of 'rebirth of the

images', and it was in fact through it as intermediary that the old mythology of Canaan entered the thinking of Judaism and Christianity and ultimately exerted its influence on European poetry and thought; see particularly Emerton's pioneer study on the origin of the Son of Man imagery.

[5] De Moor lays stress on this particularity in his well-documented study aimed at establishing a seasonal pattern in Elimelek's cycle, where he argues that the story of Yam's defeat by Baal should be transferred to a later position in the cycle after the concerns of autumn had been dealt with. He proposes the sequence *CTA* 3 (autumn) 1 and 2 (winter) 4 and 5 (spring) and 6 (summer). But such a sequence

possible for calm seas to return each spring. This local colouring can often be detected in the way in which the battle between the two gods is described in the text; it may *mutatis mutandis* be compared with the uniquely Israelite interest in historicizing the primaeval conflict in the Exodus from Egypt (e.g. Isa. li 10).

2. THE PALACE OF BAAL

The tablets

The tablet *CTA* **3,** discovered in 1931, consists of a large and a very small fragment which together preserve something over half of the original text; there are six columns of script, but following the first editor (Virolleaud) and Mlle. Herdner's official volume the remains are here grouped into six more convenient divisions which do not always coincide with the columns, these divisions being denoted by the letters A to F. The tablet opens with a description of a banquet, doubtless held to celebrate the victory of Baal over Yam-Nahar related in *CTA* **2**; this is followed by a scene in which the goddess Anat plays the dominant role, but by the beginning of division C the train of events is clearly set in motion which lead to the building of Baal's palace. The story of these events takes up the latter part of *CTA* **3** and almost the whole of *CTA* **4**. This tablet is with eight columns the largest and it is also one of the best preserved of all the Ugaritic texts; it was

reconstructed from six pieces found in 1930 and 1931. At the end of its seventh column the name of the god Mot is brought into the narrative, thus preparing the listeners for the ensuing conflict between him and Baal, which is the third major theme in Elimelek's cycle and the subject-matter of the next section.

Contents

3

Div. A [*Beginning lost*]
Ll. 1–25. Those present having been encouraged to lift up and not to lower their heads, a divine functionary spreads a banquet before mightiest Baal, cutting up joints of meat and giving him huge quantities of wine to drink in vessels such as no woman or even goddess can regard otherwise than with envious eyes. A minstrel with cymbals in his hands chants songs in Baal's honour as he drinks copious draughts of wine or of mead that he has himself mixed. While he sits celebrating on his mountain Zephon[1] (where the feast is being held) Baal notices the approach of his daughters Pidray and Tallay.[2]

[*End lost*]

Div. B [*Beginning lost*]
Ll. 1–16. Anat, adorned with henna and rouge and scented, closes the door of her mansion and meeting her servants in a valley where are two cities (which possibly represent

---

creates more difficulties than it resolves, notably in the matter of the building of Baal's house, which he has to argue was begun, then abandoned and only later completed; and one wonders whether it is in fact essential to have each successive stage of the narrative accurately reflect the changing seasons for the listeners to be enabled to make the necessary connections. The cycle is after all set in the mythological past when earthly time is by definition suspended and human limitations are regularly transcended. In the interpretation offered here the cycle is 'theomachic' in its primary thrust, cohering around the struggle for pre-eminence (under El) among the gods, and the seasonal implications, though everywhere evident, are in terms of structure secondary.

[1] Identified with the classical *mons Casius* (Akk. *Ḫazzi*) and modern *Jabal-al'Aqra'*, 'the bald (i.e. snow-capped) mountain', the highest peak in northern Syria, lying approx. 25–30 miles to the NNE of Ugarit, from which it could be seen. The meaning 'north' never occurs for *ṣpn* in Ugaritic and is probably a secondary development in Hebrew based on the location of this mountain, which may thus have been associated with Baal throughout the Canaanite world; cp. Ps. xlviii 3, where *ṣāpôn* is applied to Mt. Zion.

[2] Arṣay, the third of Baal's daughters, may have been mentioned in the ensuing lacuna; on their names and epithets, which as rendered in this edition associate them with various kinds of dew or precipitation, see at **3** A 23–25 C 4–5.

Ugarit and its port *Minat alBaidah*) falls on their inhabitants and those of a wide region round about. She slays guards and warriors alike and girds herself with the heads and hands of the slain; then wading through blood up to her knees, she drives away all the townspeople, including even tottering old men.

Ll. 17–30. Proceeding thence to her palace, she arranges tables and chairs for those warriors and guards who have so far escaped the slaughter and then lays about them also, laughing raucously until the palace is swimming in blood and she is at last satisfied with her savage work.

Ll. 31–44. Wiping the blood from the house and from her own person, Anat performs a rite at which a peace-offering is poured out; she replaces the furniture and scooping up dew, washes herself with it and remakes her toilet.

[*End lost*]

Div. C

Ll. 1–28. Baal, addressing his messengers (doubtless here as elsewhere Gupn and Ugar[1]), pictures his sister Anat as sitting with her lyre and singing of her affection for him and his daughters, and sends them off to do obeisance before her. They are to tell her to perform a rite similar to that which she has already performed but whose details are spelt out more fully, then to hasten with all speed to him to receive an important communication; this will be the secret of the lightning, a secret carried on the wind which sighs through the trees and is the means of converse between the firmament above and the earth and oceans beneath; neither the gods in heaven nor mankind on earth

understand this secret but only he himself.[2] Together he and she will search for the lightning on his holy hill Zephon, which (now that he has defeated Yam-Nahar) is also a place of victory.

Div. D

Ll. 29–80. Anat, seeing the divine messengers, is contorted with anxiety lest they come to announce the re-appearance of Baal's enemies; has she not herself, she asks them, slain Yam-Nahar and his various attendant monsters and obtained possession of the gold of him who has tried to oust Baal from his rightful throne?[3] The messengers assure her that none of Baal's enemies is in fact active; they then deliver his instructions word for word to her. She replies that she will perform the rite demanded of her only if Baal should first set his thunderbolt in the sky and flash forth his lightning. She also announces her intention to visit the most distant of gods (namely El) in his remote and marshy abode (sensing apparently that Baal will wish to obtain her good offices with him[4]).

Ll. 81–90. She then obeys his summons and sets out for Zephon. Baal, seeing her approach, sends away the women who are with him and sets a meal before her; she washes and oils herself and paints her face.

[*End lost*]

Div. E

Ll. 1–6. Baal complains bitterly to Anat that he has neither house nor court like other gods (implying that a king without these is in fact no king); he and his daughters have to live in the

---

[1] The first name perhaps means 'vine' (Hebr. *gepen*; Aram. *gupnâ*); the second has been connected with Akk. *ugāru* 'cultivated field', but may be that of the eponymous hero or divine patron of the city of Ugarit. Gupn and Ugar are always treated as separate deities, unlike the 'composite' deities Kothar-and-Khasis and Qodesh-and-Amrur (the servant of Athirat), who are usually construed with singular verbs, pronouns etc., though sometimes duals are employed. Such ambivalence is an interesting example of what A. R. Johnson has called 'the one and the many' (see his monograph of that title) in the ancient Semitic conception of deity; cp. in Hebr.

ĕlōhîm 'gods' and 'God'; Gen. i 26 iii 22; cp. also Mark v 9.

[2] As indeed he had already shown by the manner of his victory over Yam-Nahar (**2** iv 7ff.).

[3] See on this episode p. 7.

[4] As in fact he does (div. F); however, in a damaged passage in the summary tablet *CTA* **1** ii 17ff. (see Appendix) El calls on Anat to perform the same rite asked for here by Baal and summons her to his presence; in the cycle proper this message may already have been delivered to her (perhaps at the end of tablet **2** or in an intervening tablet).

dwelling of his 'father' El and of Athirat.[1]

Ll. 6–24. Anat promises to go to El and to threaten to trample him to the ground and make his grey hairs run with blood if he does not allow Baal to have a palace and a court; the earth quakes under her feet as she makes for his abode at the place where the rivers and oceans emerge from the earth.[2] She penetrates the high mountains surrounding it, and El hears her voice from the closed chamber where he is sitting.

Ll. 25–26. Meanwhile on earth there is no rain and the sun is scorching hot.

Ll. 27–52. Anat begins by telling El not to rejoice or exult because he has a palace; for she intends to pull it down about him and to strike him so that his grey hairs run with blood, if he will not grant her request. El replies that he knows her ruthless nature and asks her what she wants. Softening, Anat compliments the supreme god on his wisdom and kindliness and reminding him that Baal is (as he himself has recognized[3]) king and judge, announces that she and another (presumably Baal's consort Athtart) would gladly serve him as ministers at his table. However, he has no house like the other gods and in his chagrin has requested her to ask El to remedy the situation.

[End lost]

Div. F   *[Beginning lost]*

Ll. 1–25. Anat (having reported to Baal that her suit has met with no success) and Baal himself (for they are together later) despatch

Qodesh-and-Amrur,[4] the attendant of Athirat, via Byblos and Palestine to Memphis in Egypt, the home of the craftsman-god Kothar-and-Khasis, here also called Heyan;[5] falling down at his feet, he is to deliver to him a message from Baal.[6]

[End lost]

4

Col. i   *[Beginning lost]*

Ll. 1–23. Qodesh-and-Amrur delivers Baal's message, in which after complaining in the same words as before that he has no palace like the other gods but is compelled with his daughters to remain in the house of El and Athirat, he instructs Kothar-and-Khasis to fashion presents for the last-named (hoping obviously to buy her support in a bid to persuade El to change his mind).

Ll. 24–43. The craftsman-god enters his forge and smelts silver and gold in abundance, which he then uses in the manufacture of magnificent pieces of furniture, a pair of fine sandals and a beautifully decorated table and bowl.[7]

Col. ii   *[Beginning lost]*

Ll. 1–26. Athirat is performing her woman's work by the seashore, spinning at her wheel and washing and drying clothes, thinking all the while of amorous dalliance with her husband El, when lifting her eyes, she sees Baal approaching accompanied by his sister Anat.

---

[1] Though the scene is mythological, we may have here supporting evidence for the view that Dagon's temple at Ugarit was really El's (see p. 5 note 2); until he had his own, Baal would be worshipped there along with the other gods in the temple of El. Both temples pre-date the writing down (though not the origin) of the myths by many centuries, but that ascribed to Dagon is the older of the two.

[2] On the terms used in describing El's abode see the notes to **3** D 79–80 E 13ff. If it had, like Baal's Zephon, an earthly geographical counterpart, the best candidates for consideration are Aphek in Lebanon (Josh. xiii 4) at the source of the *Nahr Ibrâhîm* (Pope) and the valley of Hule near Mt. Hermon (Sirion) and the sources of the Jordan (Lipiński).

[3] Probably in a portion of the section on Baal and Yam which is now lost.

[4] A composite deity like Kothar-and-Khasis; his first name means 'holiness' (as in his mistress's title) and his second may be connected with the root *mr(r)* 'to fortify, bless'.

[5] *Hyn* is the Hurrian form of Ea, the Mesopotamian god of wisdom and a patron of craftsmen; it is vocalized *E-ya-an* (and identified with *Ku-šar-ru*) in the lexical list in *Ugaritica* V, p. 248.

[6] In view of the fact that that Qodesh-and-Amrur is delivering such a message to Kothar-and-Khasis at the beginning of tablet **4**, it seems unreasonable to disconnect tablets **3** and **4**, as on various grounds Ginsberg, Gordon, Rin and De Moor propose.

[7] Some see in this passage a description of the typical furniture of a Canaanite temple, thus supposing the gifts to be really intended for El; but 'sandals' fit ill with this suggestion.

She gives way to alarm and angrily wonders whether they have come as enemies to kill all her sons and kinsfolk.[1]

Ll. 26–47. When, however, she catches sight of the splendid gifts they are carrying, her anger turns to joy and she calls on Qodesh-and-Amrur to cast a net into the sea that she may have provisions with which to entertain such welcome visitors. He carries out her wish.

Col. iii   *[Beginning lost]*

Ll. 1–22. Anat, as they draw near to Athirat, is encouraging Baal with the prospect of an eternal kingdom; but Baal is himself still anxious and reminds his sister how because he has no house he has been treated with contumely in the assembly of the gods, where he has been served with foul and disgraceful food, though he hates all meanness and lewd conduct.[2]

Ll. 23–44. They arrive together where Athirat is and immediately present their gifts and make their entreaty. She asks why they do not first approach El himself and they reply tactfully that they intend to go to him when they have convinced her of the justice of their case. All three sit down with the other gods present to the repast which has been prepared.

[End lost]

Col. iv   *[Beginning lost]*

Ll. 1–62. Athirat bids her servant to get ready an ass for a journey. Having saddled it, he lifts her on to its back and she moves off; Qodesh-and-Amrur light up her way in front and Anat follows behind on foot, while Baal departs to Zephon. Athirat proceeds to El's distant abode and enters his presence and does homage. He, laughing and pleased to see his consort, asks whether she is hungry and thirsty after her long journey and invites her to eat and drink, supposing that it is her love of himself that has brought her thither. But Athirat, repeating Anat's words on an earlier occasion, compliments El on his wisdom and confesses

her own and Anat's desire to wait upon mightiest Baal, now that he is king and judge; however, they cannot until El who appointed him king permits him also to have a palace like the other gods, from which he may exercise his rule. El asks sarcastically whether Baal wishes himself as well as his gullible consort to become his labourers and handle the bricks and the trowel.

Cols. iv and v

Ll. 62–63. Nevertheless he gives his assent for a house to be built for Baal.

Col. v

Ll. 64–81. Athirat replies that all-wise as he is he has made the right decision; he has rendered it possible for Baal to ordain times for the appearance of the rain and the snow, the thunder and the lightning. She invites him to have the glad tidings taken to Baal, and to instruct him to collect the cedar-wood and bricks and precious metals which he will need for the building of his palace.

Ll. 82–102. Anat, delighted at Athirat's success, hurries to Baal on mount Zephon and imparts to him the good news and repeats El's instructions. Rejoicing, Baal does as he is bidden.

Ll. 103–127. Summoning Kothar-and-Khasis, he sets a meal before him, then urging the need for haste, describes the kind of palace that he wants him to build. Kothar-and-Khasis suggests that it ought to have windows in it, but Baal refuses to entertain the idea.

[End lost]

Col. vi

Ll. 1–14. Kothar-and-Khasis tells Baal that he will eventually come round to his suggestion, but he reaffirms his objection, explaining that he is afraid lest his daughters (i.e. mist and dew) may escape and, worse, lest his old enemy Yam may gain re-entry from beyond the firmament and trouble him again as he has done in

---

[1] In the Hittite myth of Elkunirsa, which as the name ('El creator of earth') implies is based on a Canaanite original, the storm-god boasts of having killed the many sons of Ashertu or Athirat; for references see Kramer, *Mythologies*, p. 155. Cp. **6** v

1ff., where these deities are apparently allies of Mot against Baal and suffer for it.

[2] Probably these insults are meant to reflect the poverty of Baal's cult at Ugarit in the period before he had a temple.

the past.[1]

Ll. 14–59. Kothar-and-Khasis still hopes that Baal will change his mind. Nevertheless work on the palace is quickly started; men are sent to Lebanon and Hermon to fetch timber and a fire is kindled, which burns for seven days, melting down the gold and silver ore which are being used in its construction. Baal, on the completion of the work, rejoices. He puts his new palace in order and holds a great feast, to which he invites his brothers and kinsfolk, Athirat's seventy sons and their consorts.

[*End lost*]

Col. vii   [*Beginning lost*]

Ll. 1–6. Baal in a speech (or someone else speaking on his behalf) recalls his triumph over Yam (which has led to this happy hour) and the gods with due respect remove themselves from Zephon.

Ll. 7–12. Baal then marches out through the land and seizes a large number of cities and towns, of which he makes himself lord (thus 'showing the flag' in his domains or, alternatively, annexing an empire to maintain his position).

Ll. 13–41. Returning home flushed with success, he puts away his former fears and resolves that he will after all have windows in his palace. Kothar-and-Khasis laughs at him but Baal, undeterred by his mirth, carries out his purpose. He then puts the windows to the test by thundering out of them; the earth reels and people far and near are terrified. Baal's enemies cling to the rocks in dismay and he mockingly calls out to them to inquire the cause of their fear; can it be because he strikes so fast or always hits the mark?

Ll. 42–52. Sitting down in his palace, he asks himself whether anyone, be he prince or commoner, will now dare to resist his royal power and resolves, should such exist, to send a courier to Mot god of death to demand that he invite his enemy into his gullet (an impressive way of willing his demise). He Baal alone is king over the gods and he alone has the means (in his rains) to satisfy the needs of teeming humanity.

Ll. 52–60. Even as he boasts to himself, however, Baal calls suddenly on his servants Gupn and Ugar to look around them; the daylight is becoming darkened and the sun obscured and flocks of birds are circling in the sky above (sure signs that night is about to fall).[2] He decides that the time has come to bind the snow and the lightning (and doubtless the rains also, though this last is not mentioned due to damage to the text).

[*End lost*]

Col. viii

Ll. 1–46. Gupn and Ugar are ordered to make their way to the two mountains marking the boundary of the earth, to lift them up with their hands and descend into the underworld;[3] there they are to search out Mot, whom they will find sitting on a throne deep in mud in a country heaped high with filth. They are warned not to come too near to him lest he consume them whole like a sheep or a goat, and are reminded also of the glowing heat of the sun which through Mot's power over Shapash is even now wearing out the sky. When after covering a huge distance they reach him, they are to deliver their master's message, which is that now he has a palace and is truly king he invites him, Mot, to a feast with their brothers; thus Mot too will acknowledge his sovereignty.

L. 47. The two messengers, having reached their destination, deliver their address and (in the lost ending) Mot begins his reply.

[*End lost*]

---

[1] That Yam has already been destroyed (**2** iv 27) but seems here again to be (potentially) active need not in the context of a myth with strong seasonal implications be regarded as illogical or cause surprise. In tablet **6** Mot likewise recovers after an even more thorough annihilation.

[2] Sc. mythological night. Many commentators find here and indeed in the whole second part of this column evidence that Mot has already begun to take hostile action against Baal; the translation of the text is difficult, but their interpretation does not seem to me to be a necessary one. Mot's name is certainly mentioned (in *ll.* 45–49 in connection with the fate Baal wishes on his enemies) but the god of death himself only appears actively on the scene when Gupn and Ugar deliver Baal's invitation to him (**5** i).

[3] On the conception of the nether-world at Ugarit and possible biblical and other parallels see the notes to this passage.

Interpretation

There are close parallels in language between the opening scene of this section of Elimelek's cycle and a passage in the Aqhat tale (**17** vi 30ff.), in which the goddess Anat speaks of the joyful celebrations that take place when Baal is brought to life. It is likely that both scenes are based on happenings in the course of Ugarit's autumnal or New Year festival at which the pilgrims, it seems, like Baal in the text drank generously of the first wine (*ḥmr*) from the recent vintage and listened to the minstrel (*nʿm*) chanting in oriental fashion the story of their god's successful battles with Yam and Mot. The festival commemorated both triumphs, but the scene is placed here in the cycle and not at the end after the defeat of Mot, because as it arranges Baal's exploits he becomes king following his victory over Yam and is probably thought of as being still king during Mot's temporary usurpation of his power. In that sense it marks one of the real high points in the drama of the whole cycle, namely Baal's accession to the kingship over gods and men.

There follows a bloodthirsty scene in which Baal recedes into the background and Anat is the chief actor, slaughtering mercilessly the inhabitants of two unnamed cities, which are probably (De Moor) to be identified with Ugarit and its port, and thereafter repeating the process with a number of guests in her own mansion. Gray compares Anat's bloodbath with the activity of the prophets of Baal on Mount Carmel (1 Kgs. xviii 25–29) who dance around the altar and lacerate themselves until the blood runs, and he relates both to a rite proper to the season of transition between the sterility of the late Syrian summer and the new season of fertility beginning with the rains of autumn. Whether there was either at Ugarit or among the Canaanites of Palestine such a formal yearly ritual during which men actually gashed themselves to induce the rains to come[1] we cannot say, but there is little doubt that the actions of the prophets of Baal do mirror (as such a ritual would) the intense anxiety

experienced in that area of the world towards the end of the dry season. We may therefore conclude that the same anxiety is reflected in this episode, in which Baal's worshippers suffer cruelly at the hands of Baal's own sister Anat, who is here as elsewhere in Ugarit's mythology the type or embodiment of divine bellicosity and savagery. In its present position it provides an admirable link between the events in which Baal won the kingship and those in which he has to exercise it. Will he in fact be able to provide the rains on which the people of Ugarit so depended?

In order to exercise his kingly power Baal has first in the logic of mythological thought to have a palace (i.e., temple), and Anat is summoned to Zephon to help him in this quest. The manner in which the summons is issued is perplexing. Anat is not told directly what Baal has in mind but is instructed to perform a peculiar ceremony involving the placing or pouring of bread, fruit, oil and honey in the earth[2] and then to come to Baal to hear a secret communication about the lightning. Since as far as we can tell (and the rest of the text of tablet **3** and that of tablet **4** are reasonably well preserved) Anat does not in fact carry out the ceremony at any later stage nor does Baal impart the aforesaid secret, the message of Baal may be no more than a ruse to get Anat to visit him. But even if this is so and the episode is therefore only an interlude in the plot, it takes up considerable space and must have at least some secondary significance for the meaning of the cycle. Anat's ceremony has often been judged to reflect some kind of rain charm used in autumn, but this is unlikely because for the parallel to be convincing the rite would have to be performed in the narrative; perhaps then the command is given simply to remind the pilgrims of the kind of benefits that they and the ground on which they laboured received from Baal (Caquot and Sznycer). We may interpret the mysterious talk about the lightning along the same lines; lightning was to the people of Ugarit a sign of Baal's might, they

---

[1] Some commentators go even further and suggest that human sacrifice may have been offered.

[2] Translations of this passage that bring in

references to the banishing of war and the coming of peace to the earth, though seductive, are probably illegitimate.

knew that it presaged the rains, but of how all this came about they had no idea; Baal, however, understood it, and the myth is content to leave it at that.

When Anat arrives on Zephon she is immediately despatched by Baal to the abode of the supreme god El to ask his permission to have a palace built. El's reply is not preserved but must have been negative or at any rate non-committal, for Baal then sends Qodesh-and-Amrur, the attendant of El's consort Athirat, to Egypt to ask Kothar-and-Khasis to make some beautiful gifts for her; with these he wins her round to his side, and she in turn persuades El to let Baal have his palace. When the work is finished, Baal holds a celebratory feast and then, like Yahweh marching from Mount Sinai (Ps. lxviii), goes out on an expedition of war to give surrounding cities a taste of his power; on returning he thunders from the windows of his palace, taunting his enemies and daring them to challenge him. He thus proves to the listeners' satisfaction that he can bring the rains whenever he wishes.

There can be little question that this long narrative, lovingly and expansively developed, is derived from a foundation-myth of Baal's temple at Ugarit, which has been worked into the corpus of traditions about him between the two primaeval conflicts with Yam and Mot.[1] Like Solomon's temple on Mount Zion (1 Kgs. v, vi 2 Chron. ii–iv) this temple is built of cedars of Lebanon and richly furnished with precious metals, and like it (cp. Isa. vi 1–4 1 Kgs. viii 27–30 Ps. xi 4 xx 3, 7) it is clearly conceived of as a kind of analogue or counterpart of a greater house in heaven. Doubtless a similar devotion was directed at it as biblical passages like Ps. xxvii 4 xliii 3–4 lxv 5 lxxxiv 2–5 etc. show was lavished on the one in Jerusalem.

An especially interesting episode is the one of the window which Baal was reluctant to have put in his palace. The tension is built up with much artifice so that those listening can be in

no doubt that not Kothar-and-Khasis nor any other god but only Baal controls the rains and decides when they should fall. Yet at the same time Baal's two foes of old, Yam and Mot, are forcefully brought into the picture; the window Baal puts in could, as he himself fears, have a dangerous as well as a beneficent effect and allow the chaos waters of Yam not long since conquered a means of re-entry to the firmament; and with hardly a break thereafter we have Baal unsuspectingly (or so it seems) inviting the second-named to visit him on Zephon. The terror and uncertainty of ancient man as he confronts the ambivalent forces of nature is vividly portrayed in this concluding scene of tablet 4.

3. BAAL AND MOT

The tablets

The invitation issued by Baal to Mot in the last column of *CTA* 4 provides the link between the theme of Baal's palace and that of his conflict with the god of death, which occupies the final two tablets of Elimelek's cycle. *CTA* 5 is made up of two fragments, found in 1930 and 1931; they supply about half the text of the first two and the last two columns but only the beginning of the lines on the middle two columns. The beginning (where the expected heading 'Of Baal' is lacking) and the end of the tablet are, however, intact. The beginning and end of *CTA* 6 are also preserved on a small fragment discovered in 1933, proving beyond doubt that it follows directly upon *CTA* 5; but the main part of this tablet was unearthed in 1930 and was in fact the first mythological text from Ugarit to be published; it comprises the bottom half of the first three columns and the top half of the last three. When the smaller and larger pieces were joined they fitted neatly, with the result that the text of cols. i and vi is all but complete. There is a space sufficient for three or four lines of writing at the foot of col. vi preceded by a colophon which is longer

---

[1] The message of Baal to Anat concerning the performance of a rite and the secret of the lightning, which as we saw above sits rather awkwardly in its present context, may have had a more central place in this foundation-myth, in which case we can assume

that only part of it was used in forming the larger cycle; possibly it also contained an actual description of the coming of the rains, which we do not get in the cycle (cp. 16 iii 2–16).

and more detailed than on any other mythological tablet; it seems reasonable to regard this colophon as marking the finish of the cycle.

Contents

5

Col. i

Ll. 1–11. Mot concludes his reply to the summons of Baal, and Gupn and Ugar take it back to Baal on mount Zephon.

Ll. 11–35. There they repeat it word for word to their master. Just as the dolphin longs for the open spaces of the sea or wild oxen are drawn to a pool or hinds to a spring, so he, Mot, like a lion in the desert, hungers constantly for human flesh and blood. If a supply of bodies is not available whenever his appetite is aroused, new ones have to be ferried to him across the river of death. Now Baal has thought fit to invite him to celebrate with his brethren and cousins, but he will give him only bread to eat and wine to drink. By so insulting him Baal has overreached himself and he will be transfixed by him in the same way as he, Baal, once transfixed Leviathan the sea-monster. Mot will cause the heavens to wilt and collapse and, breaking Baal into pieces, will swallow him down limb by limb. Far from him having to visit Baal, Baal will soon be dead and be descending into his subterranean domain.

[*End lost*]

Col. ii   [*Beginning lost*]

Ll. 1–7. Baal (or someone else speaking on his behalf) confesses his fear and dread of Mot. His gaping jaws, which he must enter, encompass both earth and heaven, reaching to the very stars, and his deathly power has already scorched the crops and the fruit of the trees.

Ll. 8–23. The speaker then bids Gupn and Ugar go back and tell Mot that Baal is eternally his slave. The messengers start without delay and finding Mot enthroned amid the mire of his customary surroundings, they report to him Baal's intention to submit. Mot rejoices and

asks sarcastically what the invitation that Baal has sent him can now mean.

[*End lost*]

Col. iii   [*Beginning lost*]

Ll. 1–26. Baal (having apparently—for the text is extensively damaged—made his way to the assembly of the gods) complains to El that the wide dominions which he has won are in danger of passing to Mot. He expresses the hope that this is not happening with El's connivance; for how in that case can he oppose it? He then despatches messengers successively to Sheger and Ithm, two deities with responsibility for cattle and sheep, to ask them to supply animals for a feast, to which he intends to invite Mot (clearly hoping therewith to provide a repast more to his liking and assuage his wrath).

Ll. 27–28. More messengers are despatched (presumably to another deity with a similar request).

[*End lost*]

Col. iv   [*Beginning lost*]

Ll. 1–26. A messenger (who can only have come from Mot) arrives in the divine assembly and demands to know where Baal is. Baal rises with his retinue and approaches the table where the other gods are dining on their usual sumptuous fare and quaffing wine from gold and silver vessels. The messenger of Mot and Baal together go up to El's house and the supreme god enquires what has been happening.

[*End lost*]

Col. v   [*Beginning lost*]

Ll. 1–17. A speaker (apparently Shapash the sun-goddess) addresses Baal (who has, we may assume, been abandoned by El to his fate). As the sequel shows (for the text at this point is missing or hopelessly damaged) she is advising him to procure a substitute in his own image, who will then be sought out and slain by Mot in his stead; the life thus lost will, it seems, be that merely of a calf.[1] Shapash (and the text here

---

[1] Note that if Baal does not in fact die but eludes death, this passage cannot be without its implications for the widespread theorizing about a dying and rising god in Near Eastern, particularly Canaanite, religion

(e.g. Hvidberg). The text is difficult, however, and partly damaged, and other commentators think that Baal is here providing himself with an heir in case he should fail to return.

becomes clearer) undertakes to bury his body and meanwhile she bids Baal himself take wind and cloud, thunder and rain, as well as his attendants and two of his daughters, and proceed to the two mountains that mark the entrance to the underworld (which she picturesquely describes as her own grave since in her journey round the world she visits it every night). Moving them aside, he is to go down into the earth and assume the condition of the strengthless shades (thus deceiving Mot and eluding his clutches until something can be done to rescue him).

Ll. 17–25. Baal listens to her counsel. He has connexion with a heifer in the fields near the realm of death (to which when Shapash caught up with him he was, it seems, already proceeding, no doubt to make abject obeisance before its ruler). The heifer is immediately delivered of a boy, whom Baal then clothes in his own robe and pronounces to be a gift or offering to the beloved one, a title often given to Mot.

[*End lost*]

Col. vi   [*Beginning lost*]

Ll. 1–10. Two deities (who are probably Baal's servants Gupn and Ugar) arrive at El's mountainous abode where the two oceans meet and doing homage, announce to him that they have been all round the earth searching for Baal and that they have just come from the land of pastures by the bank of the river of death, where they have found him lying dead.

Ll. 11–25. On hearing the news, El (not knowing that it is in fact a substitute victim that the two gods have found) descends from his throne and sits on the ground, strews dust on his head, dons sackcloth, shaves off his beard with a piece of flint, beats upon his breast and tears his arms, while he asks what will become of Baal's followers now that the prince of earth has perished; and he plaintively wishes that he himself could be with Baal in the nether-world.

Ll. 25–31. Meanwhile the goddess Anat also

has been scouring earth's mountains and hills looking for her brother and she too comes upon the substitute's dead body. She puts on sackcloth as a token of her grief.

6

Col. i

Ll. 1–8. Anat performs the same mourning rites (as El) for Baal and utters the same wish to follow him into the world below.

Ll. 8–31. Shapash meets her as she weeps without restraint and Anat requests her to lift the corpse on to her shoulder. The sun-goddess does not, as she might, tell her of the subterfuge that is being put into effect (for fear, we may suppose, lest it come to nought at a time when she is still under Mot's domination), but does as she is bidden; and thus loaded Anat proceeds to Baal's mountain Zephon[1] where she buries the body and slaughters large numbers of oxen and sheep, goats and asses as a fitting memorial to one who had been the brother-in-law of the gods.

Ll. 32–67. Anat, going on to the abode of El, enters his presence and does homage and then tells Athirat and her numerous family (many of whom have, as later transpires, been allies of Mot against Baal) that they can rejoice since Baal is dead. El thereupon asks Athirat to nominate one of her sons to be king in Baal's place, and she remarks that someone wise and understanding is required. El, suspecting that she means Athtar, doubts whether one so feeble (for all that he is named 'the terrible') can run as fast as Baal or wield Baal's weapons (that is, can harness wind and lightning so that the rains may fall when required). Nevertheless, Athirat designates Athtar. He seats himself on Baal's throne but finds that he is not tall enough to occupy it, thus confirming El's opinion. Athtar therefore admits himself unfit to reign on Zephon and descends from the throne but is allowed by the supreme god to exercise a more limited sovereignty on earth. Water is drawn in barrels and casks (evidently, though the text is

---

[1] Shapash presumably accompanies her, though this is not actually stated (cp. **5** v 5–6).

defective, a sarcastic allusion to Athtar's inability to fertilize the ground for which he is now responsible).

Col. ii [*Beginning lost*]

Ll. 1–23. Days pass, and Anat (now in the nether-world in search of her brother's shade) is filled with yearning for Baal, as a mother beast for her young, and she clutches Mot by his garment and demands that he restore him to her. After observing what an impossible request she is making of him, he answers that he like her had scoured every hill and mountain in the quest for Baal, hungry as usual for flesh to consume, and that the search had taken him to the pastures near the entrance to his own domains, where he had come upon him and peremptorily swallowed him as a wild animal carries off and swallows a kid.

Ll. 24–37. Meanwhile above, the sun is scorching hot (i.e. Mot is still supreme) and there is no rain; and days and months pass while Anat, thus rebuffed by Mot, continues her search high and low. Finally, losing patience, she seizes Mot, cleaves him with a sword, shakes him as with a riddle, burns him with fire, crushes him as with mill-stones, and then throws his remains into the open field for the birds to eat, as Mot cries out in his death-agony.

Col. iii [*Beginning lost*]

Ll. 1–21. Anat returns to El and announces that Mot is no more. She invites the supreme god to dream a dream whereby he may discover whether Baal can come back to life; if he should see the heavens raining oil and the valleys running with honey, she will know that the prince of earth yet exists. El has his dream and sees the signs that Anat desires him to see. He laughs and rejoices and declares that he can now rest from his anxiety; for Baal indeed lives.

Ll. 22–24. El now bids Anat speak to Shapash.

Col. iv

Ll. 25–49. She is to tell the sun-goddess that the earth is cracked with drought for lack of

Baal's fostering care, and to ask whether she knows where Baal is. Anat conveys El's message to Shapash, who promises that, if Anat makes preparations to welcome him back, pouring out sparkling wine and ordering wreaths for the gods to wear, she will herself go to look for Baal. Anat commits her to the gracious protection of El and commands that the aforesaid preparations be commenced.

[*End lost*]

Col. v

Ll. 1–6. Baal (now restored in full vigour to the world above) sets upon and fells the sons of Athirat[1] for their part in his downfall and resumes his seat on the throne of his dominion.

Ll. 7–25. Meanwhile, months and years pass, and in the seventh year Mot (now also resurrected) repairs to Zephon and complains to Baal of the treatment which because of him he has received (sc. at the hands of Anat). He demands that Baal surrender to him not this time himself but one of his own brothers that his appetite may be satisfied and his anger turned aside, threatening should he refuse to consume the teeming multitudes of mankind.

[*End lost*]

Col. vi

Ll. 1–8. Baal (evidently having sent Mot back to his own country while he considers this new threat) despatches an embassy to the god of death to tell him among other matters (for the text is imperfectly preserved) that he will banish him and that he, Mot, may eat his own servants if he is hungry.

Ll. 9–35. Mot in a rage asks what kind of answer this can be and returns forthwith to Zephon to have it out with Baal face to face. The two gods immediately fall to fighting savagely. They gore and bite each other and grapple together like wild beasts[2] until both fall exhausted to the ground, Baal lying across Mot. At this juncture Shapash arrives to warn Mot that fighting with Baal is useless and (in words that recall her address to Athtar on an earlier

---

[1] See above p. 11 note 1.

[2] Cp. *ANET*, p. 78 (Gilgamesh and Enkidu).

occasion[1]) tells him that El, so far from listening to his cries, is now on Baal's side and will overturn his throne and break his sceptre. Mot, at last afraid, picks himself up from the ground and declares that Baal is rightfully king.

[gap]

Ll. 41–52. The minstrel addresses a hymn to Shapash the sun-goddess in which after inviting her to partake of offerings that have been prepared, he lauds her pre-eminence over the shades and deities of the nether-world[2] and calls upon the craftsman-god Kothar-and-Khasis to protect her (as he had once done Baal) against the monsters of chaos.

Interpretation

The theme of this final section of Elimelek's cycle is the attempt by the god Mot (whose name means 'death') to usurp Baal's throne, which he had won by defeating the sea monster Yam-Nahar (*CTA* 1–2) and had consolidated by successfully completing his palace on Mt. Zephon (*CTA* 3–4). It is more accurately in fact described as a double attempt, for there are two challenges and two battles, in each of which Mot appears in a different role.

In the first challenge Mot is patently the god responsible for the summer drought, who causes the heavens to burn up and scorches earth's produce. Baal submits quickly and abjectly and has to descend for a while into the underworld (thus explaining the absence of the rains during that season); and his enemy is only repulsed and his own rescue effected through the combined efforts and ingenuity of the goddesses Anat, who slays Mot, and Shapash, who cheats him of his prey by getting Baal to provide a substitute in his own likeness. Baal is brought back to earth and after avenging himself on the gods who had been Mot's allies, takes his wonted seat on Zephon. At this point (6 v 7ff.) there is what seems to be an abrupt change of direction in the narrative, which is signalled by a brief statement about seven years elapsing. Thereafter, Mot, again in rudest strength, leaves his underground home for the first time in the myth and confronts Baal face to face on Zephon. Baal on this occasion feels sure enough of himself to dismiss Mot's challenge disdainfully, and a battle ensues in which the two antagonists fight to a draw; neither surrenders and it takes the intervention of the supreme god El to persuade Mot reluctantly to admit Baal's right to be king.

Some commentators, notably Gordon and Driver (in the first edition of the present textbook) make great play with the reference to the passing of seven years, arguing that the prolongation of the conflict is sufficient proof that the myth is not a seasonal drama about the temporary failure of the rains each year in the summer but is concerned with a rarer and to ancient man more perturbing phenomenon, namely the kind of recurring periods of famine that are also depicted in terms of a conventional seven years in the Joseph story in Genesis (xli 25ff., 47, 54ff.; cp. 19 42ff.). There is shrewd reasoning behind this theory, for if the myth had been purely seasonal in intent one would have expected it to finish when Baal was rescued from the nether-world and resumed his throne. A fresh dimension of meaning must therefore be looked for in the short narrative of Mot's second challenge to Baal, though I would question whether it has anything to do with Mot as bringer of drought or famine. Even in the much longer narrative of the first challenge, where the seasonal pattern is everywhere evident, Mot is something more than the disrupter of fertility, as the frequent and insistent descriptions of his voracious appetite for human flesh and of his gaping jaws show; and in the concluding scenes of tablet 6 it is this aspect of him that comes vividly to the fore, for he threatens should his demand for restitution against Anat be rejected to attack and consume all men on earth. Mot is there, I believe, quite explicitly what he is elsewhere implicitly, the personification of death *simpliciter*, humanity's ultimate enemy, a primaeval 'earth' monster every whit as dangerous to mankind as the primaeval 'sea' monster Yam-Nahar, one whom moreover Baal cannot defeat on his own but can only keep in check with the assistance of the distant head of the gods himself. As such, he is the prototype of a surprisingly large range of

---

[1] Cp. 2 iii 17–18.

[2] An allusion to her part in the defeat of Mot.

biblical images, as the footnotes in this edition attempt to bring out,[1] though only in the apocalyptic passage Isa. xxv 8, where in a magnificent figure the poet looks forward to a day when the swallower is himself swallowed, is there a veiled suggestion that the Hebrews knew of a mythical conflict between him and Yahweh.[2]

Apart from its general meaning, there are two smaller episodes in this section which have engendered much discussion.

The main issue in the first of these (**6** i 43ff.) is the identity of the god Athtar, whom Athirat during Baal's absence in the nether-world tries to have appointed king. This fierce yet when compared to Baal rather ridiculous deity is unable to exercise rule on Zephon and has to be content with a restricted dominion on earth below. As the reference immediately after to the drawing of water from or into barrels suggests, we are in the period of summer dryness when the rain-clouds disappear from Zephon's peak and divinity makes poor provision for man's needs; so Athtar's function must be explained in terms of that poor provision. Possibly he is the god of the desert (Gray) forcing men to conserve water carefully or the god of artificial irrigation (Gaster) compelling them to work hard for little reward. The same god appears briefly as a claimant, equally unsuccessfully, in the story of the contest between Baal and Yam-Nahar (**2** iii), but no details are given there that might allow us to assess his role further.[3]

The second episode is that at the end of the second column of *CTA* **6**, which tells of Anat's defeat of Mot. Some of the imagery in this passage is distinctly agricultural—winnowing, grinding, and if we translate the verb *dr*ᶜ by its commonest sense, sowing in the fields—and this has led most commentators to see in it a mythological counterpart to a ceremony held each year at the time of the grain harvest, in which the god Mot represents in some manner

the spirit of death within the grain, which has to be symbolically expelled so that the crop may be desacrilized for human consumption or, alternatively, so that the life of the seed may be safeguarded for the next year's planting. His role in bringing about the summer dryness is extended, as it were, into the growing process itself. It is very doubtful, however, whether such theories with their animistic and ritualistic connotations are either justified or necessary. As both Loewenstamm and Watson have pointed out, similar agricultural metaphors are used in the account of the destruction of the Golden Calf in Exod. xxxii 20, where they seem simply to be expressing the idea of total extinction. When the Ugaritic passage is read in this light, its other images (splitting with the sword and burning) need not be forcibly stretched to equate with farming activities, *dr*ᶜ may be more loosely translated to denote the 'scattering', not of seed, but of the pieces of Mot's dismembered corpse in the open fields for the birds to eat,[4] and the parallel allusion to their 'scattering' in the sea (**6** v 19), presumably for the fish to consume, is no longer awkward. The scene describes Mot's execution rather extravagantly, but there is no more to it than that.

The cycle closes fittingly with a hymn in praise of the sun-goddess Shapash, paying tribute to one who had been a spectator at much of its action and who, whether as El's plenipotentiary or on her own initiative, had intervened decisively on not a few occasions to bring about the triumph of good over evil.

4. KERET

The tablets

The legend of Keret[5] survives on three tablets, discovered in 1930 or 1931, each having three columns of text on both obverse and reverse sides. Of these tablets one (*CTA* **14**) is

---

[1] See further the detailed studies of Tromp and Miss Wakeman.

[2] Cp. also 1 Cor. xv 26, 54.

[3] See now, however, Addenda where a new reading at **6** i 66–67 removes the reference to drawing water.

[4] Cp. **2** iv 28–31 (of Yam) Ps. lxxiv 14 (of Leviathan) Ezek. xxix 5 (of Pharaoh as the monster).

[5] The pronunciation 'Keret' is precariously based on the Hebrew gentilic adjective 'Kerethite' (Virolleaud), but it is kept for convention's sake; quite likely the name is non-Semitic.

very well and one (*CTA* **16**), except for some
damage in the middle of the text, is tolerably
well preserved; the other (*CTA* **15**) is in a very
poor condition, as each column has lost over
half its text. All three tablets are from the hand
of Elimelek. As no catch-lines remain, the
sequence of the tablets is established solely by
their contents,[1] which are, however, adequate
for the purpose. There is no need to suppose
that further tablets have been lost, since the
story as we have it, though incomplete in some
important details due to lacunas, forms a
satisfactory thematic whole (Merrill); but it is
possible that the second and third tablets were
separated by and that the third was followed by
one such.

Contents

14

Ll. 1–43. The audience is invited by the
minstrel to bewail with Keret, a just king, the
loss in quick succession of seven wives by
natural death and pestilence, sea and sword,
and the ruin of his prospects, so that he is now
without royal dignity, lacking an heir. One
night, as sleep overcomes his grief, he has a
dream in which the supreme god El appears to
him and asks him why he weeps and whether
the reason is that, lacking the marks of sovereignty, he desires a kingdom like that of the
father of mankind.

[gap]

Ll. 53–58. Keret refuses the gifts with which
El with conventional words has tried to console
him and states that his only desire is for sons
and descendants.

Ll. 59–153. El in answer bids him wash and
deck himself out gaily, mount a high tower and
there offer sacrifice to himself and to Baal son
of Dagon, and then descend and prepare
provisions for a campaign, in which he shall put
a vast host[2] into the field, leaving not even the
infirm or the newly wed husband behind at
home. This army, swarming over the countryside, will in seven days reach a place called
Udm and, having frightened the working
women from the fields and the wells, must
remain quiet outside it for another six days. On
the seventh day its king Pabil, kept from his
sleep by the noise of his beasts, untended due
to the siege, will send messengers to Keret who
will try to buy him off by offering him gold,
slaves and horses. Keret, however, must send
back the messengers, refusing Pabil's gifts but
demanding his daughter Huray,[3] lovely as a
goddess, in marriage; for his only desire is a
wife by whom he may beget a family and a son
to succeed him.

Ll. 154–194. Keret, waking up, puts into
effect the instructions of his divine visitor. He
makes himself ready, sacrifices to El and Baal,
prepares provisions, and leads out his army
which overruns the countryside.

Ll. 194–206. On the third day the army comes
to a shrine at which Keret vows that, if he
obtains Huray, he will devote several times her
weight in gold and silver to the local goddess,
here given the names Athirat of Tyre and Elat
of Sidon.[4]

Ll. 207–229. Continuing another four days,
the army encamps before Udm and, having
frightened the working women into the city,
remains quiet for seven days. Pabil, unable to
sleep for the noise made by his beasts, consults
his wife.

[Damaged section]

Ll. 245–261. Pabil now sends envoys to Keret
with instructions to offer him the gifts already
mentioned if only he will not besiege Udm but
will remove himself far from it.

[Gap]

Ll. 265–306. The envoys arrive and deliver
their message to Keret who refuses the gifts
and declares that he wants only Huray; for El
has promised him issue by her. They depart to
take his answer to Pabil.

---

[1] The older numbering of the tablets (I K=**14**,
III K=**15**, II K=**16**) follows the order of their
publication (Virolleaud).

[2] Symbolic clearly of the involvement of the whole
community in the king's fate.

[3] This name has been variously read; for whether
it is a non-Semitic or a Semitic name is not known.

[4] Note that this reference would seem to locate
the action of the poem (and perhaps therefore the
origin of the legend) in or near Phoenicia; see,
however, p. 23 note 4.

15

Col. i [*Beginning lost*]

Ll. 1–8. The envoys (leading Huray out to Keret) tell him that the people of Udm will sorely miss her ministrations and that they bemoan her departure as a heifer lows for her calf or as the sons of absent soldiers cry for their mothers.

Col. ii [*Beginning lost*]

Ll. 1–28. Baal rises in the assembly of the gods (convened, it appears, at Keret's house) and urges El to bless the king. El, taking a cup in his hand, blesses Keret and promises that the wife whom he is about to marry shall bear him eight sons; one of these, called Yaṣṣib and presumably the eldest, will be suckled by Athirat and the virgin Anat, the nurses of the gods.

Col. iii [*Beginning lost*]

Ll. 1–30. Keret is told by El that he will be greatly exalted among past rulers of the city. Furthermore, his wife will bear eight daughters, of whom even the youngest shall enjoy the birth-right of a first-born child. The gods, having blessed Keret, go back to their own abodes, and in the course of seven years[1] Keret begets as many sons and daughters as have been promised to him; and Athirat asks rhetorically whether Keret means to keep the vow he had made, threatening disaster should he not.

[*End lost*]

Col. iv [*Beginning lost*]

Ll. 1–9. Keret bids his wife prepare a great feast for the lords of Khubur (apparently the name of his kingdom).

[*Gap*]

Ll. 14–28. Obeying his instructions she prepares meat and drink and admits the lords of Khubur to the palace and when they have entered it, she carves the joints and then tells them that she has invited them to make sacrifice on Keret's behalf (for, as the following columns show, he has fallen grievously ill).

[*End lost*]

Col. v [*Beginning lost*]

Ll. 1–29. A second time Huray prepares the feast as described and carves the joints and again she tells her audience (whose identity is not recoverable) the reason why she has invited them, namely that they may make sacrifice and may weep for Keret as for the dead; for it is her fear that he will soon reach the realm of death, to be replaced on the throne by Yaṣṣib, unless El should intervene to restore him to health.

[*End lost*]

Col. vi

Ll. 1–8. Huray summons another audience (perhaps this time her and Keret's children) to offer sacrifice for the king and to condole with him.

[*End lost*]

16

Col. i

Ll. 1–11. One of Keret's sons, soliloquizing, laments that he must now creep silently into his father's room like a dog and asks himself whether he is not in fact dying and it is not time for mourning women to be called. Already the mountains of Baal and their broad environs are grieving for him. Is Keret then really a son of El?

Ll. 11–23. He enters his father's presence and sorrowfully says that hitherto he has been gladdened by the thought of Keret's immortality, but now that he must creep before him like a dog he can but ask if he is indeed a son of El, whose issue do not surely die.

Ll. 24–45. Keret bids his son not to shed tears over him but to call his sister Thitmanat,[2] whom he knows to be full of pity, to weep for him. So as not to alarm her he is to wait till evening and go to inform her that he is preparing a sacrifice to which he invites her.

---

[1] Obviously a conventional number.

[2] As *ttmnt* means 'eighth', the girl so-called must be the eighth daughter of her parents; the Phoen.

'*šmn* = Greek *Esmounos* was similarly so called for the same reason (Eusebius *Praep. Evang.* i 10, 39). Cp. also Latin *Octavia*.

Meanwhile he himself is to perform a mysterious ritual at the gate of the palace which will, if successful, win divine assistance for Keret.

Ll. 46–62. This son, here called the hero Elhu, goes out to the gate. But as he arrives he is surprised by his sister, who has come to the well to draw water and who when she sees what he is doing, gives way to tears, suspecting that the king her father is ill; but Elhu apparently (for the text is damaged) answers that Keret is not sick but is summoning them both to a banquet.

Col. ii   [*Damaged section*]
Ll. 79–120. Thitmanat, from her brother's behaviour more than ever suspicious, asks him openly how long their father has been sick, and he answers that it is now three or four months; he then states bluntly that Keret is on the verge of death and that she ought to be thinking of making ready a tomb for him. After bewailing her father in soliloquy in the same words as have already been used by her brother, she proceeds weeping into his presence.
[*End lost*]

Col. iii   [*Beginning lost*]
Ll. 1–17. A ceremony is being held in Baal's abode on Mt. Zephon[1] to induce the return of the rains (which have, it seems, ceased in consequence of Keret's illness); and servants are dispatched round the earth to see the beneficent effect on the soil. The farmers look up joyfully as they plough and sow, glad that the dearth of bread, wine and oil is coming to an end. The good news is taken to Keret.
[*End lost*]

Col. iv   [*Beginning lost*]
Ll. 1–16. El, addressing someone who he says is as wise as himself (and therefore presumably Baal) tells him to fetch Elsh the steward of the gods and his wife. This done, he sends them to the top of a building (apparently, as the next column suggests, to summon the assembly of the gods).
[*End lost*]

Col. v   [*Beginning lost*]
Ll. 6–32. El calls seven times on the gods as they are gathered in assembly to see if there is any who will do anything to banish Keret's illness, but none answers him; he thereupon announces that he himself will cast a spell and provide the means to drive out the plague. He picks up a handful of mud or dung for this purpose.

[*Gap*]
Ll. 42–53. El addresses a female demon (having, it appears, fashioned her out of the mud and brought her to life) and giving her the name Sha'taqat (meaning that she 'drives away' sickness), he bids her fly in secret to Keret's city and by touching him on the head with her wand, expel the plague and then wash him clean of sweat.
[*End lost*]

Col. vi
Ll. 1–2. El announces the imminent defeat of death and the victory of Sha'taqat.
Ll. 2–24. Sha'taqat proceeds, sobbing but in stealth, to the palace of Keret and after curing him in the aforementioned manner, she washes him. He becomes hungry, and it is evident that death has been vanquished and that she, Sha'taqat, is triumphant. Thereupon Keret asks for food, which Huray supplies; after partaking of it, he resumes his seat upon the throne.
Ll. 25–58. Meanwhile Yassib (knowing nothing of what has happened) sits brooding in the palace; and he resolves to go to his father and upbraid him for neglecting his kingly duties (for, as he intends to remind him, violent men have during his illness waxed powerful and the weak have gone unprotected) and to bid him descend from his throne that he, Yassib, may ascend it in his place. Yassib goes into his father's presence and carries out his resolve. Keret, however, promptly curses him, calling upon the god Horon and the goddess Athtart[2] to break open his skull; so shall he be humbled.

---

[1] See p. 8 note 1.

[2] See on these deities p. 4 notes 5, 6.

Interpretation

The story of Keret opens with a description of the hero, king of a place called Khubur, mourning the collapse of his hopes for the future, since death has deprived him of seven wives one after another before he could have children by them. The question immediately posed is how a king without wife or heir can be truly king. For only he is fit to be such who has a wife with whom he can have connexion and prove his manhood (**2** iii 22)[1] and an heir to support him in life and perform the necessary rites after his death (**17** i 21–34) and thus ensure the continuance of his name. Keret, in response to instructions from El received in a dream, restores his position by invading a neighbouring kingdom and taking the daughter of its king in marriage and in due course begetting issue on her. As he is pictured rejoicing there is, however, an ominous hint that a vow he had made during the campaign has not been fulfilled; and soon afterwards Keret shows signs of failing health and falls so seriously ill that he is thought to be dying. He can no longer adequately administer justice and his illness seems also to affect adversely the fertility of the crops. The question posed in this latter part of the story is how the fabric of a society can be maintained and its prosperity safeguarded by a king whose health is impaired. Following divine intervention the rains which had failed return and Keret is miraculously cured and remounts his throne. The story ends with an attempt by one of the king's sons to usurp his place,[2] which Keret now recovered is easily able to quell.

The main thrust of the poem, certainly of the second and third tablets, is ideological. Keret is the typical sacral king of ancient Near Eastern belief, the channel of blessing to his community and the upholder of its order; as he suffers or prospers so do his land and people.[3] But behind the typical there seems to be some genuine historical reminiscence, at any rate in the first tablet; for the account of Keret's expedition to Udm is elaborated to a very much greater length than any other incident, and the expedition has its location, moreover, far from Ugarit in the vicinity of Tyre and Sidon. No-one now seriously espouses Virolleaud's early interpretation, which found in this account allusions to Abraham's father Terah and the Israelite tribes of Asher and Zebulon, and regarded it as depicting a Phoenician invasion of southern Palestine and Edom in the Patriarchal age; this rests on a number of mistranslations, inevitable in the first attempt to decipher these difficult texts, which have come to be recognized in the progress of knowledge as impossible. But that Keret and Pabil,[4] though neither their names nor those of their kingdoms occur in any other extant text, were actual historical figures, the story of whose clash in war and subsequent alliance became in time the basis of a myth about the nature and value of kingship, is difficult to deny.

5. AQHAT

The tablets

The story of Aqhat, son of Daniel, formerly entitled 'Danel' (Virolleaud), is now known to have been called 'Aqhat' from the superscription of one of the tablets (*CTA* **19**). What remains is contained in three tablets, all dis-

---

[1] The purpose of taking Abishag for David was not so much to keep him warm as to prove him still possessed of sexual power; when 'the king knew her not', the failure of his power was patent and his sons began to take steps to seize the throne (1 Kgs. i 1–39).

[2] When the Hebrew king Azariah or Uzziah was smitten with leprosy, his son acted for him; possibly he had been deposed (2 Kgs. xv 5).

[3] Cp. the prologue to the Code of Hammurabi (*ANET*, 164ff.) 2 Sam. xxi 17 xxiii 2–5 Ps. ii 6ff. xlv 3ff. lxxii *passim* lxxxix 20ff. cx Isa. xi 2ff. Lam. iv 20 etc.

[4] This pronunciation is supported by the Hittite *Pabili* (De Langhe) so the name like that probably of Keret himself is non-Semitic. It may be that we should deduce from this that the story of the expedition was itself originally non-Semitic, belonging for instance to northern Mesopotamia (as Astour argues on the basis of some of the place-names, notably that of Keret's kingdom Khubur, which is the name of a river in that region), and that one of the ways by which it was given a Semitic dress was to situate the incident of the king's vow (which is the link between the expedition and the more symbolic happenings of the last two tablets) in Phoenicia.

covered in 1930 and all written by Elimelek; two (*CTA* **17** and **19**) are in a tolerable state of preservation and one (*CTA* **18**) is badly damaged at both beginning and end and lacks the two middle columns (of a total of four).[1] Two columns of *CTA* **17** are also missing, but that tablet had originally six, being the exception, since *CTA* **19** also has four columns. The missing columns and the frequent losses at the top and bottom of those that survive create several gaps in the narrative, but the sequence of the three tablets as given is not in doubt, and enough of the text is preserved to reveal the general outline of the plot and a fair number of its details. We probably possess (except for a few lines) the beginning of the story, but the third tablet (**19**) breaks off in the middle of an incident and clearly at least one other tablet must have followed it.

Contents

17

Col. i   [*Beginning lost*]

Ll. 1–16. Daniel, a righteous chief or patriarch,[2] undergoes a seven-day rite of incubation in the hope of obtaining a son; for unlike other members of his family he is without issue.

Ll. 16–34. On the seventh day Baal takes pity on his misery and implores El, whom he addresses as father,[3] to grant Daniel the blessing of a son capable of performing the proper duties towards him during his life and after his death, and of rendering due honour to the ancestral gods.

Ll. 35–49. Daniel is blessed by El so that he may feel manly strength and have connexion with his wife, who will then conceive and bear a son capable of carrying out the aforesaid duties.

[*End lost*]

Col. ii   [*Beginning lost*]

Ll. 1–23. El in a dream tells Daniel what is to happen; and he is relieved and joyful to think that he, too, will have a son to carry out all filial duties.

Ll. 24–38. Daniel returns to his home and holds a feast lasting seven days in honour of the 'wise women', called the Kotharat,[4] who arrive to ensure that a son is successfully conceived.

Ll. 39–47. The Kotharat, having accomplished this, depart and Daniel sits down to reckon the months until the child (who when the text is resumed is called Aqhat) shall be born.

[*End lost*]

[*Two columns lost*]

Col. v   [*Beginning lost*]

Ll. 1–13. Daniel is sitting at the city gate, where he dispenses justice to widows and orphans, when he sees the divine craftsman Kothar-and-Khasis coming from afar with a bow and arrows for Aqhat (who is now grown to manhood).

Ll. 13–33. He at once summons his wife Danatay to prepare a feast for the divine visitor, who having given the bow and arrows to Daniel, partakes of the repast and departs.

Ll. 33–39. Daniel solemnly presents the bow to Aqhat, reminding him to offer a portion of what he catches to the gods.

[*End lost*]

Col. vi   [*Beginning lost*]

Ll. 1–19. In the course of a feast (at which apparently Aqhat is present) the goddess Anat sees the bow flashing like lightning across the ocean and, dashing her cup to the ground in vexation, offers Aqhat as much silver and gold as he wants if only he will give it to her.

---

[1] The old numbering I D (**19**), II D (**17**), III D (**18**) is that given in the original edition, in which they are arranged in order of size (Virolleaud).

[2] Daniel is only once given the title 'king' (**19** 152), though his house is called a palace; but his manner of life as described in the tablets is much simpler than that of Keret, recalling the atmosphere of the Patriarchal stories of Genesis rather than, as do the Keret texts, the urban monarchy of Jerusalem.

[3] **17** i 24 and possibly vi 29. The title may, however, only be honorific (see p. 5 note 2).

[4] Goddesses whose name means 'skilful' (cp. Kothar), associated here and in tablet **24** (q.v.) with the conception and birth of children.

Ll. 20–25. Aqhat answers that materials for making a bow and arrows abound and advises Anat to ask Kothar-and-Khasis to make a set for her.

Ll. 25–38. Anat, however, wants these very weapons and no others and offers to make Aqhat immortal and to give him a life as long as that of Baal and the other gods in return for them. Aqhat replies that she is lying;[1] she cannot confer these gifts, since old age and death are the lot of all men, including himself.

Ll. 39–41. Moreover, she must know that a bow is a soldier's weapon; can a woman use it?

Ll. 41–45. Anat, while she laughs at Aqhat's obstinacy, warns him that she finds his conduct presumptuous and will bring him to heel.

Ll. 46–55. She then hurries to El's distant abode and falling down in homage before him, complains of Aqhat's treatment of herself.

[*End lost*]

18

Col. i   [*Beginning lost*]

Ll. 1–14. Anat threatens El with violence and sarcastically bids him call upon Aqhat to save him from her wrath if he will not do what she wishes.

Ll. 15–19. El answers that he knows the ruthless character of the goddess and will not stand in her way; anyone who thwarts her will have to face the consequences.

Ll. 19–34. Anat sets out in search of Aqhat and having found him after a long journey, seeks (this time disguised as a mortal maiden) to involve him in her affairs by fair words. She conducts him to a place called Qart-Abilim (hoping no doubt to gain the weapons by some stratagem).

[*End lost*]

[*Two columns lost*]

Col. iv   [*Beginning lost*]

Ll. 1–11. Anat (having failed in this approach) obtains the services of her attendant Yatpan to procure the weapons; she tells him of Aqhat's presence at Qart-Abilim and expresses her fear lest, unless something is done immediately, the new moon will bring a change of luck and Aqhat will escape them.

Ll. 11–15. Yatpan encourages Anat to proceed, and we are given the information that Aqhat has been left behind in the mountains, where having grown tired he prepares a meal.

Ll. 16–27. Anat proposes a plan of action; she will turn Yatpan into an eagle or hawk and put him on her glove; she will then send a flock of these birds to hover over Aqhat at his meal, accompanying them herself, and will launch Yatpan against Aqhat to strike him down.

Ll. 27–42. She carries out this plan and Aqhat is killed; thereat she weeps as convention demands, chiding the fallen hero for having opposed her. The birds fly away (apparently having consumed Aqhat's corpse).

19

Ll. 1–19. The bow, however, has been broken and dropped into the sea[2] (perhaps in the struggle or accidentally as Yatpan was flying away), whereupon Anat expresses her chagrin at the collapse of her scheme and her regret at the failure of the crops, which will inevitably follow the spilling of Aqhat's blood.

Ll. 19–37. Daniel is sitting in court dispensing justice as usual (unaware that anything has happened), when he suddenly espies his daughter Pughat approaching from afar; for she has seen the eagles and hawks over her father's house, the land dried up, and the fields bare of green herbage, and divined that an important person has been slain. Weeping, she takes Daniel's robe and rends it.

Ll. 38–48. Daniel, now as a result of her action in fear lest a prolonged drought may be imminent, prays that the dew and rains may come in their proper season, so that the earth should again yield its fruits.

Ll. 49–74. Furthermore, he bids Pughat prepare his ass and, having mounted it with her help, rides round his scorched land, embracing any green blade that he can find in the hope

---

[1] Cp. the similarly daring response of Gilgamesh to Ishtar's offer of marriage (*ANET*, p. 84); cp. also *Od.* v 203ff. (Calypso and Odysseus).

[2] So Gilgamesh lost the plant of life immediately after obtaining possession of it (*ANET*, p. 96).

that it may recover and not fail; he also wishes ironically that Aqhat may be there to gather it into the granary.

Ll. 75–88. Meanwhile Pughat, looking round her, can see nobody; but suddenly two messengers, showing signs of grief, arrive; they act out in mime the killing of Aqhat and announce (by way of breaking the news) that if only victory lay with Zephon (otherwise Baal)[1] they would be bringing good tidings; then would Daniel and Pughat have been filled with joy.

Ll. 89–98. Unfortunately their news is that Aqhat is dead, slain by Anat; and hearing it, Daniel is seized with a paroxysm of rage and swears to slay the slayer of his son.

[*Gap*]

Ll. 105–112. Daniel perceives eagles coming up against the sun and cries out to Baal to bring them down with broken wings to his feet, when he will rip open their bodies to see if Aqhat's flesh and bones are in them; if they are, he will bury what remains in a grave.

Ll. 113–120. He has scarcely spoken when Baal brings the birds down, but Daniel finds nothing in their gizzards; so he asks Baal to restore them to life and bids them fly away.

Ll. 120–134. Baal brings down Hirgab the father of the eagles with the same result.

Ll. 134–147. Lastly Baal brings down Ṣumul the mother of the eagles and Daniel, on ripping her open, finds the flesh and bones of Aqhat inside and buries them in a dark vault.

Ll. 148–151. He then threatens the eagles that if they fly over Aqhat's grave and disturb his rest, Baal will again break their wings.

Ll. 151–169. Daniel curses the three towns, including Qart-Abilim, which lie nearest to the scene of the murder, calling down banishment and blindness on the inhabitants and loss of

vegetation on their fields for their share of the guilt.

Ll. 170–188. Daniel returns to his palace where he and professional mourners bewail the death of Aqhat for seven years,[2] after which he dismisses the mourners and offers sacrifice to the gods.

Ll. 189–202. Pughat then prays to the gods, to whom her father had sacrificed, to bless her intention to take vengeance on the murderer of her brother, and Daniel reiterates her plea.

Ll. 203–212. Pughat now paints her face (disguising herself as the goddess Anat), puts on male attire with dagger and sword, throwing a woman's cloak over it all, and sets out for the tent of Yatpan, arriving there at sunset.

Ll. 212–222. Her arrival is reported to Yatpan, who instructs his servants to give her wine. He pours out a libation to the local god, boasting that the hand that slew Aqhat will slay thousands more of his mistress's enemies.

Ll. 222–224. Pughat's heart is described as being like a serpent's as the servants twice give her Yatpan's mixture to drink.

Interpretation

The background to the story of Daniel and Aqhat is a righteous chief's need of a son; for otherwise there will be no-one to tend him in old age, to perform the proper rites after his death and maintain the worship of the family god. In answer to the prayers of Daniel[3] and on the intercession of his favourite deity Baal, whom he worships under the title of Rapiu or 'the shade',[4] the supreme god El grants him a son. The child is named Aqhat[5] and when he grows up, he is endowed with a magnificent bow and arrows made for him by the divine

---

[1] See at **19** 84.

[2] An exaggeration of the traditional seven days (Gen. 1 10).

[3] The name is the same as that of the sage counted as one of the three righteous men of Hebrew tradition (Ezek. xiv 14, 20 xxviii 3); it is sometimes argued that both these names are different from that of the wise man at the court of Nebuchadnezzar, since the form in Ezek. does not have a vowel letter (thought it is pointed Daniel), but the name *Da-ni-èl* is found as early as the time of the Mari letters, whereas no form Danel is known (Lipiński).

[4] Apparently a title of Baal associated with his

summer stay in the underworld; cp. *rpù b'l* (**22** B 8). Rapiu is not to be confused with the *ilîb* or 'god of the father(s)' of *l.* 27. Note that if Albright's identification of the place with which Rapiu was associated is accepted (Hermel), the original home of the Aqhat legend would seem to be Phoenicia; it may be significant in this regard that in Ezek. xxviii the recipient of the oracle is the king of Tyre.

[5] The pronunciation of the name as 'Aqhat' is conventional, since the vowel of the last syllable is unknown; it may be derived from the same root as that of the Levite 'Qohath' in the Bible (Gaster). Is it connected with the S.-Arab. *qht* 'commanded'?

craftsman Kothar-and-Khasis. His father warns him that the first-fruits of the chase must be offered in a temple. Aqhat may have failed to accord with this requirement, and this may have been a contributory cause of the disaster which subsequently befalls him. But in what survives of the narrative the chief cause is the envy of Anat, the sister of Baal; and when Aqhat refuses to give the weapons to her, a mere woman who cannot use them, she engages her henchman Yatpan to murder him and get them for her. Aqhat is killed, but the weapons are accidentally destroyed, and Anat is thwarted in her ultimate purpose. Following Aqhat's death Baal withholds the rain and the crops fail. Pughat,[1] the sister of Aqhat, perceiving the drought and observing eagles overhead (birds that may always be found where there is blood) concludes that the land has been polluted by bloodshed. She communicates her suspicion to Daniel, who goes on tour through the countryside seeking signs of vegetation and carrying out a fertility ritual upon the few solitary shoots he discovers. Meanwhile, he is apprized that the victim of the suspected crime is his own son. He therefore vows vengeance on the murderer and searching for Aqhat's remains, finds them in the gizzard of one of the eagles and duly buries them in the family vault. He then curses the cities nearest the scene of the crime, in accordance with ancient oriental custom, and holds mourning ceremonies which last seven years. Thereafter Pughat takes upon herself the duty of blood revenge, disguises herself as Anat, and is received and honoured as such at Yatpan's tent. Just as she is drinking the wine he gives her the story tantalisingly breaks off.

It is difficult to decide whether we have in these three tablets the remnant of an old Canaanite 'folk' or 'wisdom' tale about a pious chief or patriarch, the continuance of whose house is temporarily put at risk through the death of his only son at the hands of a capricious deity but is in the end safeguarded by his faithfulness to clan custom (my own view; we may compare the prose story of Job), or whether such a tale serves only as the backcloth to some kind of myth, fertility or otherwise, centering on the bow and the death and resurrection of the son (Gaster, Hillers, etc.). The fact that it is the son's name and not the father's which is attached to the tablets lends credence to the second interpretation, but it should not be forgotten that in the story as we have it, the father figures rather more prominently than the son, and we do not know what role he may have played in its dénouement. The account of the resurrection (or the replacement) of Aqhat is absent from the text, and was presumably contained, together with a description of how Yatpan met his deserts and how fertility returned to the land and prosperity to Daniel's house, in the lost final tablet or tablets. Whether the bow was also recovered (and is consequently to be considered a significant element in the meaning of the story), and whether Anat repented of her violent behaviour and took part in the reviving (or replacing) of Aqhat, or Baal as Daniel's champion alone brought this about, cannot at present be determined. Until (if ever) the missing portion of the text turns up and it is discovered how the various strands in the narrative are resolved, no satisfactory comprehensive interpretation is possible.[2]

---

[1] The Ugar. *Pġt* is the same word as the Arab. *fauġatu* 'exhalation of perfume' just as the Hebr. *Pûʿāh* (Exod. i 15) is the same as the Arab. *fauʿatu* 'aroma of perfume' (Hava), so that the two names are ultimately identical, since the Arabic words are but variant forms of each other. She is probably not to be regarded as a significant mythological figure (see at **19** 50ff.).

[2] The connection between the Aqhat legend and the three extremely fragmentary tablets containing the myth of the Rephaim or 'shades' (*CTA* **20–22**; see Appendix) remains to be elucidated. Like the Aqhat texts these were written by Elimelek. The name and titles of Daniel appear at **20** B 7–8, where

he makes a statement at a feast which the Rephaim are holding, but he does not figure again (at least by name) in the proceedings. It is unlikely that what in its original state must have been a narrative of considerable length about the activity of the Rephaim and other divine beings belongs *in toto* to the missing dénouement of the quite different kind of story about folk heroes that the Aqhat tablets contain. The most that can be hazarded as a guess is that Daniel in his attempts to have his dead son restored to life paid a visit to the underworld (cp. *Od.* xi) and that this encounter between him and the Rephaim was enough to have him assigned a small part in a mythological complex devoted to them.

6. SHACHAR AND SHALIM AND THE GRACIOUS GODS

The tablet

The text of the poem is written in a single column on both sides of the tablet *CTA* **23,** discovered in 1930; the number of lines is complete, but the upper right corner of the obverse and lower right corner of the reverse side have been broken off. Otherwise, apart from patches where the script is rubbed or partly effaced, the tablet is in good condition. The difficulty, therefore, of interpreting the text lies not so much in the state of the tablet as in the form and nature of its subject-matter. The first part is divided into sections by horizontal lines drawn across the tablet and separating portions of hymn or myth from more prosaic rubrical parts, which contain directions of a liturgical or ritual character; but the connexion between the poetical pieces and the directions is not always clear. The second part contains the narrative account of the birth of certain deities; this is only once interrupted by a short rubric. There is no superscription giving the title nor colophon giving the name of the scribe.

Contents

23

Ll. 1–7. Hymn in which the singer invokes the gracious and fair gods, recalling that they have established a city in the desert and inviting them to eat and drink of the offerings prepared for them. He then prays for peace on the king and queen (who are perhaps though not necessarily present) and on the officiating ministers.

Ll. 8–11. Excerpt from mythological text describing the destruction of the god of death, who is here given the additional title of 'prince'[1] and who carries two sceptres representing respectively the dangers of loss of children and widowhood. He is set upon by vine-dressers who prune and bind him and cast him down on the terrace like so much dead wood.

Ll. 12. Rubric stating that the above tale (or it may be the above hymn) should be repeated seven times with appropriate responses by the ministers.

Ll. 13–15. Rubric stating that a hymn about the fields of the goddesses Athirat and Rahmay (who is Anat) should be sung and that certain ritual acts involving coriander, mint and incense should be performed seven times.

Ll. 16–18. Quotation, being probably the first line, from a mythological tale (or another hymn) depicting Rahmay as out hunting, followed by further instructions for the minstrel and the ministers.

Ll. 19–22. Rubrics concerning dwellings (that is, niches or portable shrines) for the gods and concerning precious stones and vestments.

Ll. 23–27. Second hymn invoking the gracious gods who are described as sucking the breasts of Athirat. The singer prays that the sun-goddess Shapash may lead them to an abundance of grapes and asks a blessing as before on the officiating ministers.

Ll. 28–29. Rubric stating that the hymn about the fields of Athirat and Rahmay should be repeated.

Ll. 30–54. Mythological text containing the story of the birth of Shachar and Shalim. The supreme god El is out walking by the sea-shore when he sees two women performing their ablutions (or washing clothes) over a basin and happily calling out to their father and mother. His manhood is immediately and urgently aroused and he removes the women to his house. Wielding his staff like a javelin he shoots it into the air and brings down a bird, plucks it and sets it to roast over the fire. Speaking seductively, he then invites the women to tell him when the bird is ready, saying that if they address him as husband, they shall become his wives, but if as father, he will treat them merely as daughters. When the bird is browned they cry out 'Husband' and become his wives. He bends over and kisses them and after he has lain with them they conceive and give birth to two

---

[1] Or his name means 'Death and Dissolution' (Driver; √*šry*) or 'Death and Evil' (Tsumura; Arab. *šarru*). Tsumura well compares his two staffs with an Aramaic incantation bowl from Nippur which pictures the angel of death with a sword and spear in either hand.

children who are called Shachar[1] and Shalim
(names that mean 'Dawn' and 'Sunset' or
'Dusk'[2]). The news of their birth is brought to
El and he asks his wives to prepare an offering
for Shapash and the stars.

Ll. 55–76. Continuation of mythological text
containing the story of the birth of the gracious
gods (with a rubric inserted in parenthesis
stating that the opening of the story should be
repeated five times in the assembly). The wives
travail and the messenger brings the news to
El as before, adding the information that the
newly born deities, who are given the title
'cleavers of the sea' (probably as sons of
Athirat,[3] suggesting that she is one of the
women in the text) are being suckled by the
goddess Anat and that they are opening their
mouths so wide (for they have enormous
appetites) that their lips reach from earth to
heaven and birds and fishes fly or swim, as the
case may be, into them; side by side they stand
as this food is pushed into their mouths, but
they cannot be satisfied. On hearing this report
El despatches his wives and their children into
the desert, where they are to erect a sanctuary
and dwell among the stones and trees. For
seven full years, in fact for eight, the gods
search and hunt for food until they come upon
one who is called the guardian of the sown-
land. They request entry from him and he
grants their request. The story ends with him
plying them with wine.

Interpretation

It is generally held that the mythological
sections of this strange text correspond to
ritual acts, providing the libretto as it were for
a cultic play, in which first the destruction of
the god of death with his threatening powers
and then the marriage of El to two women and
their successful delivery of children were
portrayed in the liturgy. It is further assumed
that the drama was intended to promote
fertility in nature, though commentators differ
on the date of the festival at which it may have
been presented, some arguing for the spring
(when the laborious business of viticulture
began), some for the month of June (which in
Babylonian astrology belongs to Gemini or the
Twins, whose Ugaritic counterparts are sup-
posedly Shachar and Shalim), and some for the
autumn as an element in the New Year celebrations (when for example in Sumerian religion a
hieros gamos or sacred marriage, in which the
king played the role of the god Dumuzi or
Tammuz, took place); a few, noting the seven
or eight years that the gracious gods spend in
the wilderness, think it was only used occasionally during an exceptionally long spell of dryness
or famine. These interpretations, however
widely they vary in detail, have one feature in
common, a conviction that myth and ritual go
so closely together as to be two sides of the same
coin, which is not a position that is now greatly
favoured, at least outside biblical and Semitic
circles (Kirk). It seems a wiser procedure to
examine the mythological sections in their own
terms, particularly since the actual rubrics in
the text do not, unless superficially, equate with
them. These state merely that the stories should
be recited so many times or concern the singing
of hymns of praise or invocation to the deities
involved in the narrative or the carrying out of
some rather uncomplicated cultic instructions
like the burning of incense or the placing of
images in appropriate niches. Read without
them the mythological sections are in fact
capable of being regarded as extracts from a not
untransparent theogony or explanation of how
and why the gods came into existence; the
malevolent power of death is summarily
removed (we may compare the manner of Mot's
demise at the hands of Anat in **6** ii 30ff.), thus
making it possible for El, the progenitor of the

---

[1] According to Isa. xiv 12 Shachar is the father of
Hêlêl, the morning star (who is incidentally not to be
confused with *hll* in the title of the Kotharat).

[2] So-called as 'ending' the day; cp. Akk. *šalām*

šamši 'sunset'. His name probably provides the divine
element in Jerusalem.

[3] Athirat is at Ugarit especially associated with
the sea; see p. 4 note 1.

gods, to father divine offspring on two women[1] (who as the hymns cited in the text suggest may represent the goddesses Athirat and Anat). It is not certain whether Shachar and Shalim are the only children of this union and are therefore themselves the gracious gods of the accompanying hymns or whether we have a more comprehensive theogony in which Shachar and Shalim are merely the first-born[2] and the gracious gods are the gods of Ugarit in general who are born subsequently. The latter is the more probable if we follow Caquot and Sznycer's interpretation of the end of the narrative, which supplies a neat aetiological twist to the myth, namely that the appetite of deity is not satisfied with the natural provision of the created world, the birds of the air, the fishes of the sea, or the animals of the open country but requires in addition the offerings that men bring (these being represented in the story by the wine proffered by the guardian of the sown-land). It is unlikely that such a profound observation, in effect that though men are clearly dependent on the gods, they in their turn are dependent (or at any rate partially so) on men, would be confined to one particular ceremony, annual, fertility or otherwise. It is of the stuff of the religious attitude in general and doubtless found expression through the present text on numerous liturgical occasions at Ugarit.

7. NIKKAL AND THE KOTHARAT

The tablet

The poem accorded this title is written on a single tablet (*CTA* **24**) on which the script runs from the top of the obverse almost to the end of the reverse side; and it is divided into two pieces of composition by a horizontal line cutting across the tablet about half way down the latter side. There is a similar line at the end of the poem, beneath which there is a blank space sufficient for two more lines. The tablet was unearthed in 1933. Like the previous text it has neither superscription nor colophon. The tablet itself is complete, but part of the text has been effaced on the obverse side; the reverse side is almost wholly undamaged. Certain letters, notably *ġ*, have peculiar forms; and there are also some signs of dialectal divergence.[3]

Contents

24

Ll. 1–15. A hymn to the goddess Nikkal-and-

---

[1] The prominence in the myth of El as the father of the gods deserves to be specially emphasized. He is not in the translation offered in the present edition an almost impotent old man whose sexual powers have to be assiduously roused by the women before he can have intercourse with them. This frequently expressed interpretation depends on an identification not only of the 'hand' of *l.* 34 but of the 'sceptre' which is lowered (*l.* 37) with the male member of El; here, however, the sceptre is regarded as a real one, which El handles in the fashion of a javelin, simply lowering it behind him before he throws it up to pierce and bring down a bird which he then cooks on a fire (so De Moor). The symbolism of these actions is certainly erotic, but the situation has been engineered by El to rouse the women rather than the other way round. In the time-scale of Ugaritic mythology El is in this text, which is concerned with the birth of the gods, vigorous and far from senile. In the different circumstances of the Baal cycle, which deals with a period when the gods are grown, he is naturally older and less active, but he is still, as we are several times reminded, in ultimate command.

The peculiar logic of myth would enable the people of Ugarit to accommodate themselves without much difficulty to one or other picture of their supreme deity as occasion demanded.

[2] Dawn and Dusk may have been born first because they represent the division of day and night, which in Israel too (Gen. i 3–4) was considered the first act of creation.

[3] Notably in the presence of * z̆* (=*ḏ*) and *ẓ* where the other texts have *d* and *ṭ*; thus *špḏ* (45); *ẓhrm* (21); *lẓpn* (44). The first of these equations recurs in *CTA* **12** (see Appendix; thus *'ḥz̆* for *'ḥd*) and we may therefore assume that the two texts reflect the same dialect. The second equation (*ẓ* for *ṭ*) is, however, more likely to be a scribal spelling convention than a mark of phonetic difference, being found in several of the texts in *Ugaritica V* (e.g. *tpẓ* for *tpṭ*; *ẓbm* for *ṭbm*; *qbẓ* for *qbṭ*), which do not have the first equation (just as *CTA* **12** does not have the second); see further Dietrich, Loretz, Sanmartín, *UF* 7 (1975), pp. 103ff. *CTA* **12** also shows the feature *ẓ* (=*ṭ*) for the usual *ṣ* (=Arab. *ḍ*; thus *yẓḥq* for *yṣḥq*); no words where it might be expected to occur appear in the present text.

Ib[1] and to an unknown divinity (the vocalization Khirkhib is arbitrary)[2] who is entitled the king of summer. The singer recalls the successful outcome of the marriage of Nikkal to the moon-god Yarikh and as if present on that distant occasion announces to the divine mid-wives or Kotharat that a son is to be born to her and solicits their attendance at her confinement.

Ll. 16–39. Part of the story of the betrothal of Nikkal. Yarikh asks Khirkhib to procure the goddess's hand for him and undertakes to pay her father a huge sum in silver, gold and precious stones and to give him fields and vine-yards as her bride-price. Khirkhib suggests that instead he arrange a marriage for him with Pidray,[3] daughter of Baal, or if her present suitor the god Athtar should object too strongly, with another of Baal's daughters called *Ybrdmy*.[4] Yarikh replies, however, that he wishes to marry only Nikkal. He sends the gifts already mentioned to her house, where her parents and brothers and sisters carefully prepare the scales to weigh them. The extract finishes with the minstrel wishing happiness upon the engaged couple.

Ll. 40–50. A hymn to the Kotharat, who are called the daughters of the new moon and com-pared to swallows and are pictured descending with their potions and unguents. The singer commends the cause of a mortal maiden named *Prbḫt* to the supreme god El and to the Kotha-rat, claiming to know the appropriate incanta-tions with which the latter may be invoked. He asks them to applaud with the guests at her wedding.[5]

Interpretation

The mythological portion of the text relates how Khirkhib, king of summer, who behaves like a typical eastern marriage-broker, arranged the betrothal of the lunar goddess Nikkal to the moon-god Yarikh. It is probably like the narratives in the previous text an extract from a fuller theogonic myth. This tale is preceded and followed by hymns of praise and invocation to Nikkal, Khirkhib and the Kotharat, who are the 'sages-femmes' of the Ugaritic pantheon.[6] In the first hymn the Kotharat are summoned to oversee the birth of a son to the two moon deities. The last lines of the second hymn with their allusions to incantations to the Kotharat, betray the purpose of the whole poem, which is to secure for a human girl *Prbḫt* the same blessing and protection in her forthcoming marriage as had been enjoyed by the goddess Nikkal in hers. The Kotharat are in one of their titles associated with the new moon, which suggests that the girl may have presented herself in the temple at that auspicious time.

8. THE TEXTS IN THE APPENDIX

The texts in the Appendix are given in trans-literation only, though their vocabulary is represented as far as is practicable in the Glossary. Some of them are mere fragments, but a number contain substantial stretches of reasonably preserved writing and are therefore important for a comprehensive view of Ugaritic mythology (notably *CTA* **10** and **12** and the first three and the seventh of the eight more recently discovered texts (1961) published in *Ugaritica V*); these have been placed in the Appendix with some misgivings, but they have

---

[1] A composite deity like Kothar-and-Khasis. The first element is equivalent to the Sumerian *Ningal* or 'great lady' (consort of Sin the moon-god). The second element is an epithet meaning either 'clear, bright' (Akk. *ebbu*) or 'fruit' (Akk. *inbu*); the latter would reflect the Akk. title *ilat inbi* 'goddess of fruit', applied to Ningal.

[2] Probably a Hurrian deity. He seems to be entrusted with the betrothal arrangements, though some commentators think he may be Nikkal's father; but Dagon of Tuttul, a name restored in *l.* 14, is more likely to have been this.

[3] See at **3** A 23–24.

[4] This daughter does not appear in the Baal

cycle, nor is Athtar's interest in Pidray alluded to there.

[5] The clapping of hands is a feature of eastern weddings and was intended to drive away the evil spirits that were thought to threaten the happiness of the bride and bridegroom.

[6] Cp. **17** ii 26ff., where these goddesses arrive to bless the marriage-bed of Daniel and help ensure that a son is born. They may be alluded to in Ps. lxviii 7, where the form *kôšārôt* is fem. plur., although the meaning required is 'in safety', 'safe and sound' (*NEB*) or the like; perhaps the form was originally fem. sing. (so two manuscripts) and we should rather compare *ktr* in **14** 16.

almost without exception engendered wide dis-
agreement among commentators and I have
myself been unable to reach firm conclusions
on the rendering of damaged or problematic
passages or on their comprehensive interpretations. The following brief remarks may be of
some help to readers, but it is to be emphasized
that they are no more than provisional.

CTA 1 (remaining columns). See p. 3.

CTA 7. Two fragments of an alternative
version, not from the hand of Elimelek, of
portions of *CTA* 3 B and C.

CTA 8. The extant lines offer resemblances
to *CTA* 4 i 22f. iii 23ff. iv 50–51, 62 v 63
vii 52–58. The tablet (cp. *CTA* 1) probably
contained a summary in the form of a series of
catch-verses of this part of the Baal epic.

CTA 10. This tablet has often been regarded
as the final one in the Baal cycle, but it was not
written by Elimelek and should probably be
connected with a different genre of texts about
Baal describing his love-life with Anat (De
Moor and Lipiński). Anat seeks Baal in his
palace but is informed by his servants that he
is out hunting. After finding him and being
welcomed by him, she is told that she will bear
a steer to him; later following the birth she
takes the good news to him on Zephon.

CTA 11. A small fragment describing
realistically the mating of Baal and Anat; it
probably comes from another tablet in the same
series as the previous text.

CTA 12. A large fragment describing an
encounter in the desert between Baal-Hadad
and some creatures called 'the devourers'
(*àklm*). Most commentators believe that Baal is
worsted by them but Caquot and Sznycer argue
that the text relates his victory over them. Many
interpretations have been offered (e.g. Gaster
that it is a seasonal myth, Gray that it concerns
fratricide and atonement, Kapelrud that it is a
ritual to guard against a locust plague), but none
has gained wide currency. The text contains

certain notable idiosyncracies of spelling and
phonology (cp. *CTA* 24).

CTA 20–22. Three very fragmentary tablets,
probably from the hand of Elimelek, describing
certain happenings at a convocation of the
Rpùm or 'shades', the deities of the underworld.
Neither the order of the tablets nor of the
columns is certain. On the possible connection
of the text with the story of Aqhat see p. 27
note 2.

PRU II no. 3. A small fragment mentioning
the deity Yam and the word *mrym* 'the heights'
(sc. of Zephon). The word *šbm* (*l*.8) has been
compared with the difficult form *ištbm* in
3 D 37.

RS 22. 225. A mythological text describing
in picturesque and euphemistic language a love-
affair between Baal and Anat and probably to
be classified in the same genre as *CTA* 10 and
11. Only the obverse is relevant, the reverse
being occupied by part of a Babylonian
syllabary.

Ugaritica V no. 1 (RS 24. 258). A description
of a banquet to which El invites the other gods
and at which he falls outrageously drunk. The
last lines on the reverse contain an incantation
for the cure of a disease or perhaps (as Rainey
suggests) a hangover.

Ugaritica V no. 2 (RS 24. 252). A hymn to
Baal (who is given the title *rpù* or 'the shade')
and Anat, in which the worshipper (perhaps the
king of Ugarit, since the city is mentioned by
name) invites them to drink and invokes Baal's
protection.

Ugaritica V no. 3 (RS 24. 245). The obverse
has a description of Baal sitting on Mt. Zephon;
the visible lines of the reverse correspond to
3 B 31–33 and 3 C 1ff. The tablet has been
regarded as an enthronement ritual or a
description of an epiphany but is best taken as
a mythological fragment supplying a divergent
version of the events related at the beginning
of *CTA* 3; it breaks off in the middle of a line
and was clearly left unfinished.

Ugaritica V no. 4 (RS 24. 293). The obverse contains a slightly divergent and incomplete version of *CTA* **5** i 14ff.; it is followed after a line drawn across the tablet by a fragmentary mythological text, previously unknown, which is continued on the reverse. The tablet may have been used by a scribe for practice.

Ugaritica V no. 7 (RS 24. 244). A long and excellently preserved but difficult text containing in the opinion of most commentators a charm against snake-bite. The daughter of the sun-goddess Shapash (or perhaps simply a mare, as the name may be translated) calls on her to carry a message to El, Baal and various other deities in order to obtain help from them in curing the malady. Only when the god Horon is approached is a positive response forthcoming. According to Johnstone, however, the text is chiefly a mythical narrative not a charm and the serpent mentioned represents some cosmic disaster which is removed by Horon. The tablet is divided into roughly equal paragraphs or panels by horizontal lines (cp. *CTA* **23**).

Notes on texts not included:

CTA **9, 25–28** and *PRU* V nos. 2, 3 are very small with little or no continuous writing. *CTA* **13** is a difficult and ill-studied text thought to be a hymn to the goddess Anat. *PRU* II no. 1 is a long fragment dealing apparently with the combat of Baal and the monsters *tnn* and *btn*; *PRU* II no. 2 is also long but extensively damaged; both texts are frequently broken up by horizontal lines, a feature which invites comparison with *CTA* **23** or *Ugaritica* V no. 7. *PRU* V no. 1 is long but badly mutilated; it mentions the names of Baal and Athtart. *Ugaritica* V no. 5 has on its reverse a list of the kings of Ugarit; it and no. 6 may in fact not be mythological. *Ugaritica* V no. 8 is a poorly preserved text of the same kind as no. 7, perhaps its continuation.

TRANSLITERATION AND TRANSLATION
OF THE TEXTS

2

Col. iii

. . . .

1	[- - - - - - - - - - - -]b[- - - -]*n*[- - - ?]	[ ]
2	[- - - - - - - - -]r.l*r*[- - - ?]	[ ]
3	[- - - - - - - - - - -]m.t[- - - ?]	[ ]
4	[ìdk.]l*ytn*[.]pn*m*.	[Then] indeed he set (his) face
	ˁm[.ì]*l.mbk*[.nhrm.]	towards El at the source(s) [of the rivers],
	[qrb.àpq.thmtm]	[amid the springs of the two oceans];
5	[ygly.]ž*l.ì*[l].	[he penetrated] the mountain(s) of El
	wybù[.q]rš.*mlk*[.àb.šnm.]	and entered the massif of the king, [fathers of years];[1]
	[lpˁn.ìl] (6) [yhbr.]*wyql*[.]	[he did homage at El's feet] and fell down,
	[y]š*thw*[y.]*wykb*[dnh.]	he prostrated himself and did [him] honour[2]
	[- -]r y[- - - - - -] (7) [- - -]	[ ]
	[k]*tr.wh*[ss.t]bˁ.	'Kothar-and-Khasis, depart,
	b[n.]*bht.ym*[.]	'build a mansion for Yam,
	[rm]*m.hkl.tpt* *n*h[r]	'[raise] a palace for judge Nahar
8	[- - -]hrn.w[- - -]	'[ ]
	*t*bˁ.*k*[t]*r* w[ḫss.]	'Depart, Kothar-and-[Khasis],
	[t]b*n.bht zbl ym*	'[do you] build a mansion for prince Yam,
9	[trm]*m.hk*[l.tpt].*nhr*[.]	'[do you raise] a palace [for judge] Nahar,
	bt.k.[- - - -]š*p*[- - - -]	'a house like [ ]
10	[ḥš.bh]tm *tbn*[n.]	'[Quickly] let the [mansion] be built,
	[ḥ]š.*trm*[mn.hklm.]	'quickly let [the palace] be raised
	[- - - - - - -]*bt*	'[ ] house
11	[- - - -]k.*mnh*[- - - -]š *bš*[- -]*t*[-]	'[ ]
	ǧlm.lš*dt*[-]*ymm*	
12	[- - -]b*ym.ym.y*[- -].*yš*[-]*n*	'[ ] in the sea Yam [ ]'
	à*pk*.ˁ*ttr*.*d*m[lk]	Thereupon Athtar, the possessor [of kingship][3]
13	[- - -]*ḫrḫrtm.wl*[- - -]*n*[- -]*ìš*[- - -]*h*	[ ] a torch and [ ] fire [
	[- -]*ìšt*	] fire
14	[- - -]*y.yblmm.ù*[- - - - - - -]*k.y*rd	[ ] carried [ ] went down
	[- -]*ì*[- - -]*n.b*n	[ ]

---

ii 4–6: cp. **4** iv 20–26   **6** i 32–38

5 *žl* error for *šd*

6–7 Herdner [*dḫ*]*r* y[ˁ*n.tr.ìl.àbh*] (7) [*šm*ˁ.*l*] (cp. **1** iii 26)

7–10 Herdner (cp. **4** v 113–116); alternatively these lines may contain a complaint by Athtar about the building of Yam's palace

8 [–] *hrn.w* (Herdner) or [*b*]*ìrtk* (Driver *a*. Virolleaud) 'in accordance with (or against) your will' (cp. **18** i 18–19)

9 *bt.k* (Herdner) or *btk* (Virolleaud) 'within' (cp. **4** v 117)

10 [*bh*]*tm* (cp **4** v 115) or [*bh*]*th*

12 à*pk* error for or variant of à*pnk* (cp. **6** i 56); *dm*[*lk*]: cp. **18** and **4** iii 9

[1] See on El's abode at **3** E 12ff.

[2] Cp. Ps. lxxxvi 9.

[3] If this title is taken literally, Athtar and not Baal or Yam is king at the opening of the cycle.

15 [- - - -]*nn*[.]*nrt*[.]*ı̇lm*[.]*špš*.
    tšù̇.gh.wt[*šḥ*.]
    [*šm*]ʿ.*m*ʿ[   ]
16 [*lyt*]*ı̇r*[.]*tr il.ȧbk*[.]

    l.pn.zbl.ym
    lpn[.*t*]*pṭ*[.*n*]h*r*
17 [*ı̇k.ȧ*]*l.yšmʿk.tr.*[*ı̇*]*l.ȧbk*.
    lysʿ.[*ȧlt.*]*ṯ*[*btk.*]
    [*ly*]h*pk* (18) [*ksȧ.*]*mlkk*.
    lytbr.ḥt[.]*mṭpṭk*.
    wyʿn[.ʿ*ttr*].*dm*[*l*]*k*
19 [- - -]*h.by.tr.il.ȧby*.
    ȧnk.ı̇n bt[.*l*]*y*[.*km.*]*ı̇lm*[.]
    [*w*]*ḥẓr*[.*kbn*] (20) [*qd*]*ṧ*.
    lbùm.ȧrd[.]*bn*[*p*]*šny*.
    trḥṣn.ktrm[.]
    [*yt*]*b b*[*ht*] (21) [*zbl.*]*ym*.
    bhkl.ṭpṭ.nh[*r*].
    ytı̇r.tr.il[.]*ȧbh*
    lpn[.*zb*]*l y*[*m*]
22 [*lpn.tp*]*ṭ*[.*nhr*.]
    mlkt.[*ȧn.*]h*m.lmlkt.ȧn*[.]
    ⟨*wtʿn.nrt.ı̇lm.špš.*⟩
    ı̇n.ȧtt[.*l*]*k.k*[*m.ı̇lm*]
23 [*wġlmt.kbn.qdš.*]
    wy[- -]*zbl.ym*.
    *y*ʿ[- -]*ṭpṭ.nhr*
24 [- - - - - - - - - - - - - - - -]*yšlḥn*.
    wyʿn.ʿttr

· · · · · · · · · ·

Shapash the luminary of the gods [   ] him,
she lifted up her voice and [cried]:
'Hear, I beseech you [   ];
'the bull El your father [will indeed] cause (the table)
    to be set
'before prince Yam,
'before judge Nahar.
'[How of a truth] shall the bull El your father hear you?
'Indeed, he will pull up [the support of your seat],
'[indeed] will overturn [the throne] of your kingdom,[1]
'indeed will break the sceptre of your rule.[2]
And [Athtar], the possessor of kingship, answered:
'The bull El my father [   ] against me.
'I myself have not a house like the gods
'[nor] a court[3] [like the sons of the Holy] one.[4]
'Alone I shall go down into the grave[5] of us both
'(and) the skilful ones[6] will wash me.
'[Prince] Yam is to [dwell] in a [mansion],
'judge Nahar in a palace.
'The bull El his father will cause (the table) to be set
'before [prince] Yam,
'[before judge] Nahar.
'Am [I indeed] king or am I not king?'
⟨And Shapash luminary of the gods answered⟩:
'You have no wife[7] like [the gods]
'[nor a maiden like the sons of the Holy one].
'And prince Yam [   ]
'judge Nahar [   ]
'[   ] he sends me.'
    And Athtar answered:

· · · · · · · · · ·

---

15 Virolleaud; at the end prob. restore [*lʿttr*] or title
  (cp. **6** vi 24)
16 [*lyt*]*ı̇r*: cp. 17, 21
17–18: cp. **6** vi 26–29
18 [ʿ*ttr*].*dm*[*l*]*k*: cp. 12
19–20: cp. **4** iv 50–51 **2** i 21
20 *lbùm* error for *lbdm* or so read (Herdner); *bn*[*p*]*šny*
  Herdner *a*. Virolleaud who finds traces of *p*; [*yt*]*b*
  (De Moor)
21–22 Herdner
22 [*ȧn*]: cp. *ȧn* later in the line; Gordon *wn*; ⟨*wtʿn*⟩
  etc.: cp. [*l*]*k* (22) and *wyʿn.ʿttr* (24); *k*[*m.ı̇lm*] etc.
  Herdner after the formula in 19–20

[1] Cp. 2 Sam. vii 13   Hag. ii 22.
[2] Cp Ps. xlv 7   Ahiram inscr. *l.* 2.
[3] Or 'residence' (so in parallel passages).
[4] Lit. 'sons of Holiness', a title of Athirat (cp. **3** E
46–47 **4** iv 50–51).
[5] An extension of the metaphor whereby the
entrance to the underworld is compared to the throat
of the god of death Mot (cp. **5** i 7). The reference
here is perhaps to drowning in the sea; the sun of
course sank into the sea west of Ugarit. Cp. also **15**
v 18–20 **6** vi 50ff. The suffix is dual (cp. **4** iv 45).
[6] Presumably attendants of Yam.
[7] A wife to bear a son and heir was like a palace a
necessary mark of a king; cp. **14** i 6ff.

I

Col. iv

. . . .

1 [- -]*m.ṣ*[ ]	[ ]
2 *gm.ṣḥ.lq*[rbm]	They[1] did cry aloud to those [near]
3 *lrḥqm.lp*[ ]	to those far away,[2] to [ ]
4 *ṣḥ.il.ytb.b*[mrzḥh]	they did cry (aloud): 'El sits in [his banqueting hall]
5 *btt.ʿllmn.*[ ]	'the shame of . . . . . [ ]
6 *ilm.bt.bʿlk.*[ ]	'the gods, the house of your lord[3] [ ]
7 *dl.ylkn.ḥš.bȧ*[rṣ]	'lest he go quickly through the earth [ ]
8 *bʿpr.ḥbl.ṭṭm.*[ ]	'on the ground destruction[4] . . . . . [ ]
9 *šqy.rtȧ.tnmy.ytn*[.ks.bdhm]	He did give (them) curdled milk[5] . . . . .
	to drink, he gave [the cup into (their) hand(s)],
10 *krpn.bklȧt yd.*[ ]	the flagon into both (their) hands [ ]
11 *kmll.kḥṣ.tu̇sp*[ ]	like . . . . . like . . . . . was
	gathered [ ]
12 *tgr.il.bnh.tr*[ ]	El . . . . . his son, the bull [ ]
13 *wyʿn.lṭ⟨p⟩n.il.dp*[id]	and Latipan [kindly] god spoke [ ]
14 *šm.bny.yw.ilt*[.w]	'the name of my son is Yaw,[6] o Elat [and]
15 *wpʿr.šm.ym*[.wilt.w]	'so do you proclaim a (new) name for Yam.' [And Elat
	and]
16 *tʿnyn.lzntn*[ ]	answered: 'For our sustenance[7] [ ]
17 *ȧt.ȧdn.tpʿr*[.šmh.wyʿn.il]	'do you, sire, proclaim [his name.' And the bull El
	answered]:
18 *ȧnk.lṭpn.il*[.dpid]	'I myself, Latipan [kindly] god [ ]
19 *ʿl.ydm.pʿrt*[ ]	'on (my) hands. I have proclaimed [ ]
20 *šmk.mdd.i̇*[l]	'your name is the darling of El[8] [ ]
21 *bt kspy.d*[ ]	'my house of silver[9] which [ ]
22 *bd.ȧli̇yn* b[ʿl]	'by the hand of mightiest Baal [ ]
23 *kd.ynȧṣn*[ ]	'thus he reviles me[10] [ ]
24 *gršnn.lk*[si̇.mlkh.lnḫt.lkḫṭ]	'drive him forth from [the throne of his kingdom, from
	the cushion on the seat]
25 *drkth.š*[ ]	'of his dominion[11] [ ]

---

v 1: possibly [*g*]*m.ṣ*[*ḥ*]

2 Virolleaud; possibly *lq*[*ṣ.ilm*] (cp. *Ugaritica* V no. 1 obv. *l.* 2)

4: cp. ibid. *l.* 15

5 *ʿllmn*: cp. *ʿllmy* (**22** B 10) ‖ *zbl, mlk*

7 Virolleaud

9: cp. **3** A 10

11 *kmll.kḥṣ*: cp. *kḥṣ.kmʿr* (**16** iv 6)

12: note *l* with four vertical and *ḥ* with four horizontal wedges

13 Virolleaud

14–15: Elat seems to be accompanied by others (cp. **3** E 45)

17 Caquot and Sznycer

24: cp. **3** D 46–47

28: cp. *Ugaritica* V no. 1 obv. *ll.* 1–2

[1] Sc. Elat and her companions (cp. 14–16).

[2] Cp. Isa. xxxiii 13.

[3] Sc. Yam; this allusion suggests that Yam's palace has been built and therefore that this section belongs after **2** iii.

[4] Presumably from the sea inundating the land or the rivers overflowing.

[5] Cp. Judg. v 25.

[6] See p. 4 note 2.

[7] Cp. 2 Chron. xi 23; alternatively 'for our adornment' (Arab. *zâna*; cp. 2 Sam. i 24).

[8] A similar title is borne by Mot in **4** viii 23–24.

[9] Cp. **3** E 27ff.; or referring to Yam's palace 'the house of my silver' (sc. which I built for you).

[10] Cp. **5** iv 26.

[11] Cp. Exod. xv 17 2 Sam. vii 13 Ps. cxxxii 14.

26 *whm.åp.l*[   ]   'but if however you do not [   ]
27 *ymḫṣk.k*[   ]   'he will smite you like [   ]
28 *il dbḥ.* [   ]   El did slaughter [   ]
29 *pᶜr.b*[   ]   he did proclaim in [   ]
30 *ṭbḫ.ålp*[m.åp.ṣỉn.šql   ]   He did slay oxen, [also sheep, he did fell]
31 *trm.w*[mrỉ.ỉlm.ᶜglm.dt.šnt]   bulls and [fatted rams, yearling calves],
32 *ỉmr.*[qms.llỉm   ]   [skipping] lambs [(and) kids   ]

. . . .

2

Col. i

. . . .

1 [   ]   [   ]
2 [   ]   [   ]
3 *åt.ypᶜt.b*[- - - - - - - - - - - - - - - - - -]   'you have risen against [   ]
4 *dlỉyn.bᶜl*[- - - - - - - - - - - - - - - -]   'mightiest Baal [   ]
5 *drk.tk.mšl*[- - - - - - - - - - - - - - - -]   'your dominion [   ]
6 *brỉšk.åymr*[- - - - - - - - - - - - - - -]   'Ayyamur[1] on your head [   ]
7 *tpṭ.nhr.*   'judge Nahar.
   ytb[r.ḥrn.yymm.]   'May [Horon] break, [o Yam],
   [*ytbr.ḥrn.* (8) *rỉšk.*   '[may Horon break] your head,
   ᶜttrt.[šm.bᶜl.qdqdk.]   '(may) Athtart-[name-of-Baal (break) your crown]!
   [- - - - -] (9) [- -]*t.mṭ.*   '[   ] staff;
   tpln.bg[- - - - - - - - - - - - -]   'you will fall [   ]
10 [- -]*šnm.åttm.t*[- - - - - - - - - - - - -]   '[   ] two wives[2] [   ]
11 [m]*låkm.ylåk.ym.*   Yam sent messengers,
   [tᶜdt.- - - -.tpṭ.nhr]   [judge Nahar . . . . . an embassy], (saying):
12 *bᶜlṣ ᶜlṣm npr.š*[- - - - - - - - - - - -]   'As the jubilant rejoice,[3] let (their) [   ] be
                                                  shattered[4] [   ]
                                              '[   ] let their nose be broken![4]
13 *ùṭ.tbr.åphm.*   'Depart, pages, [do not stay].
   tbᶜ ǵlm[m.ål.ttb.]   '[Then] of a truth do you set [(your) faces]
   [*ỉdk.pnm*] (14) *ål.ttn.*   'towards the full convocation[5]
   ᶜm.pḫr.mᶜd.   'within [the mount of Lel];
   t[k.ǵr.ll.]   'do you of a truth fall down [at the feet of El],
   [*lpᶜn.ỉl*] (15) *ål.tpl.*   'do you of a truth prostrate yourselves before the [full]
   ål.tšthwy.pḫr[.mᶜd.]   convocation.

   [*qmm.åmr.åm*] (16) *r*   '[Standing up, say what you have to] say,

30–32: cp. **4** vi 40–43   **22** B 12–14

i Prob. Herdner exaggerates the number of word-
   dividers in this col. (see at **2** iv 1)
5 *drk.tk* error for *drktk*
6: perhaps complete [*.zbl.ym.bqdqdk.ygrš*] (Herdner *a.* Ginsberg; cp. **2** iv 12, 21–22)
7–8: cp. **16** vi 54–57 and below *l.* 36
9: perhaps *bg*[*bl.šntk.bḫpnk.wtᶜn*] (cp. **16** vi 57–58)
11: cp. **22**
13 *ùṭ* or *dt* (Herdner)
13–18: cp. 19–20, 30–31, 33–35; cp. also **3** D 81   F

12–13

[1] The name of a club later (iv 19) given by
Kothar-and-Khasis to Baal; it means 'Let him expel
anyhow!' or the like.
[2] Yam appears to have had two wives unlike
Athtar who had none (**2** iii 22).
[3] Cp. Prov. xxviii 12.
[4] Perfects with jussive meaning.
[5] Lit. 'the assembly' or 'totality of the appointed
meeting'. Cp. Isa. xiv 13.

ṯny.d͑tkm.   'repeat what you know;[1]
wrgm.lṯr.d̪[by.il.]   'and tell the bull [El my] father,
[ṯny.lpḫr] (17) *m͑d.*   '[repeat to the] full [convocation]:
thm.ym.b͑lkm.   ' "The message of Yam your lord,
d̪dnkm.ṯ[pṭ.nhr]   ' "of your sire judge [Nahar] (is this):
18 *tn.ilm.dtqh.*   ' "Give up,[2] gods, him whom you protect,
dtqyn.hmlt.   ' "him whom you protect, o multitude,[3]
tn.b͑l[.w͑nnh]   ' "give up Baal [and his lackeys],
19 bn.*dgn.d̪rtm.pẓh.*   ' "the son of Dagon, that I may possess his gold." '
tb͑.ġlmm.lytb.   The pages did depart, they stayed not.
[id̪k.pnm] (20) *lytn.*   [Then] indeed they set [(their) faces]
tk.ġr.ll.   towards the mount of Lel,[4]
͑m pḫr.m͑d.   towards the full convocation.
àp.ilm.l⟨l⟩ḫ[m] (21) *ytb.*   The gods also had sat down to eat,
bn qdš.lṯrm.   the sons of the Holy one to dine,
b͑l.qm.͑l.il.   (and) Baal was standing by El.
hlm (22) *ilm tphhm.*   Behold! the gods perceived them,
tphn.mld̪k ym.   they perceived[5] the messengers of Yam,
t͑dt.ṯpṭ[.nhr]   the embassy of judge [Nahar];
23 *t*[ġ]*ly.hlm.rišthm.*   the gods lowered their heads
lẓr.brkthm.   on to their knees[6]
wlkḫṭ (24) *ẓblhm.*   and (on) to their princely seats.
bhm.yg͑r b͑l.   Baal rebuked them, (saying):
lm ġltm.ilm.rišt (25) *km*   'Why, gods, have you lowered your heads
lẓr brktkm.   'on to your knees
wln.kḫṭ.ẓblkm.   'and (on) to your princely seats?
d̪ḥd (26) *ilm.t͑ny*   'Will any of the gods answer
lḫt.mld̪k.ym.   'the message[7] of the messengers of Yam,
t͑dt.ṯpṭ.nh⟨r⟩   'of the embassy of judge Nahar?
27 *šù*[.]*ilm.rd̪štkm.*   'Lift up, gods, your heads[8]
lẓr.brktkm.   'from on your knees
ln kḫṭ (28) *ẓblkm.*   '(and) from your princely seats,
wd̪nk ͑ny mld̪k.ym   'and myself I will answer[9] the messengers of Yam,
t͑dt.ṯpṭ.nhr   'the embassy of judge Nahar.'
29 *tšù ilm rd̪šthm.*   The gods lifted up their heads
lẓr.brkthm.   from on their knees
ln.kḫṭ[.]*ẓblhm.*   (and) from their princely seats.
30 *d̪ḥr.tmġyn.mld̪k ym*[.]   Thereafter the messengers of Yam arrived,
t͑dt.ṯpṭ.nhr.   the embassy of judge Nahar;
lp͑n.il (31) [lt]*pl.*   [indeed] they fell down at the feet of El,

20 *pḫr* error (phonetic) for *pḫr*; *l*⟨l⟩ḫ[m]: cp. **18** iv 19
23 *t*[ġ]*ly*: cp. 24; *hlm* error for *ilm*
26 *t͑ny* perhaps error for *d̪͑ny* (De Moor), 'Must I
    alone, gods, answer . . .?'
29: the end of the line transgresses the margin with
    the next col., which has a few letters visible at this
    point
31–32: cp. 15–16

kind) do wait' (Driver; cp. Hebr. *qiwwāh*).
    [4] See p. 5 note 1.
    [5] It is not certain whether forms like *tph* and
tphn accompanying masc. plur. (or dual) nouns
should be regarded as variants of the regular 3 masc.
plur. (or dual) forms with *y-* prefix or as 3 fem. sing.
forms with the subject nouns being treated as
collective. For dual examples see *ll.* 30–31.
    [6] Cp. 1 Kgs. xviii 42   Lam. ii 10.
    [7] Lit. 'tablets' as containing the message.
    [8] Cp. Ps. xxiv 7, 9.
    [9] Probably a partic.

    [1] I.e. what you have been told.
    [2] Cp. **6** ii 12   Hos. xi 8   Isa. xliii 6.
    [3] Or 'him on whom the multitudes (sc. of man-

ltštḥwy . pḫr . mʿd .

indeed they prostrated themselves before the full convocation.

qmm . å[mr] . åmr

Standing up, they [said] what they had to say

32 *[tn]y . dʿthm*

[(and) repeated] what they knew.

išt . ištm . yìtmr .

(Like) a fire, two fires they appeared,

ḥrb . ltšt (33) *[lš]nhm .*

(like) a sharpened sword (was) their [tongue].[1]

rgm . ltr . åbh . il .

They did tell the bull El his father:

thm . ym . bʿlkm

'The message of Yam your lord,

34 *[ådn]km . tpṭ . nhr .*

'of your [sire] judge Nahar (is this):

tn . ilm . dtqh .

'Give up, gods, him whom you protect,

dtqynh (35) *[hml]t .*

'him whom you protect, o multitude,

tn bʿl . wʿnnh .

'give up Baal and his lackeys,[2]

bn . dgn . årtm pžh

'the son of Dagon, that I may possess his gold.'

36 *[wyʿn .]tr . åbh . il .*

[And] the bull El his father [answered]:

ʿbdk . bʿl . yymm .

'Baal is your slave, o Yam,

ʿbdk . bʿl (37) *[ynhr]m .*

'Baal is your slave, o Nahar,

bn . dgn . å[s]rkm .

'the son of Dagon is your prisoner.

hw ybl . årgmnk . kilm

'Even he must bring you tribute like the gods,

38 *[hw .]ybl . wbn . qdš . mnhyk .*

'[even he] must bring you gifts[3] like the sons of the Holy one.'

åp . ånš . zbl . bʿ[l]

Prince Baal did grow angry,[4]

39 *[wyùḫ]d . byd . mšḫt .*

[and] he took a 'slayer' in his hand,

bm . ymn . mḫṣ .

a 'smiter' in (his) right hand.

ġlmm . yš[- -]

The pages [   ][5]

40 *[ymnh . ʿn]t . tùḥd .*

[Anat] took [his right hand],

šmål h . tùḥd . ʿttrt .

Athtart took his left hand, (saying):

ik[.]m[ḫṣt . ml] (41) *[åk . ym .]*

'How (is it that) you [smite the messengers of Yam],

[tʿ]dt . tpṭ nhr .

'the embassy of judge Nahar?

mlåk . mthr . yḫb[-]

'A messenger . . . . [   ]

[- - -] (42) *[- - - - - -]mlåk .*

'[   ] a messenger;

bn . ktpm . rgm . bʿlh .

'between (his) shoulders is the word of his lord,[6]

wy[- - - - - -] (43) *[- - - - -] .*

'and he [   ]'

åp . ånš . zbl . bʿl .

Prince Baal did grow angry;

šdmt . bg[- - - - - -]

the terraces[7] with [   ]

44 *[- - - - - -]dm . mlåk . ym .*

[   ] the messengers of Yam,

tʿdt . tpṭ . nh[r .]

the embassy of judge Nahar

31 *å[mr]* (De Moor)

33 *[lš]nhm* (Cross) or *[bym]nhm* (Gaster)

34–35: cp. 17–18; *dtqynh* (Herdner) or *dtqyn   h* (35) *[ml]t* (Gordon)

36 Gordon

37 *[ynhr]m*: cp. *yymm* (36); the *s* of *å[s]rkm* was visible on an earlier photograph (Herdner)

38 *[hw .]*: cp. 37; *wbn* error for *kbn* or so read (Herdner)   39 De Moor

40–41 Herdner *a*. Gordon

41 *mthr* or *mṭ ḥr* 'the staff of . . .'; *yḫb[š]* 'binds on' (Caquot and Sznycer) or *yḫb[q]* 'clasps' (De Moor)

42 Van Selms *wy[tny]* 'his lord has spoken and he can but repeat'

43 De Moor *bg[pnm]* (cp. **23** 9)

[1] Cp. Ps. lvii 5   lxiv 4   Gen. iii 24   Exod. iii 2; cp. also Qodesh-and-Amrur (**4** iv 16–17) and the divine messengers of Num. xxii 31   Josh. v 13   2 Sam. xxiv 16   1 Chron. xxi 27, 30. Similar imagery is used by Micaiah in 1 Kgs. xxii 19 and by Isaiah in Isa. vi 1ff. to add lustre to their prophetic office.

[2] Probably Gupn and Ugar are meant; cp. **3** D 76.

[3] Cp. Ps. lxxii 10. Note the 'dative' suffixes and the *mater lectionis y.*

[4] Lit. 'was companion to anger' (cp. **6** v 21 **16** vi 36).

[5] Or 'He . . . the pages'.

[6] Official messages were carried in a diplomatic bag tied round the neck.

[7] Cp. Isa. xvi 8   Hab. iii 17   **23** 10.

[- - - -] (45) [- - - - - -].
àn.rgmt.lym.bʿlkm.
ḍd[nkm.tpt] (46) [nhr.]
[šmʿ.]hwt.gmr[.]hd.
lwày[- - - - - -]
47 [- - - - - - - -]ìyrḥ.g[-]
  thbr[- - - - - - - - -]
48 [   ]

[   ]
'I myself tell Yam your lord,
'[your] sire [judge Nahar]:
'[Hear] the word of the avenger[1] Hadad:
'. . . . . [   ]
'[   ]
  'do homage [   ]
[   ]

Col. iv

.   .   (ca. 1 l.)   .   .
1 [- - - - - - - - - - - - - -]
  yd[y].ḥtt.mtt[- - -]
2 [- - - -]ḥy[- - - -]låšṣì.
  hm.àp.àmr[- -] (3) [- - - -].
  wbym.mnḥl.ḍbd.
  bym.ìrtm.m[t]
4 [tpt].nhr.tlʿm.
  tm.ḥrbm.ìts.
  ànšq (5) [-]htm.
  lḍrṣ.ypl.ùlny.
  wl.ʿpr.ʿẓmny
6 [b]ph.rgm.lysḍ.
  bšpth.hwth.wttn.gh.
  yg̱r (7) tḥt ksì.zbl ym
  wʿn.ktr.wḥss.
  lrgmt (8) lk.lzbl.bʿl.
  tnt.lrkb.ʿrpt.
  ht.ìbk (9) bʿlm.
  ht.ìbk.tmḫṣ.
  ht.tṣmt.ṣrtk
10 tqḥ.mlk.ʿlmk.
  drkt.dt drdrk
11 ktr ṣmdm.ynḥt.
  wypʿr.šmthm.

.   .   .   .
'[   ]
  [my] power is shattered [   ]
'[   ] I will not bring out.
'If moreover [   ]
'and in Yam is the sieve of destruction,
'in Yam are the lungs of [death];
'[(in) judge] Nahar "gnawers",[2]
'there "attackers" move about.
'I will kiss [   ]³
'The strength of us two[4] will fall to the earth
'and the might of us two to the ground.'
Scarce had his word(s) come forth from his mouth,
his speech and the utterance of his voice from his lips
(than) he sank under the throne of prince Yam.
But Kothar-and-Khasis answered (him):
'Truly I tell you, o prince Baal,
'I repeat (to you), o rider on the clouds.[5]
'Now (you must smite) your foes, Baal,
'now you must smite your foes,
'now you must still your enemies.[6]
'You shall take your everlasting kingdom,
'your dominion for ever and ever.'[7]
Kothar fetched down two clubs[8]
and proclaimed their names, (saying):[9]

45–46: cp. 34
46 [šmʿ.] (De Moor); lwày or lwny
v On word-divides in this col. see Horwitz UF 5 (1973),
  165ff.
1 yd[y] (Van Selms) or simply yd[.] (cp. 16 vi 32)
2 Van Selms [r]ḥy (cp. 18 iv 24–25)
3 mnḥl ḍbd (Van Selms) or mnḥ lḍbd (Virolleaud)
  'a resting-place has indeed perished'; m[t] (Van
  Selms) or m[ym] (De Moor)
5 [b]htm (Virolleaud) does not obviously suit
6 [b]ph: cp. 19 75; ttn error for ntn (16 i 4) or tn (4 v
  70) or nominal form with t prefix

¹ Or 'accomplisher'; cp. Ps. lvii 3 (Dahood).
² The normal Hebrew meaning 'worms, maggots'
hardly suits in this context.

³ Some act of submission is clearly meant; cp.
Ps. ii 12.
⁴ Dual suffix.
⁵ Cp. Ps. lxviii 5; alternatively 'cloud-gatherer', if
the root rkb originally meant 'to harness, yoke'; cp.
the title of Zeus in Homer nephelēgeretēs (Ullendorff).
⁶ Both the structure and content of this passage
are neatly parallelled in Ps. xcii 10; cp. also Ps. viii 3
cxliii 12.
⁷ Cp. Ps. cxlv 13   Dan. iii 33   iv 31.
⁸ Rather illogically the whole sentence is repeated
in l. 18.
⁹ Sc. to the first. The famous relief of Baal
(Ugaritica II pl. xxiii) has a mace or club in its right-
hand. The naming of weapons is a common motif in
mythology and folklore.

šmk ảt (12) *ygrš.*	'Your name, yours,[1] is Yagrush.
ygrš.grš ym	'Yagrush, chase away Yam,
grš ym.lksîh	'chase away Yam from his throne,
13 [n]*hr lkḥt drkth.*	'Nahar from the seat of his dominion.
trtqṣ bd bʿl	'Do you dance from Baal's hand,[2]
km nš (14) *r bừsbʿth.*	'like an eagle from his fingers.
hlm.ktp zbl ym.	'Strike the shoulders of prince Yam,
bn ydm (15) [tp]*t nhr.*	'between the arms[3] of judge Nahar.'
yrtqṣ.ṣmd.bd bʿl.	The club danced from the hand of Baal,
km.nšr (16) *b*[ừ]*ṣbʿth.*	like an eagle from his fingers.
ylm.ktp zbl ym.	It struck the shoulders of prince Yam,
bn ydm.tpṭ (17) *nhr*	between the arms of judge Nahar.
ʿz.ym lymk.	(But) Yam was strong,[4] he did not sink down,
ltnǵṣn.pnth.	his joints[5] did not quiver,
lydlp (18) *tmnh.*	his form did not crumple.
ktr ṣmdm ynḥt.	Kothar fetched down two clubs
wypʿr šmthm	and proclaimed their names, (saying):[6]
19 *šmk.ảt.ảymr.*	'Your name, yours, is Ayyamur.[7]
ảymr.mr.ym.	'Ayyamur, expel Yam,
mr ym (20) *lksîh.*	'expel Yam from his throne,
nhr lkḥt.drkth.	'Nahar from the seat of his dominion.
trtqṣ (21) *bd bʿl.*	'Do you dance from Baal's hand,
km.nšr bừṣbʿth.	'like an eagle from his fingers.
hlm.qdq (22) *d.zbl ym.*	'Strike the crown of prince Yam,
bn.ʿnm.tpṭ.nhr.	'between the eyes[8] of judge Nahar.
yprsḥ ym (23) *wyql.lảrṣ.*	'Let Yam collapse and fall to the earth!'
wyrtqṣ.ṣmd bd bʿl	And the club danced from the hand of Baal,
24 [km.]*nšr.bừsbʿth.*	[like] an eagle from his fingers.
ylm.qdqd.zbl (25) [ym.]	It struck the crown of prince [Yam],
bn.ʿnm.tpṭ.nhr.	between the eyes of judge Nahar.
yprsḥ.ym.yql (26) *lảrṣ.*	Yam collapsed (and) fell to the earth;
tnǵṣn.pnth.	his joints quivered
wydlp.tmnh	and his form crumpled.
27 *yqt bʿl wyšt.ym.*	Baal dragged out Yam and laid him down,[9]
ykly tpṭ.nhr.	he made an end of judge Nahar.
28 *bšm.tgʿrm.ʿttrt.*	Athtart rebuked the Name,[10] (saying):
bt lảlîyn.[bʿl]	'Scatter (him),[11] o mightiest [Baal]!
29 *bt.lrkb.ʿrpt.*	'Scatter (him), o rider on the clouds!
*kšbyn.z*b[l.ym.]	'For prince [Yam] is our captive,
[k] (30) *šbyn.tpṭ.nhr.*	'[for] judge Nahar is our captive.'

24–25: cp. 21–22

29: at the end [*k*] (Ginsberg) or [*w*] (Virolleaud)

[1] Note the strengthening pronoun (cp. 1 Kgs. xxi 19); the name means 'let him chase away!' (cp. Isa. lvii 20).

[2] Apparently (cp. 5) Baal was not himself strong enough to wield the weapon. The picture comes from falconry (cp. **18** iv 17ff.).

[3] Lit. 'hands'; cp. Zech. xiii 6   2 Kgs. ix 24.

[4] Cp. Ps. lxxiv 13   **6** vi 17.

[5] Possibly 'his features' (i.e. related to *pnm*; cp. the parallelism in Ps. xvii 15).

[6] Sc. to the second.

[7] See at i 6.

[8] Cp. Exod. xiii 9   Dan. viii 5.

[9] Possibly 'drank him down' (Driver, Cross).

[10] See p. 6 note 1.

[11] Possibly 'Be ashamed!' (Hebr. *bôš*; cp. i 40ff.); but the positions of envoys and defeated enemies are not the same.

wyṣả b[- - - - - - -]	And he did come forth [ ]
31 *ybt.nn.ảlỉyn.b'l.*	mightiest Baal scattered him
w[- - - - - - - - -]	and [ ]:
32 *ym.lmt.b'lm yml*[k]	'Yam is indeed dead! Baal shall be king![1]
[- - - - - - - -] (33) *ḥm.lšrr.*	'[ ] heat is indeed assured!'[2]
w[- - - - - - - - - - -] (34) *y'n.*	And [ ] answered:
ym.lmt[.b'lm.ymlk.]	'Yam is indeed dead! [Baal shall be king!]
[- - - ḥm] (35) *lšrr.*	'[heat] is indeed assured!'
wt'[n.'ttrt - - - - - - -]	And [Athtart] answered [ ]
36 *b'lm.hmt.*[- - - - - - - - - - - - ḥm]	'Baal, them [heat]
37 *lšrr.št*[- - - - - - - - - - - - -].	'is indeed assured!' He did place [ ]
38 *brỉsh.*[- - - - - - - - - - - - - -]	on his head [ ]
39 *ỉbh.mš*[- - - - - - - - - - - - - -]	his enemy [ ]
40 [b]*n.'nh*[- - -?]	between his eyes [ ]

.   .   .   .

30 Ginsberg *b*[*ph.rgm*(*h*)] (cp. 6), but the negative is missing and there is not room for the full idiom
31: perhaps *w*[*y'n.rkb.'rpt*]
32 Bauer
33: perhaps *w*[*ybt.nn.rkb.'rpt.w*] (Virolleaud)
34, 36: cp. 32–33
35 Virolleaud

39 *ỉbh* (Herdner) or (38) [*bn*] (39) *ydh* (Virolleaud; cp. 14, 16)
40: cp. 22, 25

[1] Cp. Exod. xv 18.
[2] Cp. Gen. viii 22   **19** 40.

3

A

Col. i

. . . .
. . (ca. 25 ll.) . .

1 *àl.tġl*[y.rìštkm]

2 *prdmn.ʿbd.àlì*[yn] (3) *bʿl.*
  sìd.zbl.bʿl (4) *àrṣ.*
  qm.ytʿr (5) *w.yšlḥmnh*

6 *ybrd.td.lpnwh*

7 *bḥrb.mlḥt* (8) *qṣ.mrì.*
  ndd (9) *yʿšr.wyšqynh*

10 *ytn.ks.bdh*

11 *krpn.bklàt.ydh*

12 *bk rb.ʿẓm.rì*
  dn (13) *mt.šmm.*
  ks.qdš (14) *ltphnh.àtt.*
  krpn (15) *ltʿn.àtrt.*
  àlp (16) *kd.yqḥ.bḥmr*

17 *rbt.ymsk.bmskh*

18 *qm.ybd.wyšr*

19 *mṣltm.bd.nʿm*

20 *yšr.ġzr.ṭb.ql*

21 *ʿl.bʿl.bṣrrt* (22) *ṣpn.*
  ytmr.bʿl (23) *bnth.*
  yʿn.pdry (24) *bt.àr.*
  àpn.ṭly (25) [bt.r]*b.*

. . . .

'Do not lower [your heads].'
Then *Rdmn*[1] did serve mightiest Baal,
he did wait upon the prince lord of earth.
He did rise, he set (the table) and fed him;
he divided a breast before him,
with a salted knife he did carve a fatling.
He did stand up, he spread a banquet and gave him drink;
he gave a cup into his hand(s),[2]
a flagon into his two hands,
a large jar, huge to see,
a cask of mighty men,[3]
a holy cup which no woman could regard,
a flagon which no goddess[4] could look upon;
he took a thousand pitchers of wine,[5]
ten thousand he mixed in his mixture.
One did rise, one chanted[6] and sang;
the cymbals were in the hands of the minstrel;
the sweet-voiced hero sang
over Baal in the recesses of Zephon.
Baal caught sight of his daughters,
he perceived Pidray daughter of mist,[7]
also Tallay [daughter] of showers;[8]

A 1 Aartun (cp. **2** i 24–25)
  6 De Moor *ybr d.td* (error for *dtd*) 'he cut up a suckling', lit. 'he of the teat' (Aram. *brâ* 'cut'); *lpnwh*: 'Aramaizing' form or error for *lpnnh* (D 84)
  9: this and *ll.* 11, 14 transgress the margin with col. ii
  11 *n* has been written over a second word-divider (Herdner)
  25: cp. C 4

[1] Cp. Akk. *Radmānu* (Tallqvist *Ass. Pers. Names* p. 185). Alternatively '*Prdmn* did serve', in either case a minor deity not mentioned elsewhere.
[2] Cp. Gen. xl 13.
[3] Lit. 'men of heaven'.
[4] Note the name Athirat used in a generic sense;

so sometimes El for 'god'.
[5] The term *ḥmr*, according to De Moor specifically the new wine of autumn, occurs only here and in **23** 6 in the mythological texts.
[6] Lit. 'improvised poems or songs'; the oriental singer or troubador was allowed considerable latitude within the traditional forms to vary his story. Cp. 2 Sam. xxiii 1.
[7] Cp. Job xxxvii 11 where this word may occur in Hebr.; alternatively 'daughter of light', representing the lightning (cp. Job xxxvii 15). The meaning of the personal name is unknown.
[8] Perhaps more accurately 'drizzle', regarded by the ancients as a type of dew; the second daughter's personal name means 'she of the dew'.

pdr.ydˁ (26) [- - -]t.*ìm*[-]*lt*	Pidar[1] knew [ ]
27 [- - -?]	[ ]
28 [- - - - - - - -]rt	[ ]
. . (*ca.* 12–14 *ll.*) . .	. . . .

B

Col. ii

. . (*ca.* 25 *ll.*) . .	
1 n[- - - - - - - - - - -]*š*[- -]	[ ]
2 *kpr.šbˁ.bnt.*	henna (enough) for seven girls,
rh.gdm (3) *wànhbm.*	scent of coriander and murex.[2]
klàt.tġrt (4) *bht.ˁnt.*	Anat did close the gates of the mansion,[3]
wtqry.ġlmm (5) *bšt.ġr.*	and she met the pages at the foot of the rock.
whln.ˁnt.tm (6) *ths.bˁmq*	And behold! Anat fought in the vale,
thtsb.bn (7) *qrytm*	battled between the two cities,[4]
tmhs.lìm.hpy	smote the people of . . . . . .
8 *tsmt.àdm.sàt.š*[p]*š*	silenced the men of the sun-rise.
9 *thth.kkdrt.rì*[*š*]	Head(s) were like balls[5] beneath her,
10 *ˁlh.kìrbym kp.*	palm(s) above her like locusts,
*k.qs*m (11) *ġrmn.kp.mhr.*	palm(s) of warrior(s) like avenging grasshoppers.[6]
ˁtkt (12) *rìšt.lbmth.*	She did stick the heads on her waist,[7]
šnst (13) *kpt.bhbšh.*	did bind the palms to her sash.
brkm.tġl[l] (14) *bdm.žmr.*	She plunged (her) knees in the blood of the guard(s),
hlqm.bmm[ˁ] (15) *mhrm.*	(her) skirts in the gore of the warriors.
mtm.tgrš (16) *šbm.*	With (her) shaft(s)[8] she drove forth the old men,
bksl.qšth.mdnt	with her bow[8] string the townspeople.[9]
17 *whln.ˁnt.lbth.tmġyn*	Then behold! Anat proceeded to her house,
18 *tštql.ìlt.lhklh*	the goddess started for her palace;
19 *wl.šbˁt.tmthsh.bˁmq*	but she was not sated with her fighting in the vale,
20 *thtsb.bn.qrtm.*	(her) battling between the two cities.
ttˁr (21) *ksàt.lmhr.*	She arranged chairs for the warrior(s),
tˁr.tlhnt (22) *lsbìm.*	she did arrange[10] tables for the soldiers,
hdmm.lġzrm	stools for the heroes.
23 *mìd.tmthsn.wtˁn*	Anat fought hard and looked,
24 *thtsb.wthdy ˁnt*	she battled and surveyed (the scene);[11]
25 *tġdd.kbdh.bshq.*	her liver swelled with laughter,

26–27 De Moor *hm*[.*klt*] (27)[*knyt*] (cp **4** iv 54)
7 *hpy*: Virolleaud *hp y*[*m*] 'sea-shore', but the Arab.
equivalent is *hâffatu*
9 *rì*[*š*]: sing. like *kp* (10); in 12–13 plurs. are used
11–28: **7** I 1–10 gives a slightly different version of
these lines
13–14: cp. 27–28; there is scarcely room for the
second *l* and it may have been omitted by error

[1] Cp. Akk. *Pidar* (*Ugaritica* V p. 11); the name
occurs as a divine name in *CTA* **37** 4 **38** 5 and elsewhere as an element in personal names; the context
here suggests that it is a by-name or title of Baal.
[2] I.e. purple snails, from which dye was obtained.

[3] Anat's own house, situated in a place later given
the names Ughar and Inbab (D 78).
[4] Probably Ras Shamrah and its port (*Minat
alBaidah*) in mythological guise (De Moor).
[5] Cp. Isa. xxii 18.
[6] Lit. 'of vengeance, punishment'.
[7] Lit. 'back' or perhaps more accurately 'torso'.
[8] Cp. Hab. iii 9, 14 (of Yahweh).
[9] Lit. 'town, province'. Alternatively 'foes' (lit.
'strife'; cp. Hebr. *mādôn*) or 'weaklings' (lit. 'weakness, meanness'; cp. *dnt* in **4** iii 20).
[10] Infinitive absolute or basic verbal form (3 masc.
sing. perf.); also *tˁr* (36).
[11] Or 'and rejoiced' (Hebr. *hādāh*).

ymlù (26) lbh.bšmḫt.   her heart was filled with joy,[1]
kbd.ʿnt (27) tšyt.   the liver of Anat with triumph,
kbrkm.tġll bdm (28) žmr. as she plunged (her) knees in the blood of the guard(s),
ḥlqm.bmmʿ.mhrm   (her) skirts in the gore of the warriors,
29 ʿd.tšbʿ.tmtḫṣ.bbt until she was sated with fighting in the house,
30 tḫtṣb.bn.tlḥnm. with battling between the tables.
ymḥ (31) [b]bt.dm.žmr. The blood of the guard(s) was wiped [from] the house
yṣq.šmn (32) šlm.bṣʿ. (and) oil of a peace-offering was poured from a bowl.
trḥṣ.ydh.bt (33) [l]t.ʿnt. The virgin Anat washed her hands,
ùṣbʿth.ybmt.lìmm. the sister-in-law of peoples[2] her fingers;
34 [t]rḥṣ.ydh.bdm.žmr she washed her hands of the blood of the guard(s),
35 [ù]ṣbʿth.bmmʿ.mhrm her fingers of the gore of the warriors.[3]
36 [t]ʿr[.]ksàt.lksàt. She did put (back)[4] chairs with chairs,
tlḥnt (37) [l]tlḥn⟨t⟩. tables with tables,
hdmm.ttàr.lhdmm. she put (back) stools with stools.
38 [t]ḥspn.mh.wtrḥṣ She scooped up water and washed (herself),
39 [t]l.šmm.šmn.àrṣ. dew of heaven (and) oil of earth,[5]
rbb (40) [r]kb ʿrpt. showers of the rider on the clouds,[6]
ṭl.šmm.tskh   dew that the heavens poured upon her,[7]
41 [rb]b.nskh.kbkbm [showers] that the stars did pour upon her.

Col. iii

42 ttpp.ànhb[m.]   She set off her beauty with the murex,
[dàlp.šd] (43) ẓùh.bym[.] whose source [is a thousand tracts away] in the sea,
[ṭl - - - - -] (44) [- -]rn.l[- - - - - - - -] [with dew   ]
. . (ca. 20 ll.) . . . .

C

1*[tìḫd] (1) [knrh.bydh.] '[she takes her lyre in her hand],
[t]št rìmt (2) lìrth. '[she] puts corals on her breast,
tšr.l.dd.àlìyn (3) bʿl. 'she sings of (her) love for mightiest Baal,
yd.pdry.bt.àr   'of (her) affection for Pidray daughter of mist,
4 àhbt[.]ṭly.bt.rb. 'of (her) devotion to Tallay daughter of showers,
dd.àrṣy (5) bt.yʿbdr. 'of (her) love for Arṣay daughter of . . . . . .[8]

31 Cassuto
33: this line transgresses the margin with col. iii and the final word-divider separates the last word from the first in D 34
34: cp. **7** II 8   36: cp. 21
37: cp. 36   38–43: cp. D 86–90
42–44 are written on a small fragment giving the top of col. iii and on the reverse the bottom of col. iv
C 1*–1: cp. *Ugaritica* V no. 3 rev. *l.* 6
1–26: cp. **7** II 10–21; a few letters and words from the end of B are preserved in **7** II 1–9
1: cp. **7** II 10
2 tšr: cp. *Ugaritica* V no. 3 rev. *l.* 7; Virolleaud *mšr*; this and several other lines in col. iii finish on the edge of the tablet

[1] Cp. Ps. xvi 9.
[2] Alternative renderings of the title are (Albright) 'progenitress of peoples' (from a putative √ybm) and (De Moor) 'sister-in-law, widow of the Li'mites' (an ancient dynastic or clan name).
[3] Cp. Ps. lviii 11. [4] Lit. 'did arrange'.
[5] Cp. Gen. xxvii 28 **6** iii 6.
[6] See at **2** iv 8.
[7] Note the 'dative' suffixes. In ancient belief the dew fell from the sky.
[8] The first part of the epithet of Baal's third daughter, whose personal name means 'she of the earth', is usually linked with Arab. *waʿiba* 'was spacious'; De Moor's suggestion 'ampleness of flow' (Arab. *darra*) referring to moisture in the earth seems more appropriate than Albright's 'wide-world, spacious universe' (Arab. *dawru* 'circuit'). Cp. **5** v 6ff., where this daughter does not descend with Baal into the nether-world, i.e. her function does not cease in the summer.

km ǵlmm (6) _w.ʿrbn._	'Like pages, then, enter,
lpʿn.ʿnt.hbr (7) _wql._	'do homage at the feet of Anat and fall down,
tšthwy.kbd hyt	'do you prostrate yourselves (and) honour her;
8 _wrgm lbtlt.ʿnt_	'and tell the virgin Anat,
9 _tny.lymmt.lìmm_	'repeat to the sister-in-law of peoples:
10 _thm.dlìyn.bʿl._	' "The message of mightiest Baal,
hwt (11) _dlìy.qrdm._	' "the word of the mightiest of warriors (is this):
qryy.bdrṣ (12) _mlḥmt_	' "Put an offering of loaves in the earth,
št.bʿprt.ddym	' "set mandrakes[1] in the ground,
13 _sk.šlm.lkbd.drṣ_	' "pour a peace-offering in the heart of the earth,
14 _dr bdd.lkbd.šdm_	' "honey from a pot in the heart of the fields.[2]
15 _hšk.ʿṣk.ʿbṣk_	' "Make haste! be resolute! hurry on![3]
16 _ʿmy.pʿnk.tlsmn._	' "Let your feet run towards me,
ʿmy (17) _twth.ìšdk._	' "let your legs hasten towards me.
dm.rgm (18) _ìt.ly.w.drgmk_	' "For I have a tale that I would tell you,
19 _hwt.w.dtnyk._	' "a word that I would repeat to you,
rgm (20) _ʿṣ.w.lḥšt.dbn_	' "a tale of tree(s) and a whisper of stone(s),[4]
21 _tdnt.šmm.ʿm.drṣ_	' "the sighing of the heavens to the earth,
22 _thmt.ʿmn.kbkbm_	' "of the oceans to the stars.[5]
23 _dbn.brq.dl.tdʿ.šmm_	' "I understand[6] lightning, which the heavens do not know;
24 _rgm ltdʿ.nšm._	' "(it is) a tale that mankind does not know,[7]
wltbn (25) _hmlt.drṣ._	' "nor do the multitudes of the earth understand.
dtm.wdnk (26) _ìbǵyh._	' "Come and I myself will search it out[8]
btk.ǵry.ìl.ṣpn.	' "within my rock El Zephon,[9]
27 _bqdš.bǵr.nhlty_	' "in (my) holy place, in the rock of my heritage,[10]
28 _bnʿm.bgbʿ.tlìyt_	' "in (my) pleasant place, in the hill of my victory.[11]" '

9 _ymmt_ error for or variant of _ybmt_

12 _ʿprt_ (Virolleaud; plur.?) or _ʿprm_ (Herdner; cp. D 53, 67, 73)

14 _dr bdd_ (Gaster) rather than _drb dd_ (Aistleitner) 'much love' (cp. Arab. elative)

24–25: cp. 1 iii 15 and contrast _ll._ 59–60 where the placing of the couplet is different

[1] The fruit of this plant was believed to possess erotic and fertilizing properties.

[2] This passage has often been interpreted as a call on the goddess of violence to cease from war (_mlḥmt_) and seek peace (_šlm_); but with a verb 'to pour' it is more probable that _šlm_ means 'peace-offering' as in B 32, and neither a verb _lḥm_ 'to fight' nor a noun _mlḥmt_ 'war' occurs elsewhere in Ugaritic.

[3] Lit. 'your hastening' etc.

[4] An allusion has been seen in this line to the worship of the 'high-places' with their standing poles and stones (Deut. xii 2–3 Jer. ii 27), but in conjunction with _ll._ 21–22 it is more likely to refer simply to the action of the wind, picturesquely represented as the conversation of the various natural phenomena.

[5] With the thought and language here cp. Ps. xix 2–5 xlii 8 Hos. ii 23–24.

[6] Possibly 'I will create' (√_bny_), though this disturbs the chiastic structure of _ll._ 23–25; cp. Job xxxviii 35.

[7] Cp. Job xxviii 13.

[8] Alternatively (Caquot and Sznycer) 'I will divulge it' (Arab. _faǵâ_ 'spread' (of news)).

[9] The mountain is here apparently deified (cp. 19 84 and in a sacrificial text _CTA_ 35 42) unless the phrase means simply 'my godlike, towering mountain' (Dahood; cp. Ps. xxxvi 7).

[10] Cp. Exod. xv 17 3 F 16 4 viii 13–14.

[11] Cp. Ps. lxxviii 54.

29 *hlm.ʿnt.tph.ilm.*	Behold! Anat perceived the two gods
bh.pʿnm (30) *tṯṯ.*	(and) at that[1] (her) feet stamped,
bʿdn.ksl.ttbr	she burst (her) loins round about,[2]
31 *ʿln.pnh.tdʿ.*	her face sweated above,
tǵṣ.pnt (32) *kslh.*	she convulsed the joints of her loins,
ảnš.dt.ẓrh.	the muscles of her back.
tšủ (33) *gh.wtṣḥ.*	She lifted up her voice and cried:
ỉk.mǵy.gpn.wủgr	'How (is it that) Gupn and Ugar have arrived?
34 *mn.ỉb.ypʿ.lbʿl.*	'What foe rises against Baal,
ṣrt (35) *lrkb.ʿrpt.*	'(what) enemy against the rider on the clouds?
lmḫšt.mdd (36) *ỉl ym.*	'Did I not destroy Yam the darling of El,[3]
lklt.nhr.ỉl.rbm	'did I not make an end of Nahar the great god?[4]
37 *lỉštbm.tnn.ỉštmlỉ*	'Was not the dragon captured[5] (and) vanquished?
38 *mḫšt.btn.ʿqltn*	'I did destroy the wriggling serpent,[6]
39 *šlyṭ.d.šbʿt.rảšm*	'the tyrant with seven heads;[7]
40 *mḫšt.mdd ỉlm.ảr[š]*	'I did destroy Arsh[8] the darling of the gods,
41 *ṣmt.ʿgl.ỉl.ʿtk*	'I did silence Atik[9] the calf of El,
42 *mḫšt.klbt.ỉlm.ỉšt*	'I did destroy Ishat[10] the bitch of the gods,
43 *klt.bt.ỉl.ẓbb.*	'I did make an end of Zabib[11] the daughter of El.
ỉmtḫṣ w (44) *ỉtrt.ḥrṣ.*	'He did fight and was dispossessed of gold[12]
ṭrd.bʿl ———	'who banished Baal———

Col. iv

——— (45) *bmrym.ṣpn.*	'——— from the height(s) of Zephon,
mšṣṣ.kʿṣ[r] (46) *ủdnh.*	'who pecked his ear like a bird,
gršh.lksỉ.mlkh	'who drove him forth from the throne of his kingdom,
47 *lnḫt.lkḫt.drkth*	'from the cushion on the seat of his dominion.[13]
48 *mnm.ỉb.ypʿ.lbʿl.*	'What foe (then) rises against Baal,
ṣrt.lrkb.ʿrpt	'(what) enemy against the rider on the clouds?'
49 *[w]ʿn.ǵlmm.yʿnyn.*	[And] the pages did answer (and) gave reply:
lỉb.ypʿ (50) *lbʿl.*	'No foe[14] rises against Baal,

D 29: the departure of the messengers is not related (cp. **4** v 104–105)

37 *ỉštmlỉ*: the reading is uncertain (Herdner *ỉštmlh*; Virolleaud *ỉšbm[-]h*)

38–44 are written on the rounded bottom edge of the tablet

40: cp. **6** vi 50

43: for *w* (Virolleaud) Herdner suggests *ksp*, which makes the verb difficult to translate

45 *kʿṣ[r]* (cp. Herdner); Virolleaud *wʿṣr*

46: in *ủdnh* both *ủ* and *d* have four vertical wedges

48: this and several other lines in col. iv finish on the edge of the tablet

49 *[w]ʿn* (Cassuto) or *[y]ʿn* (Virolleaud)

[1] Or 'on, in her'.

[2] Cp. Ezek. xxi 11.

[3] See further on this passage p. 7.

[4] Possibly 'god of the great (waters)'; cp. Ps. xxix 3   xciii 4.

[5] The form is 3 masc. sing. perfect Gt and the *-m* is enclitic. The meaning 'muzzle' (which Dahood also finds in Hebr. in Ps. lxviii 23) is based on an equation with Arab. *šabama*, which ought to give *sbm* in Ugar. and is in any case prob. denominative from the noun *šibâmu* (Barr).

[6] Cp. Isa. xxvii 1.

[7] Cp. Ps. lxxiv 13   Revel. xiii 1.

[8] An attendant monster of Yam mentioned also in **6** vi 50 but otherwise unknown.

[9] Meaning 'the quarrelsome one' (cp. Arab. *ʿataka* 'rushed to attack').

[10] Meaning 'fire'.

[11] Meaning perhaps 'flame' (Hebr. *šābîb*); but cp. Baal Zebub (2 Kgs. i 2).

[12] Cp. **2** i 19.

[13] Cp. **1** iv 24–25   **2** iv 12–13.

[14] Cp. Ps. lxxxix 23.

ṣrt.lrkb.ʿrpt   '(no) enemy against the rider on the clouds.

51 tḥm.ảliyn.bʿl.   'The message of mightiest Baal,

   hwt.ảliy (52) qrdm.   'the word of the mightiest of heroes (is this):

   qryy.bảrṣ.mlḥmt   'Put an offering of loaves in the earth,

53 št.bʿp[r]m.ddym.   'set mandrakes in the ground,

   sk.šlm (54) lkbd.ảrṣ.   'pour a peace-offering in the heart of the earth,

   ảr bdd.lkbd.šdm   'honey from a pot in the heart of the fields.

55 [ḥ]šk.[ʿ]sk.ʿbṣk.   'Make haste! be resolute! hurry on!

   ʿmy.pʿnk (56) [tls]mn.   'Let your feet [run] towards me,

   [ʿ]my.twtḥ.ïšdk   'let your legs hasten towards me.

57 [dm.rgm.ït.ly.]wảrgmk.   '[For I have a tale] that I would tell you,

   hwt (58) [wảtnyk.]   'a word [that I would repeat to you],

   [rgm.]ʿṣ.wlḥšt (59) [ảbn.]   '[a tale] of tree(s) and a whisper [of stone(s)],

   [rgm.ltd]ʿ.nš[m.]   '[a tale that] mankind [does not know],

   [wlt]bn (60) [hmlt.ả]rṣ.   '[nor do the multitudes of] earth understand,

   [tảnt.šmm.ʿm.ả]rṣ   '[the sighing of the heavens to] the earth,

61 thmt.[ʿmn.kbkbm.]   'of the oceans [to the stars].

   [ảbn.brq] (62) dlt[dʿ.šmm.]   '[I understand lightning] which [the heavens] do not [know].

   [ảtm.wảnk] (63) ïbǵ[yh.]   '[Come and I myself] will search [it] out

   [btk.ǵ]ry.ïl.ṣpn   '[within] my rock El Zephon,

64 bq[dš.bǵr.nḥ]lty   'in (my) holy [place, in the rock of] my heritage.'

65 wt[ʿn].btlt.[ʿ]nt.   And the virgin Anat [answered],

   ttb (66) [ybmt.]limm.   [the sister-in-law] of peoples replied:

   [ả]n.ảqry (67) [bảrṣ].mlḥmt[.]   'Shall even I put an offering of loaves [in the earth],

   [ảš]t.bʿprm (68) ddym[.]   '[shall I] set mandrakes in the ground,

   ảsk[.šlm.]lkbd.ảrṣ   'shall I pour [a peace-offering] in the heart of the earth,

69 ảr [bdd.]lkb[d.š]dm.   'honey [from a pot] in the heart of the fields?

   yšt (70) [bšmm.]bʿl.mdlh.   'Let Baal (first) set his thunder-bolt [in the heavens],

   ybʿr (71) [- - - - - - q]rnh.   'let [   ] kindle his (lightning-)flash!

   ảqry (72) [ản.]bả[r]ṣ.mlḥmt   '(Then) shall [even I] put an offering of loaves in the earth,

73 ảšt[.bʿ]p[r]m.ddym.   'I shall set mandrakes [in] the ground,

   ảsk (74) šlm.lkb[d].ảwṣ.   'I shall pour a peace-offering in the heart of the earth,

   ảr bdd (75) lkbd.š[d]m.   'honey from a pot in the heart of the fields.

   ảp.mtn.rgmm (76) ảrgmn.   'Also, one more thing[1] I will say:

   lk.lk.ʿnn.ïlm   'Go, go, lackeys of the gods.

77 ảtm.bštm.wản.šnt   'While you delay I[2] do quit

78 ủǵr.lrḥq.ïlm.   'Ughar[3] for the most distant of gods,

   ïnbb (79) lrḥq.ïlnym.   'Inbab[3] for the most distant of ghosts,

   tn.mtpdm (80) tḥt.ʿnt.ảrṣ.   'two layers beneath the wells of earth,

---

55–64: cp. C 15–27

65–66 Virolleaud (who however reads ản[k.]; but cp. 72, 77)

67–69: cp. C 11–14   70 Gaster

71 Gaster [ïl.hd.q] (cp. 12 i 41) but it hardly fills the space

72 [ản] or [ảnk] (cp. 66)

72–75: cp. C 11–14   74 ảwṣ error for ảrṣ

[1] Lit. 'the repetition of words'. Alternatively 'Moreover, messengers (lit. repeaters of words), I say (this) . . .' (Caquot and Sznycer, citing an unpublished text), though this rendering does not suit in 17 vi 39.

[2] Lit. 'You have remained and I . . .'

[3] Apparently two place-names associated with the abode of Anat.

tlt . mth . ġyrm	'three spans (beneath its) marshes[1].'
81 *ìdk . lttn . pnm .*	Then indeed she set (her) face
ʿm . bʿl (82) *mrym . ṣpn .*	towards Baal (in) the height(s) of Zephon,
bàlp . šd . rbt . kmn	across a thousand tracts, ten thousand spaces.
83 *hlk . àḫth . bʿl . yʿn .*	Baal sighted[2] his sister's coming,
tdrq (84) *ybnt . àbh .*	the swift approach of his father's daughter-in-law.
šrḥq . àtt . lpnnh	He did remove the women from his presence
85 *št . àlp . qdmh .*	(and) did set an ox before her,
mrìd . wtk (86) *pnh .*	a fatling too in front of her.
tḥspn . mh . wtrḥṣ	She scooped up water and washed (herself),
87 *tl . šmm . šmn . àrṣ .*	dew of heaven (and) oil of earth,
tl . šm[m . t]*skh*	dew that the heavens poured upon her,
88 *rbb . nskh kbkbm .*	showers that the stars did pour upon her.
89 *ttpp . ànhbm .*	She set off her beauty with the murex,
dàlp . šd[. ẓùh . bym]	[whose source] is a thousand tracts away [in the sea],
90 *tl*[- - - - - - - - - - -]	with dew [ ]³
. . (*ca.* 15 *ll.*) . .	. . . .

E

[wn . ìn] (1*) [bt] . l[bʿl . km . ìlm .]	'[But there is not a house] for [Baal like the gods],
[wḫẓr] (1) *kbn* . [àtrt .]	'[nor a court] like the sons of [Athirat].
[mtb . ìl . mẓll] (2) *bnh .*	'[The dwelling of El] is his son's [shelter];[4]
m[tb . rbt . àtrt . ym]	'[the dwelling of dame Athirat of the sea]
3 *mtb . pdr*[y . bt . àr .]	'is the dwelling of Pidray [daughter of mist],
[mẓll] (4) *tly . bt . r*[b .]	'[the shelter] of Tallay daughter of showers,
[mtb . àrṣy] (5) *bt . yʿbdr*[.]	'[the dwelling of Arṣay] daughter of . . . . . .,
[mtb . klt] (6) *knyt .*	'[the dwelling of] the noble [brides].'
wtʿn[. btlt . ʿnt]	And [the virgin Anat] answered:
7 *ytb . ly . tr . ìl*[. àby]	'The bull El [my father] will attend to me,
8 *ytb . ly . wlh .* [àrgm]	'he will attend to me and [I will tell] him (what I shall do).

Col. v

9 [mṣḫ . ì]*mṣḫ . nn . kìmr . làrṣ*	'I shall [surely] drag him like a lamb to the ground,
10 [àšhlk] . *šbth . dmm .*	'[I shall make] his grey hairs [run] with blood,[5]
šbt . dqnh (11) [mmʿm] .	'the grey hairs of his beard [with gore],
kd . l . ytn . bt . lbʿl . kìlm	'if he gives not Baal a house like the gods

84 *ybnt* error for or variant of *ybmt* (cp. C 9)
85 *mrìd*: cp. *mrà* (4 v 107; see also at 4 vi 41–42)
87: phrase perhaps omitted after *àrṣ* (cp. B 39–40);
šm[m . t]*skh*: cp. B 40
88: the final word-divider is doubtful
89: cp. B 43
E 1*–8 comprise the reverse of the small fragment
    mentioned at B 42
1*–6: cp. 46–52 and with a change of order 4 i 10–19
    iv 50–57
6 Virolleaud
7–8: cp. 17 vi 42–43; [àrgm] (Gordon) or [àtb] (De
    Moor)
9: cp. 6 v 4   10–11: cp. 32–33

¹ A reference to El's abode, described more fully in E 14ff. as being within a mountainous massif at a mysterious place (the navel of the earth?) where the waters beneath the earth meet those above the firmament and where also they gush forth to feed the seas and rivers.

² Or 'Across a thousand tracts . . . Baal sighted'.

³ There is not room in the following lacuna for the performance of Anat's rite or the imparting of the secret of the lightning (or its creation); when the text resumes Baal is already complaining about having no palace.

⁴ See p. 5 note 2.

⁵ Cp. 1 Kgs. ii 9.

12 [wḫẓ]r.kbn.åtrt[.]
[td‘ṣ.]p‘n (13) [wtr.å]rṣ.
id[k.lttn.p]nm
14 [‘m.i]l.mbk nhr[m.]
[qr]b.[åp]q (15) [thm]tm.
tgl.ẓ[d.]i̊[l.]
wtbu̇ (16) [qr]š.m[l]k.åb[.šnm.]
mṣr (17) [t]bu̇.šdm.
qn[-]å̇[-]n[- -]lt
18 qlh.yš[m‘].tr.[i̊l].åbh.
[- - -]l (19) bšb‘t.ḥdrm.
[bt]mn[t.åp] (20) sgrt.
g[-].[-]ẓ[- - -]ḥ[- - - - -]
21 ‘n.tk[- - - - - - - - - - -]
22 ‘ln.t[- - - - - - - - - - -]
23 lp‘n.ġl[m]m[- - - - - - -]
24 mi̊d.ån[- - -]sn[- - - - -]
25 nrt.i̊lm.špš[.ṣhrr]t
26 lå.šmm[.]by[d.bn.i̊lm.m]t

27 wt‘n.btlt.‘n[t.]
[bnt.]bht (28) k.yi̊lm.
bnt[.]bh[tk].å[l.tš]mḫ
29 ål.tšmḫ.br[m.h]kl[k]
30 ål.åhdhm.by[mn]y[.]
[- - -]b[-] (31) bgdlt.årkty[.]
åm[- - - - -] (32) qdqdk.
åšplk.šbt[k.dmm]
33 šbt.dqnk.mm‘m[.]
y‘ny (34) i̊l.bšb‘t.ḥdrm.
btmnt (35) åp.sgrt.

12 [ḥẓ]r: cp. 47
12–16: cp. 4 v 82–85   4 iv 20–24   6 i 32–36   17 vi
 46–49
18 Ginsberg
19: cp. 34–35
25–26: cp. 4 viii 21–24   6 ii 24–25
27–31 Herdner (cp. 18 i 7–10)
30 by[mn]y (Cassuto)
32 åšplk error for åšhlk (cp. 18 i 11)

¹ Infin. absol. or basic verbal form (3 masc. sing.
perf.). Cp. Judg. v 4   Ps. lxviii 9.
² Cp. Job xxviii 11   Gen. ii 6, 10ff. The idea is
poetically applied to Jerusalem or its Temple in Joel
iv 18   Ezek. xlvii 1ff.   Zech. xiv 8   1 Enoch xxvi 2.
³ Cp. Ezek. xlviii 2   Job xxxviii 16–17 where the
sources or springs of the sea are situated like the
entrance to Sheol in a secret and inaccessible place;
cp. also Quran Sura xviii 59–63.
⁴ Cp. 1 ii 23   iii 12 (Appendix) where El's abode
is specifically linked with a mountain (ḫršn) named
ġr ks. Alternative renderings are 'tent' (Clifford on
the basis of the parallelism in 19 212) and 'horror,

'[and a] court like the sons of Athirat.'
[She planted] (her) feet and the earth [did quake];¹
then [indeed she set] (her) face
[towards] El at the source(s) of the rivers,²
[amid the springs of the] two [oceans];³
she penetrated the mountain(s) of El⁴
and entered [the massif]⁵ of the king, father [of years]⁶
. . . . . . she entered the mountains
[   ]
The bull [El] her father heard her voice;⁷
[   ] from the seven chambers,
[through] the eight [entrances] of the closed room
[   ]
he did look [   ]
above [   ]
at the feet of the pages [   ]
much [   ]
Shapash, the luminary of the gods [did glow hot],
the heavens were wearied⁸ by the hand [of divine⁹
   Mot].
And the virgin Anat spoke:
'[(In) the building of] your mansion, o El,
'in the building of [your] mansion do not [rejoice],
'do not rejoice in the raising of [your] palace,
'lest I seize them with my [right hand],
'[   ] by the might of my long arm,¹⁰
'(lest) I [   ] your crown,
'make [your] grey hairs run [with blood],
'the grey hairs of your beard with gore.'
El answered from the seven chambers,
through the eight entrances of the closed room:

fearful place' (Lipiński; Arab. ḏâda 'drove away,
repelled'), but neither of these meanings suits in
19 220.
⁵ Or 'glacier' (Lipiński); alternatively 'pavilion'
(lit. 'planks' or 'struts') on the basis of Hebr. qereš, an
item used in the construction of the Tabernacle
(Clifford et al.; cp. Exod. xxvi 15ff.).
⁶ Cp. Isa. ix 5 Dan. vii 9; or 'father of exalted
ones, notables' (Pope; Hebr. šōnîm in Prov. xxiv 21)
or 'father of (the deity) Shunami' (30 4   Ugaritica V
no. 1 obv. l. 19; Lipiński).
⁷ Cp. 2 Sam. xxii (Ps. xviii) 7.
⁸ Possibly 'was tawny, dust-coloured . . . were
stained by' (De Moor), alternative meanings of the
verbs in the cognate languages, referring to the
Sirocco as controlled by Mot; but the words are
more likely to be a conventional description of hot
weather, or if they have significance for the myth, to
underline Mot's dominance over the sun-goddess
Shapash (cp. 6 ii 24–25).
⁹ Probably 'son of the gods' rather than 'son of El'
(with enclitic m); though cp. 5 iii 6.
¹⁰ Cp. Exod. xv 16   18 i 7ff.

yd°[tk.]*bt.kản*[št]	'[I] know, daughter, that [you] are like men[1]
36 *kin.bỉlht.ql*[ṣ]*k.*	'(and) that there exists not among goddesses contempt like yours.
mh.tảrš[n] (37) *lbtlt.°nt.*	'What do you desire, o virgin Anat?'
wt[°]*n.btlt.°n*[t]	And the virgin Anat answered:
38 *thmk.il.ḥkm*[.]	'Your decree, El, is wise,
ḥkmk (39) *°m.°lm.*	'your wisdom is everlasting.
ḥyt.ḥẓt.thmk	'A life of good fortune is your decree.
40 *mlkn.ảlỉyn.b°l.*	'Mightiest Baal is our king,
tpṭn (41) *ỉn.d°lnh.*	'our judge, over whom there is none.[2]
klnyy.qšh (42) *nbln.*	'We two[3] would carry his chalice,
klnyy.nbl.ksh	'we two would carry his cup.
43 *ảny.lyṣḥ.ṯr.ỉl.ảbh.*	'(Yet) groaning he indeed cries out to the bull El his father,
ỉl (44) *mlk.dyknnh.*	'to El the king who installed him,[4]
yṣḥ.ảṯrt (45) *wbnh.*	'he cries out to Athirat and her sons,
ỉlt.wṣbrt.ảryḥ.	'to Elat and the company of her kinsfolk:
46 *wn.ỉn.bt*[.]*lb°l.km.ỉlm*	' "But there is not a house for Baal like the gods
47 *ḥẓr.kb*[n.ả]*ṯrt.*	' "(nor) a court like the sons of Athirat.
mtb.ỉl (48) *mẓll.b*[nh.]	' "The dwelling of El is [his] son's shelter;
[m]*tb.rbt.ảṯrt* (49) *ym.*	' "the dwelling of dame Athirat of the sea
mtb.[pdr]*y.bt.ảr*	' "is the dwelling of [Pidray] daughter of mist,
50 [mẓll.]*t̠ly*[.bt.]*rb.*	' "[the shelter] of Tallay [daughter] of showers,
mtb (51) [ảrṣy.bt.y°bdr.]	' "the dwelling [of Arṣay daughter of . . . . . .],
[mtb] (52) [klt.knyt.]	' "[the dwelling of the noble brides]" '
. . (*ca. 22 ll.*) . .	. . . .

F

Col. vi

. . (*ca. 10 ll.*) . .	. . . .
1 [- - - - - - - -]b	'[ ]
2 [- - - - - - - r]*ỉšk*	'[ ] your head
3 [- - - - -]*bn °nkm*	'[ ] between your eyes
4 [- - - - -]*ảlp*	'[ ] a thousand
5 [- - - -]*ym.rbt*	'[ ] the sea, ten thousand
6 [- - -]*bnhrm*	'[ ] through the rivers.
7 [°b]*r.gbl.°br* (8) *q°l.*	'[Cross] over Byblos, cross over Keilah,[5]
°br.ỉht (9) *np šmm.*	'cross over the islands of "Noph of the heavens".[6]
šmšr (10) *ldgy.ảṯrt*	'Start away, o fisherman of Athirat,

35–36: cp. **18** i 16–17
35–37: these lines transgress the margin with col. iv
36–37 Virolleaud
45 *ảryḥ* error for *ảryh* (cp. **4** iv 50)
47–52: cp. **1***–6
F 7, 8, 11: note *l* with four vertical wedges

[1] Or (ironically) 'gentle'.
[2] Cp. Ps. xcv 3   Isa. xxxiii 22.
[3] Hardly here as in **4** iv 45 Athirat, unless the

words are conventional; perhaps Athtart, Baal's consort, was present with Anat. Note dual suffixes.

[4] Assuming that El has recognized Baal after his defeat of Yam (in a missing portion of *CTA* **2** or in a lost following tablet); alternatively 'who created him' (√*kwn*); cp. Deut. xxxii 6 where both ideas are present.
[5] In Palestine (1 Sam. xxiii 1).
[6] Noph is another name for Memphis, the islands being therefore those on the Nile delta.

11 mġ.lqdš.⟨w⟩àmrr   'proceed, o Qodesh-and-Amrur.
12 ìdk.àl.ttn (13) pnm   'Then of a truth do you set (your) face
   tk.ḥqkpt (14) ìl.klh.   'towards all broad Memphis,[1]
   kptr (15) ksù.tbth.   '(towards) Kptr[2] the throne on which he sits,
   ḥkpt (16) àrṣ.nḥlth   'Memphis the land of his heritage.[3]
17 bàlp.šd.rbt (18) kmn.   'Traversing a thousand tracts, ten thousand spaces,
   lpʿn.kt⟨r⟩ (19) hbr.wql.   'do homage at the feet of Kothar, and fall down,
   tšth (20) wy.wkbd.hwt   'prostrate yourself and do honour to him;
21 wrgm.lktr (22) wḥss.   'and tell to Kothar-and-Khasis,
   tny.lh (23) yn.dḥrš.ydm   'repeat to Heyan,[4] skilled worker by hand:[5]
24 thm.àl[ìyn.bʿl]   ' "The message of mightiest [Baal],
25 h[wt.àlìy.qrdm]   ' "the word [of the mightiest of warriors (is this)]:

    .   . (ca 20 ll.) .   .   · · · · · · · · · · · ·

                                              4

                                          Col. i

    .   . (ca. 20 ll.) .   .   · · · · · · · · · · · ·
 1 [   ]   [   ]
 2 [- - - - - - - -]y   [   ]
 3 [   ]   [   ]
 4 [àny.lyṣ]ḥ.tr (5) [ìl.àbh.]   '[(Yet) groaning he indeed cries] out to the bull [El his
                                          father],
   [ì]l mlk (6, 7) [dyknnh.]   'to El the king [who installed him],
   [yṣ]ḥ.àt (8) [rt.wbnh.]   '[he cries] out to Athirat [and her sons],
   ìlt (9) [wṣbrt.àry]h   'to Elat [and the company of] her [kinsfolk]:
10 [wn.ìn.bt.lbʿl] (11) [km.ìlm.]   ' "[But there is not a house for Baal like the gods],
   [wḥẓr] (12) [kbn.àt]r[t]   ' "[nor a court like the sons of Athirat].
13 m[t]b ìl.mẓll (14) bnh.   ' "The dwelling of El is his son's shelter;
   mtb.rbt (15) àtrt.ym.   ' "the dwelling of dame Athirat of the sea
   mtb (16) klt.knyt   ' "is the dwelling of the noble brides,
17 mtb.pdry.b⟨t.⟩àr   ' "the dwelling of Pidray daughter of mist,
18 mẓll.tly.bt rb   ' "the shelter of Tallay daughter of showers,
19 mtb.àrṣy.bt.yʿbdr   ' "the dwelling of Arṣay daughter of . . . . . ."
20 àp.mtn.rgmm (21) àrgmk.   'Also, one more thing I have to tell you:
   šskn mʿ (22) mgn.   'Make ready, I beseech you, a present
   rbt.àtrt ym   'for dame Athirat of the sea,
23 mġẓ.qnyt.ìlm   'a gift for the creatress[6] of the gods.'
24 hyn.ʿly.lmpḥm   Heyan did go up to the bellows;
25 bd.ḥss.mṣbtm   the tongs were in the hands of Khasis;

11: cp. 4 iv 8, 13 etc.
13 ḥqkpt error for or variant of ḥkpt (15)
24-25: cp. C 10-11 D 51-52
4-13: cp. iv 47-52 3 E 43-47
6-7: there is room for two lines here, but only one can
   have been inscribed, since the restorations are not
   in doubt
17: cp. iv 55
19: this and several other lines transgress the margin
   with col. ii

[1] Tell Am. Akk. (al)Ḫi-ku-up-ta-aḫ, 'the city of
Ptah', the Egyptian god of craftsmen. The phrase
means lit. 'Memphis of El, all of it'; cp. C 26 4 i
31ff. 17 vi 23.
[2] The syntax makes it unlikely that Kptr is the
same as biblical Caphtor, usually identified with
Crete.   [3] Cp. Exod. xv 17 3 C 27 4 viii 13-14.
[4] See p. 10 note 5.
[5] Lit. 'craftsman, skilled with two hands'.
[6] Or 'mistress'.

26 yṣq.ksp.yšl (27) ḫ.ḫrṣ.	he smelted silver, he plated gold,
yṣq.ksp (28) lȧlpm.	he smelted silver into thousands (of pieces),
ḫrṣ.yṣq (29) m.lrbbt	he smelted gold into ten thousands (of pieces),
30 yṣq.ḫym.wtbtḥ	he smelted a . . . . . and a couch,
31 kt.il.dt.rbtm	a divine[1] pedestal from twice ten thousand (pieces),
32 kt.il.nbt.bksp	a divine pedestal coated with silver,
33 šmrgt.bdm.ḫrṣ	overlaid with veneer of gold,
34 kḫt.il.nḫt (35) bẓr.	a divine seat with a rest at (its) back,
hdm.id (36) dpršȧ.bbr	a divine footstool whose . . . . . was . . . . . ,
37 nʿl.il.d.qblbl	divine sandals, thonged ones,[2]
38 ʿln.yblhm.ḫrṣ	which he furnished on top with gold,[3]
39 tlḥn.il.dmlȧ	a divine table whose surface[4] he did fill
40 mnm.dbbm.d (41) msdt.ȧrṣ	with creeping species from the depths[5] of the earth,
42 ṣʿ.il.dqt.kȧmr	a divine bowl whose handle was (shaped) as (in) Amurru[6]
43 sknt.kḫwt.ymȧn	(and whose) appearance was as the land of Ym'an,
44 dbḥ.rủmm.lrbbt	where are wild-oxen by the ten thousands.[7]

========   ========

. . (ca. 16 ll.) . .	**Col. ii**
1 [-]b[- - - - - - - - -]	. . . .
2 lȧbn[- - - - - -]	[ ]
3 ȧḥdt.plkh[.bydh]	on a stone [ ]
4 plk.tʿlt.bymnh	she did grasp her spindle [in her hand],
5 npynh.mks.bšrh	the spindle of (her) high-estate in her right hand;
6 tmtʿ.mdh.bym.	(she carried) her garments, the covering of her flesh,
tn (7) npynh.bnhrm	she carried her robe into the sea,
8 štt.ḫptr.lȧšt	her two garments into the rivers;[8]
9 ḥbrt.lẓr.pḥmm	she did place a cauldron on the fire,
10 tʿpp.tr.il.dpȧd	a pot upon the coals,
11 tġzy.bny.bnwt	(as) she fluttered (her eyelids) at the bull, kindly god,
12 bnši.ʿnh.wtphn	(and) winked at the creator of creatures.[9]
13 hlk.bʿl.ȧttrt (14) ktʿn.	Lifting her eyes, Athirat perceived,
hlk.btlt (15) ʿnt[.]	she surely sighted the coming of Baal,
tdrq.ybmt (16) [lȧmm].	the coming of the virgin Anat,
bh.pʿnm (17) [ttṭ.]	the speedy approach of the sister-in-law [of peoples].
	At that (her) feet [stamped],

33 šmrgt (Albright) or šmrḫt (Virolleaud; cp. Hebr. *māraḥ* 'rubbed, smeared')

35 id error for il (cp. 31, 32, 34 etc.)

40 d 'of' perhaps error for b 'from'

ii 3 Dussaud

4 tʿlt (Virolleaud) or qlt 'the spindle did fall' (Ginsberg)

13 ȧttrt error for ȧtrt (cp. 26, 28, 31) through confusion with ʿttrt

16: cp. **3** B 33 etc.

17–20: cp. **3** D 30–32

[1] Lit. 'of El' (cp. **3** F 13–14).
[2] Lit. 'possessor(s) of thong(s)'.

[3] Lit. 'above he did bring them out (as) gold'.
[4] Lit. 'which'.   [5] Lit. 'foundations'.
[6] Less likely in view of the parallelism 'like a lamb'.
[7] Lit. 'image', a word perhaps connected with Hebr. *sikkût* in Amos v 26 (Lipiński). A cup and a dish chased with animal figures was unearthed in the excavations (Schaeffer *Cuneif. Texts* p. 20).
[8] Perhaps better here 'waves'. The scene is a homely one for which a ritual counterpart need not be sought; cp. *Od.* vi 91 (Nausicaa).
[9] Since El is in fact not present, the words may be conventional; otherwise render '(that) she may, (intending) to . . .' or the like.

[bʿ]*dn.ksl* (18) [ttbr.]   [she burst] (her) loins [round]about,
[ʿln.p]*np td*[ʿ]   her face sweated [above],
19 *tǵṣ*[.pnt.ks]*lh*   she convulsed [the joints of] her loins,
20 *ȧnš.dt.ʒr*[h]   the muscles of [her] back.
21 *tšȧ.gh.wtṣḥ*[.]   She lifted up her voice and cried:
[ȧ]*k* (22) *mǵy.ȧlı̇yn*[.b]ʿ*l*   'How (is it that) mightiest Baal has arrived?
23 *ı̇k.mǵyt.b*[t]*lt* (24) ʿ*nt.*   'How (is it that) the virgin Anat has arrived?
mḫṣy hm[.m]*ḫṣ* (25) *bny.*   'Are my enemies come to smite[1] my sons
hm[.mkly.ṣ]*brt* (26) *ȧryy*[.]   'or [make an end of] the company of my kinsfolk?'
[ʒl].*ksp.*[ȧ]*trt* (27) *ktʿn.*   (But) when Athirat sighted[2] [the coverings] of silver,
ʒl.ksp.wn[b]t (28) *ḫrṣ.*   (when she sighted) the coverings of silver and the
                                                      coatings of gold,

šmḫ.rbt.ȧ[trt] (29) *ym.*   dame Athirat of the sea did rejoice.[3]
gm.lǵlmh.k[tṣḥ]   Surely [she cried] aloud to her page:
30 ʿ*n.mktr.ȧp* t[- - -]   'Look on the craftmanship, even [   ],
31 *dgy.rbt.ȧtr*[t.ym]   '[o] fisherman of dame Athirat [of the sea].
32 *qḥ.rtt.bdk.*q[dš]   'Take a net in your hand, [Qodesh],
33 *rbt.ʿl.yd*m[.ȧmrr]   'a large one[4] on (your) two hands, [Amrur];
34 *bmdd.ı̇l.*y[m - - - -]   'into Yam the darling of El [   ]
35 *bym.ı̇l.d*[- - - - bn]   'into Yam, the god of [   ]
36 *hr.ı̇l.y*[- - - - - - -]   '[into] Nahar, the god of [   ]
37 *ȧlı̇yn.*[bʿl - - - - -]   'Mightiest [Baal   ],
38 *btlt.*[ʿnt - - - - -]   'the virgin [Anat   ]
39 *mh.k*[- - - - - - - -]   'What [   ]
40 *wȧt*[- - - - - - -]   'and you [   ]
41 *ȧtr*[t - - - - - - -]   'Athirat [   ]
42 *bı̇m*[- - - - - - -]   'in [   ]
43 *bl.l*[- - - - - - -]   'not [   ]
44 *mlk*[- - - - - - -]   'the king [   ]
45 *dt*[- - - - - - - - -]   'of [   ]
46 *bṭ*[- - - - - - - - -]   [   ]
47 *gm*[- - - - - - - -]   aloud [   ]
48 *y*[- - - - - - - - -]   he [   ]

                                                  Col. iii

.   . (*ca.* 12 *ll.*)   .   .
1 [   ]   [   ]
2 [- - - - - - - - - -]*dn*   [   ]
3 [- - - - - - - -]*dd*   [   ]
4 [- - - - - -]*n.kb*   [   ]
5 [- - - - - -]*ȧl.yns*   '[   ] let him not escape[5]

18 *pnp* error for *pnh*   21: cp. 23
24–25: cp. 19 196–197, 201–202; [ṣ]*brt*: cp. 3 E 45
26 [ʒl]: cp. 27
27: cp. i 32   29: cp. vii 53 etc.
30 *ȧp* t (Herdner) or *ȧpt*[ḥ] (Bauer) 'I shall open'; at
   the end perhaps insert the vocative *l* (3 F 10)
32–33 De Moor (cp. 3 F 10–11 4 iv 16–17)
34–35: cp. 3 D 35–36; a verb meaning 'cast' is
   required (Ginsberg)
40–41 Gordon [*rbt*] (41) *ȧtr*[t.ym]

[1] Lit. 'Are my smiters the smiters of etc.?'
[2] Or 'Athirat surely sighted . . .'
[3] Infin. absol. or basic verbal form (3 masc. sing.
perf.).
[4] Perhaps a technical term for a dragnet.
[5] Anat is speaking as they approach Athirat and
referring probably to any enemy of Baal; there is no
need to seek an allusion to Mot (Cassuto) or to Yam
(Gaster).

6 [- - - - - -]ysdk .   '[   ] your foundation
7 [- - - - -]r . dr . dr   '[   ] for evermore
8 [- - - -]yk . wrḥd   '[   ] . . . . . .
9 [- - -]yilm . dmlk   '[   ] o god, possessor of kingship[1].'
10 y[t]b . aliyn . bʿl   Mightiest Baal replied,
11 ytʿdd . rkb . ʿrpt   the rider on the clouds responded, (saying):
12 [- -] . ydd . wyqlṣn   '[   ] they stood up and abased me,
13 yqm . wywptn .   'they[2] arose and spat upon me
    btk (14) p[ḫ]r . bn . ilm .   'amid the assembly of the sons of the gods.[3]
    štt (15) p[- -] . bt̄lḥny .   '[   ] was set on my table,
    qlt (16) bks . ištynh   'disgrace in the cup from which I drank.
17 dm . tn . dbḥm . šnả . bʿl .   'Truly (there are) two sacrifices Baal hates,
    tlt (18) rkb . ʿrpt .   'three[4] the rider on the clouds[5]—
    dbḥ (19) btt . wdbḥ . wdbḥ (20) dnt .   'a sacrifice of shame and a sacrifice of meanness
    wdbḥ . tdmm (21) ảmht   'and a sacrifice where handmaids debauch;[6]
    kbh . btt . ltbt̄   'for therein shameful conduct is indeed seen
22 wbh . tdmmt . ảmht   'and therein the debauchery of handmaids.'
23 ảḫr . mġy . aliyn . bʿl   Afterwards mightiest Baal did arrive
24 mġyt . btlt . ʿnt   (and) the virgin Anat did arrive;
25 tmgnn . rbt[. ả]t̄rt ym   they importuned dame Athirat of the sea,
26 tġzyn . qnyt ilm   entreated the creatress of the gods.
27 wtʿn . rbt . ảt̄rt ym   And dame Athirat of the sea answered:
28 ik . tmgnn . rbt (29) ảt̄rt . ym .   'How should you importune dame Athirat of the sea,
    tġzyn (30) qnyt . ilm .   'entreat the creatress of the gods?
    mgntm (31) t̄r . il . dpid .   'Have you importuned the bull, kindly god,
    hm . ġztm (32) bny . bnwt   'or entreated the creator of creatures?'
    wtʿn (33) btlt . ʿnt .   And the virgin Anat answered:
    nmgn (34) [ủ]m . rbt . ảt̄rt . ym   'We will importune (our) mother dame Athirat of the
                                                  sea,

35 [nġ]ẓ . qnyt . ilm   '[we] will entreat the creatress of the gods;
36 [ảḫr] . nmgn . hwt   '[thereafter] we will entreat him.'
37 [- -] . aliyn . bʿl   Mightiest Baal [   ]
38 [- -]rbt . ảt̄rt . ym   dame Athirat of the sea [   ]
39 [- - -]btlt . ʿnt   the virgin Anat [   ]
40 [ʿd . tl]ḥm . tšty (41) [ilm.]   [while the gods] ate (and) drank,
    [wtp]q . mrġtm (42) [td.]   [and they were supplied] with a suckling [of the teat];
    [bḫrb . m]lḥt . qṣ (43) [mri.]   [with] a salted [knife] they did carve [a fatling];
    [tšty . k]rpnm . yn   [they drank] flagons of wine
44 [wbks . ḥrṣ . dm] . ʿṣm   [and from cups of gold the blood] of trees[7]
    .   . (gap of 7 ll.) .   .
52 [- - - - - - - - - -]ʿln   [   ]
53 [- - - - - - - -]ln   [   ]

iii 6: note the final word-divider   [1] The phrase is used of Athtar earlier (2 iii 12, 18).
   10 Herdner   12: perhaps [dm] (cp. 17)   [2] Lit. 'one' (indef.).
   14 Virolleaud   [3] Cp. Ps. xxix 1   lxxxix 7   Job i 6   ii 1   xxxviii
   15 Gaster p[glt] 'foul meat' (cp. Hebr. piggûl)   7; alternatively 'of El'.
   19 dittography of wdbḥ   [4] Cp. Prov. vi 16ff.
   34 Gaster   35: cp. 29, 31   [5] See at 2 iv 8.
   36 Gaster   [6] Cp. Mishna Aboth ii 7 ('more maids (means)
   40–44: cp. vi 55–59   iv 36–38   more lewdness').
   41 [wtp]q (Bauer) or [wp]q (Virolleaud)   [7] Cp. Gen. xlix 11   Deut. xxxii 14   1 Macc. vi 34.

Col. iv

. . (ca. 12 *ll.*) . .   . .

[   ] (1) *tr*[.*il*.*àbn*.]   '[   ] the bull [El our father].'
[*wt‛n*.*rbt*] (2) *àtr*[*t*.*ym*.]   [And dame] Athirat [of the sea spoke]:
[*šm‛*.*lqdš*] (3) *wàm*[*rr*.]   '[Hear, o Qodesh-]and-Amrur,
[*ldgy*.*rbt*] (4) *àtrt*.*ym*[.]   'o fisherman of dame] Athirat of the sea.
[*mdl*.‛*r*] (5) *ṣmd*.*phl*.   '[Saddle a he-ass], yoke a donkey,
[*št*.*gpnm*.*dt*] (6) *ksp*.   '[put on harness of] silver,
dt.*yr*[*q*.*nqbnm*]   '[trappings] of gold,
7 ‛*db*.*gpn*.*àtnt*[*y*]   'make ready the harness of [my] she-asses.'
8 *yšm‛*.*qd*⟨*š*⟩.*wàmr*[*r*]   Qodesh-and-Amrur heard,
9 *mdl*.‛*r*.*ṣmd*.*phl*   he did saddle a he-ass,[1] did yoke a donkey,
10 *št*.*gpnm*.*dt*.*ksp*   did put on harness of silver,
11 *dt*.*yrq*.*nqbnm*   trappings of gold,
12 ‛*db*.*gpn*.*àtnth*   did make ready the harness of her she-asses.
13 *yhbq*.*qdš*.*wàmrr*   Qodesh-and-Amrur put his arms around (her)
14 *yštn*.*àtrt*.*lbmt*.‛*r*   (and) set Athirat on the back of the he-ass,
15 *lysmsmt*.*bmt*.*phl*   on the easiest part of the back of the donkey.
16 *qdš*.*yùhdm*.*šb‛r*   Qodesh took a torch,
17 *àmrr*.*kkbkb*.*lpnm*   Amrur was like a star in front.[2]
18 *àtr*.*btlt*.‛*nt*   Behind (came) the virgin Anat,
19 *wb‛l*.*tb‛*.*mrym*.*ṣpn*   but Baal did depart to the height(s) of Zephon.
20 *idk*.*lttn*.*pnm*   Then indeed she set (her) face
21 ‛*m*.*il*.*mbk*.*nhrm*   towards El at the source(s) of the rivers,
22 *qrb*.*àpq*.*thmtm*   amid the springs of the two oceans;
23 *tgly*.*šd*.*il*.   she penetrated the mountain(s) of El
     wtbù (24) *qrš*.*mlk*.*àb*.*šnm*   and entered the massif of the king, father of years.
25 *lp‛n*.*il*.*thbr*.*wtql*   She did homage at the feet of El and fell down,
26 *tšthwy*.*wtkbdh*   she prostrated herself and did him honour.
27 *hlm*.*il*.*kyphnh*   Behold! El surely perceived her,
28 *yprq*.*lṣb*.*wyṣhq*   he opened wide the passage of (his) throat[3] and
                                                    laughed,

29 *p‛nh*.*lhdm*.*ytpd*.   he placed his feet on the footstool
     wykrkr (30) *ùṣb‛th*.   and snapped his fingers,
     yšù.*gh*.*wy*[*ṣh*]   he lifted up his voice and cried:
31 *ik*.*mġyt*.*rbt*.*àtr*[*t*.*y*]*m*   'How (is it that) dame Athirat of the sea has arrived,
32 *ik*.*àtwt*.*qnyt*.*i*[*lm*]   'how (is it that) the creatress of the gods has come?
33 *rġb*.*rġbt*.*wtġt*   'Are you very hungry, having journeyed afar?
34 *hm*.*ġmù*.*ġmit*.*w‛s*[*t*]   'Or are you very thirsty, having travelled all night?
35 *lhm*.*hm*.*štym*.   'Eat and drink,
     lh[*m*] (36) *btlhnt*.*lhm*   'eat food from the tables,
     št (37) *bkrpnm*.*yn*   'drink wine from the flagons,

ⱽ 1 Herdner
2–3 Herdner (cp. 8 and ii 31–33)
4–7: cp. 9–12   8: cp. 13
29: this and several other lines are continued on the
    edge of the tablet
31–32: cp. iii 29–30   34 *w‛s*[*t*]: cp. *wtġt* (33)

[1] This passage hardly elucidates Zech. ix 9; the
donkey was the usual means of transport in the 2 mill.
B.C. and not specifically a mount of royalty.
[2] Cp. 2 i 32.
[3] Or 'smoothed his forehead' (Caquot and Sznycer
citing an unpublished text).

bk⟨s⟩.*ḥrṣ* (38) *dm.ʿṣm.*	'the blood of trees from cups of gold.
hm.yd.il m*lk* (39) *yḥssk.*	'Or does affection for El the king move you,
*ȧhbt.tr.t*ʿ*rrk*	'love of the bull rouse you?'
40 *wtʿn.rbt.ȧtrt ym*	And dame Athirat of the sea answered:[1]
41 *thmk.il.ḥkm.*	'Your decree, El, is wise,
*ḥkm*k (42) ʿ*m* ʿ*lm.*	'your wisdom is everlasting.
ḥyt.ḥẓt (43) *thmk.*	'A life of good fortune is your decree.
mlkn.ȧliy[n.]*b*ʿ*l*	'Mightiest Baal is our king,
44 *tptn.win.d*ʿ*lnh*	'our judge and there is none who is over him.
45 *klnyn.q*[š]h[.]*n*[bln]	'We two [would carry] his chalice,
46 *klnyn*[.n]*bl.ksh*	'we two would carry his cup.
47 [ȧn]*y*[.]*lyṣḥ.tr il.ȧbh*	'[(Yet) groaning] he indeed cries out to the bull El his father,
48 [i]*l.mlk.dyknnh.*	'to El the king who installed him,
yṣḥ (49) *ȧtrt.wbnh.*	'he cries out to Athirat and her sons,
ilt.wṣbrt (50) *ȧryh.*	'to Elat and the company of her kinsfolk:
*wn.in.bt.lb*ʿ*l* (51) *km ilm.*	' "But there is not a house for Baal like the gods
wḥẓr.kbn.ȧtrt	' "nor a court like the sons of Athirat.
52 *mtb il mẓll.bnh*	' "The dwelling of El is his son's shelter;
53 mtb *rbt.ȧtrt.ym*	' "the dwelling of dame Athirat of the sea
54 *mtb.klt*[.]*knyt*	' "is the dwelling of the noble brides,
55 *mtb.pdry.bt.ȧr*	' "the dwelling of Pidray daughter of mist,
56 *mẓll.tly*[.]*bt rb*	' "the shelter of Tallay daughter of showers,
57 *mtb.ȧrṣ*⟨y⟩.*bt y*ʿ*bdr*	' "the dwelling of Arṣay daughter of . . . . . ." '
58 *wy*ʿ*n ltpn il dpid*	And Latipan kindly god answered:
59 pʿ*bd.ȧn.*ʿ*nn.ȧtrt*	'So I am a slave, a lackey of Athirat,
60 pʿ*bd.ȧnk.ȧḥd ūlt*	'so I am a slave to handle the trowel,
61 *hm.ȧmt.ȧtrt.tlbn* (62) *lbnt.*	'seeing Athirat is a slave-girl to mould the bricks![2]
*ybn.bt.lb*ʿ*l* ——————	'Let a house be built for Baal ——————
	Col. v
—————— (63) *km ilm.*	'—————————————— like the gods
wḥẓr.kbn.ȧtrt	'and a court like the sons of Athirat.'
64 *wt*ʿ*n.rbt.ȧtrt ym*	And dame Athirat of the sea answered:
65 *rbt.ilm.lḥkmt*	'You are great,[3] El, you are indeed wise,
66 *šbt.dqnk.ltsrk*	'the grey hairs of your beard indeed instruct you[4]
67 *rḥntt.d*[-].*lirtk*	'. . . . . to your breast.
68 *wn ȧp.*ʿ*dn.mtrh*	'Now at last[5] Baal may appoint
69 bʿ*l.y*ʿ*dn.*	'a time for his rain,
ʿ*dn.tkt.bglt*	'a time for (his) barque (to appear) in the snow[6]
70 *wtn.qlh.b*ʿ*rpt*	'and for the sounding of his voice in the clouds,[7]

37: cp. **5** iv 16
45–47: cp. **3** E 41–43
57: cp. i 19
v 63, 69: these lines are continued on the edge of the tablet
67: perhaps *rḥnt td*[ʿ]
70 *wtn* prob. infin. (masc. form); Virolleaud *w*⟨*y*⟩*tn*

[1] See on the following lines at **3** E 38ff.

[2] Cp. Gen. xi 3   Exod. v 7.
[3] Or 'aged' (cp. Job xxxii 9).
[4] Cp. Ps. cv 22   **16** vi 26.
[5] Lit. 'And moreover'.
[6] The white snow clouds are pictured as Baal's ship; cp. the barque of the Egyptian sun-god Re. Alternatively 'waves' or 'tempest' (N. Hebr. *gālaš* 'boiled').
[7] Cp. 2 Sam. xxii (Ps. xviii) 14   Ps. xlvi 7   Jer. x 13   Joel ii 11   *ANET* p. 484 (El-Amarna letter).

71 *šrh.làrṣ.brqm* 'for him to release[1] (his) lightnings on the earth.
72 *bt.àrzm.ykllnh* '(Is it) a house of cedars?[2] He may complete it.
73 *hm.bt.lbnt.y'msnh* 'Or a house of bricks? He may construct it.
74 *lyrgm.làlìyn b'l* 'Let it indeed be told to mightiest Baal:
75 *šh.ḥrn.bbhmk* ' "Call a caravan into your mansion,
76 *'žbt.bqrb.hklk* ' "(building) wares within your palace;
77 *tblk.ġrm.mìd.ksp* ' "the rocks shall yield you much silver,
78 *gb'm.mḥmd.ḥrṣ* ' "the hills the choicest of gold,
79 *yblk.ùdr.ìlqṣm* ' "they shall yield you the noblest of gems;
80 *wbn.bht.ksp.wḥrṣ* ' "and (so) build a mansion of silver and gold,
81 *bht.ṯhrm.ìqnìm* ' "a mansion of brilliant stones (and) lapis-lazuli" '
82 *šmḥ.btlt.'nt.* The virgin Anat did rejoice,[3]
 td's (83) *p'nm.wtr.àrṣ* she planted (her) feet and the earth did quake;
84 *ìdk.lttn.pnm* then indeed she set (her) face
85 *'m.b'l.mrym.ṣpn* towards Baal (in) the height(s) of Zephon,
86 *bàlp.šd.rbt.kmn* a thousand tracts away, ten thousand spaces.
87 *šhq.btlt.'nt.* The virgin Anat did laugh,
 tšù (88) *gh.wtṣḥ.* she lifted up her voice and cried:
 tbšr b'l 'Be gladdened, Baal!
89 *bšrtk.yblt.* 'I have brought you glad tidings.[4]
 y[b]*n* (90) *bt.lk.km.àḥk.* 'A house shall be built for you like your brothers
 wḥẓr (91) *km.àryk.* 'and a court like your kinsfolk.
 šh.ḥrn (92) *bbhtk.* 'Call a caravan into your mansion,
 'žbt.bqrb (93) *hklk.* '(building) wares within your palace;
 tblk.ġrm (94) *mìd.ksp.* 'the rocks shall yield you much silver,
 gb'm.mḥmd. (95) *ḥrṣ.* 'the hills the choicest of gold;
 wbn.bht.ksp (96) *wḥrṣ.* 'and (so) build a mansion of silver and gold,
 bht.ṯhrm (97) *ìqnìm.* 'a mansion of brilliant stones (and) lapis-lazuli.'
 šmḥ.àlìyn (98) *b'l.* Mightiest Baal did rejoice,
 šh.ḥrn.bbhth he did call a caravan into his mansion,
99 *'žbt.bqrb hklh* (building) wares within his palace;
100 *yblnn ġrm.mìd.ksp* the rocks yielded him much silver,
101 *gb'm lḥmd.ḥrṣ* the hills the choicest of gold,
102 *yblnn.ùdr ìlqṣm* they yielded him the noblest of gems.
103 *y⟨l⟩àk.lktr.wḥss* He summoned Kothar-and-Khasis.

104 *wtb lmspr..ktlàkn* And again recite: When the pages
105   *ġlmm* were sent[5]

106 *àḥr.mġy.ktr.wḥss* Afterwards Kothar-and-Khasis did arrive;
107 *št.àlp.qdmh.* they did set an ox before him,
 mrà (108) *wtk.pnh.* a fatling too in front of him;
 t'db.ksù (109) *wyttb.* they made ready a seat and he was seated

---

75 *bhmk* error for *bhtk* (cp. 92)
94: note the final word-divider
95: phrase omitted (cp. 79, 102)
101 *lḥmd* error for *mḥmd* (cp. 78) or dissimilation
  (Fronzaroli)
103 Herdner (cp. 104); Virolleaud *yàkl ktr* (*l* with
  four vertical wedges)
104: notice the double word-divider

[1] Cp. Job xxxvii 3.
[2] Cp. 2 Sam. vii 2, 7.
[3] Infin. absol. or basic verbal form (3 masc. sing.
perf.); also *tr* (83) and *šhq* (87).
[4] Cp. Isa. lii 7.
[5] Rubric reminding minstrel to introduce standard
description of despatching servants, which is here
omitted.

lymn . ảlỉyn (110) *bʿl.*	on the right hand[1] of mightiest Baal,
ʿd . lḥm . ṡt[y . ỉlm]	while [the gods] did eat and drink.
111 [w]*yʿn . ảlỉy*[n . bʿl]	[And] mightiest [Baal] addressed (him, saying):
112 [- - t]*b*[ʿ . *ktr . wḫss*]	'[ ] depart, [Kothar-and-Khasis],
113 *ḥṡ . bhtm . k*[bn]	'hasten (and) surely [build] a mansion,
114 *ḥṡ . rmm . hk*[lm]	'hasten (and) raise a palace;
115 *ḥṡ . bhtm . tbn*[n]	'quickly let the mansion be built,
116 *ḥṡ . trmmn . hk*[lm]	'quickly let the palace be raised
117 *btk . ṣrrt . ṣpn*	'within the recesses of Zephon.
118 *ảlp . ṡd . ảḥd bt*	'Let the house cover[2] a thousand tracts,
119 *rbt . kmn . hkl*	'the palace ten thousand spaces.'
120 *wyʿn . ktr . wḫss*	And Kothar-and-Khasis answered:
121 *ṡmʿ . lảlỉyn bʿl*	'Hear, o mightiest Baal,
122 *bn . lrkb . ʿrpt*	'consider, o rider on the clouds:
123 *bl . ảṡt . ủrbt . bbh*[tm]	'Shall I not put a lattice in the mansion,
124 *ḥln . bqrb . hklm*	'a window in the midst of the palace?'
125 *wyʿn . ảlỉyn bʿl*	But mightiest Baal answered:
126 *ảl . tṡt . ủrbt . b*[bhtm]	'Do not put a lattice in [the mansion],
127 [ḥln] . *bqrb . hk*[lm]	'[a window] in the midst of the palace.
. . (*ca.* 3 *ll.*) . .	. . . .

	Col. vi
1 *wyʿn . k*[tr . wḫs]*s*	And Kothar-[and-Khasis] answered:
2 *ttb . bʿl . l*[hwty]	'You will come back to [my word(s)], Baal.'
3 *tn . rgm . k*[tr . w]*ḫss*	Kothar-[and]-Khasis did repeat (his) speech:
4 *ṡmʿ . mʿ . lảl*[ỉy]*n bʿl*	'Hear, I beseech you, o mightiest Baal:
5 *bl . ảṡt . ủr*[bt .]*bbhtm*	'Shall I not put a lattice in the mansion,
6 *ḥln . bqr*[b . hk]*lm*	'a window in the midst of the palace?'
7 *wʿn . ảlỉ*[yn .]*bʿl*	But mightiest Baal did answer:
8 *ảl . tṡt . ủ*[rb]*t . bbhtm*	'Do not put a lattice in the mansion,
9 *ḥln . bq*[rb . hk]*lm*	'a window in the midst of the palace,
10 *ảl . td*[. pdr]*y . bt ảr*	'lest [Pidray] daughter of mist escape,[3]
11 [-]*ht*[-ṭl]*y . bt . rb*	'[(lest) Tallay] daughter of showers [ ],
12 [- - - - - m]*dd . ỉl ym*	'(lest) the darling of El, Yam[4] [ ]
13 [- - - - -]*qlṣn*	'[ ] did abase me
wptm (14) [- - - - -]	'did spit (upon me) [ ]'
wyʿn . ktr (15) [wḫss .]	And Kothar-[and-Khasis] answered:
ttb . bʿl . lhwty	'You will come back to my word(s), Baal.'
16 [ḥṡ .]*bhth . tbnn*	[Quickly] his mansion was built,
17 [ḥṡ .]*trmm . hklh*	[quickly] his palace was raised.

110: cp. vi 55

111: cp. 125

112 De Moor (cp. **2** iii 7–8); Avishur [*ḥṡ.*]*b*[*htm . ktr*]

113–116: cp. **2** iii 7–10

113 *k*[bn] (De Moor) or *k*[tr] (Herdner)

123: cp. vi 5

126–127: cp. 123–124   vi 8–9

vi 1: cp. v 120

2: cp. 15

5–6: cp. v 123–124

10–11: cp. iv 55–56

12: cp. **3** D 35–36

16–17 [*ḥṡ*] or [*tḫṡ*] (cp. v 115–116)

[1] Cp. Ps. cx 1.

[2] Perfect with jussive sense.

[3] Cassuto, who thinks that Mot is already implicated in the plot (see at iii 5) compares Jer. ix 20; but there is no definite reference to the daughters being abducted.

[4] I.e. the chaos waters may break through; cp. Gen. vii 11.

18 *y*[tl]*k . llbnn . w*ʿ*ṣh* — Men went to Lebanon and its trees,
19 *l*[šr]*yn . mḥmd . ảrzh* — to Sirion[1] (and) its choicest cedars;
20 *ḥ*[- - l]*bnn . w*ʿ*ṣh* — they did [　　　　] Lebanon and its trees,
21 *š*[r]*yn . mḥmd . ảrzh* — Sirion (and) its choicest cedars.
22 *tšt . ỉšt . bbhtm* — Fire was set in the mansion,
23 *nb*[l]*ảt . bhklm* — flames in the palace.
24 *ḥn*[.]*ym . wtn .* — Behold! a day and a second
   tỉkl (25) *ỉšt*[.]*bbhtm .* — the fire consumed in the mansion,
   nblảt (26) *bhk*[l]*m .* — the flames in the palace.
   *tlṯ . kb*ʿ *ym* — A third, a fourth day
27 *tỉkl*[. ỉ]*št . bbhtm* — the fire consumed in the mansion,
28 *nblả*[t .]*bhklm* — the flames in the palace.
29 *ḥmš . ṯ*[d]*ṯ . ym .* — A fifth, a sixth day
   tỉkl (30) *ỉšt .*[b]*bhtm* — the fire consumed [in] the mansion,
   nblảt (31) *b*[qrb . hk]*lm .* — the flames in [the midst of the] palace.
   mk (32) *bšb*[ʿ .]*y*[mm] . — Then on the seventh day
   td . ỉšt (33) *bbhtm .* — the fire escaped from the mansion,
   n[bl]*ảt . bhklm* — the flames from the palace.
34 *sb . ksp . lrqm .* — The silver had turned into plates,
   ḥrṣ (35) *nsb . llbnt .* — the gold had been turned into bricks.
   šmḥ (36) *ảlỉyn . b*ʿ*l .* — Mightiest Baal did rejoice, (saying):
   ⟨b⟩*hty bnt* (37) *dt . ksp .* — 'I have built my mansion of silver,
   hkly[.]*dtm* (38) *ḥrṣ .* — 'my palace of gold.'
   ʿ*dbt . bht*[h . b*]*l* (39) *y*ʿ*db .* — Baal put his mansion in order,[2]
   hd . ʿ*db*[.* ʿ*d]*bt* (40) *hklh .* — Hadad did put his palace in order.
   ṭbḥ . ảlpm[. ảp] (41) *ṣỉn .* — He did slay oxen, [also] sheep,
   šql . trm[. w]*m* (42) *rỉả . ỉl*⟨m⟩ . — he did fell bulls [and] fatted rams,
   ʿ*glm . d*[t] (43) *šnt .* — yearling calves,
   ỉmr . qmṣ . l[l]*ỉm* — skipping lambs (and) kids.
44 *ṣḥ . ảḥh . bbhth .* — He did call his brothers into his mansion,
   ả[r]*yh* (45) *bqrb hklh .* — his kinsfolk into the midst of his palace,
   ṣḥ (46) *šb*ʿ*m . bn . ảtrt* — he did call the seventy[3] sons of Athirat;
47 *špq ỉlm . krm . y*[n] — he did supply the gods with rams (and) with wine,[4]
48 *špq . ỉlht . ḥprt*[. yn] — he did supply the goddesses with ewes [(and) with wine],
49 *špq . ỉlm . ảlpm . y*[n] — he did supply the gods with oxen (and) with wine,
50 *špq . ỉlht . ảrḫt*[. yn] — he did supply the goddesses with cows [(and) with wine]

---

18 Virolleaud
19: cp. 21　　　　20: cp. 18
23: cp. 25
26 *kb*ʿ error for *rb*ʿ
31: cp. 45　　　　32: cp. **17** i 16
33: this line transgresses the margin with col. v
36: cp. viii 35
39 Ginsberg
40–43: cp. **22** B 12–14
42 *mrỉả*: cp. *mrỉ* (**22** B 13; see also at **3** D 85)
44: cp. v 91
47–50, 52, 54 Virolleaud (cp. 51, 53)

[1] A name of Hermon and the Anti-Lebanon range (Deut. iii 9); cp. Ps. xxix 6.

[2] Lit. 'prepared the preparation(s) of'.

[3] Conventional for a large but indeterminate number (Exod. i 5　Judg. ix 5　2 Kgs. x 1). In the Hittite myth of Elkunirsa Ashertu (Athirat) has seventy seven or eighty eight sons.

[4] Alternatively 'he did supply the ram gods with wine etc.', the deities being specified according to their functions in presiding over the natural order (Gaster), i.e. the livestock (*ll.* 47–50), the civil authorities (*ll.* 51–52) and the vintage (*ll.* 53–54).

51 *špq.ilm.khtm.yn*   he did supply the gods with seats (and) with wine,
52 *špq.ilht.ksàt*[.yn]   he did supply the goddesses with thrones [(and) with
                                       wine],
53 *špq.ilm.rhbt yn*   he did supply the gods with tuns of wine,
54 *špq.ilht.dkrt*[.yn]   he did supply the goddesses with casks [of wine],
55 *ʿd.lhm.šty.ilm*   while the gods did eat (and) drink,
56 *wpq mrġtm.td*   and they were supplied with a suckling of the teat;
57 *bhrb.mlht.qs*[.m]r (58) *i.*   with a salted knife they did carve a fatling;
     tšty.krp[nm.y]*n*   they drank flagons of wine,
59 [bk]*s.hrs.d*[m.ʿsm]   the blood [of trees from] cups of gold.
60 [- - - - - - - - - -]*n*   [   ]
61 [- - - - - - - - - -]*t*   [   ]
62 [- - - - - - - - -]*t̬*   [   ]
63 [- - - - - - - - -]*n*   [   ]
64 [- - - - - - - - -]k   [   ]
     . . (*ca.* 1 *l.*) . .

                                     Col. vii
     . . (*ca.* 1 *l.*) . .   .   .
1 [- - - - - - *i*]*qnim*[- -]   ʿ[   ] lapis-lazuli
2 [- - - -]*àliyn.bʿl*   ʿ[   ] mightiest Baal
3 [- - - - - -]*k.mdd il*   ʿ[   ] the darling of El,
4 *y*[m - - -]*lzr.qdqdh*   ʿYam [   ] on top of his crown[1].'
5 *il*[m.]*rhq.bġr*   The gods did withdraw from the rock,
6 *km.y*[- -]*ilm.bspn*   like [   ] the gods (did withdraw) from
                                       Zephon.
7 *ʿdr.l*[ʿr].*ʿrm*   He[2] did march from [city] to city,
8 *tb.l*pd[r.]*pdrm*   he did turn from town to town;
9 *tt.lttm.àhd.ʿr*   he did seize six and sixty cities,
10 *šbʿm.šbʿ.pdr*   seventy-seven towns;
11 *tmnym.bʿl.*[- - -]   Baal did [   ] eighty,
12 *tšʿm.bʿl.mr*[-]   Baal did [   ] ninety.
13 *bkm*[.ʿ]rb *bʿl.bqrb* (14) *bt.* Forthwith Baal did enter into the house;
     wyʿn.àliyn (15) *bʿl*[.]   and mightiest Baal spoke:
     àštm.ktr bn (16) *ym.*   'I will put (it in), Kothar, this very day,
     ktr.bnm.ʿdt   'Kothar, this very hour.[3]
17 *ypth.hln.bbhtm*   'Let a window be opened in the mansion,
18 *àrbt.bqrb.*[h]*kl* (19) *m.*   'a lattice in the midst of the palace,
     wy[p]*th.bdqt.ʿrpt*   'and let a rift be opened (in) the clouds,

---

57–59: cp. iii 42–44 iv 36–38
vii 1: cp. v 81
   4: cp. vi 12
   5 *il*[m]: cp. 6; possibly *il*[m.y]*rhq*
   7 *ʿdr* error for *ʿbr* (Gaster; cp. 2 Chron. xxx 10);
   l[ʿr]: cp. 8
   13: cp. 42; De Moor *bt*[.ʿrb]
   16 *bnm.ʿdt* or (Caquot and Sznycer) *bn.mʿdt* (Hebr.
   môʿēd)
   19: cp. 17

[1] It is hardly likely that these few lines describe,

as some suppose, the final stage in the defeat of Yam;
more probably we have a statement celebrating that
triumph spoken at the feast by Baal himself or by one
of the other gods present.
   [2] Sc. Baal; cp. with this passage the descriptions
of Yahweh of hosts marching from Sinai in Deut.
xxxiii 2 Judg. v 4–5 Ps. lxviii 8–9, 18–19.
   [3] Lit. 'on the day, appointed time'; with the
parallelism cp. Jer. xlvi 21 Ezek. vii 7. Less likely,
since the titles are not found elsewhere, 'son of the
sea', 'son of the confluence (of waters)' (see apparatus),
referring to Kothar-and-Khasis.

20 *'l* h[wt] . *ktr . wḫss*	'according to the [word(s)] of Kothar-and-Khasis.'
21 *ṣḥq . ktr . wḫss*	Kothar-and-Khasis did laugh,
22 *yšù*[.]*gh*[.]*wyṣḥ*	he lifted up his voice and cried:
23 *lrgmt . lk . làlì* (24) *yn . b'l .*	'Did I not tell you, o mightiest Baal,
ttbn . b'l (25) *lhwty .*	'(that) you would come back, Baal, to my word(s).'
ypth . ḥ (26) *ln . bbhtm .*	Baal opened a window in the mansion,
ùrbt (27) *bqrb . hk*[lm .]	a lattice in the midst of the palace,
[*yp*]*th* (28) *b'l . bdqt* [. '*rp*]*t*	[he] opened a rift [(in) the clouds].
29 *qlh . qdš* [.]*b* ['*l . y*]*tn*	Baal uttered his holy voice,[1]
30 *ytny . b'l ṣ* [àt . š]*pth*	Baal repeated the [issue] of his lips;
31 *qlh . q* [dš . t]*r . àrṣ*	(he uttered) his [holy] voice [(and)] the earth did quake,[2]
32 [ṣàt . špth .]*g̣rm .*	[(he repeated) the issue of his lips (and)] the rocks (did quake);
tḫšn (33) *rḥq*[m- - - - - - - -] (34) *qdmym .*	peoples afar off[3] were dismayed [ ] the peoples of the east;[4]
bmt . à [rṣ] (35) *tttn .*	the high places of the earth[5] shook.[6]
ib . b'l . tiḥd (36) *y'rm .*	The foes of Baal clung to[7] the forests,
šnù . hd . gpt (37) *g̣r .*	the enemies of Hadad to the hollows of the rock.[8]
wy'n . àlìyn (38) *b'l .*	And mightiest Baal spoke:
ib . hdt . lm . tḫš	'Foes of Hadad, why are you dismayed,[9]
39 *lm . tḫš . ntq . dmrn*	'why are you dismayed at the weapons of *Dmrn*[10]?
40 '*n . b'l . qdm . ydh*	'(Is it because) the eye of Baal outstrips[11] his hand
41 *ktg̣ž . àrz . bymnh*	'when the "cedar"[12] is brandished in his right hand?'
42 *bkm . ytb . b'l . lbhth*	Forthwith Baal did sit down[13] in his mansion (and spoke):
43 *ùmlk . ùbl . mlk*	'Will (anyone else), whether king or commoner,[14]
44 *àrṣ . drkt* ⟨*y*⟩ *yštkn*	'occupy for himself[15] the land of ⟨my⟩ dominion?
45 *dll . àl . ilàk . lbn* (46) *ilm . mt .*	'I will of a truth send a courier to divine[16] Mot
'*dd* [.]*lydd* (47) *il . g̣zr .*	'a herald to the hero beloved of El
yqrà . mt (48) *bnpšh .*	'(to ask) that Mot invite (him) into his throat,

20 *'l* h[wt] (Herdner; cp. vi 15) or *'l* p[km] (De Moor *a*. Ginsberg)

27–28: cp. 19

29 Gaster

30 Gaster (cp. **16** i 35)

31–32: cp. 29–30; [*t*]*r* or [*wt*]*r* (cp. v 83) or (De Moor after Virolleaud's copy) [*t*]*rr* 'his holy voice made the earth quake etc.' (D)

32: this line transgresses the margin with col. vi

33: cp. **1** iv 3

34 Gaster; there is perhaps room for *l* or *k* at the end (De Moor)

38 *hdt* possibly error for *hdm* (Driver) or *hdd* (Gordon; cp. **9** rev. 6) or *t* is simply a scratch (De Moor)

42 *lbhth* perhaps error for *bbhth* (cp. 25ff.)

44: haplography

[1] See at v 70 above.

[2] Cp. (with different verbs) Judg. v 4 2 Sam. xxii (Ps. xviii) 8 Ps. lxviii 9 lxxvii 19 xcvii 4.

[3] Cp. **1** iv 3 Ps. lxv 9 Isa. xxxiii 13.

[4] Cp. Job xviii 20.

[5] Cp. Deut. xxxii 13 Amos iv 13 Mic. i 3.

[6] Cp. Ps. xcix 1.

[7] Cp. Job xxxviii 13.

[8] Cp. Isa. ii 10, 19.

[9] An ironic question as in Ps. cxiv 5–6.

[10] A name of Baal mentioned in *PRU* V no. 1 rev. *l*. 7 and in Eusebius *Praep. Evang.* i 10, 37 (Zeus Demarous).

[11] Lit. 'is before', describing the speed or accuracy of his aim.

[12] Probably signifying the lightning or a thunderbolt; cp. the stele in *Ugaritica* II pl. xxiii, where Baal grasps a mace in his right hand and a stylised tree in his left.

[13] Cp. Ps. ix 8 xxix 10.

[14] Lit. 'not king'. Cp. **2** iii 22 (Athtar) Eshmunazar inscr. *l*. 4.

[15] Cp. **14** 104, 192 Ps. lxviii 17.

[16] See at **3** E 26.

ystrn ydd (49) bgngnh.
dḥdy.dym (50) lk.ʿl.ỉlm.
lymrù (51) ỉlm.wnšm.
dyšb (52) [ʿ].hmlt.ȧrṣ.
gm.lg̃ (53) [lm]h.bʿl.kyṣḥ.
ʿn (54) [gpn].wȧgr.
bg̃lmt (55) [ʿmm.]ym.
bn.ẓlmt.r (56) [mt.prʿ]t[.]
ỉbr mnt (57) [šhrrm.]
[ḥblm.bʿ]rpt (58) [tḥt.]
[bšmm.ʿṣrm.]ht
59 [- - glt.ỉṣr - - -]m
60 [brq - - - - ymtm -]h
　. . (ca. 7 ll.) . .

'(that) the beloved one hide him within himself.[1]
'(For) I alone am he that is king over the gods,[2]
'(that) indeed fattens[3] gods and men,
'that satisfies[4] the multitudes of the earth.'
Baal surely cried aloud to his pages:
'Look, [Gupn] and Ugar,
'the daylight [is veiled] in obscurity,
'[the exalted princess] (is veiled) in darkness,
'the [blazing] pinions of . . . . .[5] (are veiled).
'[Flocks are circling round in] the clouds,
'[birds] are circling round [in the heavens]
'[　　　　I shall bind the snow　　　　]
'[the lightning　　　　　　　　　]
　. . . . .

1 ỉdk.ȧl.ttn.pnm
2 ʿm.g̃r.trg̃zz
3 ʿm.g̃r.trmg
4 ʿm.tlm.g̃ṣr.ȧrṣ
5 šȧ.g̃r.ʿl.ydm
6 ḥlb.lẓr.rḥtm
7 wrd.bt ḥptt (8) ȧrṣ.

tspr.by (9) rdm.ȧrṣ
10 ỉdk.ȧl.ttn (11) pnm.
⟨ʿm.bn.ỉlm.mt.⟩
tk.qrth (12) hmry.
mk.ksù (13) tbth.
ḥḥ..ȧrṣ (14) nḥlth.
wng̃r (15) ʿnn.ỉlm.

Col. viii

'Then of a truth do you set (your) faces
'towards the rock of Targhizizi,[6]
'towards the rock of Tharumagi,[6]
'towards the two hills bounding the earth.
'Lift up a rock on (your) two hands,
'a wooded height[7] on to (your) two palms,
'and go down (into) the house of "freedom"[8] (in) the earth,
'be counted with them that go down into the earth.[9]
'Then of a truth do you set (your) faces
'⟨towards divine Mot⟩
'within his city "Miry",[10]
'where a pit[11] is the throne on which he sits,
'filth[12] the land of his heritage.[13]
'But watch, lackeys of the gods,

50 lymrù perhaps error for dymrù (cp. 49, 51)
52 Virolleaud　　　　53–60: cp. **8** 5–15
54 bg̃lmt perhaps error for bn.g̃lmt (**8** 7)
viii 11: cp. **5** ii 14
13: note the double word-divider

1 Lit. 'in his heart, inside', prob. the same word as in **16** vi 26. Cp. Isa. v 14　Hab. ii 5　Prov. i 12 Jon. ii 3.
2 Cp. Ps. xcv 3.
3 Cp. Gen. xxvii 28　Ps. lxv 12.
4 Cp. Ps. ciii 5　cxlv 16　Job xxxviii 27　Isa. lviii 11.
5 Apparently another term denoting the sun. The passage is prob. simply a poetic description of the setting sun and the coming of evening, though it is possible (see apparatus) to translate 'the sons of obscurity, darkness have veiled etc.' and find a reference to attacks by Mot's henchmen (so also by translating 'seized' in l. 35).
6 The pronunciation of these names, which denote the twin mountains or pillars which were founded in

the earth-encircling ocean and held up the firmament (cp. Job xxvi 10–11) and also, as here, marked the entrance to the underworld, is unknown; they are thought to be Hurrian.
7 For a possible parallelism cp. Ps. lxxxi 17 ('wheat from the wooded height').
8 A euphemism for the underworld; cp. 2 Kgs. xv 5 where a similar phrase describes a leper house. Cp. also 2 Sam. xxii (Ps. xviii) 5–6　Ps cxvi 3　Jon. ii 7 of Sheol as a place of imprisonment. For other euphemisms for the realm of the dead see **5** vi 6–7.
9 Cp. Ps. lxxxviii 5 (with ḥopšī in the next verse).
10 Cp. 2 Sam. xxii 5　Ps. xl 3　lxxxviii 7–8　Job xxiv 19 (NEB)　xxvi 5.
11 Lit. 'a sunken place'; cp. Ps. lxxxviii 5　Lam. iii 55 etc. (bôr)　Ps. xvi 10　Isa. xxxviii 17　Job xxxiii 22 etc. (šaḥat).
12 So Ishtar, having descended to the netherworld, finds everything covered with dust and the denizens eating mud (ANET p. 107); cp. also Ps. xxx 10.
13 Cp. Exod. xv 17　**3** C 27　F 16.

àl (16) tqrb.lbn.ìlm (17) mt.	'(that) you come not near to divine Mot,
àl.y'dbkm (18) kìmr.bph	'lest he make you like a lamb in his mouth,[1]
19 kllì.btbrn (20) qnh.thtàn	'(and) you both be carried away like a kid in the breach of his windpipe.
21 nrt.ìlm.špš (22) shrrt.	'Shapash the luminary of the gods is glowing hot,
là (23) šmm.byd.md (24) d.ìlm.mt.	'the heavens are wearied by the hand of Mot the darling of the gods.[2]
bà (25) lp.šd.rbt.k (26) mn.	'Traversing a thousand tracts, ten thousand spaces,
lp'n.mt (27) hbr.wql	'do homage at the feet of Mot and fall down,
28 tšthwy.wk (29) bd hwt.	'prostrate yourselves and do him honour,
wrgm (30) lbn[.]ìlm.mt	'and tell to divine Mot,
31 tny.lydd (32) ìl.gzr.	'repeat to the hero beloved of El:
thm (33) àlìyn.b'l	' "The message of mightiest Baal,
34 [hw]t.àlìy.q (35) [rdm.]	' "[the word] of the mightiest of [warriors] (is this):
bhty bnt (36) [dt.ksp.]	' "I have built my mansion [of silver],
[dtm] (37) [hrs.hk]ly	' "my [palace of gold]
38 [- - - - - -]dhy	' "[ ] my brothers
39 [- - - - - -]dhy	' "[ ] my brothers
40 [- - - - - -]y	' "[ ]
41 [- - - - - -]kb	' "[ ]
42 [- - - - - -].sht	' "[ ] I have called
43 [- - - - - -]t	' "[ ]
44 [- - - - - -]ìlm	' "[ ] the gods
45 [- - - - -]ù.yd	' "[ ] hand
46 [- - - - -]k	' "[ ]
47 [- - -gpn.]wùgr	[Gupn] and Ugar
48 [ ]t	[ ]
. . (ca. 16 ll.) . .	. . . .
E. [spr.ìlmlk.t']y.nqmd.mlk.ùgrt	[The scribe is Elimelek the] master, Niqmad (being) king of Ugarit.

34–35: cp. **3** C 10–11 etc.

36–37 Herdner (cp. vi 36–38)

47: the double line indicates that the journey of the messengers to Mot is omitted (cp. v 104–105)

48ff.: the reply of Mot to Baal begins here; a version of the earlier part of this reply is preserved in

Ugaritica V no. 4; cp. also **5** i 12ff.

E.: cp. **16** vi E.

[1] Cp. Ps. cxli 7.

[2] Cp. **1** iv 20 (of Yam). Ironic?

5

2*[pnšt.bˤl.tˤn] (1*) [ìtˤnk.]

[- - - - mả - - k]

1 ktmḫṣ.ltn.btn.brḥ
2 tkly.btn.ˤqltn.[-]
3 šlyṭ.d.šbˤt.rảšm
4 ttkḫ.ttrp.šmm.
   krs (5) ìpdk.ảnk
   ìspì.ûṭm (6) ẓrqm.ảmtm.
   lyrt (7) bnpš.bn ìlm.mt.

   bmh (8) mrt.ydd.ìl.ǵzr
9 tbˤ.wl.ytb ìlm.
   ìdk (10) lytn.pnm.
   ˤm.bˤl (11) mrym.ṣpn.
   wyˤn (12) gpn.wûgr.
   tḥm.bn ìlm (13) mt.
   hwt.ydd.bn.ìl (14) ǵzr.
   pnp.š.npš.lbìm (15) thw.

   hm.brlt.ảnḫr (16) bym.
   hm.brky.tkšd (17) rùmm.
   ˤn.kẓd.ảylt
18 hm.ìmt.ìmt.npš.blt (19) ḥmr.
   pìmt.bkl⟨à⟩t (20) ydy.ìlḥm.

Col. i

'[Have you then forgotten, Baal, that I can surely transfix you],
'[you],
'for all that you smote Leviathan the slippery serpent
'(and) made an end of the wriggling serpent,
'the tyrant with seven heads?[1]
'The heavens will burn up (and) droop (helpless),[2]
'for I myself will crush you in pieces,[3]
'I will eat (you) . . . .[4] (and) forearms.[5]
'Indeed you must come down[6] into the throat of divine Mot,
'into the miry depths[7] of the hero beloved of El.'
The gods did depart and stayed not;
then indeed they set (their) faces
towards Baal (in) the height(s) of Zephon;
and Gupn and Ugar gave (him the) answer:
'The message of divine Mot,
'the word of the hero beloved of El (is this):
' "But my appetite is an appetite of lions[8] (in) the waste,[9]
' "just as the longing[10] of dolphin(s) is in the sea
' "or a pool captivates wild oxen
' "(or) a spring as it were[11] herds of hinds.[12]
' "If it is in very truth my desire to consume[13] 'clay',[14]
' "then in truth by the handfuls[15] I must eat (it),

i 2*–1*: properly the final lines of the preceding tablet (cp. below 26–27)
2: after ˤqltn the scribe apparently began to write the next word then erased it
6 ảmtm hardly '(and) I will kill (you)' (Aphel); perhaps error for tmtm '(so that) you die' (Emerton)
13: omit bn as scribal error (cp. ii 18)
14 pnp.š error for pnpš (cp. *Ugaritica* V no. 4 obv. *ll.* 2–3); lbìm: the last letter is broken off but is confirmed by ibid. obv. *l.* 3
16 brky perhaps error for brkt (ibid. obv. *l.* 6) or y is a fem. ending
16 tkšd (17) rùmm; cp. [m]šbšt krùmm (ibid. obv. *ll.* 6–7)
18 ìmt: cp. mt (ibid. obv. *l.* 9)
19: cp. 3 A 11

[1] On these lines see at 3 D 35ff.
[2] Cp. Isa. v 24.
[3] Lit. 'with a breaking in pieces'; cp. Amos vi 11

and a different metaphor Ps. cxliii 3.
[4] Cp. **18** iv 3.
[5] Seemingly the reference is to different parts of Baal's body to be consumed by Mot (Van Selms); cp. Job xviii 13–14.
[6] Lit. 'you have come down' (by assimilation from *yrdt*).
[7] Cp. Ps. cxl 11.
[8] Sc. for flesh; cp. Deut. xxxiii 20   Ps. cxxiv 3, 6   Hos. xiii 8   Isa. v 14   Hab. ii 5.
[9] Cp. Deut. xxxii 10   Job vi 18.
[10] Lit. 'Then is my appetite . . . if the longing . . .'
[11] Lit. 'like', a construction similar to the *Kaph Veritatis* of Hebrew.
[12] Cp. Ps. xlii 2.
[13] Cp. Ps. xlix 15 ('their form is for Sheol to consume').
[14] Sc. men's bodies; cp. **6** ii 17–19   Job iv 19   xxxiii 6.
[15] Lit. 'with both my hands'.

hm.šbʿ (21) ydty[.]bṣ .
hm.ks.ymsk (22) nhr[.]
k[n].ṣhn[.]bʿl.ʿm (23) ảhy[.]
qrản.hd.ʿm.ảryy
24 wlhmm.ʿm.ảhy.lhm
25 wštm.ʿm.ả[r]y⟨y.y⟩n.
26 pnšt.bʿl.[t]ʿn.iṯʿnk

27 [- - - -]mả[- -]k .
ktmhṣ (28) [ltn.btn.br]h .

tkly (29) [btn.ʿqltn.]
šlyṭ (30) [dšbʿt.rảšm.]
ttkh (31) [ttrp.šmm.]
[krs.ỉpd]k (32) [ảnk.]
[ỉspỉ.ủṭm.žrqm] (33) [ảmtm.]
[lyrt.bnpš] (34) [bn.ỉlm.mt.]

[bmhmrt] (35) [ydd.ỉl.ġzr.]

. . (ca. 12 ll.) . .

1 [- - - - - - - - - - -]m
2 [špt.lả]rṣ.špt.lšmm
3 [- - - l]šn.lkbkbm .
  yʿrb (4) [bʿ]l.bkbdh .
  bph yrd
5 khrr.zt .
  ybl.ảrṣ.wpr (6) ʿṣm .
  yrản.ảliyn.bʿl
7 ṯtʿ.nn.rkb.ʿrpt
8 tbʿ.rgm.lbn.ỉlm.mt
9 ṯny.lydd.ỉl ġzr
10 thm.ảliyn.bʿl .
  hwt.ảliy (11) qrdm .
  bht.lbn.ỉlm mt
12 ʿbdk.ản.wdʿlmk

' "whether my seven portions are (already) in the bowl
' "or whether Nahar[1] has to mix the cup.
' "[So] Baal has invited me with my brothers
' "(and) Hadad has called me with my kinsfolk!
' "But (it is) to eat[2] bread with my brothers
' "and to drink[2] wine with my kinsfolk!
' "Have you then forgotten, Baal, that I can surely transfix you,[3]
' "[   ] you,
' "for all that you smote [Leviathan the slippery serpent]
' "(and) made an end of [the wriggling serpent],
' "the tyrant [with seven heads]?
' "[The heavens] will burn up [(and) droop (helpless)],
' "[for I myself will crush] you [in pieces],
' "[I will eat (you) . . . . (and) forearms].
' "[Indeed you must come down into the throat of divine Mot],
' "[into the miry depths of the hero beloved of El]" '

. . . .

Col. ii

. . . .

'[   ]
'[A lip to the] earth, a lip to the heavens,
'[   ] a tongue to the stars![4]
'Baal must enter his innards[5]
'(and) go down into his mouth.
'Because he has scorched the olive(s),[6]
'the produce of the earth and the fruit of the trees,
'mightiest Baal is afraid of[7] him,
'the rider on the clouds is in dread of[7] him.[8]
'Depart, tell to divine Mot,
'repeat to the hero beloved of El:
' "The message of mightiest Baal,
' "the word of the mightiest of warriors (is this):
' "Hail, o divine Mot!
' "I am your servant, yes, yours for ever[9]." '

21, 23: these lines transgress the margin with col. ii
22 k[n] (cp. 12 ii 54) or k[d] 'thus' (cp. 19 14)
25 Gordon (cp. 23); Herdner ả[h]⟨y⟩ yn; note the final word-divider (or n with four wedges)
28–35: cp. 1–8
ii 2: cp. 23 61–62
3 Virolleaud
3, 5, 6, 10: these lines transgress the margin with col. iii

[1] Prob. a poetic allusion to souls being taken across river of death.

[2] Infin. absol.
[3] Sc. as you pierced Leviathan; cp. Job xl 24–26, 31 Ezek. xxix 4 Isa. lỉ 9; cp. also 10 ii 24.
[4] A poetic description of the gaping jaws of Mot; cp. Ps. lxxiii 9 and see further at 4 vii 48; cp. also 23 61–62.
[5] Lit. 'liver'.
[6] Cp. Hab. iii 17.
[7] Cp. Isa. xli 10, 23 Karatepe inscr. ii 4.
[8] Cp. 2 iv 1–7 6 vi 30–31. Note the perfect apparently followed by 'Nun energicum' suffix. On Baal's title see at 2 iv 8.
[9] Cp. Ps. cxvi 16 Job xl 28 14 55.

13 *tbʿ.wl.ytb.ilm*   The gods did depart and stayed not;

  idk (14) *lytn.pn⟨m⟩.*   then indeed they set (their) faces

  ʿm.bn.ilm.mt   towards divine Mot

15 *tk.qrth.hmry.*   within his city 'Miry',

  mk.ksù (16) *tbt.*   where a pit is the throne on which (he) sits,

  hh.àrṣ.nhlth   filth the land of his heritage.

  tšd (17) *ghm.wtṣh.*   They lifted up their voices and cried:

  thm.àlìyn (18) *bn. bʿl.*   'The message of mightiest Baal,

  hwt.àlìy.qrdm   'the word of the mightiest of warriors (is this):

19 *bht.bn.ilm.mt.*   ' "Hail, divine Mot!

  ʿbdk.àn (20) *wdʿlmk.*   ' "I am your servant, yes, yours for ever." '

  šmh.bn ilm.mt   Divine Mot did rejoice,[1]

21 [*yšù.*]*gh.wàṣh.*   [he lifted up] his voice and cried:

  ik.ylhn (22) [*bʿl.ʿm.àhy.*]   'How (is it that) [Baal] invites me [with my brothers],

  [*ìk*]*.yqrùn*[*.*]*hd* (23) [*ʿm.àryy.*]   '[how (is it that)] Hadad calls me [with my kinsfolk]?

  [- - -]*kp.mlhmy*   '[   ] my bread

24 [- - - - - - - - -]*lt.qẓb*   '[   ] he has cut up

25 [- - - - - - - - - -]*šmhy*   '[   ] . . . . .

26 [- - - - - - - - - -]*tbʿ*   '[   ] depart

27 [- - - - - - - - - - - -]*nnm*   '[   ]

. . . . . .

Col. iii

. . (*ca.* 10 *ll.*) . .

1 [- - - - -]m[   ]   [   ]

2 [-]*rbt.tbt.*[   ]   '[   ] great is the seat [   ]

3 *rbt.tbt.hš*[n   ]   'great is the seat [   ]

4 *y.àrṣ.hšn*[   ]   '[   ] the land [   ]

5 *tʿtd.tkl.*[   ]   ' . . . . [   ]

6 *tkn.lbn*[k   ]   'it shall belong to your son[2] [   ]

7 *dt.lbnk*[   ]   'of your son [   ]

8 *dk.k.kbkb*[   ]   ' . . . . like the star(s)[3] [   ]

9 *dm.mt.àṣh*[   ]   'Truly[4] I must call Mot [   ]

10 *ydd.bqr*[b   ]   'the beloved one within [   ]

11 *àl.àšt.b*[   ]   '(How) of a truth can I put [   ]

12 *àhpkk.l*[   ]   'can I overturn you [   ]

13 *tmm.wlk*[   ]   ' . . . . . And go [   ]

14 *wlk.ilm*[   ]   'and go, gods [   ]

15 *nʿm.ilm*[   ]   'the most gracious of the gods [   ]

16 *šgr.mù*[d   ]   ' "Sheger,[5] much [   ]

13–16: cp. **4** viii 10–14

18: omit *bn* as scribal error (cp. i 13)

21: cp. **4** vii 22 etc.; *àṣh* error for *yṣh* (Gordon); *ylhn* (Virolleaud) or *y.ṣhn* (Herdner) error for *yṣhn* (cp. i 22)

23 *mlhmy*: cp. *lhm* (i 24) *mlhmt* (**3** C 12 etc.)

24 Ginsberg [*bmàk*]*lt.qẓb* 'with a butcher's knife'

iii 3: cp. **4**

6: cp. **7**   10: cp. **19**

11–12: cp. **6** vi 26–28   16: cp. **17**

[1] Cp. Ps. xiii 5   xxx 2   xxxv 25–26 (all of the Psalmist's enemy or enemies)   Mic. vii 8.

[2] Sc. probably Mot, the title being used conventionally (see at **3** E 26). Baal is here complaining to El.

[3] Cp. Pyrgi inscr. *ll.* 9–11   Isa. xiv 13.

[4] Or 'For'.

[5] Sheger (whose name means 'offspring of cattle') and Ithm (24) appear together in a god-list (*Ugaritica* V p. 584).

17	*šgr . mừd*[	]	' "Sheger, much [	]
18	*dm . mt . às*[ḫ	]	' "Truly I must call Mot [	]
19	*yd*⟨d⟩*. bqrb*[	]	'the beloved one within [	]
20	*wlk . ìlm .* [	]	'And go, gods [	]
21	*wrgm . l*[	]	'and tell to [	]
22	*bmừd . ṣìn*[	]	' "with much sheep [	]
23	*mừd . ṣìn*[	]	' "much sheep [	]
24	*ìtm . mừì*[	]	' "Ithm . . . . [	]
25	*dm . mt . às*[ḫ	]	' "Truly I must call Mot [	]
26	*ydd . bqr*[b	]	'the beloved one within [	]
27	*tmm . wlk*[	]	'. . . . And go [	]
28	[- -]*ṭ . lk*[	]	'[　] go [	]
29	[- -]*kṭ . ì*[	]	[	]

. . . .

Col. iv

. . . .

1	*p . šn*[	]	[	]
2	*wlṭlb .* [	]	'and to seek [	]
3	*mìt . rḫ*[	]	'a hundred [	]
4	*ṭṭlb . d̬*[	]	'do you seek [	]
5	*yšừ . ǵh*[.wyṣḥ]		He[1] lifted up his voice [and cried]:
6	*ì . d̬p . b̬ʿ*[l	]	'Where then is Baal [	]
7	*ì . hd . d̬*[	]	'where is Hadad [	]
8	*ynpʿ . b̬ʿ*[l . bšbʿt . ǵlmh]		Baal arose [with his seven pages],
9	*bṭmnt .* [ḫnzrh]		with [his] eight ['boars'[2]	]
10	*yqrb .* [	]	he came near [	]
11	*lḥm . m*[	]	food [	]
12	[ʿ]*d . lḥm*[. šty . ìlm]		while [the gods] did eat [(and) drink]
13	*wpq*[.]*mr*[ǵtm . td]		and they were supplied with a suckling [of the teat];
14	*bḥrb .* [mlḥt . qṣ . mrì]		with [a salted] knife [they did carve a fatling],
15	*šty . kr*[pnm . yn]		they did drink [flagons of wine],
16	*bks . ḥr*[ṣ . dm . ʿṣm]		from cups of gold [the blood of trees],
17	*ks . ks*p[	]	(from) cups of silver [	]
18	*krpn .* [	]	flagon(s) [	]
19	*wtttn*[.]ḥ[	]	and they . . . . [	]
20	*tʿl . trt*[	]	they went up; new wine [	]
21	*bt . ìl . lì*[	]	the house of El [	]
22	*ʿl . ḥbš .* [	]	for a ruler [	]
23	*mn . lìk .* [	]	'Who has sent [	]
24	*lìk . tl*[	]	'has sent [	]
25	*tʿddn*[	]	'do you recount [	]
26	*nìṣ . p*[	]	'the reviler[3] [	]

. . *(ca.* 11 *ll.)* . .　　　. . . . .

18–19, 25–26: cp. 9–10
v 5: cp. ii 21 　　　8–9: cp. v 8–9
12–16: cp. **4** vi 55–59
20, 22: cp. **17** vi 7–8
21 Ginsberg *lì*[*mm*]

[1] Sc. the messenger of Mot; cp. **2** i 11ff. (of Yam).
[2] These servants of Baal are only mentioned in this part of the cycle; perhaps like his daughters they had a function in fertility.
[3] Cp. **1** iv 23.

Col. v

. . . . . .

1 [- - - - - - - - - - -]àlìyn
2 [bˁl - - - - - -]ìp.dprk
3 [- - - - - - -]mnk.ššrt
4 [- - - - -]t.npš.ˁgl
5 [- - - -]nk.
   dšt.n.bḫrt (6) ìlm.àrṣ.
   wàt.qḥ (7) ˁrptk.
   rḥk.mdlk (8) mṭrtk.
   ˁmk.šbˁt (9) ġlmk.
   tmn.ḫnzrk
10 ˁmk.pdry.bt.àr
11 ˁmk.ṭṭly.bt.rb.
   ìdk (12) pnk.àl ttn.
   tk ġr (13) knkny.
   šà.ġr[.]ˁl ydm
14 ḫlb.lẓr.rḥtm
   wrd (15) bt ḫptt.àrṣ

   tspr by (16) rdm.àrṣ.
   wtdˁ ìll (17) kmtt.
   yšmˁ.àlìyn.bˁl
18 yùḥb.ˁglt.bdbr.
   prt (19) bšd.šḥl mmt.
   škb (20) ˁmnh.šbˁ.lšbˁm
21 tš[ˁ]ly.tmn.ltmnym
22 w[th]rn.wtldn mt
23 àl[ìyn.bˁ]l šlbšn (24) ìp[dh.]
   [- - -]lh.mġz (25) y[dd.]
   [- - - - - -]lìrth
26 n[   ]
   . . (ca.11 ll.) . .

[   ] mightiest
[Baal   ] your torch[1]
ˁ[   ] your . . . . . .
ˁ[   ] the life of a calf[2]
ˁ[   ]
'I will put him in a hole of the earth-gods.[3]
'And as for you, take your clouds,
'your winds, your thunder-bolts (and) your rains,[4]
'(take) with you your seven pages
'(and) your eight "boars",
'(take) with you Pidray daughter of mist,
'(take) with you Tallay daughter of showers.[5]
'Then of a truth do you set your face
'towards the rocks (at the entrance) of my grave.
'Lift up a rock on (your) two hands,
'a wooded height on to (your) two palms,
'and go down (into) the house of "freedom" (in) the
    earth,
'be counted among those who go down into the earth,[6]
'and do you know inanition[7] like mortal men.'[8]
Mightiest Baal obeyed.
He loved a heifer in the pasture(s),
a cow in the fields by the shore of the realm of death;
he did lie with her seven and seventy times,
she allowed (him) to mount eight and eighty times;
and she conceived and gave birth to a boy.[9]
[Mightiest] Baal did clothe him with [his robe],[10]
[   ] him as a gift[11] for the [beloved one]
[   ] to his breast
[   ]
. . . .

v 1, 2, 3, 25: these lines transgress the margin with
col. iv
5 De Moor [tkn.lb]nk 'shall belong to your son' (cp. iii
6–7); dšt.n or dštn (n with four wedges)
11 ṭṭly error for ṭly (cp. 3 A 24)
13 knkny: cp. 19 147
16 ìll (Virolleaud); Herdner ìlm 'the gods shall know
that you have died' (?)
21–22 Virolleaud and Ginsberg
23: cp. 17
24 Driver (cp. Akk. epattu 'wrapper'; Hebr. ʾēpôd
'ephod')   25 y[dd]: cp. 4 vii 48

[1] Presumably to see with in the underworld; cp. 2
iii 13.
[2] A reference to the boy whose birth is related in
l. 22.

[3] Or 'in the cemetery of the gods (i.e. the shades)
(in) the earth'.
[4] Cp. Ps. cxxxv 7.
[5] The third daughter Arṣay does not go with Baal
because, it seems, her role is not affected by the
summer drought; see at 3 C 4–5.
[6] See on this passage at 4 viii 1–9.
[7] In the Bible (e.g. Ps. xcvi 5) the same root (ʾll)
is frequently applied to idols or foreign gods as
worthless or unreal.
[8] Lit. 'like, as of mortality, death'.
[9] Perhaps (with De Moor) to be related to Akk.
mašu 'twin-brother', though this hardly suits in the
case of the fem., applied to Huray and Danatay
(14 143 17 v 16).
[10] Cp. Exod. xxix 5 Num. xx 26 Isa. xxii 21.
[11] Cp. 4 i 23.

Col. vi

. . . .

3*[ìdk.lttn.pnm]   [Then indeed they set (their) faces]

2*[ᶜm.ìl.mbk.nhrm]   [towards El at the source(s) of the rivers],

1*[qrb.àpq.thmtm]   [amid the springs of the two oceans];

1 [tgly.žd.il.]   [they penetrated the mountain(s) of El]

[w]tb[à] (2) [qrš.mlk.àb.]šnm   [and] entered [the massif of the king, the father] of years.[1]

3 [tšà.ghm.wtṣ]ḥ.   [They lifted up their voices and cried]:

sbn (4) [y.ᶜd.q]ṣ[m.àrṣ.]   'We [two][2] did go round [to the edges of the earth],

ᶜdk (5) ksm.mhyt[.]   'to the limits of the watery region.[3]

[m]ǵny (6) lnᶜmy.àrṣ.dbr   'We two did reach "Pleasure"[4] the land of pasture(s),

7 lysmt.šd.šhl mmt   ' "Delight"[4] the fields by the shore of the realm of death.

8 mǵny.lbᶜl.npl.là (9) rṣ.   'We two did happen upon Baal;[5] he had fallen to the ground.

mt.àlìyn.bᶜl   'Mightiest Baal is dead,[6]

10 ḫlq.zbl.bᶜl.àrṣ   'the prince lord of earth has perished!'

11 àpnk.lṭpn.il (12) dpìd.   Thereupon Latipan kindly god

yrd.lksì.ytb (13) lhdm[.]   did come down from (his) throne (and) did sit[7] on the footstool,

[w]l.hdm.ytb (14) làrṣ[.]   [and] (he did come down) from the footstool (and) did sit on the ground.[8]

yṣq.ᶜmr (15) ùn.lrìsh.   He poured straw[9] of mourning on his head,

ᶜpr.plṭt (16) l.qdqdh.   dust of wallowing on his crown;[10]

lpš.yks (17) mìzrtm.   for clothing he covered himself[11] with sackcloth;[12]

ǵr.bàbn (18) ydy.   he scraped (his) skin with a stone,

psltm.byᶜr   with a flint for[13] a razor

19 yhdy.lḥm.wdqn   he shaved (his) side-whiskers and beard;[14]

20 ytlt.qn.žrᶜh[.]   he harrowed[15] his collar-bone,[16]

yḥrt (21) kgn.àp lb.   he ploughed (his) chest[17] like a garden,

kᶜmq.ytlt (22) bmt.   he harrowed (his) waist[18] like a valley.[19]

yšù.gh[.]wyṣḥ   He lifted up his voice and cried:

23 bᶜl.mt.   'Baal is dead!

3*–1*, 1–3: cp. 3 E 13–16   4 iv 20–24   6 i 32–36, 39

3 sbn[y]: cp. [m]ǵny (5)

4: cp. 16 iii 3; ᶜdk prob. error for ᶜd (dittography of k)

5 mhyt: cp. mìyt (16 iii 4); [m]ǵny: cp. 6 ii 19

7, 12, 15: these lines transgress the margin with col. v

[1] See on this passage at 3 E 13ff.

[2] Sc. Gupn and Ugar. The ending is dual.

[3] See at 16 iii 3–4 where there is a fuller text.

[4] Euphemisms as in 4 viii 7.

[5] It is of course the surrogate borne by the heifer (v 22) that they have found.

[6] Cp. 1 Kgs. xxii 37 (*LXX*) Ps. lxxxii 7.

[7] Cp. Isa. xlvii 1   Jer. xlviii 18.

[8] Cp. Ezek. xxvi 16.

[9] The meaning required is nearer the Mishnaic 'hay, fodder' than the biblical 'sheaves'.

[10] Cp. Ezek. xxvii 30.

[11] Cp. Ps. civ 6.

[12] Lit. 'loin-cloth'. Cp. Amos viii 10 etc.

[13] An example of what is called in Hebr. *Beth Essentiae*.

[14] Cp. *ANET* p. 88 (Gilgamesh mourning for Enkidu)   Isa. xv 2   Mic. i 16   Jer. xlviii 37.

[15] Lit. 'did for a third time', clearly a technical term for a third ploughing or harrowing.

[16] Lit. 'humeral bone of his arm'.

[17] Lit. 'front (nose) of (his) heart'.

[18] Lit. 'back' or 'torso'; cp. 3 B 12.

[19] Poetic descriptions of the cutting of flesh (cp. 1 Kgs. xviii 28   Jer. xvi 6 etc.); for a similar metaphor see Ps. cxxix 3.

my.lìm.bn (24) dgn.
my.hmlt.
àtr (25) b'l.àrd.bàrṣ.
àp (26) ʿnt.ttlk.wtṣd.
kl.ǵr (27) lkbd.àrṣ.
kl.gbʿ (28) l[k]bd.šdm.
tmǵ.lnʿm[y] (29) [àrṣ.]dbr.
ysmt.šd (30) [šhl] mmt.

t[mǵ.]lbʿl.np[l] (31) [là]rṣ[.]

[lpš]. tks.mìz[rtm]

'What[1] (will become) of the people of Dagon's son,
'what of (his) multitudes?
'After Baal[2] I would go down into the earth.'
(Then) Anat also went to and fro and scoured
every rock to the heart of the earth,
every hill to the heart of the fields.
She reached 'Pleasure' [the land] of pasture(s),
'Delight' the fields [by the shore] of the realm of
    death;
she [happened upon] Baal; he had fallen [to] the
    ground.
[For clothing] she covered herself with sackcloth;

6

1 lbʿl
2 ǵr.bàb⟨n⟩.td[.]
   [ps]ltm[.byʿr]
3 thdy.lḥm.wdqn[.]
   [ttlt] (4) qn.ǵrʿh.
   thrt.km.gn (5) àp lb.
   kʿmq.ttlt.bmt
6 bʿl.mt.
   my.lìm.bn dgn
7 my.hmlt.
   àtr.bʿl.nrd (8) bàrṣ.
   ʿmh.trd.nrt (9) ìlm.špš.
   ʿd.tšbʿ.bk
10 tšt.kyn.ùdmʿt.
   gm (11) tṣḥ.lnrt.ìlm.špš
12 ʿms mʿ.ly.àlìyn.bʿl
13 tšmʿ.nrt.ìlm.špš
14 tšù àlìyn.bʿl.
   lktp (15) ʿnt.ktšth.
   tšʿlynh (16) bṣrrt.ṣpʿn.
   tbkynh (17) wtqbrnh.
   tštnn.bḥrt (18) ìlm.àrṣ.
   tṭbḥ.šbʿm (19) rùmm.
   kgmn.àlìyn (20)[b]ʿl.

Col. i
Of Baal
she scraped (her) skin with a stone,
with a flint [for a razor]
she shaved (her) side-whiskers and beard;[3]
[she harrowed] her collar-bone,
she ploughed (her) chest like a garden,
she harrowed (her) waist like a valley, (saying):
'Baal is dead!
'What (will become) of the people of Dagon's son,
'what of (his) multitudes?
'After Baal we would go down into the earth.'
Shapash the luminary of the gods came down to her,[4]
as she sated herself with weeping
(and) drank tears[5] like wine.
She cried aloud to Shapash the luminary of the gods:
'Hoist, I beseech you, mightiest Baal on to me.'
Shapash the luminary of the gods obeyed,
she lifted up mightiest Baal,
she surely put him on to the shoulder of Anat,
(and) she took him up to the recesses of Zephon;
she wept for him and buried him,
she put him in a hole of the earth-gods.[6]
She slew seventy wild oxen
as a . . . . .[7] for mightiest Baal,

28–31: cp. 5–9   6 ii 17, 19–20
31: cp. 16–17
i 2–3: cp. 5 vi 17–20
6: notice b with three vertical wedges
7 nrd perhaps error for àrd (Bauer; cp. 5 vi 25)
16 ṣpʿn error for ṣpn (confusion with lpʿn (?) or ʿ is an
   unintentional stroke)

[1] Cp. Ruth iii 16.
[2] Cp. Gen. xxxvii 35. Alternatively 'the multi-

tude(s) of Baal's shrine' (lit. 'place').
[3] Probably conventional terminology (cp. 5 vi 19
of El), though bearded goddesses are not unknown in
mythology.
[4] Hardly 'went down with her' into the nether-
world, since Shapash has not previously been with
Anat and in any case the dead body to be buried was
lying on the ground.
[5] Cp. Ps. lxxx 6.   [6] See at 5 v 5–6.
[7] The meaning of this word is unknown.

ttbḫ.šbˁm.àlpm   she slew seventy oxen

21 [kg]mn.àlìyn.bˁl   [as a] . . . . for mightiest Baal,

22 [tt]bḫ.šbˁm.ṣin   [she] slew seventy sheep

23 [kgm]n.àlìyn.bˁl   [as a] . . . . for mightiest Baal,

24 [ttb]ḫ.šbˁm.àylm   [she] slew seventy harts

25 [kgmn.]àlìyn.bˁl   [as a . . . .] for mightiest Baal,

26 [ttbḫ.š]bˁm.yˁlm   [she slew] seventy mountain-goats

27 [kgmn.àl]ìyn.bˁl   [as a . . . . for] mightiest Baal,

28 [ttbḫ.šbˁm.]ḥmrm   [she slew seventy] asses

29 [kgm]n.àl[ì]yn[.]b[ˁl]   [as a . . . .] for mightiest Baal.

30 [- - -]ḥḥ.tšt bm.ˁ[- -]   She put his [ ] in [ ]

31 [- - -]zrḥ.ybm.lìlm   [ ] him (as befitted) a brother-in-law of the gods.

32 [ìd]k.lttn[.]pnm.   [Then] indeed she set (her) face

    ˁm (33) [ìl.]mbk nhrm.   towards [El] at the source(s) of the rivers,

    qrb (34) [à]pq.thmtm.   amid the springs of the two oceans;

    tgly.žd (35) ìl.   she penetrated the mountain(s) of El

    wtbù.qrš (36) mlk.àb.šnm.   and entered the massif of the king, father of years.

    lpˁn (37) ìl.thbr.wtql   She did homage at the feet of El and fell down,

38 tšthwy.wtkbdnh   she prostrated herself and did him honour;

39 tšù.gh.wtṣḥ.   she lifted up her voice and cried:

    tšmḥ ht (40) àtrt.wbnh.   'Now let Athirat and her sons rejoice,

    ìlt.wṣb (41) rt.àryh.   'Elat and the company of her kinsfolk;

    kmt.àlìyn (42) bˁl.   'for mightiest Baal is dead,[1]

    kḫlq.zbl.bˁl (43) àrṣ.   'for the prince lord of earth has perished!'

    gm.yṣḥ ìl (44) lrbt.àtrt ym.   El cried aloud to dame Athirat of the sea,

    šmˁ (45) lrbt.à[trt] ym.   'Hear, o dame Athirat of the sea,

    tn (46) àḥd.b.bnk[.]àmlkn   'give one of your sons that I may make him king.'

47 wtˁn.rbt.àtrt ym   And dame Athirat of the sea answered:

48 bl.nmlk.ydˁ.ylḥn   'Yes, let us make (him) king that has knowledge (and) intelligence[2].'

49 wyˁn.lṭpn.ìl dpì (50) d.   But Latipan kindly god answered:

    dq.ànm.lyrẓ (51) ˁm.bˁl.   'One feeble in strength cannot run[3] like[4] Baal

    lyˁdb.mrḥ (52) ˁm.bn.dgn.k.msm   'nor release[5] the lance like Dagon's son when the time is right[6].'

53 wˁn.rbt.àtrt ym   But dame Athirat of the sea did answer:[7]

54 blt.nmlk.ˁttr.ˁrẓ   'No! let us make Athtar the terrible king.

55 ymlk.ˁttr.ˁrẓ   'Let Athtar the terrible be king!'[8]

21-29: cp. 18-20

28 Ginsberg [y]ḥmrm 'roebucks' (Hebr. yaḥmûr) since the ass is, at least in Jewish law, ritually unclean; but cp. CTA 32 18, where the offering of a he-ass (ˁr) is mentioned

29: the small fragment ends after [kgm]; possibly it contained a further two lines (De Moor), making the total of offerings seven

32-34: cp. 4 iv 20-22   45: cp. 44, 47, 53

52 k.msm (Caquot and Sznycer) or kt msm (Dahood a. Virolleaud)

[1] See at 5 ii 20 vi 9; cp. also 4 ii 24-26 6 v 1-4.

[2] Meaning Athtar; alternatively 'one who is able (knows how) to understand'.   [3] Cp Isa. xl 29, 31.

[4] Lit. 'with' (cp. Ps. lxxiii 5).

[5] Cp. 18 iv 22 Job x 1.

[6] Lit. 'according to the opportune moment' (Caquot and Sznycer). The 'running' will refer metaphorically to the movement of the wind and the 'lance' to Baal's lightning or thunderbolt (cp. 4 vii 41). Alternatively (see apparatus) 'nor can one of scant beauty release . . .' (√ktt, ysm; Dahood; cp. 1 Sam. xvi 18 2 Sam. xiv 25).

[7] Infin. absol. or 3 pers. masc. sing. used as a basic form.   [8] Cp. Exod. xv 18 Ps. cxlvi 10.

56 *åpnk . ʿttr . ʿrẓ*   Thereupon Athtar the terrible

57 *yʿl . bṣrrt . ṣpn*   went up[1] into the recesses of Zephon;

58 *ytb . lkḫṭ[.]àlìyn* (59) *bʿl.*   he sat on the seat of mightiest Baal,

pʿnh . ltmġyn (60) *hdm[.]*   (but) his feet did not reach the foot-stool,

rìsh . lymġy (61) *åpsh .*   his head did not reach its top.

wyʿn . ʿttr . ʿrẓ   And Athtar the terrible spoke:

62 *làmlk . bṣrrt . ṣpn*   'I cannot be king in the recesses of Zephon.'

63 *yrd . ʿttr . ʿrẓ .*   Athtar the terrible came down,

yrd (64) *lkḫt . àlìyn . bʿl*   he came down from the seat of mightiest Baal,

65 *wymlk . bàrṣ . ìl . klh*   and became king over the whole broad earth.[2]

66 *[- - - t]šåbn . brḥbt*   [   ] (they) drew water from[3] casks

67 *[- - - t]šåbn . bkknt*   [   ] (they) drew water from[3] barrels.

. . *(ca. 30 ll.)* . .   **Col. ii**

1 *l[- - - - - - - - - - - -]*   [   ]

2 *wl[- - - - - - - - - -]*   [   ]

3 *kd . [- - - - - - - - - -]*   [   ]

4 *kd . t[- - - -]*   [   ]

[ym . ymm] (5) *yʿtqn .*   [A day, days] passed,

w[rḥm . ʿnt] (6) *tngth .*   and [the damsel Anat] sought him.

klb . à[rḫ] (7) *lʿglh .*   Like the heart of a [heifer] (yearning) for her calf,

klb . tå[t] (8) *lìmrh*   like the heart of a ewe (yearning) for her lamb,

km . lb . ʿn[t] (9) *åtr[.]bʿl .*   so the heart of Anat (yearned) after Baal.[4]

tìḫd . m[t] (10) *bsìn . lpš .*   She seized Mot by the hem of (his) garment,

tšṣq[nh] (11) *bqṣ . åll .*   she constrained [him] by the end of (his) robe;

tšù . gh . w[tṣ] (12) *ḥ .*   she lifted up her voice and cried:

àt . mt . tn . åḥy   'Do you, Mot, give up[5] my brother.'

13 *wʿn[.]bn . ìlm . mt*   But divine Mot did answer:

mh (14) *tàršn . lbtlt . ʿnt*   'What (is this that) you desire of me, o virgin Anat?

15 *àn . ìtlk . wåṣd .*   'I myself went to and fro and scoured

kl (16) *ġr . lkbd . àrṣ .*   'every rock to the heart[6] of the earth,

kl . gbʿ (17) *lkbd . šdm .*   'every hill to the heart of the fields.

npš . ḥsrt (18) *bn . nšm .*   'My appetite did lack[7] humans,

npš . hmlt . (19) *àrṣ .*   'my appetite (did lack) the multitudes of earth.

mġt . lnʿmy . àrṣ (20) *dbr .*   'I did reach "Pleasure" the land of pasture(s),

ysmt . šd . šḥl mmt   ' "Delight" the fields by the shore of the realm of death.

21 *ngš . ànk . àlìyn bʿl*   'I it was who confronted[8] mightiest Baal,

22 *ʿdbnn ànk . ìmr . bpy*   'I who made him (like) a lamb in my mouth,

---

66–67 Virolleaud

ii 4–9: cp. 26–31

10: or *tšṣq[nn]*

18: notice the final word-divider

22 *ìmr* or ⟨*k*⟩*ìmr* (haplography; cp. **4** viii 18)

[1] Cp. Isa. xiv 13.

[2] Lit. 'the earth of El, all of it'; cp. **3** F 13–14.

[3] Or 'into'.

[4] Cp. **15** i 5–7.

[5] Cp. **2** i 18   Hos. xi 8   Isa. xliii 6.

[6] Lit. 'liver'.

[7] Cp. Isa. xxxii 6   Ps. xxxiii 19 ('from the hungry one'?; Dahood).

[8] Lit. 'drew near to'. This and the following verb cannot be infin. absols. since the second has a suffix; they are probably 3 pers. perfs. (basic form), though the '*Nun energicum*' suffix is unusual (but cp. **5** ii 7); cp. *pʿl ʿnk* (Karatepe inscr. i 10).

23 *kllì.btbrn q⟨n⟩y.ḥtù hw*

24 *nrt.ìlm[.]špš.ṣḥrrt*
25 *là.šmm.byd.bn ìlm.mt*
26 *ym.ymm.yʿtqn.*
   lymm (27) lyrḥm.
   rḥm.ʿnt.tngth
28 *klb.àrḥ.lʿglh.*
   klb (29) tàt.lìmrh.
   km.lb (30) ʿnt.àtr.bʿl.
   tìḥd (31) bn.ìlm.mt.
   bḥrb (32) tbqʿnn.
   bḥtr.tdry (33) nn.
   bìšt.tšrpnn
34 *brḥm.tṭḥnn.*
   bšd (35) tdrʿnn.
   šìrh.ltìkl (36) ʿṣrm[.]
   mnth.ltkly (37) npr[m.]
   šìr.lšìr.yṣḥ

'(and) he was carried away like a kid in the breach of my windpipe.'

Shapash the luminary of the gods did glow hot,
the heavens were wearied by the hand of divine Mot
A day, days passed,
from days (they passed) into months
(as) the damsel Anat sought him.
Like the heart of a heifer (yearning) for her calf,
like the heart of a ewe (yearning) for her lamb,
so the heart of Anat (yearned) after Baal.
She seized divine Mot,
with a sword[1] she split him,
with a sieve she winnowed him,
with fire she burnt him,[2]
with mill-stones she ground him,[3]
in a field she scattered[4] him;
his flesh[5] indeed the birds ate,
his limbs[6] indeed the sparrows consumed.[7]
Flesh cried out to flesh[8]

Col. iii

. . (ca. 40 *ll.*) .
1 *kḫlq[.]mt[------]*
2 *whm.ḥy.à[lìyn.bʿl]*
3 *whm.ìt.zbl.bʿ[l.àrṣ]*
4 *bḥlm.lṭpn.ìl.dpìd*
5 *bžrt.bny.bnwt*
6 *šmm.šmn.tmṭrn*
7 *nḥlm.tlk.nbtm*
8 *wìdʿ.khy.àlìyn[.]bʿl*
9 *kìt.zbl.bʿl.àrṣ*
10 *bḥlm.lṭpn ìl dpì[d]*
11 *bžrt.bny.bnwt*
12 *šmm.šmn.tmṭrn*
13 *nḥlm.tlk.nbtm*
14 *šmḫ.lṭpn.ìl.dpìd*

. . . .
'for Mot has perished [   ]
'And if [mightiest Baal] is alive,[9]
'and if the prince lord [of earth] exists,[10]
'(then) in a dream of Latipan kindly god,
'in a vision of the creator of creatures,
'the heavens should rain oil,
'the ravines should run with honey,[11]
'that I may know that mightiest Baal is alive,[12]
'that the prince lord of earth exists.'
In a dream of Latipan kindly god,
in a vision of the creator of creatures,
the heavens rained oil,
the ravines ran with honey.
Latipan kindly god did rejoice;

---

23 *q⟨n⟩y*: cp. **4** viii 20
37 Herdner; De Moor restores the first line of iii [*mnt.lmnt.tṣḥ*]
i 1 *mt* (Barton); Ginsberg 1* [*kmt.àlìyn.bʿl*] (1) *kḫlq.z[bl.bʿl.àrṣ]*

[1] De Moor (wishing to keep the agrarian imagery) translates 'blade' (sc. of the threshing-sledge), comparing Syr. *ḥarbâ dpaddānâ* 'ploughshare'.
[2] Cp. Exod. xxxii 20. If the metaphor is agricultural, the burning of stubble is presumably meant.
[3] Cp. Exod. xxxii 20.
[4] Cp. Zech. x 9 for a similar metaphorical usage.

[5] Or 'his pieces, remains' (cp. Hebr. *šeʾār*).
[6] Or 'his portions' (cp. **17** i 33).
[7] Cp. Ezek. xxix 5. It is particularly difficult to see the point of this action for any agrarian rite; cp. v 19 where 'scattering' in the sea is also mentioned.
[8] Cp. Gen. iv 10   Ps. lxxxiv 3.
[9] Cp. 1 Kgs. xvii 1.
[10] This formula may be reflected in the name Eshbaal (1 Chron. viii 33; Albright).
[11] Cp. the similar images of fertility in Gen. xxvii 28   Exod. iii 8   Job xx 17   Ezek. xxxii 14   Joel iv 18.
[12] Cp. Job xix 25.

15 pʿnh.lhdm.ytpd	he placed his feet on the footstool
16 wyprq.lṣb wyṣhq	and parted (his) throat[1] and laughed;
17 yšù.gh.wyṣh	he lifted up his voice and cried:
18 àtbn.ànk.wànhn	'Even I may sit down and be at ease,
19 wtnh.bìrty.npš	'and (my) soul within me[2] may take its ease;[3]
20 khy.àlìyn.bʿl	'for mightiest Baal is alive,
21 kìt.zbl[.]bʿl[.]àrṣ	'for the prince lord of earth exists.'
22 gm.yṣh.ìl.lbtlt (23) ʿnt[.]	El cried aloud to the virgin Anat:
šmʿ.lbtlt.ʿn[t]	'Hear, o virgin Anat.
24 rgm.lnrt.ìl⟨m⟩.šp[š]	'Tell to Shapash the luminary of the gods:

Col. iv

25 pl.ʿnt.šdm.yšpš	' "The furrows in the fields are cracked,[4] o Shapash,
26 pl.ʿnt.šdm.ìl.	' "the furrows in the fields of El are cracked.
yštk[n] (27) [b]ʿl.ʿnt.mhrtt	' "Baal should be occupying the furrows in the plough-land.[5]
28 ìy.àlìyn.bʿl	' "Where is mightiest Baal,
29 ìy.zbl.bʿl.àrṣ	' "where is the prince lord of earth[6]?" '
30 ttbʿ.btlt.ʿnt	The virgin Anat departed;
31 ìdk.lttn.pnm	then indeed she set (her) face
32 ʿm.nrt.ìlm.špš	towards Shapash the luminary of the gods;
33 tšù.gh.wtṣh	she lifted up her voice and cried:
34 thm.tr.ìl.àbk	'The message of the bull El your father,
35 hwt.lṭpn.htkk	'the word of Lapitan your sire (is this):
36 pl.ʿnt.šdm.yšpš	' "The furrows in the fields are cracked, o Shapash,
37 pl.ʿnt.šdm.ìl.	' "the furrows in the fields of El are cracked.
yš[tkn] (38) bʿl.ʿnt.mhrt[t]	' "Baal should be occupying the furrows in the plough-land.
39 ìy.àlìyn.bʿl	' "Where is mightiest Baal,
40 ìy.zbl.bʿl.àrṣ	' "where is the prince lord of earth?" '
41 wtʿn.nrt.ìlm.š[p]š	And Shapash the luminary of the gods answered:
42 šd yn.ʿn.b.qbt[.]	'Pour sparkling wine[7] from a vat,
[t] (43) bl lyt.ʿl.àmtk	'let the children of your family wear wreaths,[8]
44 wàbqt.àlìyn.bʿl	'and I will seek mightiest Baal.'
45 wtʿn.btlt.ʿnt	And the virgin Anat answered:
46 àn.làn.yšpš	'Where (and) whither[9] (you go), o Shapash,
47 àn.làn.ìl.yǵr[k]	'where (and) whither (you go), may El protect [you],
48 tǵrk.š[- - - - - -]	'may [　　　　　　　] protect you!
49 yštd[.yn.ʿn.bqbt]	'Let [sparkling wine] be poured [from a vat]

21–24: these lines are written on the bottom edge of
　the tablet
24: cp. iv 32
iv 26 yštk[n]: cp. cp. **4** vii 44
37: cp. 26
38: Virolleaud's copy has mhrth (cp. 27)
42 [t]bl; the t is visible on an earlier photograph
　(Herdner)
47: cp. 48
49 De Moor (cp. 42)

　¹ See at **4** iv 28.

　² Lit. 'in my breast'.
　³ Cp. **17** ii 12–14.
　⁴ Or (a noun) 'are a waterless desert'.
　⁵ Sc. with his rains so that they may become soft
for the farmer to plough.
　⁶ Cp. Deut. xxxii 37　Ps. xlii 4　cxv 2　Jer. ii 6;
cp. also the names Jezebel and Ichabod (1 Sam. iv 21)
which may reflect this formula.
　⁷ Lit. 'wine of an eye' (cp. Prov. xxiii 31).
　⁸ Cp. Prov. i 9.
　⁹ Lit. 'where to where' (cp. 1 Kgs. ii 36, 42　Ps.
cxxxix 7　Song vi 1).

50 d*r*[- - - - - - - - -]   [   ]
51 *r*[- - - - - - - - - -]   [   ]

. . (*ca.* 35 *ll.*) . .   . .

Col. v

1 *yiḫd.bʿl.bn.àtrt*	Baal seized the sons of Athirat
2 *rbm.ymḫṣ*[.]*bktp*	he smote[1] the great ones with the broad-sword,
3 *dk ym.ymḫṣ.bṣmd*	he smote the 'pounders' of the sea[2] with the mace,
4 *ṣhr mt*[.]*ymṣḫ.làrṣ*	he dragged the yellow ones of Mot[3] to the ground.
5 [*ytb.*]*b*[ʿ]*l.lksì.mlkh*	(Then) did Baal [sit] upon the throne of his kingdom,[4]
6 [*lnḫt*].*lkḫt.drkth*	[on the cushion] on the seat of his dominion.
7 ⟨*ym.ymm.yʿtqn.*⟩	⟨A day, days passed⟩,
l[*ym*]*m.lyrḫm.*	from [days] (they passed) into months,
lyrḫm (8) *lšnt.*	from months into years.
[*m*]k.*bšbʿ* (9) *šnt.*	Then in the seventh year[5]
w[- -].*bn.ìlm.mt*	divine Mot [ ]
10 ʿ*m.àlìyn.bʿl.*	to mightiest Baal;
yšù (11) *gh.wyṣḫ.*	he lifted up his voice and cried:
ʿ*lk.b*[ʿ]*lm* (12) *pht.qlt.*	'Because of[6] you, Baal, I have suffered abasement,
ʿ*lk.pht* (13) *dry.bḫrb.*	'because of you I have suffered splitting with the sword,
ʿ*lk* (14) *pht.šrp.bìšt*	'because of you I have suffered burning with fire,
15 ʿ*lk.*[*pht.tḫ*]*n.brḥ* (16) *m.*	'because of you [I have suffered grinding] with mill-stones,
ʿ*lk.p*[ht.*dr*]*y.bkbrt*	'because [of you] I have [suffered winnowing] with the riddle,[7]
17 ʿ*lk.ph*[t.-]*l*[-] (18) *bšdm.*	'because of you I have suffered [ ] in the fields,
ʿ*lk.pht* (19) *drʿ.bym.*	'because of you I have suffered scattering in the sea.[8]
tn.àḥd (20) *bàḫk.ìspà.*	'Give one of your brothers that I may be fed,[9]
wytb (21) *àp.dànšt.*	'and the anger that I feel[10] will turn back.[11]

3 *dk ym* (Aistleitner, Dijkstra) or *dkym*
4 *ṣhr mt*[.] or *ṣhrm.* (Albright); *ymṣḫ* (Herdner; cp. **3** E 9) or *ymṣì* (Virolleaud)
5–6 Herdner (cp. vi 33–35 **16** vi 23–24 **3** D 47)
6 [*lnḫt*] or [*bn.dgn*] (cp. **10** iii 15)
7: cp. ii 26
8: cp. **4** vi 31 **15** iii 22
9 De Moor after the copy *wrk* 'softened up' (√*rkk*; cp. **10** iii 28); Virolleaud *whn*
11 Bauer
13 *dry* prob. error for *bqʿ* (cp. ii 32); the phrase with *dry* (in which the noun is different) is to be restored in 16
15: cp. ii 34
16: see at 13
17 Herdner [*ǵ*]*l*[*y*] 'sinking, wilting'

[1] Cp. Ps. cx 5–6.
[2] A name linking the sons of Athirat with their mother, whose full title is *rbt àtrt ym* 'the lady who treads upon the sea'; cp. *àgzr ym* describing the

gracious gods (**23** 58) and possibly Ps. xciii 3. There is no question of Yam himself being involved at this stage of the myth.

[3] Prob. a title of henchmen of Mot (cp. vi 8), who were aiding the sons of Athirat (cp. **4** ii 24–26) against Baal, so-called because they were parched by the sun or were pale from habitually living underground (but see now Addenda).

[4] See at **1** iv 24–25 **2** iv 8ff.

[5] See on the significance of this reference at p. 18, though perhaps too much weight should not be placed on it in view of the not dissimilar phrases in ii 4–5, 26–27, which form with it a kind of progression; in any case mythological time is meant.

[6] With the repetition of this prepos. cp. Amos i 3ff.

[7] Cp. Amos ix 9.
[8] Cp. Ps. lxxiv 13–14 (Leviathan).
[9] Cp. **6** ii 12 **5** i 5.
[10] Lit. 'am companion to' (cp. **2** i 38).
[11] Cp. Hos. xiv 5 Isa. v 25.

im (22) *dḥd.bdḥk*[.]l[tt]n

23 hn.*dḥz*[- - -]l (24) [-]*tm*[.]

dkly [.bn.nšm]

25 *dkly.hml*[t.*drṣ*]

26 *wy*[-]l.*dṭ*[- - - - - -]

27 *š*[- - - - - - - - - -]

28 *bl*[- - - - - - - -]

. .   (*ca*. 25 *ll*.)   . .

1 [- - - - - - *dt*]*rdh*

2 [- - - - - *dg*]*ršh*

3 [- - - - - - - -]*rù*

4 [- - - - - - -]h

5 [- - bn.*ilm.*]*mt*

6 [- - - - - -]*mr.lìm*m

7 [- - - - -]bn.*ilm.mt*

8 [ysp]*ù*[.]*šb*ʿt.*glmh*

9 [wy*ʿ*]n.bn.*ilm.mt*

10 ph*n.dḥym.ytn.b*ʿ*l* (11) *spủy*.

bnm.*ùmy.klyy*

12 *ytb.*ʿm.b*ʿl.ṣrrt* (13) *ṣpn*.

yšl.gh.wyṣḥ

14 *dḥym.ytnt.b*ʿl (15) *spủy*.

bnm.*ùmy.kl* (16) *yy*.

*yt*ʿn.kgmrm

17 *mt* ʿ*z.b*ʿ*l.*ʿ*z*.

ynghn (18) *krùmm*.

*mt.*ʿ*z.b*ʿ*l* (19) ʿ*z*.

yntkn.kbtnm.

20 *mt.*ʿ*z.b*ʿ*l.*ʿ*z*.

ymṣhn (21) *klsmm*.

mt.ql (22) *b*ʿ*l.ql.*ʿ*ln*.

špš (23) *tṣḥ.lmt*.

*šm*ʿ*.m*ʿ (24) *lbn.ilm.mt*.

ik.tmt[ḥ] (25) ṣ.ʿ*m.dlìyn.b*ʿ*l*

26 *ik.dl.yšm*[ʿ]*k.tr* (27) *il.dbk*.

*l.ys*ʿ.*dlt* (28) *tbtk*.

lyhpk.ksà.mlkk

'(But) if [you] do not [give] one of your brothers,

'behold I shall [   ]

'I shall consume[1] [mankind],

'I shall consume the multitudes [on earth].'

And he [   ]

[   ]

[   ]

Col. vi

'[I] will drive him forth,[2]

'[I] will banish him

'[   ]

'[   ]

'[divine] Mot

'[   ] peoples.

'[(Let)] divine Mot [   ]

'[let him eat] his seven pages!'[3]

[And] divine Mot [answered]:

'But look![4] Baal has given me my own brothers to eat,

'the sons of my mother to consume!'

He returned to Baal (in) the recesses of Zephon;

he lifted up his voice and cried:

'You have given me my own brothers, Baal, to eat,

'the sons of my mother to consume.'

They eyed each other like burning coals;

Mot was strong,[5] Baal was strong.

They gored like wild oxen;[6]

Mot was strong, Baal was strong.

They bit like serpents;[7]

Mot was strong, Baal was strong.

They tugged like greyhounds;[8]

Mot fell down, Baal fell down on top of him.

Shapash cried out to Mot:

'Hear, I beseech you, o divine Mot.

'How can you fight with mightiest Baal?

'How of a truth shall the bull El your father hear you?[9]

'Indeed he will pull up the support of your seat,

'indeed will overturn the throne of your kingdom,

22 De Moor after traces on the copy

24: perhaps [*m*]*tm* 'the dead' (De Moor); Herdner [ʿ]*nt*; [*bn.nšm*]: cp. ii 18

25: cp. ii 18–19

vi 1–2: cp. **3** D 44–46   5 Virolleaud

7: perhaps [*ykly*] (De Moor; cp. 11)

8: cp. 11   9 Driver

13 *yšl* error for *yšủ*

26: cp. **2** iii 17

[1] Cp. Hos. xi 6 Jer. x 25; cp. also Ps. xlix 15 where death is compared to a shepherd looking for his sheep.

[2] Messengers of Baal addressing Mot.

[3] Apparently here servants of Mot (contrast **5** v 8–9).

[4] Lit. 'Then behold!'.

[5] Cp. Song viii 6 **2** iv 17; cp. also the name Azmoth (*NEB*; 1 Chron. viii 36).

[6] Cp. Deut. xxxiii 17.

[7] Cp. Prov. xxiii 32.

[8] Sc. at the hare; lit. 'runners'.

[9] Possibly 'How shall . . . not hear you?' (but cp. **2** iii 17).

29 *lytbr.ḥt.mtpṭk*

30 *yrù.bn.ilm⟨.m⟩t.*

ttˁ.y (31) *dd.il.ġzr[.]*

yˁr.mt (32) *bqlh.*

y[šù.gh.wyṣḥ]

33 *bˁl.yttbn[.lksì]* (34) *mlkh.*

l[nḥt.lkḥt] (35) *drkth[.]*

[- - - - - - -]

36 [- - - -]*d*[- - - - - - -]

37 [- - - - -].*hn*[- - - - -]

38 [- - - - -]*šn*[- - - - - -]

[　　　　]*pìt*

39 [- - - - - -]*qbåt*

40 [- - - - -]*inšt* (41) [- - -]*ù.*

ltštql (42) [*lšì*]*r.try.*

åp.ltlḥm (43) [*l*]*ḥm.trmmt.*

ltšt (44) *yn.tġẓyt.*

špš (45) *rpìm.tḥtk*

46 *špš.tḥtk.ilnym*

47 *ˁdk.ilm.*

hn.mtm (48) *ˁdk.*

ktrm.ḥbrk

49 *wḥss.dˁtk*

50 *bym.årš.wtnn*

51 *ktr.wḥss.yd*

52 *ytr.ktr.wḥss*

═══════════

53 *spr.ilmlk šbny*

54 *lmd.åtn.prln.rb*

55 *khnm.rb.nqdm*

56 *tˁy.nqmd mlk ùgr*[t]

57 *ådn*[.]*yrgb.bˁl.trmn*

'indeed will break the sceptre of your rule.'[1]

Divine Mot was afraid,

the hero beloved of El was in dread.[2]

Mot roused himself at her call,

he [lifted up his voice and cried]:

'Let them seat Baal [on the throne] of his kingdom,

'on [the cushion on the seat] of his dominion!³

[　　　　　　　　　　] 　　　　]

[　　　　　　　　　　　　　　]

[　　　　　　　　　　　　　　]

[　　　　　　　　　　　　　　]

[　　　　　　] brow

[　　　　　] . . . . .

[　　　　　] . . . . .⁴ [　　　　]

'Do you indeed betake yourself [to] the fresh [meat],⁵

'yes, do you indeed eat the bread of contribution,⁶

'do you indeed drink the wine of oblation.

'Shapash, the shades are under you;⁷

'Shapash, the ghosts are under you;

'the gods (come) to you,⁸

'behold! the dead (come) to you.

'Kothar is your companion

'and Khasis your intimate.

'In the sea are Arsh and the dragon;⁹

'let Kothar-and-Khasis banish (them),

'let Kothar-and-Khasis drive (them) away!'¹⁰

═══════════

Written by Elimelek the Shubanite,¹¹

disciple of *Atn-prln*,¹² chief of the priests,

chief of the shepherds,¹³ the master,

(in the reign of) Niqmad king of Ugarit,

sire of *Yrgb* (and) lord of *Thrmn*.¹⁴

30: haplography (the title elsewhere is always *bn.ilm*; cp. iii 24)

32 De Moor　　　　33–34: cp. **3** D 46–47

37–40: the small fragment (rev.) begins at this point; according to Herdner an extra line is to be inserted after 38

42 [*lšì*]*r* (De Moor) or [*lb*]*t* (Lipiński)

45 *rpìm* perhaps error for *rpùm* (see at **21** A 9) or oblique case is used for the nominative

---

¹ See at **2** iii 17–18.

² Cp. **5** ii 6–7 (Baal).

³ See at **1** iv 24–25.

⁴ In non-mythological texts this word designates a profession.

⁵ I.e. to a ceremony in the temple. Alternatively (see apparatus) '[to the house of] freshness', i.e. to a feast in the underworld (with the euphemism cp. **4** viii 7　**5** vi 6–7).

⁶ Cp. Deut. xii 6, 11, 17.

⁷ Alternatively 'you rule the shades' (√*ḥtk*; cp. *Ugar.* V no. 2 rev. *ll.* 8, 10).

⁸ Or 'are around you' (Driver; √ˁ*wd*).

⁹ Cp. **3** D 37, 40; presumably they present a danger to her as she passes through their domain every night.

¹⁰ Cp. **2** iv 7ff., where the same deity assists Baal against Yam. Alternatively (Lipiński) 'Through the sea . . . may Kothan-and-Khasis drive (you) . . . draw (you)' (Arab. *wattara* 'stretched, drew taught'). According to Eusebius *Praep. Evang.* i 10, 11 *Chousōr* was the inventor of navigation.

¹¹ Cp. the place-name *Šubānu* (*Ugaritica* V p. 189).

¹² Or 'Elimelek . . . the (trained) singer; *Atn-prln* was chief etc.' (Cross; cp. 1 Chron. xxv 7). Cp., however, **16** vi E.

¹³ A class of functionaries appearing frequently in administrative documents; cp. Amos i 1.

¹⁴ These words may be parts of titles rather than place-names.

14

1 [lk]*rt*
2 [- - - - -]*.ml*[k- - -]
3 [- - - - -]*m.k*[- - - -]
4 [- - - - - - - - - -]
5 [- - - - -]*m.il*[- - -]
6 [- - - -]*d nhr.*
  ùmt (7) [*krt.*]*rpàt.*
  bt (8) [m]*lk.itdb.*
  dšbʿ (9) [à]*ḥm.lh.*
  tmnt.bn ùm
10 *krt.ḥtkn.rš*
11 *krt.grdš.mknt*
12 *àtt.ṣdqh.lypq*
13 *mtrḫt.yšrh*
14 *àtt.trḫ.wtbʿt*
15 *tnt.ùm.àkn lh*

16 *mtltt.ktrm.tmt*
17 *mrbʿt.zblnm*
18 *mḫmšt.yìtsp* (19) *ršp*[.]
  mtdtt.ġlm (20) *ym.*
  mšbʿthn.bšlḫ (21) *ttpl.*
  yʿn.ḥtkh (22) *krt*
  yʿn.ḥtkp rš
23 *mìd.grdš.tbth*
24 *wbtmhn.špḥ.yìtbd*
25 *wb.pḫyrh.yrt*

Col. i
[Of] Keret.
[   ] king [   ]
[   ]
[   ]
[   ] El [   ]
[   ] river.
The clan [of Keret] did die out,
the house[1] of the king did come to an end,
though there were seven brothers in it,
eight mother's sons.
Keret, our sire,[2] was crushed,
Keret was stripped of (his kingly) estate.
(One to be) his lawful wife he had not found,
(one to be) his rightful spouse.[3]
He did take a wife, but she did 'depart';[4]
a second to become a mother for him, (but she did 'depart');
the third one taken[5] died (though) in (her) prime,
the fourth (died) by plague;
the fifth Resheph[6] carried off,
the sixth the pages of Yam;[7]
the seventh of them fell by a spear.[8]
Let one look upon[9] his sire Keret,
let one look upon his sire—crushed,
utterly stripped of his (kingly) power!
So in its entirety a family came to an end,
and in its completeness a succession.[10]

14 1: cp. 6 i 1 16 i 1 19 1
  2 Virolleaud
  5: perhaps [*nʿmn.ġl*]*m* (cp. 40)
  7 [*krt*]: cp. 130–132 16 i 39–40; *rpàt* (Virolleaud) or *rwt* (Herdner)
  8 *itdb* error for *itbd* (cp. 24)
  9 Gaster
  15 *tnt.ùm* (a. Aistleitner) or *tàr ùm* (Virolleaud) 'the kin of a mother (did he get)' (cp. *tàr* 18 i 25); *àkn* error for *tkn* or so read
  20, 24: these lines transgress the margin with col. ii
  22 *ḥtkp* error for *ḥtkh*
  24 *btmhn*: the suffix is sing. with added *n* (cp. *qšthn* 10 ii 6) and therefore possibly that in *mšbʿthn* (20); Virolleaud *btm hn* 'in (its) entirety lo!'

¹ The destruction (or restoration) of Keret's

palace is not a motif in the story; the words for 'house', 'place', 'seat' in *ll.* 7, 11, 23 are therefore best understood metaphorically.

² In this introductory portion (*ll.* 1–25) 'our' refers to the story-teller and his audience.

³ With the vocabulary cp. Yehimilk inscr. *ll.* 6–7 Yehaumilk inscr. *l.* 9 Prov. xviii 22.

⁴ I.e. 'she died'.

⁵ *Ll.* 16–21 have usually been understood to refer to the death of Keret's children, e.g. 'one third died in (their) prime etc.' Note the adverbial *m* with *ktr*.

⁶ The god of pestilence; cp. 15 ii 6 Job v 7.

⁷ I.e. the waves of a storm.

⁸ Cp. Joel ii 8; or metaphorically 'lightning' (Van Selms).

⁹ Sc. each member of the audience.

¹⁰ Lit. 'heir'.

26 *y'rb.bḥdrh.ybky* He[1] entered into his chamber weeping,
27 *btn.rgmm.wydm'* as he repeated (his) tale (of woe) he shed tears;
28 *tntkn.ùdm'th* his tears streamed down
29 *km.tqlm.àrṣh* like shekels to the ground,
30 *km ḥmšt.mtth* like pieces of five upon (his) bed.
31 *bm[.]bkyh.wyšn* As he wept he fell asleep,
32 *bdm'h.nhmmt* as he shed tears (there was) slumber.
33 *šnt.tlùn* (34) *wyškb.* Sleep overpowered him and he lay down,
   nhmmt (35) *wyqmṣ.* slumber (overpowered him) and he curled up.[2]
   wbḥlmh (36) *il.yrd.* And in his dream El came down,
   bẓhrth (37) *àb àdm[.]* in his vision the father of mankind,[3]
   wyqrb (38) *bšàl.krt.* and he drew near to Keret, asking (him):
   màt (39) *krt.kybky* 'What ails Keret that he weeps,
40 *ydm'.n'mn.ǵlm* (41) *il.* 'the gracious one, page of El, that he sheds tears?
   mlk[.t]r àbh (42) *yàrš.* 'Does he wish for the kingship of the bull his father
   hm.drk[t] (43) *kàb.àdm* 'or dominion as (of) the father of mankind?'
   . . (gap of 6–7 *ll.*) . . . .
52 [lm] (53) [ànk.ksp.wyrq] '[What need have I[4] of silver and yellow metal],

Col. ii

54 [ḥrṣ.]yd.mqmh '[of gold] fresh from the mine[5]
55 [w'b]d.'lm. '[or of] perpetual[6] slaves,
   tlt (56) [ssw]m.mrkbt 'of triads[7] [of horses] (and) chariots
   btrbṣ bn.àmt 'from the stable of the son of a slave-girl[8]?
57 [- - b]nm.àqny '[   ] sons I would get[9]
58 [- - -]rm.àmìd '[   ] I would multiply.'
59 [wy'n].tr.àbh.il And the bull El his father [answered]:
60 d[- -]t.bbk.krt 'You [   ] by weeping, Keret,
61 bdm'.n'mn.ǵlm (62) il. 'by shedding tears, gracious one, page of El.
   trtḥṣ.wtàdm 'Do you wash and reddle yourself,
63 rḥṣ[.y]dk.àmt 'wash your hands (to) the elbow,
64 ùṣb['tk.]'d[.t]km '[your] fingers to the shoulder.
65 'rb [.bẓl.ḥmt] 'Enter [into the shade of the tent];[10]
66 qḥ ìm[r.bydk] 'take a sheep [in your hand],
67 ìmr.d[bḥ.bm].ymn 'a sacrificial sheep [in] (your) right hand,

---

30 *km ḥmšt* (cp. **19** 82–83); Virolleaud *tmḥ mšt* 'the covering of his bed was soaked' (Akk. *maḥāḥu* 'to pour out'; cp. Ps. vi 7)
33 *tlùn*: note *n* with five wedges; Virolleaud *tlùàn*
38 *màt* crasis of *mh àt* (Ginsberg; cp. Ps. cxiv 5) or *my àt* (Gray; cp. Ruth iii 16)
42: cp. **16** vi 24
52 (properly 50 or 51)–53: cp. 137–138
54–56: cp. 126–129
56: this line and 67 transgress the margin with col. iii
57–58 Ginsberg [*tn.b*]nm and [*tn.tà*]rm 'grant that I may get sons, multiply kin'
59 Virolleaud
60 Lipiński *d*['b]t 'you are wasting away' (cp. Ps. lxxxviii 10)
63–75: cp. 157–167

[1] Sc. Keret; the story proper begins here.
[2] Perhaps a teachnical term for resorting to incubation (Greenfield); see at **17** i 6.
[3] Cp. the title of Zeus in Homer, 'father of men and gods'. Alternatively 'the Man' as an epithet of the sacral king (Lipiński).
[4] Lit. 'Why I?'; cp. Gen. xxv 22.
[5] Lit. 'alongside its place'; cp. 1 Sam. iv 13 (*Qere*) Job xxviii 1. [6] Cp. Deut. xv 17 Job xl 28.
[7] Cp. *Od.* iv 589–90. Alternatively 'a third man, horses and a chariot'; Hebr. *šālîš* 'squire'.
[8] Sc. El himself; but the words are conventional. In *l.* 129 the reference is more appropriately to Pabil (cp. Ps. lxxxvi 16). [9] Cp. Gen. iv 1.
[10] Cp. 2 Sam. vi 17. Alternatively 'pen' for animals (Gray; Arab. *ḥummu*).

68 *llà.kl*[*àtn*]*m*
69 *klt.l*[*ḥmk.d*]*nzl*
70 *qḥ.ms*[*rr.*]*ʿṣr* (71) *dbḥ.*
　　ṣ[*q.bg*]*l.ḥtt* (72) *yn.*
　　bgl[*.ḫ*]*rṣ.nbt*
73 *ʿl lẓr.*[*mg*]*dl*
74 *wʿl lẓr.*[*mg*]*dl.rkb* (75) *tkmm.ḥm*[*t*].
　　šà.ydk (76) *šmm.*
　　dbḥ.ltr (77) *àbk.ìl.*
　　šrd.bʿl (78) *bdbḥk.*
　　bn.dgn (79) *bmṣdk.*
　　wyrd (80) *krt.lggt.*
　　ʿdb (81) *àkl.lqryt*
82 *ḥtt.lbt.ḫbr*
83 *yìp.lḥm.dḥmš*
84 *mġd*[.]*tdt.yrḫm*
85 *ʿdn*[.]*ngb.wyṣì*
86 *ṣbù.ṣbì.ngb*
87 *wyṣì.ʿdn.mʿ*
88 *ṣbùk.ùl.màd*
89 *tlt.màt.rbt*
90 *ḫpt.dbl.spr*
91 *tnn.dbl.hg*
92 *hlk.làlpm.ḥžž*
93 *wlrbt.km yr*
94 [*à*]*tr.tn.tn.hlk*
95 *àtr.tlt.klhm*
96 *yḥd.bth.sgr*
97 *àlmnt.škr* (98) *tškr.*
　　zbl.ʿršm (99) *yšù.*
　　ʿwr.mzl (100) *ymzl.*
　　wyṣì.trḫ (101) *ḥdt.*
　　ybʿr.ltn (102) *àtth.*
　　lm.nkr (103) *mddth.*

'a young beast (in) [them both];
'(take) all[1] the choicest[2] of [your bread],
'take a . . . . . , the sacrificial bird;
'pour wine [into] a vessel of silver,
'honey into a vessel of gold.
'Go up on to the tower
'and mount the shoulder of the wall;
'lift up your hands (to) heaven
'(and) sacrifice to the bull El your father,
'make Baal to come down with your sacrifice,
'the son of Dagon with your game.
'Then let Keret come down from the roof;[3]
'let him make ready[4] corn[5] for the city,
'wheat for Beth Khubur;[6]
'let him parch bread (from grain) of the fifth,
'rations[7] (from grain of) the sixth month.[8]
'Let a multitude be gathered and go forth,
'let a mighty army[9] be gathered;
'then let the multitude go forth together.
'(Let) your army (be) a numerous force,
'three hundred times ten thousand,
'peasant levies[10] without number,
'regular soldiers[10] beyond reckoning.
'Let them go by thousands (like) storm-cloud(s),[11]
'and by ten thousands like the early rains.
'After two let two go,
'after three them all;
'let the single man shut up his house (and go),
'the widowed (mother) indeed hire herself out,[12]
'the sick man take up (his) bed (and go),
'the blind man indeed stumble along behind;
'and let the newly wed husband go forth,[13]
'let him make away with his wife to another,
'with his beloved to a stranger.[14]

74: dittography of 73 or vice-versa (cp. 165–166)
94: cp. 182

[1] Or 'a measure, measures of' (Hebr. *kyl* in Isa. xl 12　Gezer inscr. *l.* 5).
[2] Properly bread offered to guests.
[3] Lit. 'roofs', i.e. roof-terraces; cp. *ANET* p. 81 (Gilgamesh) 2 Kgs. xxiii 12　Jer. xix 13　Zeph. i 5.
[4] Infin. absol. or perfect with jussive sense; so *ngb* (85), *hlk* (92, 94), *sgr* (96) and perhaps *yrd* (79).
[5] Cp. Gen. xli 35　Prov. xiii 23.
[6] Cp. **15** iv 8–9. Alternatively 'from the granary . . . from the cellar(s)' ; cp. Akk. *bīt qarîtu* 'granary', *bīt ḫubūri* 'ale-house' (Albright; cp. Prov. xxi 9　xxv 24).　[7] Cp. Gen. xlii 25　Josh. ix 14.
[8] Lit. 'of the fifth, sixth of months', being those in which respectively barley and wheat were gathered to storage (Gray). Hardly 'for five, six months', since

the campaign does not seem to have lasted long (cp. *ll.* 106ff., 114ff.).　[9] Lit. 'an army of an army'.
[10] Cp. Akk. (Alalakh) *ḫupšu*, *s/šananu*, the first referring to free-born farmers who had become tenants of the king in return for certain feudal services, the second to professional soldiers (cp. **23** 7), probably archers (Wiseman).
[11] Cp. Zech. x 1　Jer. iv. 13. Alternatively this and the following term denote military classes.
[12] Or 'hire a hireling' (Gray), in either case because her son had been taken to the war; cp. Gen. xxx 16　1 Sam. ii 5.
[13] Or 'let the newly-wed pay the bride-price (but then) etc.' (cp. *l.* 189); for another example of *yṣà* G with the meaning 'put forth' see **16** i 53.
[14] Newly married men seem to have been normally exempt from military service, as in Israel (Deut. xx 7　xxiv 5).

kìrby (104) [t]škn.šd   'Let them settle like locusts on the field,

Col. iii

105 km.ḥsn.pảt.mdbr   'like hoppers on the fringe of the wilderness.[1]
106 lk.ym.wtn.   'Go a day and a second,
    tlt.rbˁ.ym   'a third, a fourth day,
107 ḥmš.tdt.ym.   'a fifth, a sixth day;
    mk.špšm (108) bšbˁ.   'then with the sun[2] on the seventh (day)
    wtmǵy.lùdm (109) rbm.   'you shall come to great Udm
    wl.ùdm.trrt   'and to well-watered Udm;
110 wgr.nn.ˁrm.   'and do you tarry at the city,
    šrn (111) pdrm.   'encamp at the town.[3]
    sˁt.bšdm (112) ḥṭbh.   'Running in from the fields[4] (will come) the women
                                             fetching (wood),
    bgrnt.ḥpšt   'from the threshing-floors those seeking (straw);
113 sˁt.bn⟨p⟩k.šìbt.   'running in from the well (will come) the women
                                             drawing water,
    bbqr (114) mmlảt.   'from the spring those filling (buckets).[5]
    dm.ym.wtn   'Stay quiet a day and a second,
115 tlt.rbˁ.ym.   'a third, a fourth day,
    ymš (116) tdt.ym.   'a fifth, a sixth day;
    ḥẓk.ảl.tšˁl (117) qrth.   'do not discharge your arrows into the town
    ảbn.ydk (118) mšdpt.   '(nor) your sling stones (into) the citadel.[6]
    whn.špšm (119) bšbˁ.   'And behold! with the sun on the seventh (day),
    wl.yšn.pbl (120) mlk.   'then king Pabil will not sleep
    lqr.tìgt.ìbrh   'for the rumble of the roaring of his bull(s),
121 lql.nhqt.ḥmrh   'for the sound of the braying of his ass(es),
122 lgˁt.ảlp.ḥrt.   'for the lowing of his plough ox(en),
    zǵt (123) klb.ṣpr.   'the whining of his hunting dog(s).[7]
    wylảk (124) mlảkm.lk.   'And he will send messengers to you, (saying):
    ˁm.krt (125) mswnh.   ' "To Keret. . . . . . .[8]
    tḥm.pbl.mlk   ' "the message of king Pabil (is this):
126 qh.ksp.wyrq.   ' "Take silver and yellow metal,
    ḥrṣ (127) yd.mqmh.   ' "gold fresh from the mine
    wˁbd.ˁlm   ' "and perpetual slaves,
128 tlt.sswm.mrkbt   ' "triads of horses (and) chariots

104: cp. 192

106: this and several other lines of col. iii are continued on the edge of the tablet

109 rbm error for rbt (cp. 134)

112 ḥṭbh error for ḥṭbt (Pedersen)

113 n⟨p⟩k: cp. 216; bbqr error for bmqr (cp. 216–217) unless m assimilated to b

115 ymš error for ḥmš through dittography of ym (cp. 220)

[1] Cp. Judg. vi 5   vii 12 Nah. iii 15–17 Ben Sira xliii 17.

[2] It is uncertain whether this phrase means at sunrise or at sunset (cp. 118).

[3] Or 'attack' (Akk. garû) 'the villages, destroy the towns'.

[4] Or 'Swept from the fields (shall be) the women etc.' (Greenfield). The root occurs in Ps. lv 9 describing a wind.

[5] Cp. Quran Sura cxi 4   Gen. xxiv 11   1 Sam. ix 11.

[6] Cp. Num. xxxv 17; or 'your sling-stones flung in succession' (Driver; Arab. 'adaffa 'came consecutively (affairs)'.

[7] Lit. 'the ox (with which) he ploughed, the dog (to which) he whistled'. Cp. Job vi 5.

[8] Or 'he will send messengers to you, to Keret . . ., (saying):' The term mswn is variously rendered 'camp', 'colleague', 'delegate(s)' or as a place-name.

129 *btrbṣ.bn.ȧmt*   ' "from the stable of the son of a slave-girl.

130 *qḥ.krt.šlmm* (131) *šlmm.*   ' "Take, Keret, the peace-offerings, (take) the peace-offerings

  wng.mlk (132) *lbty.*   ' "and flee away, king, from my house,

  rḥq.krt (133) *lḥẓry.*   ' "keep far, Keret, from my court;

  ȧl.tṣr (134) *ủdm.rbt.*   ' "do not besiege great Udm

  wủdm trrt   ' "and well-watered Udm,

135 *ủdm.ytnȧ.ȧl*   ' "Udm the gift of El[1]

  wủšn (136) *ȧb.ȧdm.*   ' "and a present from the father of mankind."

  wttb (137) *mlȧkm.lh.*   'And do you send the messengers back to him, (saying):

  lm.ȧnk (138) *ksp.wyrq.*   ' "What need have I of silver and yellow metal,

  ḥrṣ (139) *yd.mqmh.*   ' "of gold fresh from the mine

  wᶜbd (140) *ᶜlm.*   ' "or of perpetual slaves,

  tlt.sswm.mrkbt   ' "of triads of horses (and) chariots

141 *btrbṣt.bn.ȧmt*   ' "from the stable(s) of the son of a slave-girl?

142 *pd.ȧn.bbty.ttn*   ' "So do you give (me) what is not in my house;[2]

143 *tn.ly.mtt.ḥry*   ' "give me the maiden Huray,

144 *nᶜmt.špḥ.bkrk*   ' "the most gracious of (your) family, your first-born,

145 *dk.nᶜm.ᶜnt.nᶜmh*   ' "whose grace is as the grace of Anat

146 *km.tsm.ᶜttrt.ts*[mh]   ' "(and) her fairness as the fairness of Athtart

147 *dᶜqh.ȧb.ȧqnȧ.*   ' "whose eyeballs are gems[3] of lapis-lazuli

  ᶜp[ᶜp]h (148) *sp.trml.*   ' "(and) her eyelids bowls of onyx,

  tḥgrn [ủ]*dm*   ' "(who) is girded with rubies.

149 *ȧšlw.bṣp.ᶜnh*   ' "I would repose in the glance of her eyes,

150 *dbḥlmy.ȧl.ytn*   ' "because El in my dream has granted,

151 *bẓrty.ȧb.ȧdm*   ' "the father of mankind in my vision,

152 *wld.špḥ.lkrt*   ' "the birth of a family to Keret

153 *wǵlm.lᶜbd.ȧl*   ' "and a boy to the servant of El." '

154 *krt.yḥṭ.wḥlm*   Keret awoke, and it was a dream,

155 *ᶜbd.ȧl.wḥdrt*   the servant of El—and it was a visitation.[4]

156 *yrtḥṣ.wyȧdm*   He washed and reddled himself,

157 *yrḥṣ.ydh.ȧmth*   he washed his hands to the elbow,

158 *ủṣbᶜth.ᶜd.tkm*   his fingers to the shoulder.

159 *ᶜrb.bẓl.ḥmt.*   He did enter into the shade of the tent;

  lqḥ (160) *ȧmr.dbḥ.bydh*   he did take a sacrificial sheep in his hand,

161 *llȧ.klȧtnm.*   a young beast (in) them both;

162 *klt.lḥmh.dnzl*   (he did take) all the choicest of his bread,

163 *lqḥ.msrr.ᶜṣr.db*[ḥ]   he did take a . . . . . , the sacrificial bird;

Col. iv

164 *yṣq.bgl.ḥtt.yn*   he did pour wine into a vessel of silver,

165 *bgl.ḥrṣ.nbt.*   honey into a vessel of gold.

---

135 *ytnȧ* error for *ytnt* (Virolleaud) unless *n* has four wedges

146–147: cp. 293–295

148 [ủ]*dm* (Pedersen) or [.]*dm*[-] (Herdner)

159–163 are written on the bottom edge of the tablet

160: note variation from 66–67

161: note final word-divider   163: cp. 71

[1] Cp. Eccles. iii 13 and for the thought Deut. xxxii 8.

[2] Cp. 2 Sam. ix 3.

[3] Or 'whose tresses are bloom(s)' (Arab. *ᶜaqîqatu* 'hair of new-born infant'). Cp. Song vii 5, 6.

[4] Cp. Ps. xxix 2, 'at his appearance in holiness' or the like (Cross).

w'ly (166) lẓr.mgdl.   And he did go up on to the tower,
rkb (167) tkmm.ḥmt.   did mount the shoulder of the wall;
nšả (168) [y]dh.šmmh.   he did lift up his hands to heaven
dbḥ (169) ltr.ảbḥ.ỉl.   (and) did sacrifice to the bull El his father,
šrd (170) [b'l].bdbḥh.   he did make [Baal] to come down with his sacrifice,
bn dgn (171) [bm]ṣdh.   the son of Dagon [with] his game.
yrd.krt (172) [lg]gt.   Keret did come down [from] the roof;
'db.ảkl.lqryt   he did make ready corn for the city,

173 ḥṭṭ.lbt.ḫbr   wheat for Beth Khubur;
174 yỉp.lḥm.dḫmš   he parched bread (from grain) of the fifth,
175 [mǵ]d.tdṫ.yr[ḫm]   rations (from grain of) the sixth month.
176 'dn.ngb.w[yṣỉ.]   A multitude was gathered and [went forth];
     [ṣbủ] (177) ṣbỉ.ng[b.]   [a mighty] army was gathered;
     [wyṣỉ.'dn] (178) m'[.]   [then the multitude went forth] together.
     [ṣ]bủh ủ[l.mảd]   His army (was) a [numerous] force,
179 ṫlṫ.mảṫ.rbt   three hundred times ten thousand.
180 hlk.lảlpm.ḥẓẓ   They did go by thousands (like) storm-cloud(s),
181 wl.rbt.km yr   and by ten thousands like the early rains.
182 ảtr.tn.tn.hlk   After two two did go,
183 ảtr.ṫlṫ.klhm   after three them all;
184 ảḥd.bth.ysgr   the single man shut up his house (and went),
185 ảlmnt.škr (186) tškr.   the widowed (mother) indeed hired herself out,
     zbl.'ršm (187) yšủ.   the sick man took up (his) bed (and went),
     'wr (188) mzl.ymzl   the blind man indeed stumbled along behind;
189 wybl.trḥ.ḥdt   and the newly wed husband was led off,[1]
190 yb'r.ltn.ảtth   he made away with his wife to another
191 wlnkr.mddt   and with (his) beloved to a stranger.
192 km ỉrby.tškn (193) šd.   They settled like locusts on the field,
     khsn.pảt (194) mdbr.   like hoppers on the fringe of the wilderness.
     tlkn (195) ym.wṫn.   They went a day and a second;
     ảḫr (196) šp[š]m.b[t]lt   afterwards with the sun on the third (day)
197 ym[ǵy.]lqdš (198) ả[trt.]ṣrm. he came to the sanctuary of Athirat of the two Tyres[2]
     wlỉlt (199) ṣd[ny]m.   and to (the sanctuary of) Elat of the Sidonians.
     tm (200) ydr[.k]rt.t'   There the noble[3] Keret vowed, (saying):
201 ỉ ỉtt.ảtrt.ṣrm   'As surely as Athirat of the two Tyres
202 wỉlt.ṣdynm   'and Elat of the Sidonians exists,[4]
203 hm.ḥry.bty (204) ỉqḥ.   'if I may take[5] Huray (into) my house,
     ảš'rb.ǵlmt (205) ḥzry.   'introduce[5] the lass[6] to my court,
     tnh.wspm (206) ảtn.   'I will give twice her (weight) in silver

168: cp. 75
170–172: cp. 77–80
171: note h with four horizontal wedges
172: this and several other lines of col. iv finish on the
    edge of the tablet
175–178: cp. 84–88
180: note that 90–91 are not repeated
184: note ảḥd for yḥd (96)
189: note ybl for yṣỉ (100); cp. Isa. lv 12
196–197: cp. 209–210
198–199: cp. 201–202
200: cp. 305
202: ṣdynm prob. error for ṣdnym (Baneth)

205 wspm error for kspm

[1] Or (see at l. 101) 'the newly-wed paid the bride-price (but then)' etc.'; Akk. (Amarna) abālu terḫāta.
[2] I.e. island and mainland.
[3] Or 'munificent, generous' (Driver, Gray) or 'priest' (Aistleitner), both lit. 'he who offers, presents' (t'y in religious texts).
[4] Lit. 'Where do . . .?'; note that Ugar. ỉt is inflected as a verb like Arab. laysa 'there is not'.
[5] With the terminology cp. Gen. xxiv 67   Ruth iv 11, 13.
[6] Cp. Isa. vii 14.

　　　　w.tlth.ḥrṣm
207 *ylk.ym.wtn.*
208 *tlt.rbʿ.ym.*
209 *dḥr.špšm.brbʿ*
210 *ymǵy.lùdm.rbt*
211 *wùdm[.tr]rt*
212 *grnn.ʿrm*
213 *šrn.pdrm*
214 *sʿt.bšdm.ḥtb*⟨t⟩

215 *wbgrnt.ḥpšt*

216 *sʿt.bnpk.šỉbt.*

　　　wb (217) *mqr.mmldt*
218 *d[m].ym.wtn*
219 *tlt[.]rbʿ.ym*
220 *ḥmš.tdt.ym*
221 *mk[.]špšm.bšbʿ*
222 *wl.yšn[.]pbl* (223) *mlk.*
　　l[qr.]tỉqt (224) *ỉbrh[.]*
　　[l]ql.nhqt (225) *ḥmr[h.]*
　　[lgʿt.]àlp (226) *ḥrt[.]*
　　[lz]ǵt[.]klb (227) *[s]pr[.]*
　　[àpn]k (228) *[pb]l[.mlk.]*
　　[g]m.làtt (229) *[h.k]y[ṣḥ.]*
　　šmʿ.mʿ (230) *[- -]ʿm[-]àtty*
231 *[- - - - -]tḥm*
232 *[- - - - -]t[.]r*
233 *[- - - - - -]n*
234 *[- - - - -]ḥ.lʿdb*
235 *[- - - - -]n.ydh*
236 *[- - - -].bl.ỉšlḥ*
237 *[- - - - - -]ḥ.*
　　gm (238) *[l- - - - k]yṣḥ*
239 *[- - - - -]bd.ʿr*

'and thrice her (weight) in gold.'[1]
He went a day and a second,
a third, a fourth day;
afterwards with the sun on the fifth[2] (day)
he came to great Udm
and well-watered Udm.
He did tarry[3] at the city,
did encamp[3] at the town.
Running in from the fields (did come) the women
　　fetching (wood),
and from the threshing-floors those seeking (straw);

Col. v

running in from the well (did come) the women
　　drawing (water),
and from the spring those filling (buckets).
He did stay quiet a day and a second,
a third, a fourth day,
a fifth, a sixth day;
then with the sun on the seventh (day),
king Pabil could not sleep
for [the rumble] of the roaring of his bull(s),
[for] the sound of the braying of [his] ass(es),
[for the lowing] of his plough ox(en),
[for] the whining of his hunting dog(s).
Thereupon [king] Pabil
[surely] cried aloud to [his]wife:
'Hear, I beseech you [　　　　　　] my wife
'[　　　　　　　　　　] the message
'[　　　　　　　　　　　　　　　　]
'[　　　　　　　　　　　　　　　　]
'[　　　　　　　　] to make ready
'[　　　　　　　　　] his hands
'[　　　　　　　] no, I shall send
'[　　　　　　　　　　　　　　　　]
[Surely] he [cried] aloud [to　　　　　　]:
'[　　　　　　　　] the city

207–208: note the final word-dividers
209 *brbʿ* prob. error for *bḥmš* (cp. the pattern in 106–
　　108, 195–196)
211: cp. 109
213 *šrn*: note *n* with five wedges (cp. 33, 110);
　　Virolleaud *šrnà*
214: cp. 112 (unless the masc. is used for the fem.;
　　cp. **16** i 51)
215 Virolleaud *grnm*
218: cp. 114
220: note that 116–118 are not repeated
223–227: cp. 120–123
223 *tỉqt* error for *tỉgt* (120) or variant
227–229 Ginsberg (cp. **17** v 13, 15)

230 Herdner *[ln]ʿm[t.]* 'o my gracious wife'
234: note *d* with four vertical wedges
236: this line transgresses the margin with col. iv
238: cp. 228–229

[1] Or 'two parts her (weight), the third part her
(weight)' (Herdner *a.* Pedersen); cp. Akk. *šittašu
ilu-ma šullultašu amēlūtu* (Gilgamesh), 'two parts of
him are divine, his third human'.
[2] See apparatus; the two full days of *ll.* 194–195
and the four of *ll.* 207–208 are equivalent to the six
full days of *ll.* 106ff.
[3] Apparently '*Nun energicum*' endings after perfect
verbs.

240 [- - - - - -]bb
241 [- - - - - -]lmy
242 [- - - - - -]p
243 [- - - - - - d]bḥ (244/5) t[- - - -]
    [ìd]k (246) pn[m.àl.t]tn
247 ʿm.[krt.msw]n
248 wr[gm.lkrt.]tʿ
249 tḥm[.pbl.mlk]
250 qḥ.[ksp.wyr]q
251 ḥrṣ[.yd.mqm]h
252 ʿbd[.ʿlm.]
    [tlt] (253) ss[wm.mrkbt]
254 b[trbṣ.bn.àmt]
255 [qḥ.krt.šlmm] (256) [šlmm.]

    [àl.tṣr] (257) [ùdm.rbt.]
    [wùdm] (258) [trrt.]
    [ùdm.ytnt] (259) [ìl.]
    [wùšn.àb.àdm]
260 [rḥq.mlk.lbty]
261 [ng.kr]t.lḥ[ẓ]ry

    .   .   (gap of 3 ll.)   .   .
265 [ìdk.pnm.lytn]
266 [ʿ]m[.krt.mswnh]
267 tš[àn.ghm.wtṣḥn]
268 tḥ[m.pbl.mlk]
269 qḥ[.ksp.wyrq]
270 ḥrṣ.[yd.mqmh]
271 wʿbd[.ʿlm.]
    [tlt] (272) sswm.m[rkbt]
273 btrbṣ.[bn.àmt]
274 q[ḥ.kr]t[.šlmm] (275) š[lmm.]

    àl.t[ṣr] (276) ùdm[.r]bt[.]
    wù[dm] (277) [t]rrt[.]
    ùdm.y[t]n[t] (278) ìl[.]
    ùšn[.]àb[.àd]m
279 rḥq[.]mlk[.]lbty
280 n[g.]krt[.]lḥẓ[ry]
281 wyʿn[y.k]rt[.t]ʿ
282 lm.ànk.ksp (283) wyr[q.]
    [ḥrṣ] (284) yd.mqmh.

ʿ[   ]
ʿ[   ]
ʿ[   ]
ʿ[   ] sacrifice [   ]
ʿ[Then of a truth do you set] (your) faces
ʿtowards [Keret . . . . .]
ʿand tell the noble [Keret]:
ʿ "The message [of king Pabil] (is this):
ʿ "Take [silver and yellow metal],
ʿ "gold [fresh from the mine]
ʿ "(and) [perpetual] slaves,
ʿ "[triads] of horses [(and) chariots]
ʿ "from [the stable of the son of a slave-girl].
ʿ "[Take, Keret, the peace-offerings, (take) the peace-
    offerings]
ʿ "[(and) do not besiege great Udm]
ʿ "[and well-watered Udm],
ʿ "[Udm the gift of El]
ʿ "[and a present from the father of mankind];
ʿ "[(but) keep far, king, from my house],
ʿ "[flee away, Keret,] from my court." '

Col. vi

. . . .
[Then indeed they set (their) faces]
towards [Keret . . . . . .],
they lifted up [their voices and cried]:
'The message of [king Pabil] (is this):
'Take [silver and yellow metal],
'gold [fresh from the mine]
'and [perpetual] slaves,
'[triads] of horses (and) [chariots]
'from the stable of [the son of a slave-girl].
'Take, [Keret, the peace-offerings], (take) the peace-
    [offerings]
'(and) do not [besiege] great Udm
'and well-watered Udm,
'Udm the gift of El
'(and) a present from the father of mankind;
'(but) keep far, king, from my house,
'flee away, Keret, from [my] court.'
And the noble Keret answered:
'What need have I of silver and yellow metal,
'[of gold] fresh from the mine

243 Virolleaud
244–245 are probably one line (Herdner)
244/5–246: cp. 3 F 12–13
247 Herdner (cp. 125); Ginsberg [krt.tʿ]
248 Ginsberg (cp. 16 i 38)

249–259: cp. 125–131, 133–136
260–261: cp. 279–280 and contrast 131–133
265–267: cp. 301–304
268–280: cp. 249–261
281 Herdner a. Ginsberg   283: cp. 138

w‘bd (285) ‘lm.	'or of perpetual slaves,
tlt.sswm (286) mrkbt.	'of triads of horses (and) chariots
btrbṣ (287) bn.ȧmt.	'from the stable of the son of a slave-girl?
pd.[ı̇]n (288) bbty.ttn[.]	'So do you give (me) what is not in my house;
tn (289) ly.mtt[.]hry	'give me the maiden Huray,
290 n‘mt.šbḥ.bkrk	'the most gracious of (your) family, your first-born,
291 dkn‘m.‘nt (292) n‘mh.	'whose grace is as the grace of Anat
km.tsm (293) ‘ttrt.tsmh	'(and) her fairness as the fairness of Athtart,
294 d‘qh.ı̇b[.]ı̇qnı̇	'whose eyeballs are gems of lapis-lazuli
295 ‘p‘ph.sp.trml	'(and) her eyelids bowls of onyx;
296 dbḥlmy.ı̇l.ytn	'because El in my dream has granted,
297 bẑrty[.]ȧb.ȧdm	'the father of mankind in my vision,
298 wld.šph.lkrk (299) t.	'the birth of a family to Keret
wǵlm.l‘bd (300) ı̇l.	'and a boy to the servant of El.'
ttb‘.mlȧkm (301) lytb.	The messengers departed, they did not stay;
ı̇dk.pnm (302) lytn.	then indeed they set (their) faces
‘mm.pbl (303) mlk.	towards king Pabil,
tšȧn (304) ǵhm.wtṣḥn	they lifted up their voices and cried:
305 thm.krt.t[‘]	'The message of the noble Keret,
306 hwt.[n]‘mn.[ǵlm.ı̇l]	'the word of the gracious one, [page of El], (is this):

15

Col. i

. . (ca. 40 ll.) . .	. . . .
1 [mrǵ]b.yd.m[tkt]	'[The hungry she] did [grasp] by the hand;[1]
2 mẓmȧ.yd.mtkt	'the thirsty she did grasp by the hand.
3 tttkrn.[- -]dn	'. . . . .
4 ‘m.krt.mswnh	'towards Keret . . . . . .
5 ȧrḥ tzǵ l‘glh	'(As) the heifer lows for her calf
6 bn.ḥpt.lȧmhthm	'(and) soldiers'[2] sons (cry) for their mothers,[3]
7 ktnḥn.ȧdmm	'surely the people of Udm shall bemoan her.'
8 wy‘ny.krt.t‘	And the noble Keret answered:

Col. ii

. . (ca.20 ll.) . .	. . . .
1 [ ]	'[ ]
2 [- - - - - - - -]tr	'[ ] the bull
3 [- - - - ȧlı̇y]n.b‘l	'[mightiest] Baal
4 [- - - - - - -]yrḥ.zbl	'[ ] prince Yarikh
5 [- - kt]r wḥss	'[ ] Kothar-and-Khasis
6 [- - - -]n.rḥmy.ršp zbl	'[ ] Rahmay,[4] prince Resheph

287: cp. 142

290: note b for p

295: note the omission of two phrases (cp. 148–149)

298–299 krk t error for krt (cp. 152)

305–306 Ginsberg (cp. 61–62); possibly the word ı̇l began the next tablet

i 1 Herdner and Virolleaud

ii 3, 5 Virolleaud

[1] Cp. Hos. vii 5.

[2] See at **14** 90.

[3] I.e. in the absence of their fathers; cp. **6** ii 28ff.

[4] Probably a name or title of Anat meaning 'the merciful'(!) (**23** 13).

7 [wʿ]*dt.ilm.tlth*

8 [àp]*nk.krt.tʿ.ʿ*[š]*r*

9 [ʿr]b *bth.yšt.*
ʿ*rb* (10) [bt]*h.ytn.*
wyṣù.lytn

11 [àḫ]r.*mǵy.ʿ*[d]*t.ilm*

12 [w]y*ʿn.àlìy*[n.]*bʿl*

13 [lt]*tbʿ.lltpn* (14) [ìl.d]*pìd.*
ltbrk (15) [krt.]*tʿ.*
ltmr.nʿmn (16)[ǵlm.]ì*l.*
ks.yìḫd (17) [ìl.b]*yd.*
krpn.bm (18) [ymn.]
brkm.ybrk (19) [ʿbdh.]
ybrk ìl.krt (20) [tʿ.]
[ymr]*m.nʿm*[n.]*ǵlm.ìl*

21 *d̄*[tt.tq]*h.ykrt.*
d̄tt (22) *tqh.btk.*
ǵlmt.tšʿrb (23) *hqrk.*
tld.šbʿ.bnm.lk

24 *wtmn tttmnm* (25) *lk*
tld.ysb.ǵlm

26 *ynq.ḥlb.d̄*[t]*rt*

27 *mṣṣ.td.btlt.*[ʿnt]

28 *mšnq*[t.ilm - - -]

        . . (ca.15 *ll.*) . .

1 [   ] (2) [- - - -]
[mìd.rm.]*krt*

3 [btk.rpì.]à*rṣ*

4 [bpḫr].*qbṣ.dtn*

5 [wt]*qrb.wld* (6) *bn.tlk*

7 *tld.pǵt.t*[- -]*t*

8 *tld.*pǵt[- - - -]

9 *tld.pǵ*[t - - - -]

10 *tld.pǵ*[t - - - - - - -]

'[and] the company of the gods,[1] the third thereof'.[2]

Thereupon the noble Keret did hold a banquet;
[he did enter] his house (and) drank,
he did enter his [house] (and) gave (gifts);
and he came forth, having indeed given (them).

Afterwards the company of the gods did arrive,[3]
[and] mightiest Baal spoke:
'Do [you indeed] arise,[4] o Latipan kindly [god],
'do you indeed bless the noble [Keret],
'do you indeed fortify the gracious one, [page] of El.'[5]
[El] took a cup [in] (his left) hand,
a flagon in [(his) right hand];
richly he blessed [his servant],
El blessed [the noble] Keret,
he fortified the gracious one, page of El, (saying):
'The [wife whom you] take, o Keret,
'the wife whom you take (into) your house,
'the lass whom you introduce to your court,[6]
'shall bear you seven sons,
'and get you indeed eight;
'she shall bear the lad Yaṣṣib,
'one that shall suck the milk of Athirat,
'one that shall drain the breasts of the virgin [Anat],
'the suckling nurses of [the gods].'[7]

Col. iii

. . . .

[   ]
'[Be greatly exalted], Keret,
'[in the midst of the shades] of the underworld,
'[in the assembly] where Ditan[8] gathers;
'[and she] shall approach (her time)[9] to bear daughters
    to you.
'She shall bear a girl (called) T . . . . t,
'she shall bear a girl (called) [   ]
'she shall bear a girl (called) [   ]
'she shall bear girls (called) [   ]

---

7 Herdner *a*. Virolleaud
8 [*àp*]*nk* Virolleaud; *ʿ*[*š*]*r* Sauren and Kestemont
9–10: cp. *PRU* II no. 121, *l.* 2
11–12 Virolleaud   13: cp. 14
14–18 Virolleaud
19–20 Virolleaud (cp. 17 i 35–36)
21 Virolleaud (cp. 14 204)
23 *hqrk* error for *ḫẓrk* (cp. 14 205)
26–27 Virolleaud   28 Ginsberg
2–4: cp. 13–15
5: cp. 20
6 *bn.tlk* error for *bnt.lk*
10, 11 perhaps contained two names each, making the
    total number eight

[1] Cp. Ps. lxxxii 1.
[2] Or 'the three-fold company', referring to ranks
or divisions within the pantheon.
[3] Infin. absol. or basic verbal form (3 masc. sing.
perf.).
[4] Lit. 'depart', i.e. go over to him.
[5] Cp. 17 i 24–25.
[6] See at 14 203–205.
[7] Like the Sumerian king Lugalzaggisi suckled by
Ninhursag (Gray); cp. also 23 24 *ANET* p. 62
(Marduk).
[8] Lit. 'in the assembly of the gathering of'. *Dtn* is
a prestigious tribal or dynastic name (*Ugaritica* V p.
564).   [9] Or 'shall soon'.

11   *tld.pġ[t - - - - - -]*   'she shall bear girls (called) [   ]

12   *tld.p[ġt.ttmnt]*   'she shall bear a girl (called) [Thitmanat].

13   *mìd.rm[.krt]*   'Be greatly exalted, [Keret],

14   *btk.rpì.ảr[ṣ]*   'in the midst of the shades of the underworld,

15   *bpḫr.qbṣ.dtn*   'in the assembly where Ditan gathers.

16   *ṣġrthn.ảbkr*n   'I will give the first-born's blessing (even) to the youngest of them.'[1]

17   *tbrk.ìlm.tìty*   The gods blessed (him and) returned,

18   *tìty.ìlm.lảhlhm*   the gods returned to their tents,

19   *dr ìl.lmšknthm*   the race of El[2] to their habitations.

20   *wtqrb.wld bn lh*   And she approached (her time) to bear him a son,

21   *wtqrb.wld bnm lh*   and approached (her time) to bear him sons;

22   *mk.bšbᵉ.šnt*   then in the seventh year

23   *bn.krt.km hm.tdr*   the sons of Keret (were as many) as had been promised,[3]

24   *ảp.bnt.ḥry (25) kmhm.*   moreover the daughters of Huray (were as many) as they.

     *wtḫss.ảt*rt (26) *ndrh.*   And Athirat thought on his vow

     *wìlt.*p[- - -]   and Elat on [his pledge],[4]

27   *wtšù.gh.w*[tṣḥ]   and she lifted up her voice and [cried]:

28   *ph mᵉ.ảp.k*[rt.pr]   'Consider, I beseech you: has Keret then [broken]

29   *ùtn.ndr*[h.mlk]   'or has [the king] set aside [his] vow?

30   *ảpr.*h[- - - - - - -]   '(Then) I shall break[5] [   ]

.   .   *(ca. 7 ll.)*   .   .   .   .

Col. iv

.   .   *(ca.5 ll.)*   .   .   .   .

1   *p*[ᵉnh.lhdm.ytpd]   [he placed his] feet [on the footstool];

2   *gm.*l[ảtth.kyṣḥ]   [surely he cried] aloud to [his wife]:

3   *šm*ᵉ[.lmtt.ḥry]   'Hear, [o maiden Huray]:

4   *ṭbḫ*[.]š[mn].*mrì*k   'slay the [fattest] of your fatlings,

5   *pth.*[rḥ]*bt.yn*   'open tuns of wine;

6   *ṣḥ.šbᵉm*[.]*ìry*   'call my seventy dukes

7   *tmnym.*[ẓ]*byy*   '(and) my eighty barons,[6]

8   *tr.ḫbr*[.rb]*t*   'the dukes of great Khubur,

9   *ḫbr*[.trrt]   '[well-watered] Khubur.

10   [-]ᵉ*b*[-]*.š*[- -]*m*   '[   ]

11   [- - - - -]*r*[- - -]*š*[- -]*qm*   '[   ]

12: cp. **16** i 29

13–14: cp. 2–3

20–21 Ginsberg corrects to *bn⟨m⟩* and *bnt* (cp. 23–24)

26 Ginsberg *p*[*lảh*] (Hebr. √*pl'* Piel, Hiphil 'made a special vow')

28–29 Ginsberg; [*mlk*]: cp. **14** 8

30 Ginsberg *p*[*lìy*]; Sauren and Kestemont [*hwt*]; the following gap allows for three to four lines on the bottom edge (cp. **14** 159–163)

iv 1: cp. **17** ii 11

     2: cp. **14** 228–229

     3–5: cp. **14**–16

     7: cp. 18   8–9: cp. 19–20

     10–13 are in a very poor state

[1] I.e. all will be treated as if they were the first-born; cp. Deut. xxi 16   Ps. lxxxix 28; there seems no reason why in this context the youngest should be singled out.

[2] Cp. *dr. bn. il* (**32** 17)   Phoen. *dr bn 'lm* (Karatepe inscr. iii 19).

[3] Lit. 'vowed' and thus presumably promised by Athirat in reply to his vow.

[4] See **14** 200ff. It seems that Keret had not fulfilled his side of the bargain.

[5] Cp. Ps. lxxxix 34.

[6] Lit. 'bulls' and 'gazelles'; cp. Hebr. 'bulls' (Jer. l 27), 'gazelles' (Isa. xxiii 9), 'he-goats' (Isa. xiv 9), 'rams' (Exod. xv 15), 'calves' (Ps. lxviii 31).

12 *id.ù*[- - - - -]*t*
13 *lḥn št*[- -]*àḥd*[-]
14 *tšmᵉ.mtt.*[ḥ]*ry*
15 *ttbḥ.šmn.*[m]*rìh*
16 *t*[*p*]*tḥ.rḥbt.yn*
17 *ᵉlh trh.tšᵉrb*
18 *ᵉlh.tšᵉrb.ẓbyh*
19 *tr.ḥbr*[.]*rbt*
20 *ḥbr.trrt*
21 *bt.krt.tbùn*
22 *lm.mtb*[- - - - -]
23 *wlḥmmr.tqdm*
24 *yd.bṣᵉ.tšlḥ*
25 *ḥrb.bbšr.tštn*
26 [*wt*]ᵉ*n.mtt.ḥry*
27 [*llḥ*]*m.lšty.šḥtkm*
28 [*wldbḥ.l*]*krt.bᵉlkm*

     . . (ca 15 *ll.*) . .

      . . (1 or 2 *ll.*) . .

1 [*ttbḥ.šm*]*n.*[*mrìh*]
2 [*tptḥ.rḥ*]*bt.*[*yn* - - -]
3 [- - - - *k*]*rp*[*n* - - -]
4 [- - - - *ḥ*]*br*[- - - -]
5 *bḥr*[- - -]*t*[- - - -]*h*
6 *lmtb*[- -]*t*[- - - - -] (7) [*tqdm.*]
    yd.bṣᵉ.t[*šl*]*h*
8 [*ḥrb.b*]*bš*[*r*]*.tštn*
9 [*wtᵉn*]*.mtt.ḥry*
10 [*llḥ*]*m.lšty.šḥtk*[*m*]
11 [- - -]*brk.t*[- - - -]
12 [ᵉ*l.*]*krt.tbkn*
13 [*km.*]*rgm.trm*
14 [*bk.*]*mtm.tbkn*
15 [- -]*t.wblb.tqb*[-]
16 [- -]*ml.mtm.ùṣbᵉ*
17 [-]*rt.šrk.il*
18 ᵉ*rb.špš.lymg̱* (19) *krt.*
    ṣbìd.spš (20) *bᵉlny.*

'[   ]
'[   ]
The maiden Huray obeyed;
she slew the fattest of her fatlings,
she opened tuns of wine;
she brought in his dukes to him,
she brought in his barons to him,
the dukes of great Khubur,
well-watered Khubur.
They entered (into) the house of Keret,
[   ] to the throne-room
and they advanced to the audience-chamber.
She put forth (her) hand[1] to the dish,
she put a knife to the flesh.
[And] the maiden Huray addressed (them):
'I have called you [to] eat (and) to drink,
'[and to make sacrifice for] Keret your lord.

        . . . .

Col. v

       . . . .
[she slew the] fattest [of her fatlings],
[she opened] tuns [of wine   ]
[   ] flagon(s) [   ]
[   ] Khubur [   ]
[   ]
to the throne-room [they advanced].
She put forth (her) hand to the dish,
she put [a knife to] the flesh.
[And] the maiden Huray [addressed (them)]:
'I have called you [to] eat (and) to drink
'[   ] bless [   ]
'Do you weep [over] Keret
'(with cries) [like] the roaring of bulls,
'[(as in) weeping] for the dead do you weep
'[   ] and in (your) heart . . . . . .
'[   ] the dead; the finger[2]
'. . . . . El.
'Keret shall indeed come to the setting of the sun,[3]
'the lord of us both[4] to the darkening of the sun;

15–16: cp. 4–5
26–27: cp. vi 3–4
28 [*dbḥ.l*] (Gordon; cp. vi 5) is too short and [*dbḥ.*
dbḥ.l] (Virolleaud) too long for the space
v 1–2: cp. iv 15–16
3 Ginsberg
4: cp. iv 8
7–10: cp. iv 23–27
12–13 Virolleaud and Ginsberg
14 Ginsberg

15 [- -]*t*: perhaps [ᵉ*l*]*h* or [ᵉ*l*]*n* 'over him'
16 Virolleaud [*bh*]*ml* 'with tears' (cp. Arab. *hamala*
'shed tears'); perhaps *ùṣbᵉ*[*t*]   17: prps. [*k*]*rt*
19 *ṣbìd*: cp. *ṣbà* (16 i 36) and *ṣbt* (19 209)

    [1] Cp. Judg. v 26   Job xxviii 9.
    [2] Cp. Exod. viii 15   Luke xi 20.
    [3] Where was the entrance to the underworld (cp.
2 iii 20   6 i 8ff.).
    [4] See at 2 iii 20   iv 5.

wymlk (21) [y]ṣb *ᶜln.*
wy[l]*y* (22) [kr]*t t*ᶜ.
ᶜln.bḫr (23) [- - - -].
ȧttk. *ᶜl* (24) [- - - -]k *yṣṣi*
25 [- - - - - -]*ḫbr.rbt*
26 [ḫbr.trr]*t il d*
27 [pȧd - - - - - -].*bȧnšt*
28 [- - - - - - - y]m*lu̇*
29 [- - - - - - - - - -]tm
   .   .   (*ca.* 18 *ll.*)   .   .

1 *šm*ᶜ.l[-]*mt*[-]*m* l[-]*tnm*
2 *ᶜdm.*⟨t⟩[lh]*m.tšty*
3 *wt*ᶜ*n.mtt* ḫ*ry*
4 *ll*[ḫ]*m.lš*[ty].*ṣḫtkm*
5 *d*b[ḫ.lkrt.ȧ]*dnkm*
6 *ᶜl.krt*[.]*tbu̇n.*
  km (7) *rgm.t*[rm.]*rgm.*
  hm (8) *bžrt*[- - -]*krt*
9 [   ]
   . . . . .

1 [l]*krt*
2 k[k]l*b.bbtk.n*ᶜ*tq.*
  kinr (3) *ȧp.ḫštk.*
  ȧp.ȧb.ik mtm (4) *tmtn.*
  u̇ḫštk.lntn (5) *ᶜtq.*

  bd.ȧtt.ȧb ṣrry
6 *tbkyk.ȧb.ǵr.b*ᶜ*l*
7 *ṣpn.ḫlm.qdš*
8 *ȧny.ḫlm.ȧdr.*
  ḫl (9) *rḫb.mknpt.*
  ȧp (10) [k]*rt.bnm.il.*

'and [Yaṣṣib][1] will be king over us
'and he will [replace] the noble [Keret];
'over us a youth [   ]
'your wife[2] [   ] he will drive forth
'[   ] great Khubur
'[well-watered Khubur]. May the [kindly] god
'[   ] in gentleness
'[   ] may he fill
[   ]
. . . .

Col. vi

'Hear [   ]
'once again do you eat (and) drink.'
And the maiden Huray addressed (them):
'I have called you to eat (and) to drink,
'to make sacrifice [for Keret] your lord.'
They entered into (the presence of) Keret,
(and with cries) like the roaring of bulls they did speak:
'If in a vision [   ] Keret
[   ]
. . . .

16

Col. i

[Of] Keret.
'Like a dog[3] we pass into your house,
'like a cur (through) the entrance to your chamber.[4]
'Shall you then[5] die, father, as men,[6]
'or (shall) your chamber (be made over) to an old
    man's mourning,[7]
'(to) a woman's chanting, my glorious father[8]?
'The rocks of Baal weep for you, father,
'Zephon the holy circuit,[9]
'the vast circuit is groaning (for you),
'the far-flung[10] circuit.
'Is then Keret the son of El,[11]

---

21 [y]ṣb (Aistleitner); *wy*[l]*y* (Caquot and Sznycer;
cp. Arab. *walâ(y)*)
26–28 Ginsberg
vi 1 Sauren and Kestemont [l]*mtmm* l[*q*]*tnm* 'o orphans
  (√*ytm*), o little ones'
2 Herdner   4–5: cp. iv 27–28
7 *rgm.hm* perhaps error for *rgmhm* (cp. v 13)
i 1: cp. **14** 1   2: cp. 15
3 *ik* perhaps error for *k* (cp. 17)

  [1] Keret's eldest son (ii 25).
  [2] Sc. Huray herself now addressing Keret
directly.

  [3] Dogs in the east are only allowed inside the
house on sufferance (Gray). Cp. *Ugaritica* V no. 1
obv. *l.* 13, where (with a slight emendation) the
parallelism *klb*:*inr* again occurs.
  [4] Or 'from your house . . . even from your
chamber'.
  [5] Or 'even you'.
  [6] Cp. **17** vi 38 Num. xvi 29 Ps. lxxxii 6–7.
  [7] Lit. 'giving (of voice)'; cp. Gen. xlv 2.
  [8] Lit. 'father of my brightness'.
  [9] Sc. as place of pilgrimage and processions.
  [10] Cp. Ezek. xvii 3, 7 (of a vulture).
  [11] Cp. 2 Sam. vii 14 Ps. ii 7 lxxxix 27f.

špḥ (11) *lṭpn.wqdš.*	'the progeny of Latipan and the Holy one[1]?'
ʿl (12) *dbh.yʿrṣ.*	He entered into (the presence of) his father,
ybky (13) *wyšnn.*	he wept and gnashed his teeth,[2]
ytn.gh (14) *bky.*	he uttered his voice (in) weeping (and said):
bḥyk.dbn.dšmḥ	'We rejoiced[3] in your life, our father,
15 *blmtk.ngln.*	'we exulted (in) your immortality.
kklb (16) *bbtk.nʿtq.*	'(But now) like a dog we pass into your house,
kinr (17) *dp.ḫštk.*	'like a cur (through) the entrance to your chamber.
dp.db.kmtm (18) *tmtn.*	'Shall you then die, father, as men,
uḫštk.lntn (19) *ʿtq*	'or (shall) your chamber (be made over) to an old man's mourning,
bd.dtt db.ṣrry	'(to) a woman's chanting, my glorious father?
20 *ikm.yrgm.bn il* (21) *krt[.]*	'How can it be said (that) Keret is a son of El,
špḥ.lṭpn (22) *wqdš.*	'the progeny of Latipan and the Holy one?
uilm.tmtn	'Or shall gods die?[4]
23 *špḥ.lṭpn.lyḥ*	'Shall the progeny of Latipan not live?'
24 *wyʿny.krt.tʿ*	And the noble Keret answered:
25 *bn.dl.tbkn.*	'Son, weep not,
dl (26) *tdm.ly.*	'lament not for me;
dl tkl.bn (27) *qr.ʿnk.*	'exhaust not, son, the well of your eyes
mḥ.rišk (28) *udmʿt.*	'(and) the marrow of your head with tears.[5]
ṣḥ.dḥtk (29) *ttmnt.*	'Call your sister Thitmanat,
bt.ḥmḥḥ (30) *dnn.*	'a daughter whose . . . . . is strong;
tbkn.wtdm.ly ǵ	'let her weep and lament for me.
31 *[ǵ]zr.dl.trgm.ldḥtk*	'Hero, of a truth do you speak to your sister,
32 *[t]r[gm] l[ḥ.t]dm.*	'speak to [her] (and) let [her] lament;
dḥtk (33) *ydʿt.krhmt*	'(for) I know that your sister is pitiful.
34 *dl.tšt.bšdm[.]mmh*	'Let her of a truth set her clamour in the fields,
35 *bsmkt.ṣdt npšh*	'the issue of her throat in the heights.
36 *[t]mt[n].ṣbd.rbt* (37) *špš.*	'Do [you] await the darkening of the lady Shapash
wtgh.nyr (38) *rbt.*	'and the lighting of the illuminator of myriads (of stars),[6]
wrgm.ldḥtk (39) *ttmnt.*	'and tell your sister Thitmanat:
krtn.dbḥ (40) *dbḥ.*	' "Our Keret[7] is making a sacrifice,
mlk.ʿšr (41) *ʿšrt.*	' "the king is holding a banquet."
qḥ.dpk byd	'(Meanwhile do you) take hold of your nose with (your left) hand,
42 *[b]r[lt]k.bm.ymn*	'your [throat] with (your) right hand,
43 *lk.škn.ʿl ṣrrt*	'(and) go, stand by the lintel;[8]

---

12 *yʿrṣ* error for *yʿrb* (cp. ii 112)

14 *dšmḥ* perhaps error for *nšmḥ* (cp. ii 99 but cp. also *db.ṣrry*; 5, 19)

17: this and several other lines transgress the margin with col. ii

29 Ginsberg *ḥmḥ ⟨m⟩h* 'ardour, affection'

30 *ǵ* dittography (Herdner) or read *tʿ* (Driver)

31 Ginsberg

32 Driver (cp. 31, 26)

36 Virolleaud

42 Driver *a.* Virolleaud; also possible *[g]r[gr]k* (cp. 48)

---

[1] See at **2** iii 20.

[2] The appropriate Eng. metaphor; lit. 'sharpened (his tongue)'.

[3] Or 'would rejoice etc.'.

[4] Cp. Gen. iii 22 Ps. lxxxii 6–7.

[5] Cp. Jer. viii 23.

[6] I.e. Yarikh the moon-god; cp. **24 16**, 31.

[7] Perhaps this is simply a fuller form of the name; cp. Yatp(an) (**18** iv 6, 7).

[8] Lit. 'door-pivot', associated in Mesopotamia with various ritual acts.

44	*àdnk . šqrb*[- - - -]	'bring your lord[1] near [ ]
45	*bmgnk . wḫṛṣ . lkl*	'with your entreaty, and he will consent to all.'
46	*àpnk . ǵzr ìlḫù*	Thereupon the hero Elhu
47	[m]*rḥḥ . yìḫd . byd*	took his lance in (his left) hand,
48	[g]*rgrḥ . bm . ymn*	his gorge[2] with (his) right hand,
49	[w]*yqrb . trẓẓḥ*	[and] he approached . . . . .[3]
50	[t]*k . mqyḥ . wǵlm*	[As] he reached it he was hidden;
51	[à]*ḫtḥ . šìb . yṣàt .*	his sister was drawing water (and) came out (to look);
	mrḥḥ (52) *ltl yṣb .*	he stuck his lance in (its) holder
	pnh . tǵr (53) *yṣù .*	(and) turned away[4] his face from the gate.
	hlm . àḫḥ . tph	But[5] she recognized her brother;
54	[ksl]*h . làṛṣ . ttbr*	she burst her [flank] (falling) to earth,
55	[ˁl . pn .]*àḫḥ . tbky*	she wept [in the face of] her brother, (saying):
56	[àp . m]*ṛṣ . mlk*	'[Is then] the king ill,
57	[ùdw .]*krt . àdnk*	'[or] is Keret your lord [sick]?'
58	[wyˁny .]*ǵzr . ìlḫù*	[And] the hero Elhu [answered]:
59	[lmṛṣ .]*mṛṣ . mlk*	'The king is [not at all] ill,
60	[ldw . k]*rt . àdnk*	'Keret your lord [is not sick].
61	[krt . d]*bḥ . dbḥ*	'[Keret] is making a sacrifice,
62	[mlk .ˁ]*šr . ˁšrt*	'[the king] is holding a banquet.

Col. ii

63	ˁ[- - - - - - - - - -]	'[ ]
64	*b*[- - - - - - - - -]	'[ ]
65	*tb*[- - - - - - - -]	'do you [ ]
66	*w*[- - - - - - - - -]	'and [ ]
67	*pǵ*[t . ttmnt - - -]	'the girl [Thitmanat]
68	*lk*[- - - - - - - -]	'go [ ]
69	*kì*[- - - - - - - -]	'[ ]
70	*wy*[- - - - - - - -]	'and he [ ]
71	*my*[- - - - - - - -]	'Who [ ]
72	*àt*[t - - - - - - -]	'wife [ ]
73	*àḫk*[- - - - - - -]	'your brother [ ]
74	*tr . ḥ*[t - - - - - -]	'[ ]
75	*wtṣḥ*[- - - - - -]	and she cried [ ]
76	*tšqy*[- - - - - -]	she gave (him) to drink [ ]
77	*tr . ḫt*[- - - - - -]	[ ]

44 Watson [*bḥntk*] (cp. **17** i 17)
45 *ḫṛṣ* error for *yṛṣ* or so read (Ginsberg)
47: cp. 51
48–49 Herdner a. Virolleaud
50 Ginsberg; *mqyḥ* error for *mǵyḥ*
51 *šìb* error for *šìbt* (or masc. for fem.; cp. **14** 214)
54 Virolleaud (cp. **3** D 30)
55 Virolleaud
56–57 Driver (cp. ii 81–82)
58: cp. ii 83
59–60 Driver and Lipiński
61–62: cp. 39–41
ii 66–67: perhaps [*wtˁny*] (67) *pǵ*[t . ttmnt] (cp. **15** iii 12)
69: possibly *kì*[nr] (cp. i 2)

70: perhaps *wy*[ˁny . ǵzr . ìlḫù] (cp. i 58 ii 83);
    Herdner *wḫ*
72: cp. i 5   74: cp. 77

[1] Sc. El or Baal to ask his intercession.
[2] Watson translates 'branch' (Akk. *girgiru* or *engingiru*, a plant); he compares the enigmatic passage Ezek. viii 16–17 and Akkadian rituals in which the suppliant holds a branch to his nose and in his other hand grasps a stick or spear.
[3] Presumably a place near the gate associated with Elhu's ritual.
[4] Lit. 'put forth . . . (at) the gate' (G).
[5] Lit. 'Behold!'

78 *wmsk.tr*[- - - - -]   and a mixture [   ]

79 *tqrb.àḥ*[h.wtšàl]   She approached [her] brother [and asked]:

80 *lm.tbʿrn*[- - - -]   'Why do you put me off[1] [   ]

81 *mn.yrḥ.km*[rṣ]   'How many months (is it) that he has been ill,

82 *mn.kdw.kr*[t]   'how many (months) that Keret has been sick?'

83 *wyʿny.ġzr*[.ìlḥù]   And the hero [Elhu] answered:

84 *tlt.yrḥm.km*[rṣ]   'Three[2] months (it is) that he has been ill,

85 *àrbʿ.kdw.k*[rt]   'four[2] that Keret has been sick.

86 *mndʿ.krt.mġ*[y]   'Assuredly Keret is passing away,

87 *wqbr.tṣr.*   'and you must fashion a grave,

    q[br] (88) *tṣr.*   'you must fashion a grave

    trm.tnq[t]   'you must rise (and) . . . . . ;

89 *km.nkyt tġr*[h]   'like a strong-room's[3] (let) [its] gate (be),

90 *km.škllt.*[- - - -]   'like an enclosure's [   ]

91 *ʿrym.lbl*[.sk]   'bare without [covering]

92 bl[- -]*ny*[- - - -]   'without [   ]

93 *lbl.sk.w*[- - - - -]*h*   'without covering'. And [   ]

94 *ybmh.šbʿ*[- - - - -]   her brother-in-law. Seven (days) [   ]

95 *ġzr.ìlḥù.t*[- - -]*l*   the hero Elhu [   ]

96 *trm*[.]*tṣr.trm*[.t]*nqt*   she arose (and) fashioned, she arose (and) . . . . .

97 *tbky wtšnn.*   She wept and gnashed her teeth,

    [tt]n (98) *gh.bky.*   [she] uttered her voice (in) weeping (and said):

    bḥ[yk.à]*bn* (99) *nšmḥ.*   'We rejoiced in [your] life, our father,

    *bl*mtk.*ngln*   'we exulted (in) your immortality.

100 *kklb.*[b]*btk.nʿtq*   '(But now) like a dog we pass [into] your house,

101 *kìnr*[.àp.]*ḥštk*   'like a cur [(through) the entrance to] your chamber.

102 *àp àb kmtm.tmtn*   'Shall you then die, father, as men,

103 *ùḥštk.lbky ʿtq*   'or (shall) your chamber (be made over) to an old man's weeping,

104 *bd.àtt àb.ṣrry*   '(to) a woman's chanting, my glorious father?

105 *ùìlm.tmtn*   'Or shall gods die?

    špḥ (106) [l]*ṭpn.lyḥ.*   'Shall the progeny of Latipan not live?

    t[b]*kyk* (107) *àb.ġr.bʿl.*   'The rocks of Baal weep for you, father,

    ṣ[p]*n.ḥlm* (108) *qdš.*   'Zephon the holy circuit,

    nny.ḥ[l]m.*àdr*   'the vast circuit is groaning (for you)

109 *ḥl.rḥb.mk*[npt]   'the far-flung circuit.

110 *àp.krt bn*[m.ìl]   'Is then Keret the son of [El],

111 *špḥ.lṭp*n[.wqdš]   'the progeny of Latipan [and the Holy one]?'

112 *bkm.tʿr*[b.ʿl.àbh]   Forthwith[4] she entered [into (the presence of) her father],

113 *tʿrb.ḥ*[zr.krt]   she entered the court [of Keret];

---

79 [tšàl] (Ginsberg) or [tṣḥ] (Herdner)
80 Ginsberg [àḥ]; Lipiński [lmlk]
81–85: cp. i 56–60
86 Driver   87 Virolleaud
88: cp. 96
91: cp. 93
94 Virolleaud *šbʿ* [.*ymm*]
96: cp. 88
97–98: cp. i 13–14
100–101: cp. i 2–3

106–112: cp. i 6–12
107, 108: these lines transgress the margin with col. iii
108 *nny* error for *àny* (cp. i 8)
113 Driver *a.* Virolleaud and Ginsberg; [krt] or perhaps [àdnh] (cp. vi 29)

[1] Lit. 'remove, make away with me'.
[2] Cp. Amos i 3ff. Prov. xxx 15ff.
[3] Lit. 'treasury'.
[4] Possibly here 'Weeping'.

114 *bttm.t*[- - - - - -]   with two . . . . . she [   ]
115 *šknt.*[- - - - - - -]   she did stand [   ]
116 *bkym* [- - - - - - -]   weeping [   ]
117 *ġr.y*[- - - - - - - -]   rock(s) [   ]
118 *ydm.* [- - - - - - - - -] he lamented [   ]
119 *àpn.*[- - - - - - - -]   Thereat [   ]
120 [- -]b[- - - - - - - -]   [   ]

    . . (*ca. 3 ll.*) . .

     . . (*ca. 30 ll.*) . .   *Col. iii*

1 *yṣq.šm*[*n.šlm.bṣ*]   The oil [of a peace-offering] was poured [from a bowl].
2 *°n*[*.*]*tr.àrṣ.wšmm*   They[1] did see the quaking of the earth and the
                heavens;
3 *sb.lqṣm.àrṣ*   they did go round to the edges of the earth,[2]
4 *lksm.mìyt.*   to the limits of the watery region.
  °n (5) *làrṣ.m*[*t*]*r.b°l*   A source (of blessing)[3] to the earth was the rain of Baal
6 *wlšd.mṭr.°ly*   and to the field(s) the rain of the Most High;[4]
7 *n°m.làrṣ.mṭr.b°l*   a delight[5] to the earth was the rain of Baal
8 *wlšd.mṭr.°ly*   and to the field(s) the rain of the Most High,
9 *n°m*[*.*]*lḥṭt.b°n*   a delight to the wheat in the furrow,
10 *bm*[*.*]*nrt.ksmm*   (to) the spelt in the tilth,
11 *°l tlm.°trṭrm*   (to) the . . . . . on the ridge.
12 *nšù.*[*r*]*ìš.ḥrtm*   The ploughmen did lift up (their) head(s),
13 *lẓr*[*.*]*°db.dgn*   they that prepared the corn (did lift up their heads)
                on high;
kly (14) *lḥm.*[*b*]*dnhm.*   (for) the bread had failed [in] their bins,
kly (15) *yn.bḥmthm.*   the wine had failed in their skins,
k[*l*]*y* (16) *šmn bq*[- - - - - -] the oil had failed in their [cruses].[6]
17 *bt krt.t*[*bùn* - - -]   They [entered] the house of Keret
    . . (*ca. 18 ll.*) . .

     . . (*ca. 16 ll.*) . .   *Col. iv*

1 [   ] (2) *ìl.šm°.*   '[   ] El has heard.

---

iii Fewer word-dividers are clearly visible in this col.
than Herdner marks; several lines also appear to
finish on the edge of the tablet

1: cp. **3** B 31–32 *Ugaritica* V no. 3 rev. *l.* 4

2: cp. **4** v 83; Virolleaud *°n* °[*k*]*r* 'the troubling of'
(Hebr. *°ākar*)

4 *mìyt* (Virolleaud) or *mḥyt* (Herdner; cp. **5** vi 5),
perhaps alternative forms (cp. Arab. *mâhu* and
mâ'u 'water')

9 *b°n* (Virolleaud) or *bgn* (Herdner) 'in the garden
(farm?) land'

11 De Moor; Gray *°l tl*[*m*] *k°tr trm* 'on the ridge (it
was) like perfume of . . .' (Arab. *°aṭaru*)

12 Virolleaud

14 Ginsberg; Virolleaud [*b*]*°dnhm*

16 *bq*[*lthm*] (Ginsberg; cp. Arab. *qullatu* 'earthenware

bottle') or *bq*[*rbthm*] (Gray; cp. Arab. *qirbatu*
'water-skin') or *bq*[*b°thm*] (Herdner; cp. **19** 216)

17: cp. **15** iv 21 (or dual *tbàn*); the missing lines
include four on the bottom edge (cp. **14** 159–163)

[1] Sc. probably Gupn and Ugar, the messengers
of Baal, as in the similar passage **5** vi 3ff.

[2] Cp. Ps. xlviii 11 lxv 6.

[3] Or 'They saw on the earth etc.' Note the play
on the meanings of the words *°n* (2, 4, 9) and *ksm*
(4, 10).

[4] Cp. Ps. cxlvii 8 Job v 10. With the title of
Baal cp. Hebr. *°l*, *°lw* (1 Sam. ii 10 Ps. vii 11 lxviii
35).

[5] Cp. Gen. xlix 15.

[6] Cp. **1** Kgs. xvii 14 Ps. civ 14–15 Hab. iii 17.

ȧmrk ph[t] (3) kıl.
ḥkmt . ktr . lṭpn
4 ṣḥ . ngr . ıl . ılš
ıl[š] (5) wȧtth . ngrt[. ı̇]lht
6 khṣ . kmˁr[- - - - - -]
7 yṣḥ . ngr ıl . ılš
8 ılš . ngr . bt . bˁl
9 wȧtth . ngrt . ılht
10 wyˁn . lṭpn[.]ı̇l dpı̇[d]
11 šmˁ . lngr ı̇l ı̇l[š]
12 ı̇lš . ngr bt bˁl
13 wȧttk . ngrt . ıl[ht]
14 ˁl . ltkm . bnwn
15 lnḥnpt mšpy
16 tlt kmm trry
17 [- - -]lġr . gm . ṣḥ
18 [- - - - - -]r[-]m
. .   (ca. 27 ll.)   . .

'I see (that) you[1] are percipient like El,
'(that) you are wise like the bull Latipan.
'Call Elsh the steward[2] of El,
'Elsh and his wife the stewardess of the goddesses.'
Like . . . like . . . . [   ]
he called Elsh the steward of El,
Elsh the steward of Baal's house,
and his wife the stewardess of the goddesses.
And Latipan, kindly god, addressed (them):
'Hear, o Elsh, steward of El,
'Elsh steward of Baal's house
'and your wife stewardess of the goddesses;
'go up to the shoulder of the building,
'to the parapet of the tower;
'three . . . .
'[   ] to the rock (and) cry aloud
[   ]
. . . .

Col. v

1 ˁr[- - - - - - - - - -]
2 ˁr[- - - - - - - - - -]
3 ˁr[- - - - - - - - - -]
4 wyd[- - - - - - - - -]
5 bˁd[- - - - - - - -]
6 yȧtr[- - - - - - - -]
7 bdk . b[- - - - - - - -]
8 tnnth[- - - - - - -]
9 tltth[- - -]
[wyˁn] (10) lṭpn . [ı̇l . dpı̇d .]
[my] (11) bı̇lm . [ydy . mrṣ]
12 gršm . z̧[bln .]
[ı̇n . bı̇lm] (13) ˁnyh .
y[tny . ytlt] (14) rgm .
my . b[ı̇lm . ydy] (15) mrṣ .
grš[m . zbln]
16 ı̇n . bı̇lm . ˁ[nyh .]
[yrbˁ] (17) yḥmš . rgm .
[my . bı̇lm] (18) ydy . mrṣ .
g[ršm . zbln]

[   ]
[   ]
[   ]
'and let him [   ]
'behind [   ]
'let him proceed [   ]
'with your hand [   ]
she[3] did it a second time [   ]
she did it a third time [   ]
[And] Latipan [kindly god answered]:
'[Who] among the gods[4] [will banish (his) illness]
'(and) drive out[5] the plague?'
[None among the gods] did answer him.
[A second, a third time] he [repeated] (his) speech:
'Who among [the gods will banish] (his) illness
'(and) drive out [the plague]?'
None among the gods did answer [him].
[A fourth], a fifth time he repeated (his) speech:
'[Who among the gods] will banish[5] (his) illness
'(and) drive [out the plague]?'

2 ph[t]: cp. ḥkmt (3); perhaps arrange ȧmr kph[t]
3, 4: these lines finish on the edge of the tablet
4: perhaps ı̇l[š]⟨ . ngr . bt . bˁl⟩ (cp. 8)
5: cp. 9
6: cp. kmll . kḥṣ (1 iv 11)
16: or tltkm mtrry (Gordon and Gray) 'the three of
  you, my water-providers', requiring Elsh to have
  had two wives
18: perhaps r[ù]m 'wild ox' (cp. 6 i 19)
1: perhaps ˁr[b] 'There did enter . . .' (cp. 17 ii 26)

6: perhaps yȧtr[t] 'o Athirat' (cp. 15 iii 25)
9–20 Herdner a. Virolleaud (cp. 14, 21–23)

[1] Sc. probably Baal, requesting El's aid in the
curing of Keret.
[2] Or 'carpenter' (Akk. naggāru).
[3] Sc. Athirat or some other goddess approaching
El.
[4] Cp. Exod. xv 11.
[5] Prob. participles.

19 *in.bilm.ʿn[yh.]*   None among the gods did answer [him].
    ytdt (20) *ysbʿ.rgm.*   A sixth, a seventh time he repeated (his) speech:
    [my.]*bilm* (21) *ydy.mrṣ.*   '[Who] among the gods will banish (his) illness
    gršm zbln   '(and) drive out the plague?'
22 *in.bilm.ʿnyh*   None among the gods did answer him;[1]
23 *wyʿn.lṭpn.il.bpid*   and Latipan kindly god spoke;
24 *tb.bny.lmtb[t]km*   'Sit, my sons, in[2] your places,
25 *lkḥt.zblk[m.]*   'on the seats of your princely state.
    [à]*nk* (26) *iḥtrš.w[à]škn*   'I myself will cast a spell and will create,
27 *àškn.ydt.[m]rṣ*   'I will create (what) will banish (his) illness
    gršt (28) *zbln.*   '(and) drive out the plague.'
    r[t.ydh].ymlù   He filled [his hand] with mud,[3]
29 *nʿm.rt[.ymn.]*   [(his) right hand] with a fair piece[4] of mud;
    yqrṣ (30) *dt.bpḫ[- - - -]mḫt*   he pinched into shape[5] her who [   ]
31 [- - - - - - - - - - -]*tnn*   [   ] a dragon
32 [- - - - - - - - - -]*tnn*   [   ] a dragon
    .   .   (gap of 4–5 *ll.*)   .   .   .   .
38 *bi*[- - - - - - - - - -]   [   ]
39 *lt*[- - - - - - - - -]   [   ]
40 *ks*[.yiḫd.il.byd]   [El took] a cup [in (his left) hand],
41 *kr*[pn.bm.ymn]   a flagon [in (his) right hand], (saying):
42 *àt.š*[ʿtqt - - - - -]   'You, Shaʿtaqat [   ]
43 *šʿd*[- - - - - - - -]   'remove [   ]
44 *rt.š*[ʿtqt - - - - -]   ' .   .   .   .   Shaʿtaqat [   ]
45 *ʿtr*[- - - - - - - -]   'scent [   ]
46 *bp.š*[ʿtqt - - - - -]   'in (your) mouth, Shaʿtaqat [   ]
47 *il.pd*[- - - - - - - -]   El [   ]
48 *ʿrm*[.di.mh.]   '[Fly in stealth] to[6] the city,
    [pdrm] (49) *di.š*[rr.]   'fly [in secret to the town].
    [ḫṭm.ʿmt]   '[Do you tap (him) with (your) wand];
50 *mr*[ṣ.ypṭr.ptm]   'the illness [will escape] (from his) temples,
51 *zb*[ln.ʿl.riš]   'the plague [from his head].
52 *t*[tb.trḥṣ.nn] (53) *b*[dʿt.]   '[(Then) do] you [sit down (and) wash him (clean)] of
                                                 [sweat]
    [- - - - - - -]   '[   ]
    .   .   (*ca.* 8 *ll.*)   .   .   .   .

1   [m]*t.dm.ḫt.*   *Col. vi*
    šʿtqt dt. (2) *li.*   'Death, truly be shattered!
    wttbʿ.šʿtqt   'Shaʿtaqat, truly be victorious!'
                                             And Shaʿtaqat departed;

23 *bpid* error for *dpid*   48–53: cp. vi 6–10
24–25 Virolleaud   vi 1 [*m*]*t*; cp. 13; *dt.* error for *dm* or so read
26–27 Herdner
28–29 Ginsberg; the reading *rt* is very uncertain   [1] Cp. 1 Kgs. xviii 29 Job v 1.
30 *dt* or *dm* (cp. vi 1); *mḫt* or *.ḫt* (cp. vi 1)   [2] Or 'Return, my sons, to'.
40–41: cp. **15** ii 16–18   [3] Cp. **17** i 34; or 'dung' as in Arabic (*rawtu*).
42 Ginsberg (cp. vi 1)   [4] I.e. a piece of suitable size or texture.
44: cp. 42   [5] Cp. Gilgamesh I ii 34 (*ANET* p. 74) Job
45 Ginsberg and Gray *ʿtr*[*ptm*] after vi 8   xxxiii 6.
46 Ginsberg   [6] Or 'from' or 'over cities, towns' (so in vi 6–7).

3 *bt.krt.bù.tbù*   she indeed went into the house of Keret;

4 *bkt.tgly.wtbù*   she did weep (as) she entered and went in,

5 *nṣrt.tbù.pnm*   she did sob (as) she went in within.

6 *ʿrm.tdù.mh*   She flew in stealth to the city,

7 *pdrm.tdù.šrr*   she flew in secret to the town.

8 *ḥtm.tˁmt.*   She tapped (him) with (her) wand;

    ⟨*mrṣ.*⟩*pṭr ptm*   ⟨the illness⟩ did escape (from his) temples,

9 *zbln.ˁl.rìsh*   the plague from his head.

10 *wttb.trḥṣ.nn.bdˁt*   And she sat down (and) washed him (clean) of sweat.

11 *npšh.llḥm.tptḥ*   His throat opened for food,

12 *brlth.ltrm*   his gorge for a meal.

13 *mt.dm.ḥt.*   (So) death was truly shattered,

    sˁtqt (14) *dm.làn.*   Shaˁtaqat was truly victorious.

    wypqd (15) *krt.tˁ.*   And the noble Keret gave command,

    yšù.gh (16) *wyṣḥ.*   he lifted up his voice and cried:

    šmˁ.lmtt (17) *ḥry.*   'Hear, o maiden Huray;

    ṭbḥ.ìmr (18) *wìlḥm.*   'Slay a sheep and I will eat (it),

    mgt.wìtrm   'a fatling and I will consume (it).'

19 *tšmˁ.mtt.ḥry*   The maiden Huray heard,

20 *tṭbḥ.ìmr.wlḥm*   she slew a sheep and he did eat (it),

21 *mgt.wytrm.*   a fatling and he consumed (it).

    hn.ym (22) *wtn.*   Behold! a day and a second (passed)

    ytb.krt.lˁdh   (and) Keret sat down on his dais,

23 *ytb.lksì mlk*   he sat down on the throne of (his) kingdom,

24 *lnḥt.lkḥt.drkt*   on the cushion on the seat of (his) dominion.[1]

25 *àp.yṣb.ytb.bhkl*   Yaṣṣib too sat in the palace,

26 *wywsrnn.ggnh*   and his heart instructed him:[2]

27 *lk.làbk.yṣb.*   'Go to your father, Yaṣṣib,

    lk (28) [*là*]*bk.wrgm.*   'go [to] your father and speak,

    tny (29) *lk*[*rt.àdnk.*]   'repeat (your speech) to Keret [your lord], (saying):

    ìštm[ˁ] (30) *wtqġ*[.*ùdn.*]   ' "Hearken and let [(your) ear] be attentive.

    [*kġz.ġzm*] (31) *tdbr.*   ' "[While bandits raid] you turn (your) back,

    w[*ġ*]*rm.*[*ttwy*]   ' "and [you entertain] feuding rivals.

32 *šqlt.bġlt.ydk*   ' "You have been brought down by your failing power.[3]

33 *ltdn.dn.àlmnt*   ' "You do not judge the cause of the widow,[4]

34 *lttpṭ.tpṭ.qṣr npš*   ' "you do not try the case of the importunate.[5]

35 *km.àḥt.ˁrš.mdw*   ' "Because you have become brother to a bed of sickness,[6]

36 *ànšt.ˁrš.zbln*   ' "companion to a bed of plague,

37 *rd.lmlk.àmlk*   ' "come down from the (throne of your) kingdom

6 *mh* (Herdner); Virolleaud *mt*; Ginsberg *mì*, perhaps error for *mìt* 'over a hundred cities' (Driver)

8 ⟨*mrṣ*⟩; cp. v 50; *pṭr ptm* (Virolleaud) or *ˁṭrptm* (Ginsberg and Gray after v 45) 'wrapping, bandage' (lit. 'surrounding of the brow'; cp. Hebr. *ˁāṭar*)

14 *làn* error for *làt* (cp. 2)

20 Virolleaud *w*⟨*y*⟩*lḥm*

28: cp. 39–40

29 [*àdnk*] (Herdner); *ìštm*[ˁ]: cp. 42

30–31: cp. 42–44

[1] See at **1** iv 24–25.

[2] Cp. **4** v 66 Ps. xvi 7; or 'his *jinn* or personal demon' (Kutscher).

[3] Lit. 'the drooping of your hand(s)'.

[4] Cp. **17** v 7–8 Deut. x 18 Isa. i 17 Job xxix
12–13 Ben Sira iv 10 *ANET* p. 178 (Hammurabi).

[5] Cp. Judg. xvi 16.

[6] Cp. Job xvii 14 Ps. xli 4.

38 *ldrktk . ảtb . ản*

(that) I may be king,
' "from (the seat of) your dominion (that) even I may sit (on it)" '

39 *ytb͑ . yṣb ǵlm .*
   ͑l (40) ảbh . y͑rb .
   yšủ gh (41) wyṣḥ .
   šm͑ m͑ . lkrt (42) t͑ .
   ỉštm͑ . wtqǵ ủdn
43 *kǵz . ǵzm . tdbr*
44 *wǵrm . ttwy .*
   šqlt (45) bǵlt . ydk .
   ltdn (46) dn . ảlmnt .
   lttpṭ (47) ṭpṭ qṣr . npš .
   ltdy (48) tšm . ͑l . dl .
   lpnk (49) ltšlḥm . ytm .
   b͑d (50) kslk . ảlmnt .
   km (51) ảḥt . ͑rš . mdw .

   ảnšt (52) ͑rš . zbln .
   rd . lmlk (53) ảmlk .

   ldrktk . ảtb . (54) ản .

   wy͑ny . krt t͑ .
   ytbr (55) ḥrn . ybn .
   ytbr . ḥrn (56) rỉšk[.]
   ͑ttrt . šm . b͑l (57) qdqdr
   tqln . bgbl (58) šntk .
   bhpnk . wt͑n

The lad Yaṣṣib departed,
he entered into (the presence of) his father,
(and) he lifted up his voice and cried:
'Hear, I beseech you, o noble Keret,
'hearken and let (your) ear be attentive.
'While bandits raid you turn (your) back,
'and you entertain feuding rivals.
'You have been brought down by your failing power.
'You do not judge the cause of the widow,
'you do not try the case of the importunate.
'You do not banish the extortioners of the poor,[1]
'you do not feed the orphan before your face
'(nor) the widow behind your back.[2]
'Because you have become brother to a bed of sickness,
'companion to a bed of plague,
'come down from the (throne of your) kingdom (that) I may be king,
'from (the seat of) your dominion (that) even I may sit (on it).'
And the noble Keret answered:
'May Horon[3] break, o my son,
'may Horon break your head,
'(may) Athtart-name-of-Baal[3] (break) your crown!
'May you fall down at the frontier of your years,[4]
'with your hands empty[5] and (so) be humbled!'

E. *spr ỉlmlk t͑y*

The scribe is Elimelek, the master.

---

38 *ảtb . ản* (Herdner; cp. 53–54) or *ảtbnn* (Virolleaud)
54: this line transgresses the margin with col. v
57 *qdqdr* error for *qdqdk*

[1] Cp. Amos v 11.

[2] With *ll.* 48–50 cp. Job xxii 7–9   xxxi 16–17   Isa. x 2   Ps. lxxxii 2–4   Ben Sira xxxv 13–14.
[3] On these deities see p. 4 notes 5, 6.
[4] Alternatively 'from the peak of your loftiness' (Driver; Arab. *jabalu*; Hebr. *šᵉnôt* in Prov. v 9).
[5] Lit. 'the hollow of your hands' (Lipiński).

17

Col. i

. . . .

1 [åpnk] (2) [dnil.mt.rp]ì.
ȧpn.ǵz[r] (3) [mt.hrnmy.]
ȧzr ìlm.ylḥm

4 [ȧzr.yšqy.]bn.qdš.
yd (5) [ṣth.yʿl.]wyškb.
yd (6) [mìzrt.]pynl.
ḥn[.]ym (7) [wtn.]
[ȧzr.]ìlm.dnìl.

8 [ȧzr.ìlm.]ylḥm.
ȧzr (9) [yšqy.b]n.qdš
ṭlt rbʿ ym

10 [ȧzr.ì]lm.dnìl.
ȧzr (11) [ìlm.y]lḥm.
ȧzr.yšqy bn (12) [qdš.]
[ḫ]mš[.]tdt.šym.
ȧzr (13) [ìlm].dnìl.
ȧzr.ìlm.ylḥm

14 [ȧzr.]yšqy.bn qdš.
yd.ṣth (15) [dn]ìl.
yd.ṣth.yʿl.wyškb

16 [yd.]mìzrt pyln.
mk bšbʿ.ymm

17 [w]yqrb.bʿl.bḥnth.
ȧbynt (18) [d]nìl.mt.rpì
ȧnḫ.ǵzr (19) [mt.]hrnmy.
dìn.bn.lh (20) km.ȧḫh.
w.šrš.km.ȧryh

[Thereupon Daniel, man of Rapiu],
thereat the hero, [man of He-of-Harnam],
gave the gods . . . . .[1] to eat,
[gave] the holy ones[2] [. . . . . to drink].
He put aside [his cloak, he ascended] and lay down,
he put aside [his loincloth], and so he passed the night[3].
Behold! a day [and a second]
Daniel (gave) the gods [. . . . .],
he gave [the gods . . . . .] to eat,
[he gave] the holy ones . . . . [to drink].
A third, a fourth day
Daniel (gave) the gods [. . . . .],
[he] gave [the gods] . . . . to eat,
he gave the [holy] ones . . . . to drink.
A fifth, a sixth day
Daniel (gave) [the gods] . . . . . ,
he gave the gods . . . . . to eat,
he gave the holy ones [. . . . .] to drink.
Daniel put aside his cloak,
he put aside his cloak, he ascended[4] and lay down,
[he put aside] his loincloth, and so he passed the night.
Then on the seventh day
Baal drew near with his supplication:
'The misery[5] of Daniel, man of Rapiu![6]
'The groaning of the hero, [man] of He-of-Harnam![7]
'For he has no son like his brothers,
'nor offspring like his kinsmen.[8]

1–3: cp. ii 27–29
2 ȧpn perhaps error for ȧphn (cp. ii 28 v 14, 34)
4: cp. 11   5–6: cp. 15–16
6 ynl error for yln (cp. 16)
7ff.: cp. 22–23
9: this and several other lines transgress the margin with col. ii
12 šym: the scribe apparently began to write šbʿ, then erased it
16: cp. 14, 15
17 [w] (Virolleaud); ȧbynt or ȧbyn t[-], the final letter transgressing the margin, or possibly ȧbynm

[1] Precise meaning of ȧzr unknown; it should not be too hastily connected with the disputed Punic sacrificial term 'zrm, which may be Berber in origin.

Some translate 'ate the . . . of the gods etc.' (G)

[2] Or 'the sons of the Holy one' (Athirat); see at 2 iii 19.

[3] For biblical allusions to the practice of incubation see 1 Sam. iii 1ff. Ps. xvii 3, 15; cp. also 14 31ff.

[4] Perhaps to a special cell or loft.

[5] Or (see apparatus) 'Miserable is . . . groaning is'; or 'because of his compassion for the misery of etc.' or 'because of his (Daniel's) plea, (because of) the misery of etc.', the address of Baal then beginning at l. 21.

[6] Lit. 'the shade'; see p. 26 note 4.

[7] Perhaps Hermel east of Byblos in Phoenicia (Albright); cp. the biblical epithet Shaddai, 'He-of-the-mountain' (Cross), applied to El.

[8] Cp. Num. xxvii 4 2 Sam. xviii 18 Isa. xi 10.

21 *bl.ìt.bn.lh.wm àḥh.*	'(Because) he has not[1] a son like his brothers,
wšrš (22) *km.àryh.*	'nor offspring like his kinsmen,
ùzrm.ìlm.ylḥm	'he gives the gods . . . . . to eat,
23 *ùzrm.yšqy.bn.qdš*	'he gives the holy ones . . . . . to drink.
24 *ltbrknn ltr.ìl àby*	'Do you indeed bless him, o bull El my father,
25 *tmrnn.lbny.bnwt*	'do you fortify him, o creator of creatures,[2]
26 *wykn.bnh bbt.*	'that he may have a son in (his) house,
šrš.bqrb (27) *hklh.*	'offspring within his palace;
nṣb.skn.ìlìbh.	'one to stand as steward of his father's god,[3]
bqdš (28) *ztr.ʿmh.*	'in the sanctuary as . . . . . of his ancestors;[4]
làrṣ.mšṣù.qṭrh	'one to free his spirit[5] from the earth,
29 *lʿpr.žmr.àtrh.*	'to protect his tomb[6] from the dust;
ṭbq.lḥt (30) *nìṣh.*	'one to shut the jaws[7] of his detractors,
grš d.ʿšy.lnh	'to drive away those who turn against him;[8]
31 *àḥd.ydh.bškrn.*	'one to hold his hand in drunkenness,
mʿmsh (32) [k]*šbʿ yn.*	'to carry him [when] filled with wine;[9]
spù.ksmh.bt.bʿl	'one to supply his (offering of) corn in the house of Baal,
33 [wm]*nth bt.ìl.*	'[and] his portion[10] in the house of El;
ṯḫ.ggh.bym (34) [tì]*ṭ.*	'one to plaster his roof in the [muddy] season,[11]
rḥṣ.npṣh.bym.rt	'to wash his garments when the weather is foul[12].'
35 [- - y]*ìḥd.ìl ʿbdh.*	[ ] El took his servant,
ybrk (36) [dnì]*l mt rpì.*	he blessed [Daniel], man of Rapiu,
ymr.ġzr (37) [mt.hr]*nmy*	fortified the hero, [man] of He-of-Harnam, (saying):
npš.yḥ.dnìl (38) [mt.rp]*ì*	'In spirit let Daniel, [man of Rapiu], revive,
brlt[.]*ġzr.mt hrnmy*	'in breath the hero, man of He-of-Harnam.
39 [- - - - -]*.hw.mḥ.*	'Let him [ ] vigour;
lʿršh.yʿl (40) [- - - - - -].	'his couch let him mount [ ];
bm.nšq.àtth (41) [- - - - -]	'as he kisses his wife [ ],
bḥbqh.ḥmḥmt	'as he embraces her let her become pregnant,[13]
42 [- - - - - -]*kn ylt.*	'[ ] let her be with child;[13]
ḥmḥmt (43) [àtt.mt.r]*pì.*	'let [the wife of the man of] Rapiu become pregnant,
wykn.bnh (44) [bbt.]	'so that he may have a son [in (his) house],

21 *wm* error for *km*
32–34: cp. ii 6–7, 20–22
35 Virolleaud [*byd.y*]; Gaster [*bkm.y*]; Dijkstra and
De Moor [*ks.y*]*ìḥd.ìl bdh* (ʿ being an unintentional
stroke; cp. **15** ii 16–17)
39 *hw.mḥ*: cp. *hy*[.]*mḥ* (**19** 201)
40–43: cp. **23** 51–53, 56
42 *ylt* from *yldt* (cp. **23** 53; *yrt* **5** i 6)
43: cp. 40
44ff.: cp. 26ff.

1 Cp. Hebr. *'ên yeš* (1 Sam. xxi 9   Ps. cxxxv 17).
2 Cp. Akk. *bān binûti*, a title of Nebo. On El as
Baal's 'father' see p. 5 note 2. With the passage cp.
15 ii 12ff.
3 Daniel's ancestral or clan deity; cp. the patriarchal 'god(s) of the fathers'. Alternatively 'one to set
up the effigy of the god of his fathers' (Akk. *šiknu*), in
which case compare perhaps the biblical Teraphim
(Judg. xvii 5).
4 Or 'in the sanctuary (to set up) the sun-emblem
of his kindred deity' (Tsevat; Hittite *šittar(i)*; West
Semitic *ʿm* in proper names).
5 Cp. **18** iv 26; alternatively 'his incense'.
6 Cp. *mqm* (Hadad inscr. *l.* 14).
7 Cp. Ps. lxiii 12.
8 Cp. Ezek. xxix 20 (Driver); or 'those who abuse
his guests' (√*lw/yn*; Gray; cp. Gen. xix 1–11 Judg. xix
22–26).
9 Cp. Isa. li 18.
10 Cp. 1 Sam. i 4   2 Chron. xxxi 3.
11 When the rains come the Arab peasant rolls his
roof with a light limestone roller (Gray). Alternatively
'when it leaks'.
12 Or 'when they are soiled'; lit. 'on the day of
dirt'.
13 Perfects with jussive sense; the first may be a
noun '(let there be) pregnancy' (cp. **23** 51).

[šrš] . *bqrb hkllh*
45 [nṣb . skn . ì]*lìbh* .
   bqdš (46) [ztr . ʿmh.]
   [là]rṣ . *mṣṣù* (47) [qtrh.]
   [lʿpr . ž]*mr . đ*[t]*rh*
48 [ṭbq . lḥt . nìṣh.]
   [gr]*š . đ . ʿšy* (49) [lnh.]
   [åḥd . ydh . bškrn]
50 [mʿmsh . kšbʿ . yn.]
   [spù] (51) [ksmh . bt . bʿl.]

   [wmnth] (52) [bt . ìl.]
   [ṭḫ . ggh . bym . tìt]
53 [rḥṣ . npšh . bym . rt.]

   . . . .

   . . . .
 3*[wykn . bnk] (2*) [bbt.]
   [šrš . bqrb . hklk]
 1*[nṣb . skn . ìlìbk.]
   [bqdš] (1) z[tr . ʿmk.]
   [làrṣ . mṣṣù . qtrk]
 2 *l . ʿpr . žm*[r . åtrk.]
   [ṭbq] (3) *lḥt . nìṣk*.
   gr[š . đ . ʿšy . lnk]
 4 *spù . ksmk . bt .* [bʿl.]

   [wmntk] (5) *bt . ìl.*
   åḥd . ydk[.]*b*[škrn]
 6 *mʿmsk . kšbʿt . yn.*
   ṭ[ḫ] (7) *ggk . bym . tìṭ.*
   rḥṣ (8) *npšk . bym rt.*
   bùnì[l] (9) *pnm . tšmḫ.*
   wʿl . yṣhl pì[t]
10 *yprq . lṣb . wyṣḥq*
11 *pʿn . lhdm . yṭpd.*
   yšù (12) *gh . wyṣḥ.*
   åtbn . ånk (13) *wånḫn.*
   wtnḫ . bìrty (14) *npš.*
   kyld . bn . ly . km (15) *åḫy.*
   wšrš . km åryy
16 *nṣb . skn . ìlìby.*
   bqdš (17) *ztr . ʿmy.*
   ⟨ *làrṣ . mṣṣù . qtry .* ⟩

'[offspring] within his palace;
'[one to stand as steward] of his father's god,
'in the sanctuary [as . . . . . of his ancestors];
'one to free [his spirit from] the earth,
'to protect his tomb [from the dust];
'[one to shut the jaws of his detractors],
'[to drive away] those who turn [against him];
'[one to hold his hand in drunkenness],
'[to carry him when filled with wine];
'[one to supply his (offering of) corn in the house of
    Baal],
'[and his portion in the house of El];
'[one to plaster his roof in the muddy season],
'[to wash his garments when the weather is foul].'

   . . . .

Col. ii

   . . . .
'[and you will have a son in (your) house],
'[offspring within your palace];
'[one to stand as steward of your father's god],
'[in the sanctuary] as . . . . . [of your ancestors];
'[one to free your spirit from the earth],
'to protect [your tomb] from the dust;
'[one to shut] the jaws of your detractors,
'to drive [away those who turn against you]
'one to supply your (offering of) corn in the house of
    [Baal],
'[and your portion] in the house of El;
'one to hold your hand in [drunkenness],
'to carry you when filled with wine;
'one to plaster your roof in the muddy season,
'to wash your garments when the weather is foul.'
Daniel's face lit up with joy
and (his) brow above gleamed;[1]
he parted (his) throat and laughed;[2]
he placed (his) feet on the footstool,
he lifted up his voice and cried:
'Even I may sit down and be at ease,
'and my soul within me may take its ease;[3]
'for a son's to be born to me[4] like my brothers
'and offspring like my kinsmen;
'one to stand as steward of my father's god,
'in the sanctuary as . . . . . of my ancestors;
'⟨one to free my spirit from the earth⟩,

ii 3*ff.: cp. i 26ff.
   3 [lnk] or possibly [lk]
   4ff.: note the change of order (cp. i 31ff.   ii 19ff.)
   8 *bùnì*[l] error for *bdnì*[l] (Ginsberg)
   17: phrase restored (cp. i 28)

[1] Cp. Ps. civ 15.
[2] Cp. Gen. xxi 6. For an alternative rendering of
the first phrase see at **4** iv 28.
[3] Cp. **6** iii 18–19   Gen. v 29.
[4] Cp. Isa. ix 5.

l*pr[.]žmr.àtr[y] 'to protect [my] tomb from the dust;
18 ṭbq lḥt.nìṣy. 'one to shut the jaws of my detractors,
   grš (19) dᵉšy.ln. 'to drive away those who turn against me;
   àḥd.ydy.bš (20) krn. 'one to hold my hand in drunkenness,
   mᵉmsy kšbᵗt yn 'to carry me when filled with wine;
21 spù.ksmy.bt.bᶜl 'one to supply my (offering of) corn in the house of Baal

   [w]mn[t] (22) y.bt.ìl. '[and] my portion in the house of El;
   ṭḫ.ggy.bym.ṭiṭ 'one to plaster my roof in the muddy season,
23 rḥṣ.npṣy.bym.rt 'to wash my garments when the weather is foul.'
24 dn.ìl.bth.ymǵyn Daniel proceeded to his house,
25 yštql.dnìl.lhklh Daniel betook himself to his palace.
26 ᶜrb.bbth.ktrt. There did enter into his house the Kotharat,
   bnt (27) hll.snnt. the swallow-like[1] daughters of the crescent moon.[2]
   àpnk.dnìl (28) mt.rpi. Thereupon Daniel, man of Rapiu,
   àp.hn.ǵzr.mt (29) hrnmy. thereat the hero, man of He-of-Harnam,
   àlp.yṭbḥ.lkt (30) rt. slaughtered an ox for the Kotharat.
   yšlḥm[.]ktrt.wy (31) ššq. He fed the Kotharat and gave drink to
   bnt.[hl]l.snnt the swallow-like daughters of the crescent moon.
32 hn.ym.wtn. Behold! a day and a second
   yšlḥm (33) ktrt.wyš[š]q. he fed the Kotharat and gave drink to
   bnt.hl[l] (34) snnt. the swallow-like daughters of the crescent moon.
   tlt[.r]bᶜ ym. A third, a fourth day
   yšl (35) ḥm ktrt[.]wyššq he fed the Kotharat and gave drink to
36 bnt hll[.]snnt. the swallow-like daughters of the crescent moon.
   ḥmš (37) tdt.ym. A fifth, a sixth day
   yšlḥm.k[t]rt (38) wy[ššq]. he fed the Kotharat and gave drink to
   bnt.hll.snnt the swallow-like daughters of the crescent moon.
39 mk.bšb[ᶜ.]ymm. Then on the seventh day
   tbᶜ.bbth (40) ktrt. the Kotharat did depart from his house,
   bnt.hll.snnt the swallow-like daughters of the crescent moon,
41 [y]d[ᶜ]t.nᶜmy.ᶜrš.h[r]m those [artful] in pleasure(s) of the bed of conception,
42 ysmsmt.ᶜrš.ḫlln delight(s) of the bed of childbirth.
43 ytb.dnìl.[ys]pr yrḫh Daniel sat down (and) [counted] her months.[3]
44 yrs.y[- - - - - - - -] A month [(passed)   ]
45 tlt.rb[ᶜ - - - - - - - - -] a third, a fourth [(month)   ]
46 yrḥm.ymǵy[- - - - - -] month passed [   ]
47 ḫ[- -]r[   ] [   ]

  . . . .

19: perhaps read ln⟨y⟩; cp. the lines of poetry in 15–18

24: note dn.ìl for dnìl

28 àp.hn: cp. àphn (v 14, 34 **19** 20)

41 [y]d[ᶜ]t (Virolleaud); h[r]m (Dijkstra)

43 [ys]pr; Herdner [ls]pr; the p is very uncertain

44 yrs perhaps error for yrḫ with thereafter y[mǵy] (cp. 46)

[1] Lit. 'the swallows', so-called because these birds are commonly associated with domestic bliss and fertility (Driver).

[2] Hardly in view of **24** 41–42 'the daughters of melody, praise' (though cp. Eccles. xii 4). The moon is generally regarded in mythology and popular belief as propitious to child-birth.

[3] I.e. the months till the child was born (cp. Job xxxix 2).

Col. v

. . . .

1 [   ](2)[- - - -]   [   ]
àbl.qšt tmn[-]   'I shall bring the bow of eight (parts),[1]
3 àšrb& lsquo;[.]qṣ‘t.   'I shall have four times as many arrows.'[2]
  whn šb[‘] (4) bymm.   And behold! on the seventh day,
  àpnk.dnil.mt (5) rpi.   thereupon Daniel, man of Rapiu,
  à⟨p⟩hn.ġzr.mt.hrnm[y]   thereat the hero, man of He-of-Harnam,
6 ytšu.ytb.bàp.tġr.   raised himself up (and) sat at the entrance of the gate[3]
  tḥt (7) àdrm.dbgrn.   beneath the trees which were by[4] the threshing-floor;[5]
  ydn (8) dn.àlmnt.   he judged the cause of the widow,
  ytpṭ.tpṭ.ytm   tried the case of the orphan.[6]
9 bnši ‘nh.wyphn.   Lifting his eyes, he saw
  bàlp (10) šd.rbt.kmn.   a thousand tracts away, ten thousand spaces,
  hlk.ktr (11) ky‘n.   the coming of Kothar surely he sighted
  wy‘n.tdrq.ḫss   and he sighted the swift approach of Khasis.
12 hlk.qšt.ybln.   Behold! he carried the bow,
  hl.yš (13) rb‘.qṣ‘t.   lo! he had four times as many arrows.
  àpnk.dnil (14) mt.rpi.   Thereupon Daniel, man of Rapiu,
  àphn.ġzr.mt (15) hrnmy.   thereat the hero, man of He-of-Harnam,
  gm.làtth.kyṣḥ   surely cried aloud to his wife:
16 šm‘.mtt.dnty.   'Hear, maiden Danatay,
  ‘d[b] (17) imr.bpḫd.   'make ready a lamb from the youngling(s)
  lnpš.ktr (18) wḫss.   'for the desire of Kothar-and-Khasis,
  lbrlt.hyn d (19) ḥrš yd.   'for the appetite of Heyan, skilled worker by hand;
  šlḥm.ššqy. (20) ilm   'feed, give drink to the gods,[7]
  sàd.kbd.hmt.   'wait upon (and) do them[7] honour,
  b‘l (21) ḥkpt.il.klh.   'the lord(s)[7] of all broad Memphis.'[8]
  tšm‘ (23) mtt.dnty.   The maiden Danatay heard,
  t‘db.imr (23) bpḫd.   she made ready a lamb from the youngling(s)
  lnpš.ktr.wḫss   for the desire of Kothar-and-Khasis,
24 lbrlt.hyn.dḥrš (25) ydm.   for the appetite of Heyan, skilled worker by hand.
  àḫr.ymġy.ktr (26) wḫss.   Afterward Kothar-and-Khasis arrived;[7]
  bd.dnil.ytnn (27) qšt.   he gave the bow into the hand of Daniel,
  lbrkh.y‘db (28) qṣ‘t.   he left the arrows upon his knees.
  àpnk.mtt.dnty   Thereupon the maiden Danatay
29 tšlḥm.tššqy ilm   fed, gave drink to the gods,
30 tsàd.tkbd.hmt.   she waited upon (and) did them honour,
  b‘l (31) ḥkpt il.klh.   the lord(s) of all broad Memphis.
  tb‘.ktr (32) làhlh.   Kothar did depart to[9] his tent,
  hyn.tb‘.lmš (33) knth.   Heyan did depart to his dwelling.
  àpnk.dnil.m[t] (34) rpi.   Thereupon Daniel, man of Rapiu,

2 tmn: cp. **19** 5
5 à⟨p⟩hn: cp. **14**, 34; ii 28

[1] Perhaps referring to the parts or layers of a composite bow (cp. vi 20ff.).
[2] Lit. 'make four(fold)'. 'Arrows' rather than 'arc' in view of vi 23.
[3] Where justice was dispensed in eastern cities (e.g. Deut. xxi 19 Amos v 10, 12, 15).

[4] Lit. 'mighty ones'; cp. Ezek. xvii 23 (of a cedar). Possibly 'below the notables who were (sitting) in' (Gordon).
[5] Cp. 1 Kgs. xxii 10 Mishna *Sanhedrin* iv 3.
[6] See **16** vi 33–34 and references there.
[7] Note the oscillation between sing. and dual; see p. 9 note 1.   [8] See at **3** F 12ff.
[9] Probably not in view of **15** iii 18–19 'from his (Daniel's) tent etc.'.

ảphn . ǧzr . m[t] (35) *hrnmy .* | the reat the hero, man of He-of-Harnam,
qšt . yqb . [- - -] (36) *rk .* | . . . . the bow [   ],
ʿl . ảqht . kyq[- - -] | over Aqhat surely he [   ], (saying):
37 *prʿm . ṣdk . ybn*[- - -] | 'The choicest of your game, o son [   ],
38 *prʿm . ṣdk . hn* pr[ʿm] | 'the choicest of your game, behold! the [choicest]
39 *ṣd . bhk*lh[- - - - - - -] | 'of (your) game in his temple[1] [   ]

. . . .

Col. vi

. . . .

1 [   ] | [   ]
2 [- - - - - - - - - -l]*ḥm*[- - - - -] | [   ] food [   ]
3 [- - - - - - - - - - -] . *ảy* š[- - - -] | [   ]
4 [- - - - - - -] | [   ]
[*bḥ*]*rb . mlḥ*[t . qṣ] (5) [mrỉ .] | [With] a salted knife [they did carve a fatling];
[*tšty . krpnm*] . *yn .* | [they drank flagons] of wine,
bks . ḫ[*rṣ*] (6) [dm . ʿṣm .] | from cups of [gold the blood of trees]
[- - - - -]*n . krpn . ʿl .* [k]*rpn* | [   ] flagon upon flagon
7 [- - - - - - - -]*qym . ktʿl* | [   ] surely they ascended;
trt (8) [- - - - - - - - -] . | new wine [   ]
yn . ʿšy lḥbš | wine fit[2] for a ruler [   ]
9 [- - - - - - - - -]*ḥtn*[.]*qn . yṣbt* | [   ]
10 [- - - - - - - - -]*m .* | [   ]
bnšỉ[.]ʿnh[.]*wtphn* | Lifting her eyes, she perceived
11 [- - - - - - - - -]*ml . kslh . kb*[r]*q* | [   ] its string like lightning
12 [- - - - - - - - -]*mḫ gʿt . thmt . brq* | [   ] the ocean(s) the lightning
13 [- - - - - - - - -] . *tṣb . qšt . bnt* | [   ] she coveted the bow[3] [   ]
14 [- - - - - - - -] | [   ]
[ʿ]*nh . km . bṭn . yqr* | her eyes like a serpent that hisses.
15 [- - - - - - - l]*ảrṣ* | [to] the earth,
ksh . tšrm (16) [lʿpr .] | her cup she hurled [to the ground];
[*tšủ . gh .*]*wtṣḥ .* | [she lifted up her voice] and cried:
šmʿ . mʿ (17) [*lảqht . ǧzr .*] | 'Hear, I beseech you, [o hero Aqhat],
[ỉ]*rš . ksp . wảtnk* | 'ask silver and I will give (it) you,
18 [*ḫrṣ . wảš*]*lḥk*[.] | '[gold and I will] bestow (it) on you;
wtn . qštk . [l] (19) [ʿnt .] | 'but give your bow [to Anat],
[*tq*]*ḫ*[. q]*ṣʿtk . ybmt . lỉmm* | '[let] the sister-in-law of peoples[4] [take] your arrows.'
20 *wyʿn . ảqht . ǧzr .* | But the hero Aqhat answered:
ảdr . tqbm (21) b*lbnn .* | 'Most splendid of ash trees from Lebanon,
ảdr . gdm . brủmm | 'most splendid of sinews from wild oxen,
22 *ảdr . qrnt . byʿlm .* | 'most splendid of horns from mountain-goats,

---

38: cp. 37
vi 7 *ktʿl* or *wtʿl*
7-8: cp. **5** iv 20-22
9: the text is very uncertain
10: this line transgresses the margin with col. v
11 Virolleaud (cp. 12)
13: possibly *bnth* (Virolleaud) 'within herself' (?)
14 [ʿ]*nh* (Ginsberg) or [*qr*]*nh* 'its (the bow's) horns'
(Virolleaud)
15 *ksh* or *kst* 'the cups'; *tšrm* (Ginsberg) or *tšpkm*

(Herdner) 'she emptied'
16 Herdner *a.* Ginsberg
17-18: cp. 26-28
18-19 Herdner (cp. 24)
21 *blbnn* or *dlbnn*

[1] Sc. that presumably of Baal.
[2] Or 'manufactured wine'.
[3] Or 'the bow was set between'.
[4] See at **3** B 33.

mtnm (23) *bʿqbt.tr.*	'of tendons from the hocks of a bull,[1]
* àdr.bǵl il.qnm*	'most splendid of stalks from vast reed-beds,[2]
24 *tn.lktr.wḫss.*	'do you give to Kothar-and-Khasis;
ybʿl.qšt lʿnt	'let him fashion a bow for Anat,
25 *qṣʿt.lybmt.limm.*	'arrows for the sister-in-law of peoples.'
wtʿn.btlt (26) *ʿnt.*	And the virgin Anat answered:
irš ḥym.làqht.ǵzr	'Ask life, o hero Aqhat,
27 *irš ḥym.wàtnk.*	'ask life and I will give (it) you,
blmt (28) *wàšlḥk.*	'immortality and I will bestow (it) on you;[3]
àšsprk.ʿm.bʿl (29) *šnt.*	'I will cause you to count the years with Baal,
ʿm.bn il.tspr.yrḫm	'with the sons of El[4] you shall count the months.[5]
30 *kbʿl.kyḥwy.*	'As if he were Baal when he comes alive,
yʿšr.ḥwy.	'(when) men[6] feast the living one,
yʿš (31) *r.wyšqynh.*	'feast and give him drink,
ybd.wyšr ʿlh (32) *nʿm[.]*	'(and) the minstrel chants and sings over him'
[*wt*]*ʿnynn.*	—and she answered him—
àp ànk.àḥwy (33) *àqht[.ǵz]r.*	'so will even I give life to the [hero] Aqhat[7].'
wyʿn.àqht.ǵzr	But the hero Aqhat answered:
34 *àl.tšrgn.ybtltm.*	'Do not lie, o virgin;
dm.lǵzr (35) *šrgk.ḫḫm.*	'for to a hero your lying is unseemly.[8]
mt.ùḥryt.mh.yqh	'As (his) ultimate fate[9] what does a man get?
36 *mh.yqh.mt.àtryt.*	'What does a man get as (his) final lot?
spsg.ysk (37) [*l*]*riš.*	'Glaze will be poured [on] (my) head,
ḥrṣ.lẓr.qdqdy	'quicklime on to my crown;[10]
38 [*w*]*mt.kl.àmt.*	'[and] the death of all men I shall die,[11]
wàn.mtm.àmt	'even I indeed shall die.
39 [*àp.m*]*tn.rgmm.àrgm.*	'[Also], one thing further[12] I will say;
qštm (40) [- - -]*mḥrm.*	'a bow [[(is the weapon of)] warriors;
ht.tṣdn.tìntt (41) [*bh.*]	'shall now womenfolk hunt [with it]?'
[*g*]*m.tṣḥq.ʿnt.*	Anat laughed [aloud],
wblb.tqny (42) [- - -]	and in (her) heart she forged [(a plot)]:
tb ṣy.làqht.ǵzr.	'Attend to me, o hero Aqhat,
tb ly wlk (43) [àrgm.]	'attend to me and [I will tell] you (what I will do).

30 *ḥwy.yʿš* (31) *r*: perhaps dittography (cp. **3** A 9)
32 *nʿm* (De Moor: cp. **3** A 19) or *nʿm[t]* 'men sing over him pleasant songs' (Gaster); [*wt*]*ʿnynn* (Herdner) or [*wy*]*ʿnynn* 'and make(s) responses to him' (Virolleaud) or [*à*]*tnynn* '—I repeat it—' (De Moor)
35 *mt*: the *t* with word-divider looks more like *m*
38 [*w*] (Ginsberg); there is perhaps room for two letters
39: cp. **3** D 75–76 **4** i 20–21
41 [*bh.g*]*m* (Ginsberg) or [*bh.bk*]*m* (Gaster)
42: there is not room for [*tḥblt*] (Albright; cp. Prov. i 5), but a word of similar meaning is required; *ṣy* error for *ly*
43 [*àrgm*] (Gordon) or [*àtb*] (De Moor); cp. **3** E 8

[1] On the structure of such 'composite' bows see McLeod, *Composite Bows from the Tomb of Tutʿankhamun.*
[2] Lit. 'of El', i.e. divine or in this context vast;

cp. Ps. xxxvi 7 lxxx 11. The stalks are obviously for making arrows.
[3] Cp. Ps. xxi 5.
[4] Cp. **4** iii 14 **10** i 3. Possibly 'son of El', though immortality was a property of all gods (cp. Gen. vi 2–4) and not only of Baal; see further p. 5 note 2.
[5] Cp. Ps. cxxxix 18.
[6] Lit. 'one, he', unless *nʿm* is the subject.
[7] Cp. 2 Kgs. v 7. The allusion is to the celebrations in honour of Baal's victory in the autumn, a heavenly counterpart of which may be being described in **3** A 1–22.
[8] Lit. 'rubbish'.
[9] Cp. Num. xxiii 10 Eccles. vi 12.
[10] There is evidence from Jericho of the plastering of skulls before burial (Gordon), but it comes from Neolithic times; it is safer to take the phrases as a poetic description of the white hair of old age.
[11] Cp. **16** i 3–4 Num. xvi 29 Ps. lxxxii 7.
[12] Lit. 'the repetition of words'.

h*m.ldqryk.bntb.pš°*

44 [- - - -].*bntb.gdn.*
dšqlk.tht (45) [p°ny.d]n*k.*
n°mn.°mq.nšm

46 [td°ṣ.p°n]*m.wtr.drṣ.*
idk (47) [lttn.pn]*m.*
°*m il.mbr.nhrm*

48 [qrb.dp]q.*thmtm*
tgly.šd il

49 [wtbu.qr]š*.mlk.db*[.]*šnm*

50 [lp°n.il.t]h*br.wtql.*
tšth (51) [wy.wtkbd]n*h.*
tlšn.dqht ġzr

52 [- - - - kdd.dn]*il mt.rpi.*
wt°n (53) [btlt.°nt.]
[tšu.g]*h.wtṣh.*
hwt (54) [- - - - - - - - - - -]
dqht.yš[- -] (55) [- - - -]
[- - - - - - - -]*n.ṣ*[- - - - -]

. . . . . .

E. [spr.ilmlk.šbny.lmd.dtn.]*prln*

'If ever I meet you on the path of transgression,
'[   ] on the path of presumption,
'I shall fell you beneath my very own [feet],[1]
'you charming, strongest one of men!'
[She planted] (her) feet and the earth did quake;
then [indeed she set (her)] face
towards El at the source(s) of the rivers,
[amid the springs] of the two oceans;
she penetrated the mountain(s) of El
[and entered the massif] of the king, father of years.[2]
[At the feet of El she] did homage and fell down,
she prostrated [herself and did] him [honour].
She denounced[3] the hero Aqhat,
[the child of] Daniel, man of Rapiu.
[The virgin Anat] spoke,
[she lifted up] her [voice] and cried:
'Him [   ]
'Aqhat [   ]
[   ]

. . . .

[The scribe is Elimelek, the Shubanite, disciple of Atn-]*prln.*

18

Col. i

1 [   ]
2 [   ]
3 [   ]
4 [- - - - -]h.*dt*[   ]
5 [- - - - -]b*h.dp.*[   ](6) [- - - - -].
wt°n.[btlt.°nt]

7 [bnt.bht]*k.yilm*[.]
[bnt.bhtk] (8) [dl.tšmh.]
dl.tš[mh.brm.h] (9) [klk.]
[dl.]*dhdhm.*[bymny]

10 [- - - b.b]*gdlt.dr*[kty.]
[dm - -] (11) [- - - qdq]*dk*
dšhlk[.šbtk.dmm]

12 [šbt.dq]*nk.mm°m.*
w[qrd] (13) *dqht.wypltk.*

[   ]
And [the virgin Anat] answered:
'[(In) the building of] your [mansion], o El,
'[(in) the building of your mansion do not rejoice],
'do not rejoice [in the raising of your palace],[4]
'[lest] I seize them [with my right hand],
'[by] the might of my long [arm],[5]
'[(lest) I   ] your [crown],
'make [your grey hairs] run [with blood],
'[the grey hairs of] your beard with gore.
'So [call upon][6] Aqhat and let him deliver you,

45: cp. **19** 109, 115–116 etc. and for the reinforcing
   prepos. **2** iv 11, 19
46–51: cp. **3** E 12–16   **4** iv 20–26   v 82–83
47 *mbr* error for *mbk*
52: cp. **19** 174   E.: cp. **6** vi 53–54
i 6–12: cp. **3** E 27–33 as reconstructed by Herdner
12 [qrd]: cp. **21** A 2

[1] Cp. **19** 109.
[2] On *ll.* 46–49 see at **3** E 12ff.
[3] Cp. Prov. xxx 10.
[4] A conventional address, more appropriate to the
context in **3** E 27ff. than here.
[5] Cp. Exod. xv 16.
[6] Cp. **1** Kgs. xviii 24   Job v 1.

bn[.dnìl] (14) wy῾ẓrk.
byd.bṯlt.[῾nt]

15 wy῾n[.]lṭpn.ìl dp[ìd]
16 yd῾tk.bt kàmšt.
    wì[n.bìlht] (17) qlṣk.

tb῾.bt.ḥnp.lb[k.]
[tì] (18) ḥd.dìt.bkbdk.
tšt.d[ìt.b] (19) ìrtk.
dt.ydt.m῾qbk.
[ttb῾] (20) [bt]lt.῾nt.
ìdk.lttn.[pnm]

21 [῾m.à]qht.ġzr.
bàlp.š[d] (22) [rbt.]kmn.
wṣḥq.bṯlt.[῾nt]

23 [tšù.]gh.wtṣḥ.
šm῾.m[῾.là] (24) [qht.ġ]zr.
àt.àḥ.wàn.à[ḥtk]

25 [- - - - -].šb῾.ṯìrk.ṣ[   ]
26 [- - lbt.]dby.ndt.ànk[   ]

27 [- - - - - -]dmlk.tlk.bṣd[   ]
28 [- - - - - -]mt.ìšryt[   ]
29 [- - - - - -]r.àlmdk.ṣ[   ]
30 [- - - - - -]qrt.àblm.à[blm]
31 [qrt.zbl.]yrḥ.dmgdl.š[   ]
32 [- - - - - - -]mn.῾rhm[   ]
33 [- - - - - - - -]ìt[   ]
34 [- - - - - - - -]῾ṗ[   ]

. . . . . .

. . . . . .

1 [- - - -]pṣ[   ]
2 [- - -].ytbr[   ]
3 [- - -]àṯm.ẓr[qm   ]
4 [bṯl]t.῾nt.lkl.[   ]
5 [tt]b῾.bṯlt.῾nt[.]
    [ìdk.lttn.pnm]
6 ῾m.yṭpn.mhr.š[t.]

'the son [of Daniel], and let him preserve you
'from the hand of the virgin [Anat].'
And Latipan, kindly god, answered:
'I know, daughter, that you are like men[1]
'and there exists not [among goddesses] contempt like
    yours.
'Depart, daughter, haughty is [your] heart;
'[you] take what is in your mind,[2]
'you carry out[2*] what [is in] your breast.
'He who hinders you[3] shall be utterly struck down.'
[The virgin] Anat [departed];
then indeed she set [(her) face]
[towards] the hero Aqhat,
a thousand tracts away, [ten thousand] spaces.
And the virgin [Anat] did laugh,[4]
[she lifted up] her voice and cried:
'Hear, [I beseech you, o] hero [Aqhat],
'you are my brother, and I am [your sister][5]
'[   ] your seven kinsfolk[6] [   ]
'[   ] I myself have fled [from] my father's [house
    ]
'[   ] of a king. Go you on the chase? [   ]
'[   ] a man of Ishriyyat [   ]
'[   ] I will teach you [   ]
'[   ] Qart-Abilim, [Abilim]
'[city of prince] Yarikh, whose tower [   ]
'[   ] their city [   ]
[   ]
[   ]

. . . .

Col. iv

[   ]
'[   ] may he break [   ]
'[   ] . . . . [   ]'
'[the virgin] Anat to all [   ]'
The virgin Anat departed;
[then indeed she set (her) face]
towards Yatpan, warrior of the [Lady];

13: cp. iv 19
16–17: cp. 3 E 35–36 16 v 22
17 qlṣk: Virolleaud qlṣ w and in 3 E 36 qlṣt 'there is no
    contumely among goddesses' or 'there can be no
    scoffing at goddesses'; [tì]ḥd (Obermann)
18 d[ìt.b] (Obermann) or b[m] (Virolleaud) or b[qrb]
    (Gordon) 'you place (it) within'
19 [ttb῾] (cp. 17) or [tb῾] or [šmḥ] (cp. 4 v 82)
20–23: cp. 4 v 84–87
23–24 Gordon
26 Gaster
29: perhaps ṣ[d] (cp. 27) but cp. 17 vi 40

30–31: cp. 19 163–164
32 ῾rhm (Herdner) or ῾rpt (Virolleaud)
iv 3: cp. 5 i 5–6
4 lkl (Herdner) or ùkl (Virolleaud)
5–6: cp. i 19ff.; š[t]: cp. 27

[1] Or (ironically) 'you are gentle'.
[2] Lit. 'liver'; cp. 2 Sam. vii 3. 2* Cp. 19 221
[3] Cp. Job xxxvii 4.
[4] Infin. absol. or basic form (3 masc. sing. perf.).
[5] Cp. Song iv 9 et passim.
[6] Or there is a reference here to blood-revenge.

[tšù.gh] (7) *wtṣḥ.*
ytb.yṭp.[åqht.]
[ytb.b] (8) *qrt.åblm.*
åblm.[qrt.zbl.yrḫ]
9 *ìk.ål.yḥdt.yrḫ.*
b[- - - - -] (10) *bqrn.ymnh.*
bånšt[- - - - -] (11) *qdqdh.*
wy°n.yṭpn.[mhr.št]
12 *šm°.lbtlt.°nt.*
åt.°[l.qšth] (13) *tmḫsh.*
qṣ°th.hwt.lt[ḥwy]
14 *n°mn.ġzr.št.trm.*
w[- - -] (15) *ištir.bẓdm.*

wn°rs[- - -]
16 *wt°n.btlt.°nt.*
tb.yṭp.w[årgm] (17) *lk.*
åštk.km.nšr.bḥb[šy]
18 *km.dìy.bt°rty.*
åqht.[km.ytb] (19) *llḥm.*
wbn.dnìl.ltrm[.]
[°lh] (20) *nšrm.trḫpn.*
ybṣr.[ḥbl.d] (21) *ìym.*
bn.nšrm.årḫp.ån[k.]
[°]l (22) *åqht.°dbk.*
hlmn.tnm.qdqd
23 *tlt ìd.°l.ùdn.*
špk.km.šìy (24) *dm.*
km.šḥt.lbrkh.
tṣì.km (25) *rḥ.npšh.*
km.ìtl.brlth.
km (26) *qtr.båph.*
båp.mprh.
ånk (27) *låḥwy.*
tqḥ.yṭpn.mhr.št
28 *tštn.knšr.bḥbšh.*
km.dìy (29) *bt°rtp.*

[she lifted up her voice] and cried:
'[Aqhat] is dwelling, Yatp,[1]
'[he is dwelling at] Qart-abilim,
'Abilim [city of prince Yarikh].
'How may the moon be not renewed
'with [   ] in its right horn,[2]
'with gentleness [   ] its crown?'
And Yatpan, [warrior of the Lady], answered:
'Hear, o virgin Anat,
'for [his bow] you yourself should smite him,
'(for) his arrows you should not let him [live].[3]
The gracious hero had set a meal
and [   ] was left behind in the mountains,
and he did grow tired [   ].[4]
And the virgin Anat spoke:
'Attend, Yatp, and [I will tell] you (what we will do).
'I will put you like an eagle on [my] wristlet,
'like a hawk on my glove.[5]
'[As] Aqhat [sits down] to meat,
'and the son of Daniel to a meal,
'[above him] eagles shall hover,
'[a flock] of hawks look down.
'Among the eagles I myself will hover;
'[over] Aqhat I will release you;[6]
'strike him twice (on) the crown,
'three times on the ear;
'spill (his) blood like a . . . . . ,[7]
'like a "killer", on to his knees.
'Let his breath go forth like a wind,[8]
'his life like spittle,
'like a vapour from his nose
'—(and) from his warriors'[9] noses!
'I will not let (him) live.'
She took Yatpan, warrior of the Lady,[10]
she put him like an eagle on her wristlet,
like a hawk on her glove.

---

7 Driver and Gaster; a restoration as in 16 does not give a connection with the following lines
8: cp. **19** 164   11: cp. **27**
12–13: cp. **27**, 40–41 **19** 14–16
16 [*årgm*] (Gaster) or [*åtb*] (De Moor); cp. **3** E 8
17–21: cp. **28**–32
22 *°dbk*: perhaps error for *å°dbk* (cp. 33)
26 *båp* perhaps dittography (Ginsberg), i.e. '(nor) shall I let his warriors live'; *mprh* error for *mhrh*
29 *t°rtp* error for *t°rth* (cp. 18)

---

1 A shorter form of the name (cp. *l.* 16).
2 Cp. Akk. *qarnu imittašu* 'the horn on its right side', said of the moon; apparently Anat wished the deed to be done quickly before the moon waxed and

Aqhat was protected by its beneficence.
  3 Cp. Deut. xxxii 39   2 Kgs. v 7.
  4 Perhaps these lines belong to Yatpan's speech.
  5 Cp. **2** iv 12ff.   Isa. xlvi 11   Zech. ix 13. The picture is derived from falconry (Watson).
  6 Cp. Job x 1. The verb is prps. a partic. (cp. **2** i 28), masc. for fem., or basic form.
  7 This and the next adjective may refer to classes of hunting hawks.
  8 Cp. Ps. cxlvi 4.
  9 Servants of Aqhat who escape and later inform his father (**19** 77ff.). Alternatively, giving another meaning to *mhr* here, 'his ready courage I will not revive' (Driver; see apparatus for omission of *båp*).
  10 I.e. Anat herself; cp. *mhr °nt* (**22** B 9).

àqht.km.ytb.llḥ[m]
30 bn.dnìl.ltrm.
ʿlh.nšr[m] (31) trḥpn.
ybṣr.ḥbl.dìy[m.]
[bn] (32) nšrm.trḥp.ʿnt.
ʿl[.àqht] (33) tʿdbnh.
hlmn.tnm[.qdqd]
34 tlt ìd.ʿl.ùdn[.]
š[pk.km] (35) šìy.dmh.
km.šḥ[ṭ.lbrkh]
36 yṣàt.km.rḥ.npš[h.]
[km.ìtl] (37) brlth.
km.qṭr.[bàph.]
[w - - -] (38) ʿnt.bṣmt.mhrh.

[- - - - - - - -] (39) àqht.
wtbk. yl [k. àqht.]
[- -] (40) dbn.dnk.
wʿl.[qštk.ìmḥṣk]
41 qṣʿtk.àt.lḥ[wt.]
[- - - - - - - -] (42) wḥlq.
ʿpmm[- - - - - - - - - - -]

As Aqhat sat down to meat,
the son of Daniel to a meal,
above him eagles hovered,
a flock of hawks looked down.
[Among] the eagles Anat hovered;
over [Aqhat] she released him;
he did strike him twice [(on) the crown],
three times on the ear;
he [did spill] his blood [like] a . . . . .
like a 'killer', [on to his knees].
[His] breath did go forth like a wind,
his life [like spittle],
like a vapour [from his nose].
[And] Anat [   ] at the stillness of his warriors,
[   ] Aqhat.
And she wept, (saying): 'Woe to [you, Aqhat]!
'[(Life for you)] I myself would have created;
'but for [your bow I smote you],
'(for) your arrows you do not [live]'.
[   ] and he did perish.[1]
Flying [   ]

19

1 [là]q[h]t
2 wtrd.[- - - - - -]lqrb[.]mym.

3 tql.[- - - - - - -]lb.tt[b]r
4 qšt[- - - - - - -]r.y[t]br

5 tmn.[- - - - - -]btlt.[ʿ]nt
6 ttb.[- - - - - -]šà
7 tlm.km[- - -]ydh.kšr
8 knr.ùšbʿth[.]ḥrṣ.
dbn (9) ph.tìḥd.
šnth.wàkl.bqmm. (10) tšt

hrṣ.klb ìlnm

Col. i
[Of] Aqhat.
and (the bow) came down [   ] in the midst of the waters
it fell [   ] the bow
was broken [   ] the eight [
                    ]
were broken [   ] the virgin Anat
sat down [   ]
. . . . . [   ] her hand . . . . .
a lyre, her fingers . . . . .
The stones of her mouth she clenched,
her teeth (she clenched) and food in . . . . .
she placed
. . . .[2]

29–36: cp. 18–25
37: cp. 26; thereafter w with a fem. verb
39: cp. 19 152, 157, 165; at the end perhaps [ḥyk]
40–41: cp. 12–13   19 14–16   41 Gordon
19 1: cp. 6 i 1   16 i 1
2 wtrd (Driver) or tkrb (Herdner); this line transgresses upon the next col. and the word-divider separates the last word from the first in 50; similarly in 9, 11, 14, 17, 23, 28, 37, 41
5 tmn: cp. 17 v 2
6 šà: Driver [t]šà error for [t]šù

7: perhaps km[r] (cp. 12)
9 wàkl or kàkl; bqmm: Gaster bmʿmm 'in (her) bowels' (Hebr. mēʿîm)
10 tšt ḥrṣ or tštḥrṣ 'she whetted (her tongue)' (Cassuto; cp. Exod. xi 7)

[1] Cp. 5 vi 10.
[2] A reference has been found here to 'the hound of the gods' (Cassuto), a kind of Canaanite Cerberus. For an attempt to reconstruct this whole difficult sect. see Dijkstra and De Moor UF 7 (1975) 197ff.

11 *wtn.gprm.mn gprh.š[- -].*   . . . .

    . . . . . .

12 *aqht.yʿn.kmr.kmr[- -]*   'Aqhat has been humbled[1] . . . .

13 *kap̊ʿ.il.bgdrt.*   'surely I cry (like) a ram in the fold,

    klb l (14) *ḥth.*   '(like) a dog for its stick.

    imḥṣh.kd.   'I smote him thus,

    ʿl.qšth. (15) *imḥṣh*   'for his bow I smote him,

    ʿl.qṣʿth.hwt (16) *l.aḥw.*   'for his arrows I did not let him live.

    ap.qšth.lttn (17) *ly.*   'Yet his bow has not been given to me,

    wbmt[.y]ḥmṣ ṣ[- - -].   'and through (his) death [   ] shall be soured,[2]

18 *prʿ.qẓ.yb[l].*   'the shoots of summer will wither,

    šblt (19) *bg̣lph.*   'the ear(s) of corn in their husk(s)[3].'

    apnk.dnil (20) *[m]t.rpi.*   Thereupon Daniel, man of Rapiu,

    ap[h]n.g̣zr (21) *[mt.hrn]my.*   thereat the hero, [man of He-of-]Harnam,

    ytšu (22) *[ytb.bap.t]g̣r[.]*   raised himself up [(and) sat at the entrance of the] gate

    [t]ḥt (23) *[adrm.dbgrn.]*   beneath [the trees which were by the threshing-floor];

    [y]dn[.] (24) *[dn.almnt.]*   [he] judged [the cause of the widow],

    [ytpt.]tpt (25) *[ytm.]*   [tried] the case [of the orphan].

    [bnši.ʿn]h (26) *[wyphn.]*   [Lifting] his [eyes, he saw]

    [bal]p (27) *[šd.rbt.kmn]*   [a thousand tracts away, ten thousand spaces],

28 *hlk.[pg̣t.kyʿn.]*   the coming [of Pughat surely he sighted].

    [bn]ši. (29) *ʿnh.wtphn[.]*   [Lifting] her eyes, she perceived

    [- - - - -] (30) *bgrn.yḥrb[.]*   (that) [   ] on the threshing-floor was dried up,

    [- - - - -] (31) *yg̣ly.*   [   ] had wilted,

    yḥsp.ib[- - - -]   the blossom[4] [   ] was shrivelled,

32 *ʿl.bt.abh.nšrm.trḥ[p]n*   (that) eagles hovered over her father's house,

33 *ybṣr.ḥbl.diym*   a flock of hawks looked down.[5]

34 *tbky.pg̣t.bm.lb*   Pughat wept in (her) heart,

35 *tdmʿ.bm.kbd[.]*   she sobbed in (her) inward parts.[6]

36 *tmzʿ.kst.dnil.mt* (37) *rpi.*   She rent the cloak of Daniel, man of Rapiu,

    al⟨l⟩.g̣zr.mt hrnmy.   the robe of the hero, man of He-of-Harnam.

38 *apnk.dnil.mt* (39) *rpi.*   Thereupon Daniel, man of Rapiu,

    yṣly.ʿrpt.b (40) *ḥm.un.*   prayed (that) the clouds in the heat of the season,

    yr.ʿrpt (41) *tmṭr.*   (that) the clouds might give the early rains,

    bqẓ.ṭl.ytll. (42) *lg̣nbm.*   (that) in summer[7] the dew might distil upon the grapes, (saying):

12: perhaps *kmr[t]* 'I have overthrown'
17: perhaps *bmt[.]dḥ* (or *lyḥ*) *mṣṣ[.ʿnt]* (cp. **15** ii 27)
18 Virolleaud and Ginsberg
20–28: cp. **17** v 4–11; there may be room for a further line between 27 and 29 (cp. **4** ii 13–15)
32: cp. **18** iv 20, 31
35: there seems to be a word-divider at the end of this short line
37: cp. **48**

[1] Cp. **16** vi 58. Alternatively (Gaster), 'Because he has indeed been laid low' (Hebr. *yaʿan*; Akk. *kamāru* 'to overthrow').

[2] Or (see apparatus) 'and in death the fosterling of Anat is cast down' (cp. Prov. xiv 32); or 'from death . . . shall not revive'.

[3] The basic thought here and in *ll.* 30–31, 38ff. is of the land under a curse because it has been polluted by bloodshed; cp. Gen. iv 11–12   Num. xxxv 33   2 Sam. xxi 1   Jer. xii 4.

[4] Cp. Job viii 12.

[5] For the association of birds of prey with death and drought see Hos. viii 1   Jer. xii 9   Job xxxix 30   Matt. xxiv 28.

[6] Lit. 'liver' (cp. Lam. ii 11).

[7] Alternatively (i) (De Moor) 'Thereupon Daniel

šbˤ . šnt (43) *ysrk . bˤl.*
tmn . rkb (44) *ˤrpt.*
*bl . ṭl . bl r*bb
45 *bl . šrˤ . thmtm.*
bl (46) *ṭbn . ql . bˤl.*
ktmzˤ (47) *kst . dnil . mt . rpi*
48 *ảll . ǵzr .* m[t .]hr[nmy]
49 *gm . lbt*[h . dnil . kyṣḥ]

50 *šmˤ . pǵt . tkmt*[. my]
51 *ḥspt . lšˤr . ṭl.*
yd[ˤt] (52) *hlk . kbkbm.*
mdl . ˤr (53) *ṣmd . pḥl.*
*št . gpny dt k*sp
54 *dt . yrq . nqbny.*
tš[mˤ] (55) *pǵt . tkmt . my.*
ḥspt . l[šˤ]r . ṭl
56 *ydˤt . hlk . kbkbm*
57 *bkm . tmdln . ˤr*
58 *bkm . tṣmd . pḥl.*
bkm (59) *tšủ . ảbh.*
tštnn . l[b]mt *ˤr*
60 *lysmsm . bmt . pḥl*
61 *ydn*⟨ . dn⟩*il . ysb . pảlth*
62 *bṣql . yph . bpảlt.*
bṣ[q]l (63) *yph . byǵlm.*
bṣql . y[ḫb]q (64) *wynšq.*
ảḫl . ản bṣ[ql] (65) *ynpˤ . bpảlt.*

'For seven years[1] shall Baal fail,[2]
'for eight the rider on the clouds,[3]
'without dew, without showers,
'without watering by the two deeps,[4]
'without the sweet sound of Baal's voice?[5]
'For rent is[6] the cloak of Daniel, man of Rapiu,
'the robe of the hero, [man of He-of-]Harnam.'
[Surely Daniel cried] aloud to [his] daughter:

Col. ii

'Hear, Pughat, who carry [water] on your shoulders,[7]
'who skim the dew from the barley,[8]
'who [know] the course of the stars,[9]
'saddle a he-ass,[10] yoke a donkey,
'put on my harness of silver,
'my trappings of gold.'
Pughat heard, she who carried water on her shoulders,
who skimmed the dew from the [barley],
who knew the course of the stars.
Forthwith[11] she saddled a he-ass,
forthwith she yoked a donkey;
forthwith she lifted up her father,
she put him on the back of the he-ass,
on the easiest part of the back of the donkey.
Daniel approached, he went round his parched land,
a ripening stalk[12] he descried in the parched land,
a ripening stalk he descried in the scrub.
He embraced the ripening stalk and kissed it,[13] (saying):
'May, oh! may (this) ripening [stalk] shoot up in the
        parched land,

[cont.]
adjured the clouds (and) cast a spell on the heat, (saying): Let the clouds pour rain on the summer-fruit etc.' (Hebr. *'āwen* 'evil'; *yry* 'to shoot, throw'); (ii) (Dietrich and Loretz) 'Thereupon Daniel prayed, (saying): May the clouds (rain) a downpour on the heat, may the clouds rain on the summer-fruit etc.' (*ủn yr* = 'downpour'; cp. Hebr. *'ôn* 'strength').

44: the second *b* of *rbb* is only partially formed
49: cp. **17** v 15
50–51: cp. 55–56
53: this and several other lines in col. ii are continued on the edge of the tablet
54–55: cp. 50–51
59: cp. 60
60: possibly *ysmsm*⟨*t*⟩ (cp. **4** iv 15)
61: ⟨*dn*⟩*il*: cp. 68
63, 70 *yḫbq*: cp. **17** i 40–41

[1] Cp. Gen. xli 26   2 Kgs. viii 1   Sefire inscr. i A 27.
[2] Or 'For seven years Baal failed etc.' (cp. 176–177). Alternatively *ll.* 38–43 may be translated (cp.

Ginsberg, Rin) 'Thereupon Daniel cursed the clouds (that gather) in the heat of the season of early rains, the clouds that bring rain in summer, the dew that distils upon the grapes, (saying): For seven years let Baal fail etc.'. Cp. *Ugaritica* V p. 245 where in a lexical list the verb *ṣly* is given the Akk. meaning 'to curse'.
[3] See at **2** iv 8.
[4] Cp. 2 Sam. i 21   1 Kgs. xvii 1   Hab. iii 10.
[5] Cp. **4** vii 29.
[6] Or 'When she rent etc.' Cp. Gen. xxxvii 34   1 Kgs. xi 30.
[7] Cp. **14** 113–114.
[8] Possibly 'for (her) hair' (cp. Hebr. *śēˤār*; Aram. *saˤrâ*); cp. **3** B 38.
[9] I.e. who is skilled in the spells associated with midwifery.
[10] Hardly in this homely context as the mount of royalty (Zech. ix 9); cp. **4** iv 9ff. (Athirat).
[11] Possibly 'weeping'.
[12] Cp. 2 Kgs. iv 42 ('grain (in) its ripeness'?).
[13] Possibly a rite of sympathetic magic to restore fertility to the crops.

bṣql yṗ bẏǵlm

66 *ủr.tỉspk.yd.ảqht* (67) *ǵzr.*
    tštk.bqrbm.ảsm

68 *ydnh.ysb.ảklth.*
    yph (69) *šblt.bảk⟨l⟩t.*
    šblt.yṗ (70) *bḥmdrt.*
    šblt.yḥ[bq] (71) *wynšq.*
    ảḥl.ản.š[blt] (72) *tṗ.bảklt.*

    šblt.tṗ[.bḥm]drt

73 *ủr.tỉspk.yd.ảqht.ǵz[r]*
74 *tštk.bm.qrbm.ảsm*
75 *bph.rgm.lyṣả.*
    bšpth[.hwth]
76 *bnšỉ ʿnh[.]wtphn.*
    ỉn.[- - -] (77) *[-]hlk.ǵlmm*

    bddy.yṣ[ả - -]

78 *[l]yṣả.wl.yṣả.*
    hlm.[tnm] (79) *[q]dqd.*
    tlt ỉd.ʿl.ủd[n]
80 *[- - ả]sr.pdm.rỉšh[m]*

81 *ʿl.pd.ảsr.[- - -]*
    [-]l[- - -] (82) *mḫlpt.*
    wl.ytk.[d]m[ʿt.]
    km (83) *rbʿt.tqlm.*
    ttp[- - - - -]
    bm (84) *yd ṣpn hm.tlỉyt[.]*
    [byd.ṣ]pn hm (85) *nṣhy.*
    šrr.m[- - - - -]ảy

86 *nbšrkm.dnỉl.[w]p[ǵt.]*
    [- -] (87) *rỉš.r[- -]⟨- - - - -⟩*
    ⟨btlt.ʿnt.ššảt.⟩

'(this) ripening stalk shoot up in the scrub!
'O herb, may the hand of the hero Aqhat gather you,
'put you within the granary!'
He approached, he went round his blighted[1] land,
he descried an ear of corn in the blighted land,
an ear of corn he descried among the shrivelled grain.
He embraced the ear of corn and kissed it, (saying):
'May, oh! may (this) ear [of corn] shoot up in the blighted land,
'(this) ear of corn shoot up [among the shrivelled] grain!
'O herb, may the hand of the hero Aqhat gather you,
'put you within the granary!'
Scarce had (his) word(s) come forth[2] from his mouth,
[his speech] from his lips,
(than) lifting her eyes, she perceived
(that) there was no [   ] the coming of two youths.[3]
(Mournful) singing[4] did come [forth (from their mouth)],
it indeed did come forth unceasingly.[5]
They did strike (each other) [twice] (on) the crown,
three times on the ear.
[   ] they did bind the locks of their head(s),
over (their) lock(s) they did bind [   ],
[   ] (their) tresses;
and (their) tears indeed flowed
like quarter shekels[6]
[   ] (as they said):
'If only (our) victory was in the hand of Zephon,[7]
'if only our[8] triumph was [in the hand] of Zephon,
'(if only) our[8] [   ] was sure,
'we would give you good news, Daniel [and Pughat],
'[   ] (your) head [   ]
'⟨(But) the virgin Anat has caused⟩

69 *ảk⟨l⟩t*: cp. 68, 72; *yṗ* error for *yph* (cp. 68, 72)
71–72: cp. 69–70   75: cp. 113, 142
77: a letter visible before *h* may belong to *l.* 29 (see apparatus at 2), or supply *w*; at the end perhaps *[bphm]* (cp. 75), continued on the edge of the tablet
78–79: cp. **18** iv 33–34
80 *[--ả]sr* (cp. 81); the two (or one) letters before this may belong to *l.* 31
81: perhaps *[ʿ]l* as earlier in the line
82 *[d]m[ʿt]* (Herdner) alternant of or error for *ủdmʿt* (cp. **14** 28)
85 *ảy* or *ny* (cp. 88)
86 *nbšr* or *ảbšr*; Pughat's name is required in the lacuna (Driver)
87: a line written on the edge (see *CTA* p. 88 n. 17 and fig. 60 *bis*) probably supplies an omission after *rỉš.r[--]*; it repeats (though with a different suffix)

part of this line, and reads *[- - - - - btlt.ʿ]nt.[š]ṣảt [k]rḥ.npšhm* (cp. 91–92 and more fully **18** iv 24–26)

[1] Lit. 'eaten, consumed (by drought)'; cp. Gen. xxxi 40.
[2] Lit. 'did not come forth'; cp. Ps. cxxxix 4.
[3] Or 'behold two youths'. These were servants of Aqhat who had been attacked with him (**18** iv 26, 38) but had escaped; they act out his killing in mime and repeat his dying words.
[4] Or 'garbled sounds'.
[5] Lit. 'and indeed it did come forth' (continuity indicated by repetition).   [6] Cp. **14** 28–30.
[7] See at **3** C 26; cp. also Phoen. *Bdṣpn* as personal name.
[8] Lit. 'my'; with the changes of person cp. **17** v 20ff.

[kr]ḥ[.npšn]y
88 kı̇tl.brltny[.]
[kqtr.bȧpny]
89 tmǵyn.tšd̂.ǵh[m.wtṣhn]
90 šm°.ldnı̇l.[mt.rpı̇]
91 mt.ȧqht.ǵzr.
[ṣṣȧt] (92) btlt.ʿnt.
k[rḥ.npš]
93 kı̇tl.brlth.
[kqtr.bȧph.]
[bh.pʿnm] (94) tṭṭ.
ʿl[n.pnh.td°.]
[b°dn] (95) ksl.y[tbr.]
[yǵṣ.pnt.kslh]
96 ȧnš.[dt.ẓrh.]
[yšủ.ǵh] (97) wyṣ[ḥ.]
[- - - - - - - - - - -]
98 mḥṣ [- - - - - - - - - - - -]
99 š[   ]
    .   .   (gap of 5 ll.)   .   .
105 bnšı̇[.ʿnh.wyphn.]
[yḥd] (106) lʿrb š[pš.nšrm.]
[yšủ]————————————

———— (107) [ǵh.]wyṣḥ[.]
[knp.nšrm] (108) b°l.ytb⟨r⟩.
b°l.ytb[r.dı̇y.hmt]
109 tqln.th⟨t.⟩pʿny.
ı̇bq[°.kbdthm.w] (110) ȧhd.
hm.ı̇t.šmt.hm.ı̇[t] (111) °ẓm.
ȧbpy.w.ȧqbrnh.
112 ȧšt.bhrt.ı̇lm.ȧrt
113 bph.rgm.ly.ṣd̂.
bšpth hwt[h]
114 knp.nšrm.b°l.ytbr
115 b°l.tbr.dı̇y hmt.
tqln (116) tht.pʿnh.

'[the breath] of us both ⟨to go forth⟩ [like] a wind,
'the life of us both like spittle,
'[like a vapour from our nose].'
They came on, they lifted up their voices [and cried]:
'Hear, o Daniel, [man of Rapiu],
'the hero Aqhat is dead;
'the virgin Anat [has caused]
'[his breath to go forth] like [a wind],
'his life like spittle,
'[like a vapour from his nose]'.
[At that (his) feet] stamped,
[his face sweated] above,
he [burst] (his) loins [round about],[1]
[he convulsed the joints of his loins],
the muscles [of his back].
[He lifted up his voice] and cried:
'[   ]
'the smiter [   ]
[   ]
.   .   .   .
Lifting [his eyes, he perceived],
[he saw eagles] (coming) from the west[2]
[he lifted up] ————————————

Col. iii
———————— [his voice] and cried:
'[The wings of the eagles] let Baal break,
'let Baal break [the breast-bones of them];
'they shall fall beneath my feet,[3]
'I will rip open [their gizzards and] see (into them).
'If there is fat or is bone,
'I shall weep and bury him,
'I shall put (him) in a hole of the earth-gods.'[4]
Scarce had (his) word(s) come forth from his mouth,
his speech from his lips,
(than) the wings of the eagles Baal broke,[5]
Baal did break the breast-bones[6] of them;
they fell beneath his feet,

89 Virolleaud
91–93: see apparatus at 87; it is assumed that 93
finishes on the edge of the tablet
93–97: cp. 3 D 29–33   4 ii 16–21
97–99: perhaps restore as in 196–197, 201–202 (with
bny for ȧḫy), though the long space in 97 and the
first letter of 99 hardly fit
105–109: cp. 120–125, 134–139
106 Virolleaud (cp. 210); Ginsberg b°rpt[.nšrm] (cp.
8 11)
108 and 123 ytb⟨r⟩ (cp. 137) or ytb 'let Baal pluck'
(Watson; cp. Arab. nataba (?), natafa)
111 ȧbpy error for ȧbky (cp. 126, 140)
112 ȧrt error for ȧrṣ (cp. 141)

113 ly.ṣd̂ error for lyṣd̂ (cp. 75); this and several other
lines in col. iii transgress the edge of the tablet

[1] Cp. Ezek. xxi 11.
[2] Lit. 'from the setting of the sun', i.e. towards
the east, reflecting perhaps a superstition that eagles
can fly into the sun without being dazzled or
blinded (Gaster); cp. Shakespeare 3 *Henry the
Sixth* II i 91–92; cp. also Prov. xxiii 5.
[3] Cp. 17 vi 45   2 Sam. xxii (Ps. xviii) 39.
[4] Cp. 5 v 5–6   6 i 17–18.
[5] Cp. Adapa B 5–6 (*ANET* p. 101).
[6] Possibly 'pinions' (from the root 'to fly').

ybqˁ . kbdthm . w[yḥd]	he ripped open their gizzards[1] and [saw (into them)],
117 *ỉn . šmt . ỉn . ˁẓm.*	(but) there was no fat nor bone.
yšủ . gh (118) *wyṣḥ.*	He lifted up his voice and cried:
knp . nšrm . ⟨bˁl.⟩ ybn	'The wings of the eagles let ⟨Baal⟩ (re)make,
119 *bˁl . ybn . dỉy hm*t	'let Baal (re)make the breast-bones of them;
nšrm (120) *tpr . wdủ.*	'eagles, flee and fly away.'
bnšỉ . ˁnh . wyp⟨h⟩n	Lifting his eyes, he perceived,
121 *yḥd . hrgb . ảb . nšrm*	he saw Hirgab the father of the eagles.
122 *yšủ . gh . wyṣḥ.*	He lifted up his voice and cried:
knp . hr[g]b (123) *bˁl . ytb⟨r⟩.*	'The wings of Hirgab let Baal break,
bˁl . y[tb]r . dỉy[.h]wt	'let Baal break the breast-bones of him;
124 *wyql . tḥt . pˁny.*	'and he shall fall beneath my feet,
ỉbqˁ . kbd[h] (125) *wảḥd.*	'I will rip open [his] gizzard and see (into it).
hm . ỉt . šmt . hm . ỉt[.ˁẓm]	'If there is fat or is [bone],
126 *ảbky . wảqbrn.*	'I shall weep and bury him,
ảšt . bḫrt (127) *ỉ[lm . ảrṣ.]*	'I shall put (him) in a hole of the [earth-gods].'
[bph . rgm . lyṣả.]	[Scarce had (his) word(s) come forth from his mouth],
[bšp] (128) *th[.]hwth.*	his speech [from] his lips,
knp . hrgb . bˁl . tbr	(than) the wings of Hirgab Baal did break,
129 *bˁl . tbr . dỉy . hwt.*	Baal did break the breast-bones of him;
wyql (130) *tḥt . pˁnh.*	and he fell beneath his feet,
ybqˁ . kbdh . wyḥd	he ripped open his gizzard and saw (into it),
131 *[ỉ]n . šmt . ỉn . ˁẓm.*	(but) there was no fat nor bone.
yšủ . g[h] (132) *wyṣḥ.*	He lifted up [his] voice and cried:
knp . hrgb . bˁl . ybn	'The wings of Hirgab let Baal (re)make,
133 *[b]ˁl . ybn . dỉy . hwt.*	'let Baal (re)make the breast-bones of him;
hrg[b] (134) *tpr . wdủ.*	'Hirgab, flee and fly away.'
bnšỉ . ˁnh[.] (135) *[w]yphn.*	Lifting his eyes, he perceived,
yḥd . ṣml . ủm . nšrm	he saw Ṣumul the mother of the eagles.
136 *yšủ . gh . wyṣḥ.*	He lifted up his voice and cried:
knp . ṣml[.] (137) *bˁl . ytbr.*	'The wings of Ṣumul let Baal break,
*bˁl . ytb*r . dỉy (138) *hyt.*	'let Baal break the breast-bones of her;
tql . tḥt . pˁny.	'she shall fall beneath my feet,
ỉbqˁ (139) *kbdh . wảḥd.*	'I will rip open her gizzard and see (into it).
hm . ỉt . šmt . ⟨hm.⟩ỉt (140) *ˁẓm.*	'If there is fat ⟨or⟩ is bone,
ảbky[.]wảqbrnh.	'I shall weep and bury him,
ảštn (141) *bḫrt . ỉlm . ảrṣ.*	'I shall put him in a hole of the earth-gods.'
bph . rgm . l[yṣ]ả	Scarce had (his) word(s) come forth from his mouth,
142 *bšpth . hwth.*	his speech from his lips,
knp . ṣml . bˁ[l]⟨.tbr⟩	(than) the wings of Ṣumul Baal ⟨did break⟩,
143 *bˁl . tbr . dỉy . hyt.*	Baal did break the breast-bones of her;
tq[l . tḥt] (144) *pˁnh.*	she fell [beneath] his feet,
ybqˁ . kbdh . wyḥd	he ripped open her gizzard and saw (into it).
145 *ỉt . šmt . ỉt . ˁẓm.*	There was fat, there was bone;

116: cp. 130, 144

118 ⟨*bˁl*⟩: cp. 132

123–125: cp. 138–140

127: cp. 112–113, 141–142

131: cp. 117

134, 136: according to Herdner there is a word-

divider at the end of these lines

139 ⟨*hm*⟩: cp. 110, 125

142 ⟨*tbr*⟩ (cp. 128) or ⟨*ytbr*⟩ (cp. 114)

143: cp. 138

[1] Lit. 'livers'.

wyqḥ bhm (146) àqht.   and he took Aqhat from them,
yb.llqẓ.   he scraped out . . . . .
ybky.wyqbr   he wept and buried (him),
147 yqbr.nn.bmdgt.bknk[n]   he buried him in a dark chamber in a grave.
148 wyšù.gh.wysḥ.   And he lifted up his voice and cried:
    knp.nšrm (149) bˁl.ytbr.   'The wings of the eagles let Baal break,
    bˁl.ytbr.dìy (150) hmt.   'let Baal break the breast-bones of them,
    hm.tˁpn.ˁl.qbr.bny   'if they fly over the grave of my son
151 tšḥṭnn.bšnth.   '(and) wake him out of his sleep.'
    qr.[mym] (152) mlk.yṣm.   The king cursed Qor-[mayim],[1] (saying):
    ylkm.qr.mym.   'Woe to you, Qor-mayim,
    dˁ[lk] (153) mḥṣ.àqht.ǵzr.   '[near] whom the hero Aqhat was struck down![2]
    àmd.gr bt ìl   'Be continually a seeker of sanctuary.[3]
154 ˁnt.brḥ.pˁlm.h.   'Be a fugitive[4] now and evermore,
    ˁnt.pdr[.dr]   'now and to all [generations];[5]
155 ˁdb.ùḥry mṭ.ydh   'let every last one[6] make ready a staff for his hand.'[7]
156 ymǵ.lmrrt.tǵll.bnr   He proceeded to Mararat-tughullal-bnar,[8]
157 yšù.gh.wysḥ.   he lifted up his voice and cried:
    ylk.mrrt (158) tǵll.bnr.   'Woe to you, Mararat-tughullal-bnar,
    dˁlk.mḥṣ.àqht (159) ǵzr.   'near whom the hero Aqhat was struck down!
    šršk.bàrṣ.àl (160) ypˁ.   'May your root not shoot up in the earth,
    rìš.ǵly.bd.nsˁk   'may (your) head droop at the touch of him that
                                                   plucks you!'[9]
161 ˁnt.brḥ.pˁlmh   'Be a fugitive now and evermore,
162 ˁnt.pdr.dr.   'now and to all generations;
    ˁdb.ùḥry mṭ ydh   'let every last one make ready a staff for his hand.'

                                             Col. iv
163 ymǵ.lqrt.àblm.   He proceeded to Qart-Abilim,[10]
    àbl[m] (164) qrt.zbl.yrḥ.   Abilim city of prince Yarikh,
    yšù.gh (165) wysḥ.   he lifted up his voice and cried:
    ylk.qrt.àblm   'Woe to you, Qart-Abilim,
166 dˁlk.mḥṣ.àqht.ǵzr   'near whom the hero Aqhat was struck down!
167 ˁwrt.yštk.bˁl.lht⟨.⟩   'May Baal this instant render you blind!'[11]

---

146 Driver yd.llqh 'he laid out his . . .'
147 bknk[n] (cp. **5** v 13) or bknrt 'in a shroud' (Gray; Arab. kinnâratu)
151 tšḥṭnn: note n with five wedges; Virolleaud tšḥṭànn
152: cp. 158, 166
153 àmd error for tmd (Gaster) or has same meaning
154 ˁlm.h error for ˁlmh; pdr[.dr]: cp. 161–162, 168
160 nsˁk: note n with four wedges
162 pdr: note d with four vertical wedges

¹ The name means 'source of waters'. On the custom of cursing cities near the scene of a crime see Deut. xxi 1–9 Driver and Miles *Bab. Laws* I, 110–111; cp. also 2 Sam. i 21 (Gilboa).
² Or 'upon whom (the guilt rests for) the smiting etc.'.
³ Lit. 'sojourn, be a client in the house of a god'

(cp. Ps. lxi 5). Alternatively '(Aqhat) who dwelt ever in the sanctuary', i.e. like the child Samuel (1 Sam. i 22).
⁴ Cp. Jer. iv 29.
⁵ Cp. Exod. iii 15 Ps. xxxiii 11 etc.
⁶ Or '(even) the youngest'. The verb is infin. absol. or perfect with jussive sense (so also ǵly in l. 160).
⁷ Cp. Gen. xxxviii 18 Exod. xii 11 Mark vi 8.
⁸ The name has the suggestive meaning 'The bitter place which was plunged in fire' or the like (or could be so understood).
⁹ Cp. Eshmunazar inscr. ll. 11–12 Amos ii 9 Job xviii 16.
¹⁰ Where Aqhat had in fact been murdered (**18** i 30 iv 7ff.); the name means (or could be taken to mean) 'city of mourners'.
¹¹ Cp. Deut. xxviii 28 Sefire inscr. i A 39.

⟨ʿnt.brḥ⟩ (168) wʿlmh.   '⟨Be a fugitive now⟩ and evermore,
      lʿnt.pdr.dr   'now and to all generations;
169 ʿdb.ủḥry.mṭ.ydh   'let every last one make ready a staff for his hand.'
170 dnỉl.bth.ym.ǵyn   Daniel proceeded to his house,
      yšt (171) ql.dnỉl.lhklh.   Daniel betook himself to his palace.
      ʿrb.b⟨bth.b⟩ (172) kyt.   Weeping women[1] did enter into ⟨his house⟩,
      bhklh.mšspdt.   wailing women into his palace,
      bḥẓrh.pẓ (173) pẓǵm.ǵr. men that gashed (their) flesh[2] into his courtyard;
      ybk.lảqht (174) ǵzr.   they wept for the hero Aqhat,
      ydmʿ.lkdd.dnỉl (175) mt.rpỉ. shed tears for the child of Daniel, man of Rapiu;
      lymm.lyrḥm   from days to months,
176 lyrḥm.lšnt.   from months to years
      ʿd (177) šbʿt.šnt.   for seven years[3]
      ybk.lảq (178) ht.ǵzr.   they wept for the hero Aqhat,
      yd[mʿ.]lkdd (179) dnỉl.mt.r[pỉ.] shed [tears] for the child of Daniel, man of Rapiu.
      [mk].bšbʿ (180) šnt.   [Then] in the seventh year
      wyʿn[.dnỉl.mt.]rpỉ   [Daniel, man of] Rapiu spoke,
181 ytb.ǵzr.m[t.hrnmy.]   the hero, [man of He-of-Harnam], addressed (them),
      [y]šủ (182) gh.wyṣḥ.   [he] lifted up his voice and cried:
      t[bʿ.bbty] (183) bkyt.   '[Depart from my house], weeping women,
      bhk[l]y.mšspdt   'from my palace, wailing women,
184 bḥẓry pẓǵm.ǵr.   'from my courtyard, men that gash (your) flesh.'
      wyq[ry] (185) dbḥ.ỉlm. And he presented a sacrifice to the gods,
      yšʿly.dǵth (186) bšmym. he sent up his incense among the heavenly ones,
      dǵt hrnmy[.bk] (187) bkbm. He-of-Harnam's incense[4] [among] the stars
      ʿd[- - - - - - - -]   [   ]
188 [-]lh.yd ʿd[- - - - mṣ]   [   ] hand [   ] cymbals,
189 ltm.mrqdm.dš[n - -]   castanets[5] of ivory [   ]
190 wtʿn.pǵt.tkmt.mym   And Pughat spoke, she who carried water on her shoulders:

191 qrym.ảb.dbḥ.ỉlm   'My father has presented a sacrifice to the gods,
192 šʿly.dǵth[.]bšmym   'he has sent up his incense among the heavenly ones,
193 dǵt.hrnmy.bkbkbm   'He-of-Harnam's incense among the stars.
194 ltbrkn.ảlk brkt   'Let them indeed bless me[6] (that) I may go blessed,
195 tmrn.ảlkn mrrt   'fortify me (that) I may go fortified,
196 ỉmḥṣ.mḥṣ.ảḥy.   '(that) I may smite the smiter of my brother,
      ảkl[.m] (197) kly[.ʿ]l.ủmty. 'make an end of [him] that made an end of the child of my family.'

---

167 ⟨ʿnt etc.⟩ (cp. 154, 161) or ⟨lʿnt⟩ (cp. 168)
170 ym.ǵyn error for ymǵyn
171 b⟨bth.b⟩ Herdner (cp. 182–184)
172: note dittography of pẓ (cp. 184)
178–179: cp. 174–175; [mk]: cp. 17 i 16   ii 39
182 t[bʿ.bbty]: cp. 17 ii 39
184 Gordon (cp. 191)
186: cp. 193
188–189: cp. *Ugaritica* V no. 2 obv. *ll.* 4–5
190: the second and third epithets have been omitted (cp. 50–52, 199–200)
193 (and 186) Herdner dkbkbm '(among) the lords of the stars'

195 alkn mrrt (Virolleaud) or ảlk nmr[rt] (Herdner; N partic.)
196–197: cp. 202

[1] The professional mourners familiar in the east; cp. Jer. ix 17–18   16 i 5.
[2] Cp. 5 vi 17ff.   1 Kgs. xviii 28. The practice was frowned upon in Israel (Deut. xiv 1   Jer. xvi 6).
[3] Cp. 6 v 7–9.
[4] Or 'incense for He-of-Harnam'.
[5] For the use of castanets in mourning see Mishna *Kelim* xvi 7.
[6] Or 'Do you indeed bless me etc.'

wy‘n[.dn] (198) *ìl.mt.rph*
npš[.]tḥ[.*pġt*]
199 *t*[km]*t.mym.*
  ḥspt.lš‘r (200) *ṭl.*
  yd‘t[.]h*lk.kbkbm*
201 *à*[- -].*hy*[.]*mḥ.*
  tmḥṣ.mḥṣ[.*àḥh*]
202 *tkl.*m[k]*ly.‘l.ùmt*[h.]

  [- -] (203) [- - - - -].b*ym.*
  trtḥ[ṣ] (204) [wt]*àdm.*
  tàùm.bġlp y[m]
205 *dàlp šd.ẓùḥ.bym.*
  t[ḥt] (206) *tlbš.npṣ.ġzr.*
  tšt.ḥ[- - -] (207) *nšgh.*
  ḥrb.tšt.bt‘r[th]
208 *w‘l.tlbš.npṣ.àtt.*
  [*lm.*] (209) *ṣbì nrt.ìlm.špš.*
  [-]*r*[- -] (210) *pġt.mìnš.šdm.*

  lm ‘[rb] (211) *nrt.ìlm špš.*
  mġy[t] (212) *pġt.làhlm.*
  rgm.lyṭ[pn.y] (213) *bl.*
  àgrtn.bàt.bždk.
  [‘nt] (214) *bàt.b*⟨à⟩*hlm*[.]
  wy‘n.ytpn[.mhr] (215) *št.*
  qḥn.wtšqyn.yn.
  qḥ (216) *ks.bdy.*
  qb‘t.bymny[.]
  [t]*q* (217) *ḥ.pġt.wtšqynh.*
  tp[ḥ.ks.]*bdh*
218 *qb‘t.bymnh.*
  wy‘n.yṭ[p]*n*[.mh]*r* (219) *št.*
  byn.yšt.ìlà.
  ìl š[- -]*ìl* (220) *dyqny.šdm.*

Then Daniel, man of Rapiu, spoke:
'In spirit let [Pughat] revive,
'she who carries water on her shoulders,
'who skims the dew from the barley,
'who knows the course of the stars;
'let her [   ] vigour;
'let her smite the smiter of [her brother],
'make an end of him that made an end of the child of
    [her] family.'
[   ] in the sea,
she washed herself [and] roughed herself
with rouge from the shell of the [sea],[1]
whose source is a thousand tracts away in the sea.
[Beneath] she put on the garments of a hero,
she put [   ] (in) its sheath,
put (her) sword in [its] scabbard,
and on top she put on the garments of a woman.
[At] the darkening of Shapash the luminary of the gods
Pughat [   ] to the gathering-place in the
    fields;
at the setting of Shapash the luminary of the gods
Pughat did arrive at the tents.
Word [was] brought to Yatpan:
'She that hired us[2] has come into your mountain(s),
'[Anat] has come among (your) tents.'
And Yatpan, [warrior] of the Lady, answered:
'Bring her and give her wine to drink;
'take the cup[3] from my hand,
'the goblet from my right hand.'
They brought Pughat and gave her (it) to drink;
they took [the cup] from his hand,
the goblet from his right hand.
And Yatpan, [warrior] of the Lady, spoke:
'May our god drink of the wine,[4]
'El [   ], the god who owns (these) mountains![5]

197–198 Gordon (cp. **17** i 37); *rph* error for *rpì*
199: cp. 50, 55
201 *hy*[.]*mḥ*: cp. *hw.mḥ* (**17** i 39)
201–202: cp. 196–197
203–204: cp. **14** 62, 156; *tàùm* error for *tìdm*
205 De Moor; Virolleaud *t*[‘*l*]; Gaster *t*[*ḥgr*]
206 Gaster *ḥ*[*lp.b*] 'a dagger' (cp. Syr. *ḥlāpâ*)
207: cp. **18** iv 18   208 [*lm*] or [*bm*]
209 De Moor [‘]*r*[*bt*]
210 *šdm* perhaps error for *ždm* (213, 220); *lm* ‘*rb* (cp.
  106) or *lm‘rb* (Virolleaud)
212 Gordon
213 *ždk* perhaps error for *šdk* (cp. 210); De Moor
  [‘*nt*]; Ginsberg [*pġt*]
214 *b*⟨à⟩*hlm* (cp. 212) or *bhlm* 'hither' (Lipiński; cp.
  Hebr. *‘ad hălōm*); [*mhr*]: cp. **18** iv 6
215 possibly *tqḥ*; the reading is uncertain
217 *tp*[*ḥ*] error for *tq*[*ḥ*]; this and *ll.* 218, 222 transgress the margin with col. iii
219 *ìlà* error for *ìln* or so read; Gaster completes
  š[*mm.*]

[1] Probably a member of the murex family, from
which dye was obtained. Pughat disguises herself as a
courtesan or serving maid (Gray) or more appropriately as Anat (De Moor; cp. **3** B 42–43; **18** iv 5ff.).
[2] Or (without 'Anat' in the lacuna) 'our hired
woman.'
[3] Or (see apparatus) 'Bring her and let her give me
wine to drink; let her take etc.' (similarly in 217).
Cp. Judg. iv 19 v 25 (Jael).
[4] Yatpan makes a libation to the El of the district
before uttering his boast (Lipiński; cp. Hadad inscr.
ll. 15–17.
[5] Possibly (see apparatus) 'El of [heaven], El who
created the mountains'; cp. Gen. xiv 19.

yd[.]mḫṣt.ḋ[qh]t.ġ (221) zr. 'The hand that smote the hero Aqhat
tmḫṣ.ḋlpm.ỉb.št[.]   'shall smite thousands of (my) Lady's foes,
[t]št (222) ḥršm.lḋhlm.   'shall work¹ magic² against (their) tents.'
p[- - -]km (223) [-]bl   [   ] like [   ],
lbh.km.bṭn.y[- -]lḋh.   her heart (was) like a serpent's (as) he [   ] her.
224 tnm.tšqy.msk.ḥwt.   Twice they gave (her) his mixture to drink,
tšqy[.]w[they gave (her it) to drink and [

E. whnḋt.yṭb.lmspr   And this he shall recite again.³

---

221 [t]št: cp. tmḫṣ; possibly the previous št is infin. absol. 'shall indeed work'
222 Virolleaud k[bdh]
223 Gaster [s]bl (cp. Arab. šiblu 'lion's whelp')
224 is a continuation of 223 (note the final word-divider) at the foot of col. iii
E. hnḋt (cp. Herdner) perhaps fem. form of hnd 'this'

(Gordon, *Textbook*, 39); Virolleaud hn.bt

¹ Cp. Exod. x 1.
² Lit. 'spells, charms'; cp. Isa. iii 3.
³ The rubric may have reference to the passage in *ll.* 171–184, alongside which it is written.

Obv. 1 *i̇qrȧ.ı̇lm.n[ʿmm - - - -]*   I would call on[1] the gracious gods [   ]
    2 *wysmm.bn.šp[- - - - - - -]*   and fair, sons of [   ]
    3 *ytnm.qrt.lʿly[- - - - - - -]*   who established a city on high[2] [   ]
    4 *bmdbr.špm.yd[- - - - - - -]r*   in the desert, who . . . . .[3] [their] hands [   ]
    5 *lrı̇šhm.wyš[- - - - - -]m*   for their head(s) and [   ]
    6 *lḥm.blḥm.ȧy.*   Eat of any bread
      wšty.bḥmr yn ȧy   and drink of any foaming wine.[4]
    7 *šlm.mlk.*   Peace to the king!
      šlm.mlkt.ʿrbm.wtnnm   Peace to the queen, the ministers[5] and the guards![6]

    8 *mt.wšr.ytb.*   Mot-and-Shar[7] sat down,
      bdh.ḥt.tkl.   in his one hand the sceptre of bereavement,
      bdh (9) *ḥt.ȧlmn.*   in his other hand the sceptre of widowhood.[8]
      yzbrnn.zbrm.gpn   The pruners of the vine pruned him,
   10 *yṣmdnn.ṣmdm.gpn.*   the binders of the vine bound him,
      yšql.šdtmth (11) *km gpn*   they felled (him) on the terrace[9] like a vine.

   12 *šbʿd.yrgm.ʿl.ʿd.wʿrbn.tʿnyn*   Seven times shall (this) be recited on the dais, and the
      ministers shall make response.

   13 *wšd.šd ı̇lm.*   Then (shall be sung) 'The field(s), the field(s) of the
      gods,
      šd ȧtrt.wrḥm⟨y⟩   'the field(s) of Athirat and Rahmay[10].'
   14 *ʿl.ı̇št.šbʿd.ǵzrm.ṭb[- g]d.bḥlb.*   Seven times over the fire let the heroes . . . . .
      ȧnnḥ bḥmȧt   coriander in milk,[11] mint in butter;

1: cp. 23, 60, 67
2 Virolleaud *šr[m]* (cp. 22 and Ps. lxxxii 6, 7);
Herdner *šp[š]*
3 Ginsberg *ʿly[nm]* 'the most high (gods)'
6: this and several other lines on the obv. are continued on the edge of the tablet (particularly 14)
13 *rḥm⟨y⟩*: cp. 28
14 Virolleaud *ṭb[ḥ.g]d*; Caquot and Sznycer *ṭb[ʿ.g]d* 'let (them) plunge' (D); De Moor *ǵzrm.g.ṭb* '(let) the sweet-voiced youth(s) (sing)' (referring to the hymn; cp. 3 A 20)

[1] Cp. Deut. xxxii 3.
[2] Perhaps a reference to the sanctuary of *l.* 65. Alternatively (Xella *a.* Ginsberg) 'Let glory be given to the most high gods' (√*yqr*; cp. Esth. i 20).
[3] Alternatively 'in the desert of the dunes' (Hebr. *šᵉpāyîm*).
[4] Cp. Prov. ix 5. The last phrase may refer to a mixture of *ḥmr*, the new wine from the early grapes (3 A 16) with older wine (*yn*).
[5] Lit. 'those who enter'; cp. Akk. *ērib bīti* of a minister in a temple.   [6] See at 14 91.

[7] I.e. 'prince'; see p. 28 note 1.
[8] Cp. Isa. xlvii 8–9 Jer. xv 7–8; cp. also Ps. cxxv 3.
[9] Cp. 2 i 43 Deut. xxxii 32; the interpretation of this word as a compound ('field(s) of death'; cp. Hebr. *ṣalmāwet*) can only be sustained if it is assumed that the Massoretic tradition (pl. *šᵉdēmôt*) with initial *š* is wrong.
[10] Apparently another name for Anat meaning 'the merciful' (!; 15 ii 6). The prominence of Anat and Athirat in the preliminary hymns makes it not unlikely that they are the two unnamed women of the mythological text; and the present hymn and the story (or hymn) mentioned in *ll.* 16–17 may in fact be alluding to the events of *ll.* 66–68.
[11] See apparatus; the text is difficult but a verb (presumably perf. with jussive sense) seems to be required. Virolleaud's suggestion, widely accepted, '(let them cook) a kid in butter' (cp. Exod. xxiii 19 xxxiv 26 Deut. xiv 21) is not suitable in the context; and in any case *ṭbḥ* is 'slaughter' rather than 'cook' (the Hebr. has a verb 'to boil' and adds 'of its mother' after 'milk').

15 wʿl.ảgn.šbʿdm.dǵ[t - - - - -]t

and seven times over the basin incense [   ]

---

16 tlkm.rḥmy.wtṣd[.]
[- - - -] (17) tẖgrn
ǵzr[.]nʿm[- - - - -]
18 wšm.ʿrbm.yr[   ]

'Rahmay went and hunted,
'[   ] she girded herself.'
The hero minstrel [   ]
and the name[1] shall the ministers [   ]

---

19 mtbt.ỉlm.tmn.t̠[mn - - - -]
20 pảmt.šbʿ

Niches for the gods eight [by eight   ]
seven times.

---

21 ỉqnủ.šmt
22 tn.šrm.

Lapis-lazuli, cornaline,
the scarlet of princes.[2]

---

23 ỉqrản.ỉlm.nʿmm[.]
[ảgzr ym.bn]ym
24 ynqm.bảp zd.
ảtrt.[wrḥmy]
25 špš.mṣprt.dlthm[.]
[- - - - -] (26) wǵnbm
šlm.ʿrbm.tn[nm]
27 hlkm.bdbḥ nʿmt

I would call on the gracious gods,
['cleavers' of the sea,[3] children] of the sea,[4]
who suck the teats of the breasts
of Athirat[5] [and Rahmay]
May pale Shapash lead them[6]
[   ] and (to) the grapes!
Peace to the ministers (and) the guards,
those who come with the sacrifice of grace!

---

28 šd⟨.šd⟩[ỉ]lm.
šd.ảtrt.wrḥmy
29 [- - - -].y[t̠]b

'The field(s) ⟨the field(s)⟩ of the gods,
'the field(s) of Athirat and Rahmay,'
shall again[7] [   ]

E. 30 [ỉl.yṣ]ỉ.gp ym.
wyṣǵd.gp.thm.
31 [- - -]ỉl[.]mštʿltm.
mštʿltm.lrỉš.ảgn

[El went out] to the shore of the sea
and advanced to the shore of the ocean.
El [(perceived)] two women moving up and down,[8]
two women moving up and down over a basin.

15: cp. **19** 185
18: perhaps yr[gm] (cp. 12)
19 De Moor t̠[mn.bgg] 'on the roof' (cp. *CTA* **35** 50–51 and **14** 80)
22 tn or bn (Virolleaud; cp. 2); notice the word-divider after šrm
23: cp. 58–59, 61; ảgzr ym or ảgzrym
24 [wrḥmy] (cp. 59, 61) or (beginning the next phrase) [nrt.ỉlm] (Bauer; cp. **2** iii 15 etc.)
25 mṣprt (Herdner) or myprt (Bauer, Gaster etc.) 'Shapash (who) makes their tendrils abound with . . .' (Driver; √ypr D; cp. Arab. *wafara* 'was plentiful'; Arab. *dalâ(w)* V 'hung down' of fruit)
26: cp. 7
28 ⟨šd⟩: cp. 13
29 De Moor [lmspr] (cp. **19** E.)
30 [yṣ]ỉ (De Moor; the final letter is doubtful) or similar verb
31 Gordon [yqḥ] (cp. 35) but on the interpretation advanced here a verb of seeing is assumed; this line on the bottom edge finishes on the side of the tablet

[1] Perhaps that of Rahmay (cp. **2** iv 28); or 'the names(s) of the ministers shall be . . .'

[2] Or 'singers'.
[3] Cp. Ps. cxxxvi 13; the form is probably 'broken' plur. (sing. gzr; 63); or (if Shachar and Shalim are being described) 'those who cut off the day' (Gray). Alternatively ảgzrym (with unexplained y; a *mater lectionis*?) 'greedy, gluttonous' (Xella, De Moor; cp. Isa. ix 19).
[4] Or (of Shachar and Shalim) 'born in one day' (Driver).
[5] Cp. **15** ii 26ff. Note zd and šd (61) for the td of the other texts, unless these are variants of a different word related to Hebr. zîz, parallel to šōd in Isa. lxvi 11.
[6] Perf. with jussive sense.
[7] Lit. 'one shall return . . .'
[8] Lit. 'those raising themselves up' (Št partic. fem. dual), perhaps describing the act of washing clothes; cp. **4** ii 5ff. (Athirat). Most commentators (restoring 'took' in the lacuna) assume El is performing some kind of ceremony to restore his virility; e.g. 'two handfuls' (Albright; cp. Hebr. šōʿal), 'two kindlings' (Gordon), 'lids' (Largement), 'scales' (De Moor). Caquot and Sznycer render 'two women who made (sc. the water) rise', i.e. who were filling the basin.

32 h*l*h.[t]*šp̌l*.
   hlh.trm.
   hlh.tṣḥ.ảd ảd

33 hlh.tṣḥ.ủm.ủm.
   tỉrkm.yd.ỉl.kym

34 wyd ỉl.kmdb.
   ảrk.yd.ỉl.kym

Rev. 35 w.yd.ỉl.kmdb.
   yqḥ.ỉl.mštˁltm

36 mštˁltm.lrỉš.ảgn.

   yqḥ.yš⟨t⟩.bbth

37 ỉl.ḫth.nḫt[.]
   ỉl.ymnn.mṭ.ydh.
   yšủ (38) yr.šmmh.
   yr.bšmm.ˁṣr.
   yḫrt yšt (39) lpḥm.
   ỉl.ảttm.kypt.
   hm.ảttm.tṣḥn

40 ymt[.]mt.nḥtm.ḥtk.

   mmnnm.mṭ ydk

41 h[l.]ˁṣr.thrr.lỉšt.
   ṣḥrrt.lpḥmm

42 ả[t]tm.ảtt.ỉl.
   ảtt.ỉl.wˁlmh.
   whm (43) ảttm.tṣḥn.
   y.ảd ảd.nḥtm.ḥtk

44 mmnnm.mṭ ydk.
   hl.ˁṣr.thrr.lỉšt

45 wṣḥrrt.lpḥmm.
   btm.bt.ỉl.
   bt.ỉl (46) wˁlmh.
   whn.ảttm.tṣḥn.
   y.mt mt (47) nḥtm.ḥtk.

   mmnnm.mṭ ydk.
   hl.ˁṣr (48) thrr.lỉšt.
   wṣḥr⟨r⟩t.lpḥmm.
   ảttm.ả[tt.ỉl]

49 ảtt.ỉl.wˁlmh.
   yhbr.špthm.yš[q]

50 hn.špthm.mtqtm.

One[1] moved down,
the other moved up;
one cried 'Father, father!'
and the other cried 'Mother, mother!'
The organ[2] of El grew long as the sea
and the organ of El as the flood.
The organ of El did grow long[3] as the sea
and the organ of El as the flood.
El took the two women who moved up and down,
(he took) the two women who moved up and down
   over the basin,
he took (them and) set (them) in his house.
El did lower his sceptre,
El . . . . the staff in his hand.
He raised (it and) shot heavenward,
he shot a bird in the heavens,
he plucked (it and) put (it) on the coals.
Surely El seduced[4] the two women, (saying):
'If the two women should cry out
' "O husband, husband, who have lowered your
   sceptre,
' "who have . . . . . the staff in your hand,
' "look! the bird is roasted on the fire,
' "it has browned on the coals,"
'the two women (will be) wives of El,
'wives of El even for ever.
'But if the two women should cry out
' "O father, father, who have lowered your sceptre,
' "who have . . . . . the staff in your hand,
' "look! the bird is roasted on the fire
' "and has browned on the coals,"
'the two girls (will be) daughters of El,
'daughters of El even for ever.'
And behold! the two women cried out:
'O husband, husband, who have lowered your
   sceptre,
'who have . . . . . the staff in your hand,
'look! the bird is roasted on the fire
'and has browned on the coals.'
The two women (became) wives [of El],
wives of El even for ever.
He stooped (and) kissed their lips;
behold! their lips were sweet,[5]

---

32 Gaster
36 Virolleaud
38: this and several other lines on the reverse finish
   on the edge of the tablet
41: cp. 44   42: cp. 48
48: cp. 41–42
49: cp. 55

[1] Lit. 'Behold she'.
[2] Lit. 'hand'; cp. Isa. lvii 8. Xella resists this
interpretation.
[3] Infin. absol. or 3 masc. sing. perf. used as basic
form.
[4] Cp. Exod. xxii 15.
[5] Cp. Prov. xvi 21.

mtqtm . klrmn[m]   sweet as pomegranate[s].

51 bm . nšq . whr .   In the kissing (there was) conception,

    bḥbq . ḥmḥmt .   in the embracing (there was) pregnancy;[1]

    tqt[nṣn] (52) tldn . šḥr . wšlm .   they travailed[2] (and) gave birth to Shachar and Shalim.

    rgm . lil . ybl .   Word was carried to El:

    å[tty] (53) il . ylt .   '[The two] wives of El have given birth.'[3]

    mh . ylt .   'What did they bear?'

    yldy . šḥr . wšl[m]   'Two have been born,[4] Shachar and Shalim.'

54 šu . ʿdb . lšpš . rbt .   'Raise (and) prepare (an offering) for lady Shapash

    wlkbkbm . kn[m]   'and for the fixed stars.'[5]

55 yhbr . špthm . yšq .   (Once more) he stooped (and) kissed their lips;

    hn . [š]pthm . mtqtm   behold! their lips were sweet.

56 bm . nšq . whr .   In the kissing (there was) conception,

    [b]ḥbq . wḥ[m]ḥmt .   [in] the embracing (there was) pregnancy—

    ytb[n] (57) yspr . lḥmš . lṣ[- - - - -]   this shall be recited again[6] five times for [   ]

    šr . pḫr .   the assembly—

    klåt (58) tqtnṣn . wtldn .   Both of them travailed and gave birth,

    tld . [ilm .]nʿmm .   they gave birth to the gracious [gods],

    ågzr ym (59) bn . ym .   'cleavers' of the sea, children of the sea,

    ynqm . bå[p .]ž[d .]⟨št . ⟩   who suck the teats of the breasts ⟨of the Lady⟩.[7]

    [r]gm . lil . ybl   Word was carried to El:

60 åtty . il . ylt .   'The two wives of El have given birth.'

    mh . ylt .   'What did they bear?'

    ilmy nʿmm   'The gracious gods,

61 ågzr ym . bn ym .   ' "cleavers" of the sea, children of the sea,

    ynqm . båp . žd . št .   'who suck the teats of the breasts of the Lady,

    špt (62) lårṣ .   'One lip (reached) to the earth,

    špt lšmm .   'one lip to the heavens,[8]

    w[l]ʿrb . bphm .   'and there did [indeed] enter their mouth

    ʿṣr . šmm   'the birds of the heavens

63 wdg bym .   'and the fish from the sea.

    wndd . gzr . l⟨g⟩zr .   'And they did stand, 'cleaver' by 'cleaver',

    yʿdb . uymn (64) ušmål . bphm   '(as) or right or left they were put[9] into their mouth,

    wl[.]tšbʿn[.]   'but they were not satisfied.'

    y . ått . itrḥ   'O wives whom I have married,

65 ybn . åšld[.]   'o sons whom I have begotten,

---

50 Ginsberg or read sing.

51: perhaps ⟨w⟩ḥmḥmt (cp. 56); tqt[nṣn]: cp. 58

52: cp. 60

54 Gaster and Largement; De Moor knt, 'establish for Shapash a large (city) and for the stars a stable one' (cp. 3, 65)

55–56: cp. 49–51; ytb[n]: cp. 29

58: cp. 1

59: cp. 61, 52

60 ilmy error for ilm; there are traces at the end of this line, perhaps ågzr erased for lack of room

62 w[l]ʿrb (Virolleaud) or wʿrb (Herdner)

63 l⟨g⟩zr Ginsberg

[1] Cp. 17 i 40ff.

[2] Lit. 'crouched, stooped'.

[3] Apparently -y is a dual construct ending; this is better than supposing the news to have been brought by an unknown husband of the two women, 'My two wives, El, etc.' Note the assimilation in the verbal form.

[4] A passive dual perfect form (Driver); alternatively (the husband speaking), 'My two children...'

[5] Cp. Ps. viii 4; or 'Raise (and) prepare regular (offerings) for ...'; or 'Raise an offering (lit. something prepared) for ...'

[6] Lit. 'one shall recite again'.

[7] I.e. Anat (cp. 18 iv 6, 27).

[8] Cp. 5 ii 2–3 (of the appetite of Mot).

[9] Lit. 'one put (them)'.

šù.ʿdb.tk.mdbr qdš

 'raise (and) prepare a sanctuary in the midst of the desert,[1]

66 *tm.tgrgr.làbnm.wl.ʿṣm.*
 'there dwell among[2] the stones and the trees.'

šbʿ.šnt (67) *tmt.*
 Seven years did come to an end,

tmn.nqpt.ʿd.
 eight revolutions of time,

ìlm.nʿmm.ttlkn (68) *šd.*
 (as) the gracious gods went about in the field(s)

tṣdn.pàt.mdbr.
 (and) hunted on the fringe of the desert;

wngš.hm.nǵr (69) *mdrʿ.*
 and they did come upon the watchman of the sown land,[3]

wṣh hm.ʿm.nǵr.mdrʿ.
 and they did cry to the watchman of the sown land:

y.nǵr (70) *nǵr.ptḥ.*
 'O watchman, watchman, open!'

wptḥ hw.prṣ.bʿdhm
 And he did open a breach for them

71 *wʿrb.hm.*
 and they did enter, (saying):

hm[.ìt - - l]ḥm.
 'If [there is   ] bread,

wt[n] (72) *wnlḥm.*
 'then give (us it) that we may eat;

hm.ìt[- - yn.]
 'if there is [wine],

[w]tn.wnšt
 '[then] give (us it) that we may drink.'

73 *wʿnhm.nǵr.mdrʿ[.]*
 And the watchman of the sown land did answer them:

[ìt.lḥm.dʿrb]
 '[There is bread for him who enters];

74 *ìt.yn.dʿrb.*
 'there is wine for him who enters

bìk[- - - - - - - - - -]
 '[   ]

75 *mǵ hw.lhn.lg ynh[- - - - - - - - -]*
 'let him approach[4] here, his pint of wine [ ]

76 *wḥbrh.mlà yn.[- - - - - - - - -]*
 'let him fill[4] his companion(s) with wine [ ]

71: cp. 72; perhaps [*ày*] (cp. 6)
73: cp. 71, 74

[1] Or 'raise an offering within the holy desert'.
[2] Or 'open your throat for' (De Moor; denom. from *grgr*).

[3] Nothing else is known about this enigmatic figure; cp. however, the guardian cherubim of Gen. iii 24 and the gatekeeper in the Descent of Ishtar *ll.* 12ff. (*ANET* p. 107).
[4] Perfects with jussive sense. Alternatively *ll* 75–76 are narrative, though *lhn* is then difficult to translate.

Obv. 1 *àšr nkl wìb*
    2 *ḫrḫb.mlk* qẓ
    ḫrḫb m (3) *lk àǵzt.*
    bsǵsǵ špš (4) *yrḫ*
    ytkḫ yḫ[bq.]d (5) *tld*

    bt.[- -]t.ḫ[- - -]
    [lk] (6) *ṭrt.lbnt.ḫll*[.snnt]

    7 *hl ǵlmt tld b*[n.]
    [- - -]n (8) ʿnhà
    lydh tzd[- - -]
    9 *pt lbšrh.dm*
    à[- - - -]ḫ (10) *wyn.*
    kmtrḫt[- - - -]ḫ
    11 *šmʿ ìlht ktr*[t.]
    [- -]*mm* (12) nh
    lydh tzdn[- - - -]n
    13 *làd*[nh- - - - - - -]
    14 *dgn tt*[l - - - - - - - - - -]l (15) ʿ.
    lktrt⟨.lbnt⟩ *hl*[l.sn]*nt*

    16 *ylàk yrḫ ny*[r] *šmm.*
    ʿm (17) *ḫr*[ḫ]*b mlk qẓ.*
    tn nkl y (18) *rḫ ytrḫ.*
    ìb tʿrbm bbh (19) *th.*
    wàtn mhrh là (20) *bh.*
    àlp ksp wrbt ḫ (21) *rṣ.*

    ìšlḫ ẓhrm ìq (22) *nìm.*

I sing (of)[1] Nikkal-and-Ib
(and of) Khirkhib king of summer,
Khirkhib king of . . . . .[2]
At the going down of the sun Yarikh
was inflamed (and) embraced her who[3] would give
    birth,
the daughter [   ]
[O] Kotharat, o [swallow-like] daughters of the
    crescent-moon,
behold! a maiden shall bear a son.[4]
[(May)] their eye[5] [   ] her!
For her use[6] may they get sustenance [   ]
. . . . . for her flesh blood
[   ] and wine;
for the betrothed one [   ]
Hear, goddesses the Kotharat,
[   ],
for her use do you get sustenance [   ]
to [her] sire [   ]
Dagon of Tuttul[7] [   ]
o Kotharat, swallow-like[8] ⟨daughters⟩ of the crescent-
    moon.
Yarikh lamp of heaven sent (word)
to Khirkhib king of summer, (saying):
'Give Nikkal (that) Yarikh may marry (her),
'(give) Ib (that) she may enter into his mansion;
'and I will give as her bride-price[9] to her father
'a thousand (pieces) of silver and ten thousand (pieces)
    of gold,
'I will send brilliant (stones of) lapis-lazuli,

2: this and several other lines on the obv. finish on
    the edge of the tablet
3 *àǵzt* or *tǵzt*: note the single word-divider closing
    the line of poetry (similarly in *ll.* 16–22, 23, 29–33,
    35–38, 42–43, 46)
4 Herdner *a.* Virolleaud and Ginsberg; the *d* is by no
    means certain and *l* is possible; *dtld* may be an
    error for *dt tld*
5: perhaps ḫ[rḫb]   5–6: cp. 15, 41
7 Herdner
8 ʿnhà error for ʿnhn
13 Virolleaud (cp. 33)
14 *tt*[l]: cp. *Ugaritica* V no. 7 *l.* 15
14–15 *l*ʿ: perhaps [š]*m*ʿ (cp. 11)
15: cp. 6, 41; the *k* of *ktrt* is only partially formed
16: cp. 31   17: cp. 2

[1] Cp. Isa. v 1   Ps. lxxxix 2   ci 1.
[2] Possibly 'the raiding season', i.e. autumn
(*ǵzy*; cp. **16** vi 43).
[3] Note *d* for *ž* of *l.* 45; the text, however, is
doubtful.
[4] Cp. Isa. vii 14.
[5] Or 'Look! behold!' followed by 2 pers. verbs.
[6] Lit. 'hand(s)'.
[7] In NE Syria, known from the period of the Mari
letters as a centre of the cult of Dagon; he seems to
be the father of Nikkal. The Hurrian sounding names
of Khirkhib and *Prbḫt* (49) point also to this region
as the original home of the myth.
[8] Lit. 'swallows'; on this and the following title
see at **17** ii 26–27.
[9] Cp. Gen. xxxiv 12   Exod. xxii 15–16.

átn šdh krm[m]

23 *šd ddh ḥrnqm.*

w (24) *yʿn ḫrḫb mlk qẓ*[.]

[l] (25) *nʿmn.ìlm*

E. *lḥt*[n] (26) *m.bʿl*

trḥ pdry b[th]

27 *áqrbk ábh bʿ*[l]

28 *yġtr.ʿttr*

Rev.   *t* (29) *rḥ lk ybrdmy.*

b[t] (30) *bh lbb yʿrr.*

wyʿ[n] (31) *yrḫ nyr šmm.*

wn ʿ[n] (32) *ʿmá nkl ḥtny.*

áḫr (33) *nkl yrḫ ytrḫ.*

ádnh (34) *yšt mṣb. mznm.*

ùmh (35) *kp mznm.*

ìḫh ytʿr (36) *mšrrm.*

áḫtth lá (37) *bn mznm.*

nkl wìb (38) *dášr.*

ár yrḫ.wy (39) *rḫ yárk*

40 [*ášr ìlht ktrt*]

[*bn*] (41) *t hll.snnt.*

bnt h (42) *ll bʿl gml.*

yrdt (43) *bʿrgzm.*

bgbzt dm

44 *lldy.ʿm lẓpn ì* (45) *l špìd.*

hn bpy ṣ*p* (46) *rhn.*

bšpty mn (47) *thn*

tlḥh wmlgh

y (48) *ttqt ʿmh bqʿt*

49 *tqʿt ʿm prbḫt*

50 *dmqt ṣġrt ktrt*

'I will give vineyards (to be) fields for him,

'. . . . (to be) fields for him to delight in[1].'

And Khirkhib king of summer answered:

'[O] gracious one of the gods,

'o son-in-law (to be) of Baal,[2]

'bring a betrothal gift for Pidray [his] daughter

'(and) I will introduce you to her father Baal.

'(But if) Athtar is jealous,

'bring you a betrothal gift for *Ybrdmy*,

'a daughter by whom (any) heart would be stirred.'

But Yarikh lamp of heaven answered,

indeed he did answer: 'With Nikkal (shall) my marriage (be).'

Thereafter Yarikh brought the betrothal gift for Nikkal;

her sire set the base of the scales,

her mother the trays[3] of the scales;

her brothers arranged the hinges,

her sisters (saw) to the weights of the scales.

Nikkal-and-Ib (of) whom I sing,

light of Yarikh,[4] may Yarikh give light to you![5]

[I sing (of) the goddesses the Kotharat],

the swallow-like [daughters] of the crescent-moon,

the daughters of the crescent-moon, lord of the sicle,[6]

that come down with . . . . . ,

with . . . .[7]

Surely my victory is with Latipan kindly god!

Look! in my mouth is their incantation,[8]

on my lips their formula.

Her dowry[9] and her wedding gift(s)

will be . . . . . in her presence with shouting.

In the presence of *Prbḫt*[10]

let the good young Kotharat applaud![11]

22, 24, 25, 29–31: the signs at the ends of these lines have disappeared but were visible when Virolleaud's copy was made

26 *b*[th] (Herdner) or *b*[*t ár*] (cp. **3** A 24)

27: perhaps insert [*hm*] at the end (construe with 28)

29 *b*[t] (Herdner) or *b*[*t á*] (30) *bh* (Virolleaud, Gordon)

30 *lbb* or *lbù* 'lion', thought to be a title of Athtar or Baal; this and several other lines on the rev. finish on the edge of the tablet

32 *ʿmá* error for *ʿmn*

36 *dḫtth* error for *áḫth* (Virolleaud) or reduplicated form (Gordon, Driver)

40: this line read by Virolleaud has now disappeared

47–48 *yttqt* perhaps error for *yttql* 'will be weighed out' (Gaster)

[1] Lit. 'of his love'.

[2] I.e. if you agree to my proposal.

[3] Lit. 'palms'.

[4] Or 'may Yarikh give light' (perf. with jussive sense).

[5] Note the 'dative' suffix and (if *ár* in l. 38 is a verb) the chiastic arrangement of the couplet.

[6] Presumably the emblem of the new moon.

[7] Apparently drugs or potions for use at childbirth; the first appears in the hippiatric text *CTA* **161** 10 and the second was perhaps an agent to prevent haemorrhage (cp. the element *dm*).

[8] Lit. 'number'.

[9] Cp. 1 Kgs. ix 16.

[10] The girl for whom intercession is being made.

[11] Perf. with jussive sense.

8. APPENDIX: FRAGMENTARY AND RECENTLY DISCOVERED TEXTS

I

Col. ii

. . . .

[ḥšk.ʿṣk.ʿbṣk.ʿ]m*y.p*[ʿ]nk
[tlsmn.ʿmy.twt]*ḥ.ỉšdk*
[tk.ḫršn - - - -]r.[-]*ḥmk.wšt*
[- - - - - - - - - -]ẓ[- -]*rdyk*

5 [- - - - - - - - - - -*ỉ*]*qnỉm*
[- - - - - - - - - - -]*šủ.bqrb*
[- - - - - - - - - - -].*ảsr*
[- - - - - - - - - - -]*m.ymtm*
[- - - - - - - - - - -]*kỉtl*

10 [- - - - - - - - - -]*m*[.]ʿ*db.lảrṣ*
[- - - - - - - - - -]*špm.ʿdb*
[- - - - - - - - - -]*tʿtqn*
[- - - - - - - - - -]*b.ỉlk*
[lytn.pnm.ʿm.]*ỉn.bb.bảlp ḥẓr*

15 [rbt - - - lpʿ]*n.ʿnt*
[yhbr.wyql.yšt]*ḥwyn.wy*
[kbdnh.yšủ.gh.wy]*ṣḥ.thm*
[tr.ỉl.ảbk.hwt.l]*ṭpn.ḥtkk*
[qryy.bảrṣ.mlḥ]*mt.št bʿp*

20 [rm.ddym.sk.šlm]*.lkbd.ảrṣ*
[ảr bdd.lkbd.š]*dm.ḥšk*
[ʿṣk.ʿbṣk.ʿmy.pʿ]*nk.tlsmn*
[ʿmy.twtḥ.ỉšd]*k.tk.ḫršn*
[- - - - - - - - - -]*bdk. spr*

25 [- - - - - - - - - - -]*nk*

. . . . . .

Col. iii

1* [*ỉdk.ảl.ttn.pnm.tk.ḥkpt.ỉl.klh*]

[kptr.]*ks*[*ủ.tbth.ḥkpt.ảrṣ.nḥlth*]
*bảlp.šd.*r[bt.kmn.lpʿn.ktr]
hbr.wql.t[štḥwy.wkbd.hwt]
w.rgm.lk[tr.wḫss.tny.lhyn]

5 *dḥrš.y*[dm.tḥm.tr.ỉl.ảbk]
hwt.lṭpn[.ḥtkk*
yh.ktr.b[
št.lskt.n[
ʿ*db.bġrt.t*[

10 *ḥšk.ʿṣk.ʿ*b[ṣk.ʿmy.pʿnk.tlsmn]
ʿ*my tktḥ.ỉ*[šdk.tk.ḫršn
ġr.ks.dm.r[gm.ỉt.ly.wảrgmk]
hwt.wảtnyk[.rgm.ʿṣ.wlḫšt.ảbn]
tủnt.šmm.ʿm[.ảrṣ.thmt.ʿmn.kbkbm]

15 *rgm.ltdʿ.nš*[m.wltbn.hmlt.ảrṣ]
ảt.w.ảnk.ỉb[ġyh
wyʿn.ktr.wḫss[.lk.lk.ʿnn.ỉlm]
ảtm.bštm.wản[.šnt.kptr]
lrḥq.ỉlm.ḥkp[t.lrḥq.ỉlnym]

20 *tn.mṭpdm.tḥt.*[ʿnt.ảrṣ.tlt.mtḥ]
ġyrm.ỉdk.lyt[n.pnm.ʿm.lṭpn]
ỉl dpỉd.tk ḫrš[n - - - - - ġr.ks]
ygly šd.ỉ[l.wybủ.qrš.mlk]
ảb.šnm.l[pʿn.ỉl.yhbr.wyql]

25 *yštḥwy*[.wykbdnh
tr.ỉl[.ảbh
ḥš b[htm.tbnn.ḥš.trmmn.hklm]
btk.[
bn.[

30 *ả*[

. . . .

ii 1–2: cp. **3** C 15–17
3: cp. **23**   5: cp. **4** v 81
9: cp. **18** iv 25
13 *ỉlk* error for *ỉdk*
13–17: cp. **3** F 12–20
17–18: cp. **6** iv 33–35; for *yšủ* perhaps read *yšả* (dual; Gordon)
19–23: cp. **3** C 11–17
25 Virolleaud [*ym*]*nk*
iii 1*–5: cp. **3** F 12–23
5–6: cp. **6** iv 34–35

10–11: cp. ii 1–3
11 *tktḥ* error for *twtḥ*
12–16: cp. **3** C 17–26
14: note *ủ* with four vertical wedges
17: the arrival of the messengers and delivery of the message are not given
17–20: cp. **3** D 76–80
21–22: cp. **2** iii 4 ii 13–14 iii 11–12
23–25: cp. **4** iv 23–26 **6** i 34–38
26: cp. **3** E 18
27: cp. **4** v 115–116

Col. iv (see p. 39)

Col. v

. . . . . .

```
[                    ]b
[              wym.ym]m
[y°tqn         ymg°y.]npš
[              h]d.tngtnh
5 [            ḥmk].bṣpn
[             ].nšb.b°n
[             ]bkm.y°n
[             yd°.l]yd°t
[             t]ảsrn
10 [t.ỉl        ]trks
[            b]n ảbnm.ủpqt
[             ]l wǵr mtny
[ảt.zd        ]rq.gb
[             ]kl.tǵr.mtnh
15 [           ]b.wym ymm
[y°tqn        ].ymǵy.npš
[            ]t.hd.tngtnh
[            ]ḥmk bṣpn
[            ]ỉšqb ảylt
20 [          ]m.bkm.y°n
[            ].yd°.lyd°t
[            ]tảsrn.tr ỉl
[            ]rks.bn.ảbnm
[            ]ủpqt.°rb
25 [          wǵ]r.mtny ảt zd
[            ]t°rb.bšỉ
[            ]l tzd.ltptq
[            ].g[- -]lảrṣ
```

. . . . . .

7

I obv. . . . . . .

```
bḥb]šh.°tkt r[ỉšt]
]hy bth t°rb
tm]tḥṣ.b°mq
5            ]lṣbỉm
```

```
                wt]°n.tḥtṣb
               bṣh]q.ymlủ.lbh
                k]kdrt[.]rỉš
               br]k⟨m⟩.tǵll.bdm
10             ]td[-]rǵb
                            ]k
                            ]h
```

. . . . . .

Rev. A few signs are visible

II obv. . . . . . .

```
[-]p[-]l[
kllỉ.[
kpr.[
wtqr[y
5 [°]d tš[b°
klyn[
špk.l[
trḥṣ.yd[h
[- -]yṣt žm[r
10 tšt[.r]ỉmt[
[ảhb]t pdr[y
ảrṣy bt.y[°bdr
rgm lbtl[t
E. ḥw[t
15 [b°]pr[m
lkbd[.]š[dm         tls]
[m]n °my t[wtḥ
Rev. [h]wt.dảt[nyk
wlḥšt.ảbn[
20 °m kbkbm[
wảnk.ỉb[ǵyh
[-].ly°mdn[.]ỉ[
kpr.šb° bn[t
klả[t.tǵ]r[t
25 ảp °nt tm[tḥṣ
lỉm ḥ[py
ỉ[-]m.t[-]t[
m[-]mt[
[
30 t[
```

v 2–3: cp. **6** ii 4–5, 26; [ymǵy]: cp. 16
  4: cp. 17   5: cp. 18
  8: cp. 21
  9–10: cp. 22
  11: cp. 23
  13: cp. 25
  17: note final *h* with four horizontal wedges
I 2: cp. **3** B 11–13
  3: perhaps [tm]ǵy (cp. **3** B 17)
  4–7: cp. **3** B 19–26

  8: cp. **3** B 9
  9: cp. **3** B 13, 27
II 3: cp. **3** B 2
  4: cp. **3** B4
  5: cp. **3** B 29
  8: cp. **3** B 32, 34
  10–12: cp. **3** C 1–5
  13–21: cp. **3** C 8–26
  23–26: cp. **3** B 2–7
  27 Virolleaud ỉ[l]m

t[
k[
. . . . . .

8

[ì]k.mgn.rbt.ảtrt
[ym].mǵẓ.qnyt.ỉlm
wtn bt.lbᶜl.km
[ì]lm.whẓr.kbn
5 [à]trt.gm.lǵlmh
bᶜl.yṣḥ.ᶜn.gpn[.]
wủgr.bn.ǵlmt
ᶜmm ym.bn.ẓlm[t]
rmt.prᶜt.ỉbr[.mnt]
10 ṣhrrm.ḥbl[m.b]
ᶜrpt.tḥt.[bšm]
m ᶜṣrm.ḥ[t - -]
glt.ỉsr[- - -]
m.brq[- - - -]
15 ymtm[- - - - -]
šṭ[- - - - - -]
m[- - - - - - -]
. . . . . .

10

Col. i
. . (ca. 20ll.) . .
                ]btlt.ᶜnt
                ]pp.hrm
                ].dlydᶜ bn ỉl
                ]pḥr kkbm
5   ]dr dt.šmm
                àl]ỉyn bᶜl
                ].rkb.ᶜrpt
                ]ǵš.llìmm
                ]lytb.lảrṣ
10   ].mtm
                ]yd mhr.ủr
                ]yḥnnn
                ]t.ytn
            btlt.]ᶜnt
15   ybmt.]lìmm

]l[.]lìmm
]b.lảrṣ
]l.šỉr
]dtm
20]ydy
]y
]lm
r]ủmm
. . (ca.15ll.) . .

Col. ii
. . (ca.20ll.) . .
[- - - -bᶜl.bbhth]
[ỉl.hd.bqr]b.hklh
wtᶜnyn.ǵlm.bᶜl
ỉn.bᶜl.bbhtht
5 ỉl hd.bqrb.hklh
qšthn.ảḥd.bydh
wqṣᶜth.bm.ymnh
ỉdk.lytn pnm
tk.ảḥ.šmk.mlả[t.r]ủmm
10 tšủ knp.btlt.ᶜn[t]
tšủ.knp.wtr.bᶜp
tk.ảḥ šmk.mlảt rủmm
wyšủ.ᶜnh.ảlỉyn.bᶜl
wyšủ.ᶜnh.wyᶜn
15 wyᶜn.btlt.ᶜnt
nᶜmt.bn.ảḥt.bᶜl
lpnnh.ydd.wyqm
lpᶜnh.ykrᶜ.wyql
wyšủ.gh.wyṣḥ
20 ḥwt.ảḥt.wnảr[-]
qrn.dbảtk.btlt[.]ᶜnt
qrn[.]dbảtk bᶜl.ymšḥ
bᶜl.ymšḥ.hm.bᶜp
nṭᶜn.bảrṣ.ỉby
25 wbᶜpr.qm.ảḥk
wtšủ.ᶜnh.btlt.ᶜnt
wtšủ.ᶜnh.wtᶜn
wtᶜn.ảrḥ.wtr.blkt
tr.blkt.wtr.bḫl
30 [b]nᶜmm.bysmm.ḥ[- -]kǵrt
[ql].lbᶜl.ᶜnt.ttnn

8 1–2: cp. **4** i 22–23 iii 28
    4–5: cp. **4** iv 51
    5ff.: cp. **4** vii 52ff.
    11 [b]ᶜrpt . . . [bšm]m De Moor (cp. **19** 106; app.)
i 2: perhaps part of verb √ᶜwp 'to fly' (cp. ii 10–11)
    17: cp. 9
    20–21: cp. ii 6–7
    23: cp. ii 12

ii 1–2: cp. **4**–5
    4 bhtht error for bhth
    20 Herdner nảr[k] 'may (sc. your days) be prolonged':
        Driver wn ảr[m] error for tr[m] 'and now you shall
        be exalted'
    30 Gaster g[bᶜ.]wǵr (cp. iii 32); Caquot and Sznycer
        ḥ[bl.]ktrt (cp. **11** 6)
    31: cp. iii 33

[- -]ỉ . b‘lm . dỉpỉ[- -]
[ỉl .]hd . d‘nn[.]n[- -]
[- - - -]ảlỉyn . b[‘l]
35 [- - - btl]t . ‘n[t -]ph
[- - - - - - - - - -]n
[- - - - - - - - - -]y
[- - - - - - - - - -]
[- - - - - - - - - - -]lk[- -]t

Col. iii

. . (ca. 20 ll.) . .
[- - -]ảrḥt . tld[n]
ả[lp] . lbtlt . ‘nt
wypt lybmt . lỉ[mm]
5 wy‘ny[.]ảlỉyn[. b‘l]
lm . kqnym . ‘l[m]
kdrd⟨r⟩ . dyknn[
b‘l . ysg̣d . mlỉ[
ỉl pd . mlả . ủṣ[
10 blt . pbtlt . ‘n[t]
wp . n‘mt . ảḥt[. b‘l]
y‘l . b‘l . bg̣[r
wbn . dgn . bš[
b‘l . ytb . lks[ỉ . mlkh]
15 bn dgn . lkh[t . drkth]
lảlp[.]ql . ẓ[
lnp ql[.]nd . [
tlk . wtr . b[
bn‘mm . bys[mm
20 ảrḫ . ảrḫ . [
ỉbr . tld[. lb‘l
wrủm . l[rkb . ‘rpt]
tḥbq . [
tḥbq[
25 wtksynn . btn[
y[- -]šrh . wšḥph

[- -]šḥp . ṣg̣rth
yrk . t‘l . b[-]g̣r
mslmt . bg̣r . tlỉyt
30 wt‘l . bkm . bảrr
bm . ảrr . wbṣpn
bn‘m . bg̣r . t[l]ỉyt
ql . lb‘l . ttnn
bšrt . ỉl . bš[r . b‘]l
35 wbšr . ḥtk . dgn
k . ỉbr . lb‘l[. yl]d
wrủm . lrkb[.]‘rpt
yšmḥ . ảlỉyn . b‘l

11

[   ] . ytkḥ . wyỉḥd . bqrb
[t]tkḥ . wtỉḥd . bủšk
[b]‘l . ynbd . lảlp
[bt]lt . ‘nt
5 [   ]q . hry . wyld
[   ]m . ḥbl . kt[r]t
[bt]lt . ‘nt
[ảlỉ]yn . b‘l
[   ]m‘n
10 [   ]
[   ]
[   ]r
[   ]qk
[   ]ỉk
15 [   ]
[   ]ảlp
[   ]ḥ
[   ]d
[   ]t

. . . . . .

39 lk[tr]t (Driver a. Virolleaud)
iii 2 Ginsberg [‘glm]
3 Virolleaud
6–7 Ginsberg
8 Ginsberg [. ydh] 'with his member erect'
9 pd error for hd; Ginsberg uṣ[b‘(t)h]
12: cp. 28
13 w has apparently been written over a defective b (Herdner)
14–15: cp. 6 v 5–6
17: perhaps lả⟨l⟩p (Herdner)
18–19: cp. ii 29–30
20–22: cp. 36–37
21: perhaps [ỉbr . lb‘l] or [lb‘l . whd] (Virolleaud)

26 Caquot and Sznycer y[nq]
28: the letter visible after b has been erased (Herdner)
32: cp. 29
34: cp. 35
36 Ginsberg and Gordon
11 1–3: if the fragment belongs to the same tablet or series as 10 there is only room at the beginning for a small particle
1–2: perhaps bqrb[h] and bủšk[h]
2 ủšk (Virolleaud) or ủšr 'penis' (Caquot and Sznycer; cp. Akk. išaru)
3: or yảbd
5: perhaps [bnš]q (cp. 23 51, 56)
6: cp. 10 ii 30, 39

12

Col. i

. . . . . .

[- - - - - - - - -]m
[- - - - - -]
[- - - - - -]dảrṣ
[- - - - -]ln
5 [- - - -]nbhm
[- - -]kn
[- -]ḫrn . km . šḫr
[- -]ltn . km . qdm
[k]bdn . il . ảbn
10 kbd kiš . tikln
ṯdn . km . mʀm . tqrṣn
il . yẓḫq . bm
lb . wygmẓ . bm kbd
ẓi . ảt . ltlš
15 ảmt . yrḫ
ldmgy . ảmt
ảṯrt . qḫ
ksảnk . ḫdgk
ḫtlk . wzi
20 bảln . tkm
btk . mlbr
il šiy
kry ảmt
ʿpr . ʿẓm yd
25 ủgrm . ḫl . ld
ảklm . tbrkk
wld ʿqqm
ủm[.]ypʿr
šmthm
30 bhm . qrnm
km . trm . wgbtt
km . ibrm
wbhm . pn . bʿl
bʿl . ytlk wyṣd
35 yḫ pảt . mlbr
wn . ymǵy . ảklm

wymẓả . ʿqqm
bʿl . ḫmdm . yḫmdm
bn dgn . yhrrm
40 bʿl . ngthm . bpʿnh
wil . hd . bḫrẓʿh
=

Col. ii

[
[- - -]t . [
[- -]ʿn[
pnm[
5 bʿl . n[
il . hd[
ảt . bl[. ảt
ḫmdm . [
10 il . hr[r
kb[
ym . [
yšḫ[
yikl[
15 km . s[
tš[
t[
[
[
20 b[
wb[
bʿl . [
il hd . b[
ảt . bl . ảt[
25 yisphm . b[
bn . dgn[
ʿẓbm . [
ủḫry . l[
mṣt . ksh . t[
30 idm . ảdr[
idm . ʿrẓ . tʿr[ẓ
ʿn . bʿl . ả[ḫ]š[
ẓrh . ảḫẓ . qš[t

---

i   1, 3: these lines finish on col. ii between *ll.* 5–6 and 6–7 (=8) respectively

7: this and *ll.* 8–11, 13, 26, 38, 40 transgress upon col. ii; the scribe has drawn a wavy line to indicate the separation

9: cp. 10

11: or *trm*

21 *mlbr* (cp. 35) apparently a variant of *mdbr*

22 *il šiy* or *ilšiy* (a place-name)

41 *ḫrẓʿh* perhaps error for *ḫrẓh* (Gray); he renders 'in his haste'

ii   The width of the col. is indicated by *ll.* 47, 49, 54–56 where at the most two or three letters are missing

5: perhaps *n[pl]* (cp. 54)

7: this line is to be suppressed; it is really the continuation of i 3

8: cp. 24

10: cp. i 39

25: perhaps *b[ʿl]*

31 Herdner; Virolleaud *ʿrẓ . q[*

32: cp. 33

33 Herdner; Gaster *ảḫẓq . š[* , 'I will fasten . . .'?

p˓n.b˓l.aḫẓ[
35 wṣmt.ġllm[
aḫẓ.aklm.k[
npl.bmšmš[
anpnm yḫr[r
bmtnm.yšḫn.[
40 qrnh.km.ġb[
hw km.ḥrr[
šn mtm.dbṭ[
tr˓.tr˓n.a[
bnt.šdm.ṣḫr[
45 šb˓.šnt.il.mla.[
wtmn.nqpnt.˓d
klbš.km lpš.dm a[ḫh]
km.all.dm.aryh
kšb˓t.lšb˓m.aḫh.ym[
50 wtmnt.ltmnym
šr.aḫyh.mzah
wmzah.šr.ylyh
bskn.sknm.b˓dn
˓dnm.kn.npl.b˓l[
55 km tr.wtkms.hd.p[
km[.]ibr[.]btk.mšmš dṣ[
ittpq.lawl
išttk.lm.ttkn
štk.mlk.dn
60 štk.šibt.˓n
štk.qr.bt[.]il
wmṣlt.bt.ḥrš
═══

]b wt˓rb.sd
5]n bym.qẓ
]ym.tlḥmn
rp]um.tštyn
]il.d˓rgzm
]dt.˓l.lty
10]tdbḥ.amr
. . . . . .

Col. B

tmn.bqrb.hkly.[atrh.rpum]
tdd.atrh.tdd.iln[ym
asr.sswm.tṣmd.dg[
t˓ln.lmrkbthm.ti[ty.l˓rhm]
5 tlkn.ym.wta aḫr.š[pšm.btlt]
mġy[.]rpum.lgrnt.i[lnym.l]
mṯ˓t.wy˓n.dnil.[mt.rpi]
ytb.ġzr.mt hrnmy[
bgrnt.ilm.bqrb.m[ṯ˓t.ilnym]
10 dtit.yspi.spu.q[
tpḫ.tṣr.shr[
mr[
. . . . . .

21

Col. A

[- - - - - - - - -]rz˓y.lk[.]bty
[rpim.rpim.b]ty.aṣḥkm[.]iqra
[km.ilnym.bh]kly.atrh.rpum
[ltdd.atrh].ltdd.ilnym
5 [- - - - - - -]rz˓y.apnnk.yrp
[- - - - - - -]km.r˓y.ht.alk
[- - - - - - -]tltt.amġy.lbt
[y - - - - bqrb].hkly.wy˓n.il
[- - - - - rz˓]y.lk.bty.rpim
10 [rpim.bty.aṣ]ḥkm.iqrakm

20

Col. A

rp]um.tdbḥn
]b˓d.ilynm
]l km amtm

37: cp. 56
38: cp. 41 and 23 41
45: there may (despite the word-divider) be no
further writing after mla (cp. 55)
47: cp. 49
49 Gaster ym[li]; Gray ym[d] 'he measured, appointed'; Caquot and Sznycer ym[ġy]
51 aḫyh prob. error for aḫh (49) or aryh (48)
54-55: it is not certain whether there is writing at the
end of these lines, as the p in 55 seems to have been
erased; Gaster restores [tr] in 54 and i[br] in 55
56-57 Herdner dṣ or dl; Gaster š[in] 'mire' (cp. Ps.
xl 3); Gray mšmš dt(57)i ttpq (ti 'waterhole'; cp.
Arab. ta'ta'a 'watered beasts')
20A 1, 7 Virolleaud

3 Caquot and Sznycer kmt mtm
B 1-2: cp. 21 A 3-4
4: cp. 22 A 23-24
5 ta error for tn; š[pšm.btlt]: cp. 14 196
6: cp. 22 A 25-26
7: cp. 17 i 18 etc.
9 Virolleaud (cp. 6-7)
21A 1, 5: there does not seem to be room for [wy˓n.il] and
the required space as in 8-9
2-4: cp. 9-12 20 B 2
5: perhaps yrp (6) [um]
8: cp. 20 B 1; perhaps [alk.bqrb] (Herdner)
9 rpim perhaps error for rpum (thus also in 2, 10; cp.
3); cp. also 6 vi 45

[ı̊lnym.bhkl]y.átrh.rpùm
[ltdd.átr]h.ltdd.ı̊[lnym]
[   ]rn[   ]

· · · · · ·

Col. B

· · · · · ·

[yt]b.lárṣ

22

Col. A

· · · · · · ·

[- -].[-]l̊[
b.hkly.[
lk.bty.r[pı̊m.rpı̊m.bty.aṣḥ]
km.ı̊qr[ákm.ı̊lnym.bhkly]
5 átrh.r[pùm.ltdd.átrh]
ltdd.ı̊l[nym
mhr.bᶜl̊[mhr]
ᶜnt.lk b[ty.rpı̊m.rpı̊m.bty]
àṣḥ.km.[ı̊qràkm.ı̊lnym.b]
10 hkly.átr[h.rpùm.ltdd]
átrh.lt[dd.ı̊lnym.tm]
yḥpn.ḥy[ly.zbl.mlk.ᶜllmy]
šmᶜ.ntm[
ym.lm.qd[
15 šmn.prst[
ydr.hm.ym[
ᶜṣ àmr.yù[ḫd.ksà.mlkh]
nḫt.kḫt.d[rkth.bty]
àṣḥ.rpı̊[m.ı̊qrà.ı̊lnym]
20 bqrb.h[kly.átrh.rpùm.l]
tdd.átr[h.ltdd.ı̊lnym]
àsr.mr[kbt
tᶜln.lmr[kbthm.tı̊ty.l]
ᶜrhm.tl[kn.ym.wtn.àḫr.spšm]
25 btlt.mġy.[rpùm.lgrnt]
ı̊[ln]y[m.lmṭᶜt

· · · · · · ·

Col. B

· · · · · ·

[-]m[   ]

---

h.hn bnk.hn[- - - - - - - -]
bn bn.átrk.hn[- - - - - -]
ydk.ṣġr.tnšq.šptk.tm
5 tkm.bm tkm.àḥm.qym.ı̊l
blsmt.tm.ytbš.šm.ı̊l.mtm
yᶜbš.brkn.šm.ı̊l.ġzrm
tm.tmq.rpù.bᶜl.mhr bᶜl
wmhr.ᶜnt.tm.yḥpn.ḥyl
10 y.zbl.mlk.ᶜllmy[.]km.tdd
ᶜnt.ṣd.tštr.ᶜpt.šmm
ṭbḫ.àlpm.àp ṣı̊n.šql.trm
wmrı̊ ı̊lm.ᶜglm.dt.šnt
ı̊mr.qmṣ.llı̊m.kksp
15 lᶜbrm.zt.ḥrṣ.lᶜbrm.kš
dpr.tlḥn.bqᶜl.bqᶜl
mlkm.hn.ym.yṣq.yn.tmk
mrt.yn.srnm.yn.bld
ġll.yn.ı̊sryt.ᶜnq.smd
20 lbnn.ṭl mrt.yḥrt.ı̊l
hn.ym.wtn.tlḥm.rpùm
tštyn.tlt.rbᶜ.ym.ḥmš
tdt.ym.tlḥmn.rpùm
tštyn.bt.ı̊kl.bprᶜ
25 yṣq[.]bı̊rt.lbnn.mk.bšbᶜ
[ymm.àpn]k.àlı̊yn.bᶜl
[- - - - - -].rᶜh àby[-]
[- - - - - - - -]ᶜ[- - - -]

· · · · · ·

PRU II no. 3

[- - - -]r[- - - -]
[- - -]ı̊l.[- - -]
[- -]ùn.bárṣ
mḥnm.trp ym.
5 lšnm.tlḥk.
šmm.ttrp
ym.žnbtm.
tnn.lšbm
tšt.trks
10 lmrym.lb[-]
pl.tbᶜ[- - -]
hmlt ḫt.[- -]

B Virolleaud (cp. **5** vi 13–14 **10** i 9)
22A 3–6, 8–11, 18–21: cp. **21** A 1–4, 9–12
7: cp. B 9
11–12: cp. B 9–10
13 ntm error for àtm; at the end perhaps [ı̊ln] (14) ym
14 Virolleaud qd[qd.àlı̊yn.bᶜl]
16 Virolleaud ym[lk]

17 ᶜṣ prob. error for ᶜl
17–18 Virolleaud after **3** D 46–47
22–26: cp. **20** B 2–7
B 7 yᶜbš perhaps error for ytbš (6) or vice-versa
9–10 ḥyly or (De Moor) ḥyl ḥḥ 'the host of filth'
26: cp. **17** v 4
(PRU) 4, 6: note t; ᶜ is also possible

l.tp[- -]m[- - -]
n[-]m[- - - -]

RS 22.225

ʿnt.ḥlkt.wšnwt
tp.àḥḥ.wnʿm.àḥḥ.
kysmsm.tspì.sìrh
l.bl ḥrb.tšt.dmḥ.
5 lbl.ks.tpnn.ʿn
bty.ʿn btt.tpnn
ʿn.mḥr.ʿn.pḥr
ʿn.tǵr.ʿn tǵr
ltǵr.ttb.ʿn[.]pḥr
10 lpḥr.ttb.ʿn.mḥr
lmḥr.ttb.ʿn bty
lbty[.t]tb.ʿn[.]btt
lbtt.[ttb   ]

Ugaritica V no. 1

Obv. ìl dbḥ.bbth.mṣd.ṣd.bqrb
ḥkl[ḥ] ṣh.lqṣ.ìlm.tlḥmn
ìlm.wtštn.tštn y⟨n⟩ʿd šbʿ
trt.ʿd.škr.yʿdb.yrḥ
5 gbh.km.[- - -]yqtqt.tḥt
tlḥnt.ìl.dydʿnn
yʿdb.lḥm.lh(dmṣd).wdlydʿnn
ylmn(bqrʿ).ḥtm.tḥt.tlḥn
ʿttrt.wʿnt.ymǵy
10 ʿttrt.tʿdb.nšb lh
wʿnt.ktp[.]bhm.ygʿr.tǵr
bt.ìl.pn.lmgr lb.tʿdbn
nšb.lìnr.tʿdbn.ktp
bìl[.]àbh.gʿr.ytb.ìl.kb[n]
15 àt[rt.]ìl.ytb.bmrzḥḥ
yšt[.ìl.y]n.ʿd šbʿ.trt.ʿd škr
ìl.hlk.lbth.yštql.
lḥẓrh.yʿmsn.nn.tkmn
wšnm.wngšnn.ḥby.
20 bʿl.qrnm.wẓnb.ylšn
bḥrìh.wtnth.ql.ìl

il.kyrdm.àrṣ.ʿnt
wʿttrt.tṣdn[- - - - -]
[- - -]b[   ]
· · · ·

Rev. · · · · ·
[ʿt]trt.wʿnt[   ]
wbhm.tttb[- -]dh[-]
kmt rpà.hn nʿr
_____
dyšt.llṣbh ḥš ʿrk lb
5 [w]rìš.pqq.wšrh
yšt.àḥdh.dm zt.ḥrpnt

Ugaritica V no. 2

Obv. [- -]n.yšt.rpù.mlk.ʿlm.wyšt
[- -]gtr.wyqr.ìl.ytb.bʿttrt
ìl tpẓ.bhd rʿy.dyšr.wyẓmr
bknr.wtlb.btp.wmṣltm.bm
5 rqdm.dšn.bḥbr.ktr.ẓbm
wtšt.ʿnt.gtr.bʿlt.mlk.bʿ
lt.drkt.bʿlt.šmm.rmm
[bʿl]t.kpt.wʿnt.dì.dìt.rḥpt
[- - - -]rm.àklt.ʿgl ʿl.mšt
10 [- - - - -]r.špr.wyšt.ìl
[- - - - - -]n.ìl ǵnt.ʿgl ìl
[- - - - - - - -]d.ìl.šd yṣd mlk
[- - - - - - - - - -]yšt.ìlh
[- - - - - - - - - - - - -]ìtmh
· · · · ·

Rev. · · · · ·
[- - - - - - - - - - -]mǵy
[- - - - - - - - - -]drh
[- - - - - - - - -]rš.lbʿl
[- - - - - - - -]ǵk.rpù mlk
5 [ʿlm - - -]k.ltštk.lìršt
[- - - - -]rpì.mlk ʿlm.bʿz
[rpì.m]lk.ʿlm.bẓmrh.bl
[ành.]bhtkh.bnmrth.lr
[- -]àrṣ.ʿzk.ẓmrk.là

Rev. 4: the letters in this line may be variously divided

1 Obv. 7, 8: the words in brackets are glosses written in
   small characters under the words which they here
   follow
   12 Probably the r before *lb* should be read as *k*, giving
   klb parallel to *ìnr* (cp. **16** i 2); Dietrich and others
   hn.lm.klb (. for *g*) (see Addenda)
   14 De Moor *wb*[n]
   18 Virolleaud wrongly reads *lḥṭrh* (see p. 30 note 3)

2 Obv. 3, 5 *tpẓ, ẓbm*: see p. 30 note 3
   9 De Moor [*bšmm*.] (cp. *CTA* **13** 12); 'l error for *ìl*
   (the ʿ has been circled by the scribe; cp. 11)
   12: perhaps *mlk* (13) [ʿlm] (cp. rev. l. 6)
Rev. 3: perhaps [ì]rš (cp. 5)
   5: cp. 6
   8–10: as corrected by Fisher

10 *nk . ḥtkk . nmrtk . btk*
ùgrt . lymt . špš . wyrḫ
wnʿmt . šnt . ìl

Ugaritica V no. 3

Obv. *bʿl . ytb . ktbt . ǵr . hd . r[- -]*
kmdb . btk . ǵrh . ìl ṣpn . b[tk]
ǵr . tlìyt . šbʿt . brqm . [- -]
tmnt . ìṣr rʿt . ʿṣ brq y[- -]
5 *rìš . tply . tly . bn . ʿn[h]*
ùzʿrt . tmll . ìšdh . qrn[m]
dt . ʿlh . rìš . bglt . bšm[m]
[- -]ìl . tr . ìt . ph . ktt . ǵbm[- - - -]
[- - - - -]kyn . ddm . lb[- - - - -]
10 *[- - - - - - - -]ṣyt š[- - - - -]*

. . . .

Rev. . . . .
[- - - - - - - -]àhl[- - - - - -]
[- - - - - -]mṭr . ùr[- - - - - -]
[- - n]skt . nʿmn . nbl[m - - - -]
[- -]yṣq šmn . šlm . bṣ[ʿ . trḫṣ]
5 *ydh . btlt . ʿnt . ùṣbʿt[h . ybmt]*
lìmm . tìḫd . knrh . byd[h . tšt]
rìmt . lìrth . tšr . dd àl[ìyn]
bʿl . àhbt .

(unfinished)

Ugaritica V no. 4

Obv. *wyʿny . bn*
ìlm . mt . npš
npš . lbìm
thw . wnpš
5 *ànḫr . bym*
brkt . [m]šbšt
krùmm . hm
ʿn . kžd . àylt
mt hm . ks . ym
10 *sk . nhr hm*

šbʿ . ydty . bṣʿ
—————————————
[- -]šbʿ . rbt[- -]
[- - -]qbẓ . tm
E. *[- - -]m ẓbm tr*
Rev. 15 *[- - -]bn . ìlm*
[mt .]šmḫ . pydd
ìl[. ǵ]zr .
bndn . ʿ . ẓ . w
rgbt . ẓbl

Ugaritica V no. 7

Obv. *ùm . pḫl . pḫlt . bt . ʿn[.]bt . àbn . bt šmm wthm*
qrìt . lšpš . ùmh . špš . ùm . ql . bl . ʿm
ìl . mbk nhrm . bʿdt . thmtm
mnt . ntk . nḥš . šmrr . nḥš
5 *ʿqšr . lnh . mlḫš . àbd . lnh . ydy*
ḥmt . hlm . ytq . nḥš . yšlḥm . ⟨nḥš . ⟩ʿqšr
yʿdb . ksà . wytb
—————————————
tqrù . lšpš . ùmh . špš . ùm . ql bl
ʿm . bʿl . mrym . ṣpn . mnty . ntk
10 *nḥš . šmrr . nḥš . ʿqšr . lnh*
mlḫš . àbd . lnh . ydy . ḥmt . hlm . ytq
nḥš . yšlḥm . nḥš . ʿqšr . y⟨ʿ⟩db . ksà
wytb
—————————————
tqrù . lšpš . ù⟨m⟩h . špš . ùm . ql . bl . ʿm
15 *dgn . ttlh . mnt . ntk . nḥš . šmrr*
nḥš . ʿqšr . lnh . mlḫš . àbd . lnh
ydy[.]ḥmt . hlm . ytq . nḥš . yšlḥm
nḥš . ʿqšr . yʿdb . ksà . wytb
—————————————
tqrù lšpš . ùmh . špš . ùm . ql . bl . ʿm
20 *ʿnt wʿ . ttrt ìnbbh . mnt . ntk*
nḥš . šmrr . nḥš . ʿqšr . lnh . ml
ḫš . àbd . lnh . ydy . ḥmt . hlm . ytq
nḥš . yšlḥm . nḥš . ʿqšr[. yʿ]db ksà
wytb
—————————————
25 *tqrù . lšpš . ùmh . špš . [ùm . ql] bl . ʿm*

---

3 Obv.   1: perhaps *r[ʿy]* (cp. no. 2 obv. *l.* 3)
          8 *ǵbm* or *ǵbt* (Hebr. has both plurals)
   Rev.   3: cp. RS 24.249 A 8 (*Ugaritica* V p. 588; Virolleaud)
          4–5: cp. **3** B 31–33
          6–7: cp. **3** C 1–2
4 Obv.   6 De Moor
          13, 14 *qbẓ, ẓbm*: see p. 30 note 3
   Rev.   18 ʿ . *ẓ* prob. error for ʿ*z*
7 Obv.   1: the end of this line transgresses the margin sub-

stantially; several other lines finish with one or two
letters on the edge of the tablet
6: cp. 12, 17–18 etc.
12: cp. 7, 18 etc.
14: cp. 2, 8 etc.
20 ʿ . *ttrt* error for ʿ*ttrt*; the ʿ appears to have been
written over original *t* or *à* (for *àtrt*?)
23: cp. 6–7, 18 etc.
25–26: cp. 2–4, 8–10 etc.

yrḫ.lrgth.mnt.ntk.[nḫ]s.šmrr
nḫš.ʿqšr.lnh.mlḫš.ȧbd.lnk.ydy
ḥmt.hlm.yṭq.nḫš[.]yšlḥm.nḫš
ʿqšr.yʿdb.ksȧ.wyṯb

───────────────────

30 tqrù.lšpš.ȧmh.špš.ȧm.ql b⟨l⟩.ʿm
ršp.bbth.mnt.ntk.nḫš.šmrr
nḫš.ʿqšr.lnh.mlḫš.ȧbd.lnh.ydy
ḥmt.hlm.yṭq.nḫš.yšlḥm.nḫš.ʿq
š⟨r⟩.yʿdb.ksȧ wyṯb

───────────────────

35 tqrù lšpš.ȧmh.špš.ȧm.ql bl ʿm
ẓẓ.wkmt.ḥryth.mnt.ntk nḫš.šm
rr.nḫš.ʿqšr.lnh.mlḫš ȧbd.lnh
ydy.ḥmt.hlm.yṭq nḫš yšlḥm.nḫš
ʿq.šr.yʿdb.ksȧ.wyṯb

───────────────────

40 [t]qrù lšpš ȧmh špš ȧm ql.bl.ʿm
mlk.ʿttrth.mnt.ntk.nḫš.šmrr
nḫš.ʿqšr.lnh.mlḫš ȧbd.lnh.ydy
ḥmt.hlm.yṭq.nḫš.yšlḥm.nḫš
Rev. ʿqšr.yʿdb.ksȧ.wyṯb

───────────────────

45 tqrù.lšps.ȧmh.špš.ȧm.ql bl.ʿm
ktr.wḫss.kptrh.mnt.ntk.nḫš
šmrr.nḫš.ʿqšr.lnh.mlḫš.ȧbd
lnh.ydy.ḥmt.hlm yṭq.nḫš
yšlḥm.nḫš.ʿqšr.yʿdb ksȧ
50 wyṯb

───────────────────

tqrù lšpš.ȧmh.špš.ȧm.ql.bl[.]ʿm
šḥr.wšlm šmmh mnt.ntk.nḫš

šmrr.nḫš ʿqšr.lnh.mlḫš
ȧbd.lnh.ydy ḥmt.hlm.yṭq
55 nḫš.yšlḥm.nḫš.ʿqšr.yʿdb
ksȧ.wyṯb

───────────────────

tqrù.lšpš.ȧmh špš.ȧm.ql bl
ʿm ḥrn.mṣdh.mnt.ntk nḫš
šmrr.nḫš.ʿqšr.lnh.mlḫš
60 ȧbd.lnh.ydy.ḥmt.

bḥrn.pnm.trġnw[.]wttkl
bnwth.ykr.ʿr.dqdm
ȧdk.pnm.lytn.tk ȧršḫ.rbt
wȧršḫ.trrt.ydy.bʿṣm.ʿrʿr
65 wbšḫt.ʿṣ.mt.ʿrʿrm.ynʿrnh
ssnm.ysynh.ʿdtm.yʿdynh.yb
ltm.yblnh.mġy.ḥrn.lbth.w
yštql.lḥẓrh.tlù.ḥt.km.nḫl
tplg.km.plg

───────────────────

70 bʿdh.bhtm.mnt.bʿdh.bhtm.sgrt
bʿdh.ʿdbt.ṯlt.pth.bt.mnt
pth.bt.wùbȧ.hkl.wištql
tn.km.nḫšm.yḥr.tn.km
mhry.wbn.bṯn.ȧtnny
75 ytt.nḫšm.mhrk.bn bṯn
ȧtnnk

E. ȧtr ršp.ʿttrt
ʿm ʿttrt.mrh
mnt.ntk.nḫš

30: cp. 2, 8 etc.
36 ẓẓ: Virolleaud ṭṭ
39 ʿq.šr prob. error for ʿqšr (cp. 5, 10 etc.)
41–43: these lines are written on the bottom edge of the tablet
Rev. 65: Virolleaud's copy (but not his transcription) wrongly has ynʿrȧh (Fisher)
68 ḥẓrh: see at no. 1 obv. l. 18

72 wùbȧ (Fisher); the copy and transcription have wùbn

E. These lines are written on the left edge of the tablet alongside ll. 30–40, and refer to a section omitted; there may be some connection with the list of deities in no. 8 obv. ll. 13ff., where [ʿtt]r.wʿttpr follows ršp and precedes ẓẓ.wkmt

NOTE ON THE PHONOLOGY
OF UGARITIC

THE mutation of the troublesome interdental/dental and velar/pharyngal consonants as between Ugaritic and other Semitic languages is summarized in the following table; consonants in brackets are occasional but well-attested variants.

P.-Sem.	Ugar.	Aram.	Hebr.	Akk.	Arab.
ṯ	t	t	š	š	ṯ
d̠	d/ẓ	d	z	z	d̠
ṱ	ẓ(ġ)[1]	ṭ	ṣ	ṣ	ẓ
ḍ	ṣ(ẓ)[2]	'	ṣ	ṣ	ḍ
ś	š	s	ś	š	š
ḥ	ḥ	ḥ	ḥ	ḥ	ḥ
ġ	ġ(')[3]	'	'	—	ġ

[For the position in the Old Aramaic dialects, which has many similarities to Ugaritic, see my *Textbook of Syrian Semitic Inscriptions*, vol. II, p. xix.]

Examples:
[1] yqġ, mġd, nġr, ġmi, ġr 'rock'
[2] ḥẓr (2nd etym.), ẓù, ġẓy, qẓb
[3] n'm 'tunefulness', 'mm 'darkened', 'ms, 'mr, 'rb, 'rpt (if connected Arab. ġarafa 'ladled')

The second of the above features (ẓ for ṣ) is shown regularly by *CTA* **12**; this text and *CTA* **24** also have ẓ regularly for d of the other texts; see further p. 30 note 3.

Irregular or exceptional mutations are evidenced by the following words (they mostly involve the interdental/dental and velar/pharyngal consonants): ẓbb (see p. 50 note 11), ẓd 'mountain', ẓd/zd 'breast' (but see p. 124 note 5), ẓhrt, ẓmr 'made music', ḥdy (see also p. 47 note 11), ḥsp, ḥp (see p. 47 app.), ktr, mġy, mtk, 'db 'left, released' (if connected Arab. 'azaba 'was, went far away'), ġnb, ġṣr (if connected Arab. 'aṣara 'pressed grapes'), pàm, pd 'crushed', pẓġ (if connected Arab. faṣa'a 'squeezed grapes'), ṣġd (if connected Arab. ṣa'ida 'ascended'), qlṣ, šbm (see p. 50 note 5), tdt, tš.

The following show mutation within Ugaritic: ẓhrt/ẓrt; ẓd/ẓd/td (but see p. 124 note 5); ḥm 'if'/im; miyt/mhyt; mdbr/mlbr; tigt/tlqt.

Note also these cognate verbs: yṣd/yẓd (ẓù); ytn/ntn; mḥs/mḥš; nġs/nġš; ġmi/ẓmi; šmḥ/šmḫ (?); t'r/tdr.

Interchange of the labial consonants p, b, m (sometimes within Ugaritic) is shown in the following: bk, b'l, brd (but see p. 46 app.), brlt, bš, btn, zbr, ybmt/ymmt, lbš/lpš, mbk/npk, mqr/bqr, nbt, nqbn (2nd. etym.), ph (2nd. etym.), ṣph/šbh, špš, tlb. Interchange of m, n: bkm, ybmt/ybnt, km/kn 'so, thus', p'n. Interchange of n, l: ḥsn.

On the (non-phonological) replacement of t by ẓ in *CTA* **24** and certain of the texts in *Ugaritica* V see p. 30 note 3.

Metathesis of consonants is evidenced in the following: irt, glt, ḥprt, mzl, mrḥ, qṣm, šr', t'r.

The role of the stress in Ugaritic is different from its role in the first millennium 'Canaanite' and Aramaic dialects. In Ugaritic (as in Arabic) vowel quantity is distinctive and the stress is attracted to a penultimate or previous open syllable containing a long vowel (or its equivalent, a closed syllable containing a short vowel). In Hebrew, Phoenician and Aramaic, on the other hand, the stress is free and therefore distinctive, deciding the quality (rather than the quantity) of the vowels in its environment. This change in the role of the stress was closely associated with the dropping of final short vowels in grammatical forms and occurred sometime between the age of the Ugaritic texts and the appearance of the earliest Phoenician and Hebrew inscriptions (*c.* 1000 B.C.); see further my remarks in *Journal of Linguistics* 2 (1966), 35ff. There are, it should be noted, important corollaries here for theories of Ugaritic and Hebrew metre; syllable counting may be a viable undertaking for Ugaritic where differences in vowel quantity are phonologically relevant, but is hardly meaningful in the case of a stress-orientated language like Hebrew.

GLOSSARY

Notes: 1. The order of letters follows that in Gordon's *Textbook* and Whitaker's *Concordance*, i.e. ǵ (=ḏ) after d and ẓ (=ṭ) after ṭ

2. In the case of common words selected references only are given; Whitaker's *Concordance* should be consulted for the fuller picture.

3. Etymologies are as a general rule added only where a word or a meaning cannot be easily attested from classical Hebrew.

4. A number of alternative etymologies may be found in the footnotes to the translation.

5. A list of verbal forms whose roots are uncertain is given at the end of the Glossary.

6. Obvious truncated forms are not included.

ảb 'father' **2** i 33 iii 17   **3** E 43 etc.

ảbd G 'perished, was lost, lacking'   *Ugar* V no. 7 *ll.* 5ff.   Gt 'perished' **14** i 8, 24

ảbd 'destruction' **2** iv 3

ảbynt 'misery' **17** i 17 [M.-Hebr. *'ebyônût* 'poverty']

ảblm element in place-name **18** i 30

ảbn 'stone' **3** C 20   **5** vi 17 etc.

ảgn 'basin' **23** 15, 31

ảgrt 'one hiring' (fem.) or 'hired woman' **19** 213

ảd 'father, daddy' **23** 32, 43 [child's term of endearment]

ảdm N 'reddled, rouged oneself' **14** 62   **19** 204

ảdm 'mankind, men' **3** B 8   **14** 37, 43

ảdn 'lord, sire' **1** iv 17   **2** i 17   **15** vi 5   **16** i 44 etc.

ảdr 'vast, noble' **16** i 8   **17** v 7 vi 20

ảhb G 'loved' **5** v 18

ảhbt 'love' **3** C 4   **4** iv 39

ảhl 'tent' **15** iii 18   **17** v 32   **19** 212

ảḥd 'one, alone' **2** i 25   **4** vii 49   **6** i 46 v 19   **14** 184

ảḥdh 'together' *Ugar.* V no. 1 rev. *l.* 6

ảḥl 'oh that!' **19** 64, 71 [Hebr. *'aḥălay, 'aḥălēy*]

ảḫ 'brother' **4** v 90   **16** i 53 etc.

ảḫ [√ʾḫy] G 'was a brother to' **16** vi 35, 51

ảḫ 'bank, shore' **10** ii 9, 12 [Akk. *aḫu* 'arm, side']

ảḫd, also ảḫẓ G impf. *yỉḫd, yủḫd* 'took, seized' **2** i 40   **3** E 30   **6** ii 30 etc.

ảḫẓ, also ảḫd G 'seized' **12** ii 33, 34

ảḫr 'afterwards' **2** i 30   **14** 195   **24** 32 etc.

ảḫt 'sister' **3** D 83   **10** ii 16 etc.

ảy 'any' **23** 6 [Arab. *'ayyu* 'which?, what?']

ảyl 'hart, stag' **6** i 24

ảylt 'doe, hind' **1** v 19   **5** i 17

ảymr name given to club **2** i 6 iv 19

ảkl G 'ate, devoured' **4** vi 24   **6** ii 35   **12** i 36 etc.

ảkl 'food' **14** 81   **19** 9

ảklt 'blighted earth' **19** 68

ảl 'not' in prohibitions **3** E 29   **14** 116, 133   **19** 159   in questions **18** iv 9   'lest' in subordinate clauses **3** E 30   **4** vi 10 viii 17

ảl 'surely, of a truth' in commands **2** i 14–15   **4** viii 1   **17** vi 34   in questions **6** vi 26   in statements **4** vii 45 [Hebr. *'al* 'surely' in Mic. i 10; the etymology of this particle and its connection with the preceding are uncertain]

ảlỉy [√ʾl'y] 'mightiest' **3** C 11   **4** viii 34   **5** ii 10

ảlỉyn [√ʾl'y] 'mightiest' as title of Baal **1** iv 22   **2** i 4   **3** A 2   **4** ii 22 etc.

ảll 'robe' **6** ii 11   **12** ii 48   **19** 37, 48 [Akk. *alālu* 'to hang']

ảlmnt 'widow' **14** 97   **16** vi 33, 50   **17** v 8

ảln **12** i 20

ảlp 'ox' **3** D 85   **4** vi 40 etc.

ảlp 'thousand' **3** A 15 D 82   **4** v 86 etc.

ảlt [√?] 'mainstay, prop' or similar **6** vi 27 [Arab. *'âlatu* 'tool, instrument' or Hebr. *'allāh* 'pole' (Josh. xxiv 26)=Arab. *'allatu* 'spear' or Akk. *alālu* 'to hang']

ảmr G 'saw' **16** iv 2 'said' **2** i 15, 31 Gt 'caught sight of' **3** A 22 'was seen, appeared' **2** i 32 [Akk. *amāru* 'to see'; Hebr. *'āmar* 'said']

ảmr 'saying, command' **2** i 15, 31   **22** A 17

ảmr variant of ỉmr 'lamb' **20** A 10

ảmr 'Amurru' **4** i 42

ảmrr name of Athirat's servant **4** iv 17 more fully qdš-w-ảmrr (q.v.)

ảmt pl. ảmht 'slave-girl' **4** iii 21 iv 61   **12** i 15   **14** 56

ảmt 'fore-arm, elbow' **5** i 6   **14** 63

ản, also ảnk 'I' **2** i 45 iii 22   **3** D 77 etc.

ản 'where, whither' **6** iv 46 [Hebr. *'ān*]

ản 'ah! now' **19** 64 [Hebr. *'annâ*]

ảnhb 'murex' **3** B 3 D 89 [Akk. *yanibu, nibu* 'shell-fish']

ảnḫ 'sighing' **17** i 18 [Akk. *inḫu*]

ảnḫr 'dolphin' **5** i 15 [Akk. *nāḫiru*]

ảny G 'groaned' **3** E 43 **16** i 8

ảnk, also ản 'I' **2** iii 19   **3** C 25 etc.

ảnm [√ʾwn] pl. 'strength' **6** i 50

ảnnḫ 'mint' **23** 14 [Akk. *nānaḫu*]

ảnp, also ảp dual 'nostrils, face' **12** ii 38

ảnš G 'was like a man' or 'was gentle' **3** E 35   **18** i 16 D 'made someone a companion' or L 'was familiar with' **2** i 38   **6** v 21   **16** vi 36 [Arab. *'anisa, 'ânasa*]

ảnš broken pl. 'muscles' **3** D 32 [Hebr. *nāšeh*]

ảnšt 'gentleness' **15** v 27   **18** iv 10

ảsm 'granary' **19** 67, 74

ảsp G 'gathered' **1** iv 11   **12** ii 25   **19** 66 Gt 'gathered to oneself, carried off' **14** 18

ảsr G 'bound' **1** ii 7 v 9, 22   **8** 13   **19** 81   **20** B 3   **22** A 22

ảsr 'prisoner' **2** i 37

ảǵzt **24** 3

ảp, also ảpn 'also, moreover, even, yet' **1** iv 26   **2** i 20   **6** vi 42   **16** i 3, 9   **19** 16 etc.

ảp, also *ảnp* 'nostril, nose' **2** i 13 **18** iv 26
  'anger' **2** i 38 **6** v 21 'tip'**23** 24 'front'**5** vi 21
  'entrance' **3** E 35 **17** v 6
ảphn, also *ảpn*, *ảpnk* 'thereupon' **17** ii 28 v 14
ảpy G 'baked' **14** 83
ảpn, also *ảp* 'also' **3** A 24
ảpn, also *ảphn*, *ảpnk* 'thereupon' **17** i 2 **16** ii 119
ảpnk, also *ảphn*, *ảpn* 'thereupon' **5** vi 11 **6** i 56
  17 ii 27 *ảpnnk* **21** A 5
ảps 'end, top' **6** i 61
ảpq 'channel, spring' **4** iv 22 **6** i 34
ảqht name of Daniel's son **17–19** *passim*
ảr [√'*wr*] 'light' **24** 38
ảr [√'*wr*] G 'gave light to' **24** 39
ảr 'mist, moisture' **3** A 24 **4** i 17 **5** v 10 [Arab.
  '*aryu* 'dew, rain']
ảr 'honey' **3** C 14 etc. [Arab. '*aryu*]
ảrb' 'four' **16** ii 85
ảrgmn 'purple stuff, tribute' **2** i 37
ảrz 'cedar' **4** v 72 vi 19 vii 41
ảrḫ pl. *ảrḫt* 'cow, heifer' **4** vi 50 **6** ii 6, 28 **10** ii 28
  iii 2, 20 [Akk. *arḫu*]
ảry 'kinsman, dependent' **3** E 45 **4** ii 26 vi 44
  12 ii 48 **17** i 20 [Egyp. *ỉry* 'companion']
ảrk G 'was, grew long' **23** 33, 34
ảrkt 'long arm' **3** E 31 [‖ *ymn*]
ảrṣ 'earth, ground, land' **2** iv 23 **3** C 13 **4** v 83
  6 i 65 etc. 'underworld' **3** D 80 **4** viii 8, 9
  15 iii 3 **19** 112 etc.
ảrṣy name of one of Baal's daughters **3** C 4 **4** i 19
  iv 57 **7** II 12
ảrr place-name **10** iii 30
ảrš G 'asked, desired' **3** E 36 **14** 42 **17** vi 26
  [Akk. *erēšu*]
ảrš name of sea-monster **3** D 40 **6** vi 50
ảršḫ place-name *Ugar.* V no. 7 *l.* 63
ảt 'you' (sing.) **1** iv 17 **2** iv 11 etc.
ảtw G 'came' **3** C 25 **4** iv 32 **15** iii 17 **20** B 4, 10
ảtm 'you' (dual) **3** D 77
ảtn pl. *ảtnt* 'she-ass' **4** iv 7, 12
ảtn-prln name of chief-priest **6** vi 54 **17** vi E
ảtr G 'proceeded, advanced' **16** v 6 [Hebr. '*āšar*]
ảtr 'after' **5** vi 24 **14** 94 etc. [Aram. *bâtar*]
ảtr 'place, shrine' **17** i 29 [Aram. '*atrâ*]
ảtryt 'destiny, final lot' **17** vi 36 [Arab. '*atrîyatu*]
ảtrt 'Athirat' consort of El **3** E 44 **4** i 15 **23** 13 etc.
  'goddess' **3** A 15
ảtt [√'*nt*] 'woman, wife' **2** iii 22 **3** D 84 **16** i 5 etc.

ỉ, also *ỉy* 'where?' **5** iv 6 **14** 201
ỉb [√'*bb*] 'blossom' **19** 31 'gem, jewel' **14** 147
ỉb [√'*yb*] 'enemy' **2** iv 8 **3** D 34 **4** vii 35 **10** ii 24
  19 221
ỉb element in name of composite deity *Nkl-w-ỉb*
  24 18
ỉbr 'buffalo, bull' **10** iii 21 **12** i 32 **14** 120 [Hebr.
  '*abbîr*]
ỉbr 'pinion' **4** vii 56 **8** 9 [Hebr. '*ēber*]
ỉd 'time' **18** iv 23 [Hebr. '*az* 'time; then' = Arab. '*iḏ*
  'then']
ỉd **15** iv 12

ỉdk 'then' **3** D 81 **4** viii 1 etc.
ỉdm **12** ii 30
ỉht pl. of *ỉy* 'islands' **3** F 8 [Neiman, *JNES* 30, 64]
ỉḥ 'brother, cousin' **24** 35 [Zenjirli inscrs. '*yḥ*]
ỉy, also *ỉ* 'where?' **6** iv 28
ỉk 'as, like' **16** 1 3 [cp. *k*]
ỉk(m) 'how?' **2** i 40 **3** D 33 **6** vi 26 **16** i 20 etc.
ỉl 'god' **1** iv 13 **3** D 36 **4** ii 10, 35 **10** ii 5 **12** i 41
  19 153, 219 etc.   name of 'El' as supreme god
  1 iv 12, 28 **2** i 21 iii 19 **3** E 47 **4** iv 23 etc.
  dual and pl. 'gods' **1** iv 6 **2** i 18, 20 **3** D 40, 78
  17 v 20 etc. expressing superlative **3** F 14 **4** i 31ff.
  6 i 65 **10** iii 34 **12** i 22 **17** vi 23
ỉl-ṣpn title of Baal *Ugar.* V no. 3 obv. *l.*2 of Mt.
  Zephon **3** C 26 D 63
ỉl [√'*wl*] 'ram' **4** vi 42 **19** 13 **22** B 13
ỉlỉb 'father's god' **17** i 27 ii 16 [from *ỉl* and *ỉb* ⟨*ảb*]
ỉlh a deity *Ugar.* V no 2 obv. *l.* 13 [Hebr. '*ĕlōah*]
ỉlhù name of son of Keret **16** i 46 ii 83
ỉll 'inanition' **5** v 16 [Syr. '*alîl* 'weak'; Hebr. '*ĕlîl*
  'worthlessness']
ỉlmlk name of scribe **6** vi 53 **16** vi E
ỉlnym 'ghosts' particularly of gods of underworld
  6 vi 46 **20–22** *passim* but also of El **3** D 79
  [Phoen. '*lnm* 'gods']
ỉlnm **19** 10
ỉlqṣ 'gem' **4** v 79 [‖ *ỉqnủ*]
ỉlš name of divine steward or herald **16** iv 4
ỉlt 'goddess' **3** B 18 'Elat' as name or title of Athirat **1** iv 14 **3** E 45 **14** 198 **15** iii 26 pl. *ỉlht*
  'goddesses' **3** E 36 **4** vi 48 **16** iv 5 **24** 11
ỉm, also *hm* 'if' **6** v 21
ỉmr, also *ảmr* 'lamb' **3** E 9 **4** vi 43 viii 18 etc.
ỉmt, also *mt* [√'*mn*] 'truly' **5** i 18 [Zenjirli inscrs. *mt*]
ỉn [√'*yn*] 'there is not, was not' **2** iii 22 **3** E 36 etc.
ỉnbb place associated with Anat **3** D 78 *Ugar.* V
  no. 7 *l.* 20
ỉnr 'cur' **16** i 2, 16 *Ugar.* V no. 1 obv. *l.* 13 [‖ *klb*]
ỉnšt name of profession **6** vi 40
ỉpủ 'mist, clouds' **10** ii 32 [Akk. *upû*]
ỉṣr 'bundle' *Ugar.* V no. 3 obv. *l.* 4 [Arab. '*iṣru*]
ỉqnủ 'lapis-lazuli' **4** v 81 **14** 147 [Akk. *uknû*]
ỉrby [√*rby*] 'locust(s)' **3** B 10 **14** 103
ỉršt 'request' *Ugar.* V no. 2 rev. *l.* 5 [Akk. *erištu*]
ỉrt 'breast, lung' **2** iv 2 **3** C 2 **6** iii 19 **22** B 25
  [Akk. *irtu* 'breast'; cognate Arab. *ri'atu* 'lung']
ỉš, also *ỉšt* 'fire' **12** i 10 [Hebr. '*ēš* and Akk. *išātu*]
ỉšd 'leg' **3** D 56 *Ugar.* V no. 3 obv. *l.* 6 [Akk. *išdu*]
ỉšryt place-name **18** i 28 **22** B 19
ỉšt, also *ỉš* 'fire' **2** i 32 iii 13 **4** vi 22 **23** 14, 41
ỉtnn [√*ytn*] 'salary, fee' *Ugar.* V no. 7 *l.* 74
ỉt 'there is, was' **3** C 18 **6** iii 3 **14** 201 etc. [Aram.
  '*ỉt(ay)*]
ỉtl 'spittle' **1** ii 9 **18** iv 25 [Hittite *iššali*]
ỉtm deity of cattle **5** iii 24
ỉtm *Ugar.* V no. 2 obv. *l.* 14

ủ 'or' **4** vii 43 **15** iii 29 **16** i 4, 22 **23** 63
ủbả [√*bw*'] 'entrance' *Ugar.* V no. 7 *l.* 72
ủgr name of second servant of Baal [see *gpn*]
ủgr 'field, soil' **12** i 25 [Akk. *ugāru*]

ủgrt 'Ugarit' **4** viii E **6** vi 56 *Ugar.* V no. 2 rev. *l.* 11

ủdm name of Pabil's city **14** *passim*

ủdmm inhabitants of Udm **15** i 7

ủdmˁt pl. 'tears' **6** i 10 **14** 28 **16** i 28

ủdn 'ear' **3** D 46 **16** vi 42 **18** iv 23

ủdr 'most noble' **4** v 79

ủẓˁrt Ugar. V no. 3 obv. *l.*6

ủẓr **17** i 3ff.

ủḫry 'coming after, last, last-born' **12** ii 28 **19** 155, 162, 169

ủḫryt 'latter end' **17** vi 35

ủṭ **2** i 13 **5** i 5 **18** iv 3

ủl [√*ˀwl*] 'force, strength' **2** iv 5 **14** 88

ủlmn 'widowhood' **23** 9

ủlt implement of metal **4** iv 60

ủm pl. *ủmht* 'mother' **6** vi 11 **15** i 6 **23** 33 etc.

ủmt 'family, clan' **6** iv 43 **14** 6 **19** 197 [Arab. *ˀummatu*]

ủn 'evil, sorrow' **5** vi 15 [Hebr. *ˀāwen*]

ủn 'season' **19** 40 [Arab. *ˀānu*]

ủgr place associated with Anat **3** D 78

ủpqt **1** v 11, 24

ủṣbˁ pl. *ủṣbˁt* 'finger' **2** iv 14 **3** B 35 **14** 158 **15** v 16

ủr 'herb' **19** 66, 73 [Hebr. *ˀôrāh*]

ủr **10** i 11

ủrbt 'lattice, sluice' **4** v 123 vii 18 [Hebr. *ˀărubbāh*]

ủšk 'testicle' **11** 2 [Hebr. *ˀešek*]

ủšn 'gift' **14** 135 [Arab. *ˀawsu*]

b, also *bm* and *bn* 'in, into, at, among, on, by, with' *passim* 'as' **5** vi 18 'from, out of' **2** iv 6 **3** B 34 C **14** D 45 **4** iv 36 vi 33 vii 5 **6** i 46 v 20 **14** 56, 111 **16** vi 10 **17** ii 39 **19** 183, 219 **23** 6, 59, 63 [Hebr. *bᵉ* 'from' in Ps. xviii (2 Sam. xxii) 9 Job v 21 xx 20 Prov. ix 5 etc.]

bả [√*bw*] G 'came in, went in' **2** iii 5 **3** E 15 **15** iv 21 **16** vi 3 **19** 213

bbr **4** i 36 [or *b+br*]

bbt place-name *Ugar.* V no. 7 *l.* 31 [or *b+bt*]

bd [√*bdd*] G 'chanted, recited' **3** A 18 **17** vi 31

bd 'chanting' **16** i 5

bd [√*bdd*] in *lbdm* 'alone' **2** iii 20

bd [<*byd*] 'by the hand of' **1** iv 22 **19** 160 'in(to) the hand of' **3** A 10 **4** i 25 **17** v 26 **23** 8 'from the hand of' **2** iv 13

bddy 'chanting' **19** 77

bdqt 'breach, rift' **4** vii 19, 28 [Hebr. *bedeq*]

bht 'hail!' **5** ii 11, 19 [Arab. *bahata* 'welcomed']

bḥr 'youth' **15** v 22 [Hebr. *bāḥûr*]

bk 'beaker, jar' **3** A 12 [Hebr. *pak*]

bky G 'wept' **6** i 9 **14** 26 **15** v 12 **16** i 6, 12, 14 vi 4 **19** 111 etc. 'bewept' **6** i 16

bkyt 'weeping woman' **19** 171-172

bkm 'forthwith' **4** vii 13, 42 **16** ii 112 **19** 57 [cognate Hebr. *bᵉkēn* = Aram. *bkēn* 'then']

bkm **10** iii 30

bkr 'first-born' **14** 144

bkr D 'treated as first-born' **15** iii 16

bl 'not' **4** v 123 vii 43 **17** i 21 etc. 'nay, but' or 'yea' **6** i 48 [Hebr. *bal* 'not' = Arab. *bal* 'nay, but' and *balâ(y)* 'yea']

bl 'without' **14** 91 **19** 44 [*b+l*]

bld 'country' **22** B 18 [Arab. *baladu*]

bly G 'became worn, withered' **19** 18 D 'wore out, consumed' **5** i 18

blmt 'immortality' **16** i 15 **17** vi 27

blt 'nay, but' **6** i 54 [cp. *bl*]

blt **10** iii 10

bm, also *b* and *bn* 'in etc.' **2** i 39 **10** iii 31 **12** i 12 **14** 31 **19** 34, 83 **23** 51 [Hebr. *bᵉmô*]

bmt 'torso, back' **3** B 12 **4** iv 14 **5** vi 22 [Akk. *bamtu* 'rib-cage, chest'; Hebr. *bāmāh* in Deut. xxxiii 29]

bmt 'high place' **4** vii 34 [Hebr. *bāmāh* 'high-place'; Akk. *bamātu* 'open country']

bn, also *b* and *bm* 'in' **4** vii 15, 16 (*bnm*), 55 **8** 7-8 [S.-Arab.*bn* 'from']

bn 'son' **1** iv 12 **2** i 19, 21 **3** E 12 **5** i 7 etc.

bn [√*byn*] G 'understood' **3** C 23, 24 **4** v 122

bn [√*byn*] 'between' **1** v 23 **2** i 42 iv 14 **3** B 6 etc.

bn [√*bny*] G 'built, made, re-made' **2** iii 10 **4** iv 62, 80 vi 36 **19** 118 etc.

bnwn [√*bny*] 'building, structure' **16** iv 14

bnwt [√*bny*] 'creature(s)' **4** ii 11 **6** iii 5 **17** i 25 *Ugar.* V no. 7 *l.* 62

bny 'creator' **4** ii 11 **6** iii 5 **17** i 25

bnt **12** ii 44 **17** vi 13

bˁd, also *bˁdn* 'behind, around' **16** v 5 vi 49 *Ugar.* V no. 7 *l.* 70 'for' **23** 70 [Hebr. *baˁad*]

bˁdn, also *bˁd* 'behind, round about' **3** D 30

bˁl 'lord' **1** iv 6 **2** i 17 **3** A 3 **6** vi 157 **17** v 20 **24** 42 elsewhere title of Baal, chief god of Ugarit

bˁl G 'made' **17** vi 24 [Hebr. *pāˁal*]

bˁlt 'mistress' *Ugar.* V no. 2 obv. *l.* 6

bˁr D 'kindled' **3** D 70 'removed, made away with' **14** 101 **16** ii 80 [Hebr. *biˁˁēr*; perhaps two roots]

bġy G 'sought out' **3** C 26 D 63 [Aram. *bˁâ*]

bṣql 'green, ripening stalk' **19** 62 [Hebr. *biṣqālôn*]

bṣr 'looked, regarded' **18** iv 20 **19** 33 [Arab. *baṣira*]

bqˁ G or D 'split, ripped open' **6** ii 32 **19** 109, 116

bqr, also *mqr* [√*qwr*] 'well' **14** 113

bqt D 'sought' **6** iv 44 [Hebr. *biqqēš*]

brd G 'carved' **3** A 6 [Hebr. *pārad*]

brḥ G 'fled' **19** 154

brḥ 'fleeing, slippery' **5** i 1

brk D 'made to kneel' **12** i 26 'blessed' **15** ii 18 **17** i 24, 35 **19** 194

brk adj. 'blessed' **19** 194

brk pl. *brkt* 'knee' **2** i 23 **3** B 13 **17** v 27 **18** iv 24

brky, also *brkt* 'pool' **5** i 16

brkn 'blessing' **22** B 7

brkt, also *brky* 'pool' *Ugar.* V no. 4 *l.* 6

brlt 'breath, life, appetite, throat' **5** i 15 **16** vi 12 **17** v 18 **18** iv 25 [‖ *npš*; perhaps cognate Akk. *mēriltu*, *mērištu* 'request, desire']

brq 'lightning' **3** C 23 **4** v 71 etc.

bš [√*bwš*] G 'remained, delayed' **3** D 77 [Hebr. *bôšēš*; Syr. *pāš*]

bšr G 'was gladdened' **4** v 88 **10** iii 34 D 'brought good news' **19** 86 [Hebr. *biśśar*]

bšr 'flesh' **4** ii 5 **15** iv 25 **24** 9

bšrt 'good news' **4** v 89 **10** iii 34

bt 'house' **1** iv 6 **3** E 46 **4** v 72 **19** 32 etc. pl. *bht* 'mansion, palace' **2** iii 8 **3** B 4 **4** v 75, 92 etc.

bt pl. *bnt* 'daughter' **3** A 23 B 2 C 3 D 43 etc.

btlt 'virgin' as title of Anat **3** B 32 **4** ii 14 etc.

bt[√*btt*] G 'scattered' **2** iv 28 [Arab. *batta*]

bty RS **22.225** *l.* 5

btn 'serpent' **5** i 1 **6** vi 19 **17** vi 14 **19** 223 *Ugar* V no. 7 *l.* 74 [Hebr. *peten*; Arab. *batanu*]

btt [√*bwt*] 'shame' **1** iv 5 **4** iii 19 [Hebr. *bōšet*]

btt RS **22.225** *l.* 5

g 'voice' **2** iii 15 **3** D 33 **16** i 13 etc.

gản [√*g'y*] 'pride' **17** vi 44

gb **1** v 13 *Ugar.* V no. 1 obv. *l.* 5

gbb N 'was gathered' **14** 85, 176 [M.-Hebr. *gibbēb* 'gathered']

gbzt **24** 43

gbl 'frontier' **16** vi 57 [Hebr. *g*ᵉ*bûl*]

gbl 'Byblos' **3** F 7 [Hebr. *g*ᵉ*bal*; Akk. *Gubli*]

gb' 'hill' **3** C 28 **4** v 78 **5** vi 27

gbtt 'hump(s)' or the like **12** i 31 [from context]

gg pl. *ggt* 'roof, roof-terrace' **14** 80 **17** i 33

ggn, also *gngn* 'heart' **16** vi 26 [cp. Arab *janânu*]

gd 'coriander' **3** B 2 **24** 13 [Hebr. *gad*=Aram. *giddâ*]

gd 'sinew' **17** vi 21 [Hebr. *gîd*]

gdlt 'might' **3** E 31 **18** i 10

gdrt 'fold' **19** 13 [Hebr. *g*ᵉ*dērāh* 'wall, hedge, sheep-fold']

gzr broken pl. *ảgzr* 'cutter, cleaver' **23** 58, 63

gl [√*gyl*] G 'rejoiced' **16** i 15 ii 99

gl 'vessel' **14** 71, 164 [Hebr. *gullāh* 'basin, bowl']

gly G 'penetrated' **1** iii 23 **3** E 15 **16** vi 4 [Hebr. *gālāh* 'went into exile'=Arab. *jalâ* 'emigrated']

glt 'snow' **4** v 69 **8** 13 *Ugar.* V no. 3 obv. *l.* 7 [Hebr. *šeleg*=Arab. *talju*]

gmẓ G 'laughed' or similar **12** i 13 [‖ *ẓḥq*]

gml 'sickle' **24** 42 [Akk. *gamlu*]

gmn **6** i 19ff.

gmr 'avenger' **2** i 46 [Hebr. *gōmēr* in Ps. lvii 3]

gmr 'burning coal' **6** vi 16 [Aram. *gumartâ*=Arab. *jamratu*]

gn 'garden' **5** vi 21

gngn, also *ggn* 'heart' **4** vii 49

g'r G 'rebuked' **2** i 24 iv 28 *Ugar.* V no. 1 obv. *ll.* 11, 14

g't [√*g'y*] 'lowing' **14** 122

gp [√*gdp*] 'shore' **23** 30 [Aram. *gadpâ*=Syr. *geppâ* 'wing, flank']

gpn wản gr names of Baal's two servants **3** D 33 **5** i 12 etc.

gpn 'vine' **23** 9

gpnm pl. 'reins, harness' **4** iv 7, 10 **19** 53 [possibly vine-tendrils serving as such (cp. Gen. xlix 11)]

gpr **19** 11

gpt pl. 'hollows' **4** vii 36 [Arab. *jawfu*]

gr [√*gwr*] G 'sojourned, tarried' **14** 110 **19** 153

[*g*]*rgr* 'throat' **16** i 48

grgr [√*gwr*] 'sojourned' **23** 66

grdš pass. 'was stripped, deprived' **14** 11, 23 [Syr.

gardēš 'gnawed, scraped (bones)' cognate with *grad* 'scraped' and *gardî* 'was lacking, was deprived of']

grn pl. *grnt* 'threshing-floor' **14** 112 **17** v 7 **20** B 6

grš G 'drove out' **1** iv 24 **2** iv 12 **16** v 12, 27 **17** i 30

gtr 'strong, mighty' *Ugar.* V no. 2 obv. *ll.* 2, 6 [Akk. *gašru*]

d 'who, which' after masc. sing. **3** C 23 D 89 **4** i 39, 44 **14** 8, 90 **19** 220 after fem. sing. **14** 145, 147 **24** 38 after dual or pl. **4** i 37 **17** v 7 'he who, that which' **2** i 18 **3** E 41 **5** ii 12 **14** 142 **17** i 30 'she who' **24** 4 fem. *dt* 'she who' **16** v 30 [Aram. *dî, d*]

d, also *ẓ* 'of, possessor of' after masc. sing. **2** iii 12 **3** F 23 **4** iii 9 **5** i 3 **14** 69, 83 **23** 74 after pl. **4** i 40 (?) *dt* after fem. sing. **2** iv 10 **4** i 31 after pl. **3** D 32 **4** iv 10, 11 **4** vi 37 *dtm* after pl. **4** vi 37 (?) [Aram. *dî, d*]

d, also *dm* 'that, because' **1** iv 7 **14** 150 **17** i 19 [Aram. *dî, d*]

dả [√*d'y*] G 'flew' **16** v 48 vi 6 **19** 120 *Ugar.* V no. 2 obv. *l.* 8

dỉy 'hawk, kite' **18** iv 18, 20 **19** 33 [Hebr. *dā'āh*]

dỉy 'breast-bone' **19** 115ff. [Arab. *da'yu* 'ribs of breast']

dbảt 'strength' **10** ii 21 [Hebr. *dōbe* in Deut. xxxiii 25]

dbb G 'moved, crept (animal)' **4** i 40 [Arab. *dabba*]

dbḥ G 'sacrificed' **1** iv 28 **14** 76 **16** i 39 **20** A 1, 10 etc.

dbḥ 'sacrifice' **4** iii 17 **14** 71 **23** 27 etc.

dbṭ **12** ii 42 [or *d*+*bṭ*]

dbr G 'turned the back' **16** vi 31 [Arab. *dabara*]

dbr 'open country, pasture' **5** v 18 **6** ii 20 [Hebr. *dōber*; Aram. *dabrâ*]

dg 'fish' **23** 63

dgy 'fisherman' **3** F 10 **4** ii 31

dgn 'grain' **16** iii 13

dgn the god 'Dagon' **2** i 19 **5** vi 24 *Ugar.* V no. 7 *l.* 15 etc.

dd [√*dwd*] N 'stood up' **3** A 8 **4** iii 12 **10** ii 17 **23** 63 [Akk. *uzuzzu*]

dd 'pot, jar' **3** C 14 *Ugar.* V no. 3 obv. *l.* 9 [Hebr. *dûd*]

ddy 'mandrake' **3** C 12 D 68 [Hebr. *dûdāy*]

ddm pl. 'love' **3** C 2 **24** 23 [Hebr. *dôdîm*]

dw [√*dwy*] 'sick' **16** ii 82

dk 'pounder, crusher' **6** v 3 [Hebr. *dākāh* 'crushed']

dk **5** iii 8 [truncated?]

dkrt pl. vessels for wine **4** vi 54 [‖ *rḥbt*]

dl [√*dll*] 'poor' **16** vi 48

dl [√*dll*] G 'guided, led' **23** 25 [Arab. *dalla*]

dll 'courier, agent' **4** vii 45 [Arab. *dalîlu* 'guide, pilot', *dallâlu* 'broker']

dlp G 'crumbled' **2** iv 17, 26 [Hebr. *dālap* 'crumbled away; flickered']

dm, also *d* 'because' **3** C 17 **16** i 32 **17** vi 34

dm 'truly' **4** iii 17 **16** vi 1, 13 [Syr. *dam* 'lest; is not . . .?']

dm 'blood' **3** B 14 E 10 **4** iv 38 **18** iv 24 etc.

dm [√*dmm*] 'plating, veneer' **4** i 33 [Arab. *damma*

'smeared, tarred']

dm [√*dmm*] G 'lamented' **16** i 26 [Akk. *damāmu*]

dm [√*dmm*] G 'was silent, still' **14** 114 [Hebr. *dāmam*]

dm [√*dmm*] D 'acted disgracefully, lewdly' **4** iii 20 [Arab. *'adamma* 'behaved vilely']

dmgy name of Athirat's handmaid **12** i 16

dm' G 'shed tears' **14** 27 **19** 35, 174

dmq 'good, fine' **24** 50 [Akk. *damqu*]

d'mrn name or title of Baal **4** vii 39

dn [√*dyn*] G 'judged' **16** vi 33 **17** v 7

dn 'cause' **16** vi 33 **17** v 8

dn [√*dny*] G 'approached' **19** 61, 68 [Arab. *danâ*]

dn 'powerful' **12** ii 59 [Akk. *dannu*]

dn 'large cask' **3** A 12 **16** iii 14 [Akk. and Arab. *dannu*]

dnıl 'Daniel' father of Aqhat **17–19** *passim*

dnn 'strong' **16** i 30 [cp. *dn*]

dnt [√*dny*] 'meanness' **4** iii 20 [Arab. *daniya* 'was base']

dnty name of Daniel's wife **17** v 16

d't [√*yd'*] 'knowledge' **2** i 16 'acquaintance' **6** vi 49

d't [√*yd'*] 'sweat' **16** vi 10

d'ṣ G 'planted (feet)' **4** v 82 [Syr. *d'aṣ* 'fixed']

dġt 'incense' or the like **19** 185 **23** 15 [Hittite *tuḫḫueššar* 'substance for cultic purification']

dpr 'torch' **5** v 2 [Akk. *dipāru*]

dpr **22** B 16 [or *d*+*pr*]

dqn 'chin, beard' **3** E 10 **4** v 66 **5** vi 19

dq [√*dqq*] 'fine, feeble' **6** i 50

dr [√*dwr*] 'generation, race' **2** iv 10 **4** iii 7 **15** iii 19 **19** 154 *Ugar.* V no. 2 rev. *l.* 2

dry G 'winnowed' **6** ii 32 v 13

drkt 'dominion' **2** iv 10, 13 **4** vii 44 **14** 42 **16** vi 38

dr' G 'sowed, scattered' **6** ii 35 v 19

dt fem. of *d* (q.v.)

dtn dynastic name **15** iii 4

dt [√*dtt*] G pass. 'was struck down' **18** i 19 [Arab. *datta*]

ẓ, also *d* 'of, possessor of' **24** 45

ẓbb name of monster **3** D 43

šd 'mountain' **2** iii 5 **3** E 17 **4** iv 23 **19** 213, 220 [Akk. *šadû*; cp. Hebr. *šadday* as divine title; perhaps connected *td*, *šd* 'breast']

šd, also *td* and *zd* 'breast' **23** 61 [see p. 124 note 5]

šd, 'herd' **5** i 17 [Arab. *dawdu* 'small herd of camels']

šhrt, also *šrt* 'vision' **6** iii 5 **14** 36, 151 [Hebr. *šûr* 'saw, gazed']

šmr G 'guarded' **17** i 29 [S.-Arab. *dmr*; Hebr. *zimrāh* 'protection']

šmr 'guard' **3** B 14

šmr 'protection' *Ugar.* V no. 2 rev. *ll.* 7, 9

šmr D 'made music' *Ugar.* V no. 2 obv. *l.* 3 [Hebr. *zimmēr*; Arab. *zamara* 'piped']

šnb pl. *šnbt* 'tail' *PRU* II no. 3 *l.* 7 *Ugar.* V no. 1 obv. *l.* 20

šr' 'arm' **5** vi 20 **6** i 4

šrq **5** i 6

šrt see *šhrt*

—*h* adv. of direction, **14** 29, 117 **23** 10, 38 etc.

of time **19** 154 **23** 42

hbr G 'bowed down, stooped' **2** i 47 **3** C 6 **4** iv 25 **23** 49 [Arab. *habru* 'depressed ground']

hg [√*hgy*] 'reckoning' **14** 91 [Aram. *hgâ* 'mused, spelled']

hd 'Hadad' the personal name of Baal **2** i 46 **4** vii 36 **10** ii 5 **12** i 41 etc.

hdy G 'cut off, shaved' **5** vi 19 [Arab. *hadâ*]

hdm 'foot-stool' **3** B 22 **4** i 35 iv 29 etc.

hdrt 'glory, divine visitation' **14** 155

hw obl. *hwt* 'he, him' **2** i 37 **3** F 20 **6** ii 23 etc.

hwt 'word, speech' **2** i 46 **3** C 10, 19 **19** 113 etc. [Hebr. *hawwāh* 'desire' and possibly Akk. *awatu* 'word']

hy obl. *hyt* 'she, her' **3** C 7 **19** 138, 201

hyn 'Heyan' name of Kothar-and-Khasis **3** F 22 **4** i 24 **17** v 18

hkl 'palace' **2** iii 7 **3** B 18 **4** v 93 etc. [possibly pl. when ‖ *bht*; cp. **4** vi 37 (with *dtm*)]

hl, also *hlk*, *hlm*, *hln* 'behold, look here!' **17** v 12 **23** 32, 41 **24** 7 [*hl* in Arab. *halâ* 'forward!'; Aram. *lhallâ*, Syr. *lhal*, Hebr. *hāl'āh* 'thither, onwards, further etc.']

hlk, also *hl* etc. 'behold, look here!' **17** v 12 **19** 77

hlk G 'went, came' **1** iv 7 **3** D 76 **14** 92 **19** 194 etc. 'flowed' **6** iii 7 Gt or tD 'went to and fro' **5** vi 26 **6** ii 15 **23** 67 Š 'made to flow' **3** E 32 **18** i 11

hlk 'course' **19** 52

hll 'crescent moon' **17** ii 27 **24** 6 [Arab. *hilālu*]

hlm, also *hl* etc. 'behold, look here!' **2** i 21 **3** D 29 **4** iv 27 **16** i 53 *Ugar.* V no. 7 *l.* 6 [Hebr. *hălōm* 'hither'; Arab. *halumma*, 'hither!, come here!']

hlm G 'beat, struck' **2** iv 14, 16 **18** iv 22 **19** 78 *Ugar.* V no. 1 obv. *l.* 8

hln, also *hl* etc. 'behold, look here!' **3** B 5, 17

hm obl. *hmt* 'they, them' **17** v 20 **19** 115 **23** 68

hm, also *im* 'if, or' **4** ii 24 iv 34, 35, 61 **5** i 15ff. **6** iii 2 **19** 84, 110ff., 150 **23** 39, 42 etc.

hmlt 'multitude' **2** i 18 **3** C 25 **4** vii 52 *PRU* II no 3 *l.* 12 [Hebr. *hămullāh* in Ezek. i 24]

hmry 'miry, watery' **4** viii 12 **5** ii 15 [cp. *mhmrt*]

hn 'behold!' **4** vi 24 **6** vi 47 **14** 118 **23** 46 etc.

hn 'hither' **23** 75 [Hebr. *hēnnāh*]

hndt 'this' (fem.) **19** E

hpk G 'overthrew' **5** iii 12 **6** vi 28

hr 'hill, mountain' **10** i 2

hr [√*hry*] 'conception' **17** ii 41 **23** 51

hrgb name of male eagle **19** 121

hry G 'conceived' **5** v 22 **11** i 5

hrnmy epithet of Daniel's god **17–19** *passim*

hrr **12** i 39

ht 'now' **2** iv 8 **6** i 39 **17** vi 40 **19** 167 **21** A 6 [‖ *'nt*]

w 'and, but, so' *passim* 'even' **17** vi 38 'that, so that' **6** iii 8 **16** vi 18 **17** i 26, 43 **23** 72 'then' etc, *in apodosi* **4** ii 12 **6** v 9 **14** 27, 108 **16** i 50 **17** v 9 **19** 76, 180 pleonastic **3** C 6 D 85 **4** v 108

wḥ [√*wḥy*] Gt 'hurried' **3** C 17 D 56 [Arab. *waḥâ*

and *tawwaḥâ*]

wld 'birth' **14** 152   **15** iii 5, 20

wn 'but, and now' **3** E 46   **4** iv 50 v 68   **12** i 36
24 31 (from *whn* or *w+n*]

wsr G 'instructed' **4** v 66   D 'instructed' **16** vi 26
[Hebr. *yāsar* and *yissēr*]

wpt D 'spat upon' **4** iii 13 vi 13 [cognate Arab.
nafata 'spat']

zbl 'highness, prince' **2** i 38 iii 8   **3** A 3   **19** 164
22 B 10 etc. [Hebr. personal names *zᵉbûl* and
'îzebel]

zbl 'princely state' **2** i 24   **16** v 25 [Hebr. *zᵉbûl* in
Isa. lxiii 15]

zbl 'sick' **14** 98 [Akk. *zabālu* 'to carry, bear, suffer']

zbln 'sickness, plague' **14** 17   **16** v 21 vi 36

zbr G 'pruned' **23** 9 [Hebr. *zāmar*=Arab. *zabara*]

zd, also *td* and *šd* 'breast' **23** 24 [see p. 124 note 5]

zd [√*zwd*] G 'got sustenance' **1** v 27   **24** 8, 12
[Arab. *zâda* 'supplied oneself with provisions']

znt [√*zwn*] 'provision, sustenance' **1** iv 16

zġ [√?] G 'lowed' **15** i 5 [cp. Arab. *zaġzaġa* 'spoke
faintly']

zġt 'whining' **14** 122

zt 'olive(s)' **5** ii 5   **22** B 15   *Ugar.* V no. 1 rev. *l.* 6

ztr **17** i 28 ii 17

ḥby *Ugar.* V no. 1 obv. *l.* 19

ḥbl 'band, flock' **8** 10   **11** i 6   **18** iv 31

ḥbq G 'embraced' **4** iv 13   **10** iii 23   **17** i 41   **19** 63,
70   **23** 51   **24**

ḥbr 'companion' **6** vi 48   **23** 76   *Ugar.* V no 2 obv. *l.* 5

ḥbš 'belt, sash' **3** B 13   'thong, wristlet' **18** iv 17, 28

ḥbš 'governor' **5** iv 22   **17** vi 8 [Hebr. *ḥôbēš* in
Isa. iii 7]

ḥgr G 'girded (oneself)' **14** 148   **23** 17

ḥdg 'litter' **12** i 18 [Arab. *ḥidâjatu*]

ḥdy G 'saw, regarded' **3** B 24   **19** 110, 121 [‖ *'n*;
cognate Hebr. *ḥāzāh*]

ḥdr 'chamber' **3** E 19   **14** 26

ḥdt G 'became new, was renewed' **18** iv 9

ḥdt 'newly-wed' **14** 101

ḥwy G 'lived, came alive' **10** ii 20   **16** i 23   **17** i 37
vi 30   D 'let live, gave life to' **17** vi 32   **18** iv 27
19 16

ḥwt 'land' **4** i 43 [Hebr. *ḥawwôt* 'tent-villages']

ḥṭb G 'gathered firewood' **14** 112, 214

ḥṭt [√*ḥnṭ*] 'wheat' **14** 82   **16** iii 9

ḥẓ [√*ḥẓẓ* or *ḥẓy*] 'arrow' **14** 116 [Hebr. *ḥēṣ* and
ḥēṣî]

ḥẓr 'court' or 'dwelling, residence' **1** ii 14   **2** iii 19
3 E 47   **14** 133, 205   **19** 184   *Ugar.* V no. 1
obv *l.* 18 [Hebr. *ḥāṣēr* and Arab. *ḥaẓîratu* 'court'
or Hebr. *ḥāṣērîm* 'settlement(s)' and Arab. *ḥaḍaru*
'village']

ḥẓt [√*ḥẓẓ* or *ḥẓy*] 'good fortune' **3** E 39   **4** iv 42
[Arab. *ḥaẓẓa* and *ḥaẓiya* 'was lucky, fortunate';
ḥuẓwatu 'fortune']

ḥy 'living, alive' **6** iii 2

ḥyly **22** B 9 [but see apparatus]

ḥym pl. 'life' **16** i 14   **17** vi 26

ḥyt 'life' **3** E 39   **4** iv 42

ḥkm G 'is, was wise' **4** v 65   **16** iv 3

ḥkm 'wise' **3** E 38   **4** iv 41

ḥkm 'wisdom' **3** E 38   **4** iv 41

ḥkpt and *ḥqkpt* 'Memphis' **3** F 15   **17** v 21

ḥl [√*ḥwl*] 'circuit, district' **16** i 8 ii 108 [Arab. *ḥâla*
'changed, turned', *taḥawwala* 'went from place to
place'; Hebr. *ḥêl* 'surrounding wall']

ḥlb 'milk' **15** ii 26   **23** 14

ḥlm 'dream' **6** iii 4   **14** 35, 150, 154

ḥln 'window' **4** v 124 vi 9 vii 17

ḥlq 'skirt' or other garment **3** B 14 [M.-Hebr. *ḥālûq*
'under-garment'; Arab. *miḥlaqu* 'coarse garment']

ḥm [√*ḥmm*] 'heat' **2** iv 33   **19** 40

ḥmd G 'coveted, desired' **12** i 38 ii 9

ḥmdrt 'shrivelled plant' **19** 70 [Akk. *ḥamadîru*
'withered']

ḥmḥ **16** i 29

ḥmḥm [√*ḥmm*] 'was pregnant' **17** i 41

ḥmḥmt 'pregnancy' **23** 51, 56 [‖ *hr*]

ḥmṣ G 'is, was sour' **19** 17 [Arab. *ḥamuḍa*]

ḥmr 'ass' **6** i 28   **14** 121

ḥmr 'clay' **5** i 19

ḥmt [√*ḥmy*] 'wall' **14** 75, 167

ḥmt 'venom' *Ugar.* V no. 7 *ll.* 6ff. [Hebr. *ḥēmāh*]

ḥmt 'vessel of skin' **16** iii 15 [Hebr. *ḥemet*]

ḥnn G 'showed favour' **10** i 12

ḥnt [√*ḥnn*] 'favour, pity, supplication' **17** i 17

ḥsn coll. 'locusts' **14** 105 [Hebr. *ḥāsîl*]

ḥsp G 'skimmed' **3** B 38 D 86   **19** ii 51, 199 [Hebr.
ḥāśap]

ḥpn 'hollow of hand' **16** vi 58

ḥpn **22** A 12 B 9

ḥpš G 'sought out (sc. straw)' **14** 112 [Hebr. *ḥāpaś*]

ḥṣ **1** iv 11   **16** iv 6

ḥqkpt, also *ḥkpt* 'Memphis' **3** F 1

ḥrb 'sword, knife' **2** i 32   **3** A 7   **6** v 13 etc.

ḥrb 'attacker' **2** iv 4

ḥrḥrt [√*ḥrr*] 'torch, brand' **2** iii 13

ḥry name of Keret's wife **14–16** *passim*

ḥryt place-name *Ugar.* V no. 7 *l.* 36

ḥrn the deity 'Horon' **16** vi 55   *Ugar.* V no. 7 *l.* 58

ḥrnq **24** 23

ḥrṣ 'quicklime' **17** vi 37 [Arab. *ḥuruḍu*]

ḥrṣ **19** 8, 10

ḥrr D 'scorched' **5** ii 5 pass. 'was roasted' **23** 41
'was inflamed, flushed' **12** ii 38, 41

ḥrš 'craftsman' **3** F 23   **17** v 19

ḥrš Gt 'cast a spell' **16** v 26 [Syr. *ḥar(r)ēš* 'practised
magic']

ḥrš 'spell, magic art' **19** 222 [Hebr. *ḥărāšîm*]

ḥrš **12** ii 62

ḥrt G 'ploughed' **5** vi 20   **14** 122   **22** B 20

ḥrt 'ploughman' **16** iii 12

ḥš [√*ḥwš*] G 'hastened' **1** ii 21   **3** C 15   **4** v 113

ḥš 'quickly' **1** iv 7   **2** iii 10   **4** v 115 [Hebr. *ḥîš*]

ḥšn **5** iii 4

ḥt [√*ḥwt*] G 'flew around (birds)' **4** vii 58   **8** 11
[Arab. *ḥâta*]

ḥt **16** ii 77   *Ugar.* V no. 7 *l.* 68

ḥtk 'parent, sire' **1** ii 18   **6** iv 35   **14** 10, 21 [cp.

Hebr. *ḥātak* 'cut, determined']

ḥtk 'son, scion' **10** iii 35

ḥtk 'rule, sway' *Ugar.* V no. 2 rev. *ll.* 8, 10

ḥtl 'wrapper' **12** i 19 [Hebr. *ḥătullîm* 'swaddling-bands']

ḥtt 'silver' **14** 71 [Hittite *ḥattuš*]

ḥbl 'destruction, mischief' **1** iv 8 [Hebr. *ḥebel*]

ḥbr name of Keret's kingdom **14** 82 **15** iv 8

ḥbrt 'pot, cauldron' **4** ii 9 [Hittite *ḥuprušḥu*]

ḥẓẓ 'rain-cloud' **14** 92 [Hebr. *ḥăzîzîm*]

ḥḥ 'filth, rubbish' **4** viii 13 **17** vi 35 [Akk. *ḥaḥû* 'slag'; *ḥaḥḥu* 'spittle']

ḥṭ 'stick, sceptre' **2** iii 18 **16** vi 8 **19** 14 **23** 8, 37 [Akk. *ḥaṭṭu*]

ḥṭ [√*ḥyṭ*] G 'awoke' **14** 154 Š 'awakened' **19** 151 [Akk. *ḥâṭu* 'to watch']

ḥym **4** i 30

ḥl [√*ḥw/yl*] G 'was in labour' **12** i 25 'danced, trembled' **10** ii 29 [Akk. *ḥâlu*, Hebr. *ḥāl*; perhaps two different roots combined]

ḥlb 'wooded height' **4** viii 6 **5** v 14 [‖ *ġr*; Akk. *ḥalbu* 'forest']

ḥlln [√*ḥw/yl*] 'labour, child-birth' **17** ii 42

ḥlq G 'perished' **5** vi 10 **18** iv 42 [Akk. *ḥalāqu*]

ḥmảt 'curdled milk, butter' **23** 14

ḥmmr 'audience chamber' or the like **15** iv 23 [‖ *mtb*]

ḥmr 'wine' **3** A 16 **23** 6

ḥmš 'five' **23** 57 'fifth' **4** vi 29 **14** 83, 107 **17** i 12

ḥmš D 'did for fifth time' **16** v 17 'took as fifth' **14** 18

ḥmšt pl. 'pieces of five' **14** 30

ḥmt 'tent' **14** 159 [Arab. *ḥaymatu*]

ḥnzr 'boar' **5** v 9

ḥnp 'haughty' **18** i 17 [Arab. *ḥânifu*]

ḥss G 'thought of, remembered, was intelligent' **15** iii 25 D 'reminded, moved' **4** iv 39 [Akk. *ḥasāsu*]

ḥss name of divine craftsman meaning 'clever' **4** i 25 **17** v 11 more fully *ktr-w-ḥss* (q.v.)

ḥsp G 'withered, was shrivelled' **19** 31 [Arab. *ḥasafa* 'was emaciated']

ḥsr G 'lacked' **6** ii 17

ḥpy **3** B 7

ḥprt 'ewe' **4** vi 48 [Akk. *ḥuraptu*, Arab. *ḥarûfatu* 'she-lamb']

ḥptr 'pot, cauldron' **4** ii 8 [‖ *ḥbrt*]

ḥpt 'peasant, common soldier' **14** ii 90 **15** i 6 [Akk. (Alalakh) *ḥupšu*; Hebr. *ḥopšî*]

ḥptt 'peasant status, freedom' **4** viii 7 **5** v 15

ḥṣb Gt 'hewed about one, battled' **3** B 6, 30 **7** I 6

ḥrả 'dung' *Ugar.* V no. 1 obv. *l.* 21

ḥrb G 'became dry' **19** 30

ḥrḥb name of deity **24** 2

ḥrṭ G 'plucked' **23** 38 [Arab. *ḥaraṭa* 'stripped (leaves), planed (wood)']

ḥrẓʿ **12** i 41

ḥrn 'caravan' **4** v 75, 91 [Akk. *ḥarrānu* 'highway; caravan']

ḥrpnt 'autumn' *Ugar.* V no. 1 rev. *l.* 6 [Hebr. *ḥōrep*,

Arab. *ḥarîfu*]

ḥrṣ 'gold' **3** D 44 **4** i 27 **14** 126 etc.

ḥršn 'mountain' **1** ii 23 [Akk. *ḥuršānu*]

ḥrt [√*ḥrr*] 'hole' **5** v 5 **19** 112

ḥš [√*ḥyš*] G 'was dismayed, troubled' **4** vii 32, 38 [Akk. *ḥâšu* 'to worry'; Hebr. *yāḥîš* in Isa. xxviii 16]

ḥš 'troubled, worried' *Ugar.* V no. 1 rev. *l.* 4

ḥšt 'place of confinement, sickroom' **16** i 3, 4, 17 etc. [cp. Arab. *ḥayyasa* 'humbled, confined']

ḥt [√*ḥtt*] G 'was shattered' **2** iv 1 **16** vi 1

ḥt *PRU* II no. 3 *l.* 12

ḥtả G pass. and Gt 'was carried off, snatched away' **4** viii 20 **6** ii 23 [Arab. *iḥtata'a* 'carried away']

ḥtn 'son-in-law' **24** 25

ḥtn 'marriage' **24** 32

ḥtr 'sieve' **6** ii 32 [M.-Hebr. *ḥāšar* 'sifted, scattered']

ṭb, also *ẓb* 'good, pleasant' **3** A 20

ṭbḥ G 'slaughtered' **1** iv 30 **6** i 18 **15** iv 4 etc.

ṭbn 'goodness, sweetness' **19** 46

ṭbq G 'shut' **17** i 29 [Arab. *ṭabiqa* 'was shut (hand)' and *ṭabbaqa* 'shut (a book)']

ṭhr, also *ẓhr* 'clean, brilliant (of jewel)' **4** v 81

ṭḥn G 'ground' **6** ii 34

ṭḥ [√*ṭwḥ*] 'plastered' **17** i 33

ṭl [√*ṭll*] 'dew' **3** B 40 **19** 41, 44, 51 **22** B 20

ṭlb G 'sought' **5** iv 2, 4 [Arab. *ṭalaba*]

ṭly name of daughter of Baal **3** A 24 C 4 *Ugar.* V no. 3 obv. *l.* 5 etc.

ṭll D 'gave dew, bedewed' **19** 41

ṭʿn G 'pierced' **5** i 26 **10** ii 24

ṭrd G 'drove away' **3** D 44 [Aram. *ṭrad*]

ṭry 'fresh (meat)' **6** vi 42

ṭtm **1** iv 8

ẓủ [√*yzả*=*yṣả*] 'outgoing, source' **3** B 43 **19** 205

ẓb, also *ṭb* 'good, pleasant' *Ugar.* V no 2 obv. *l.* 5 no 4 *l.* 14 (?)

ẓby 'gazelle, baron, lord' **15** iv 7, 18 [Arab. *ẓabyu*]

ẓhr, also *ṭhr* 'clean, brilliant (stone)' **24** 21

ẓḥq, also *ṣḥq* G 'laughed' **12** i 12

ẓẓ-w-kmt name of composite deity *Ugar* V no. 7 *l.* 36

ẓl [√*ẓll*] 'shadow' **14** 159 'covering' **4** ii 27

ẓlmt 'darkness' or 'shadow of death' **4** vii 55 **8** 8 [Hebr. *ṣalmāwet*]

ẓr [√*ẓhr*] 'back, top' **2** i 23 **3** D 32 **4** i 35 **14** 73 *lẓr* 'upwards' **16** iii 13 [Arab. *ẓahru*]

y 'O!' of vocative **2** i 36 **3** E 28 **4** iii 9 etc. with following *l* 'woe to!' **19** 152 [Arab. *yā*]

ybl G 'brought, carried, yielded, wore' **2** i 37 **3** E 42 **4** i 38 v 77 **6** iv 42 **14** 189 *Ugar.* V no. 7 *ll.* 2ff.

ybl 'produce' **5** ii 5

yblt 'tuber, growth' *Ugar.* V no. 7 *l.* 66 [M.-Hebr. *yabbelet*]

ybm 'brother-in-law' **6** i 31 **16** ii 94

ybmt, also *ybnt* and *ymmt* 'daughter-in-law' **3** B 33 **4** ii 15 **17** vi 19 etc.

ybnt, also *ybmt* 'daughter-in-law' **3** D 84

ybrdmy name of daughter of Baal **24** 29

ygrš name given to club **2** iv 12

yd pl. *ydt* 'hand' **1** iv 19 **2** i 39 **3** B 34 F 23
4 vii 40 etc. 'left hand' **10** ii 6 **15** ii 17 **16** i 41,
47 etc. 'power' **2** iv 1 **16** vi 32 'portion, share'
5 i 21 'membrum virile' **23** 33 [Hebr. *yad* 'left
hand' in e.g. Judg. v 26 Ps. lxxxix 26]

yd prep. 'beside' **14** 54

yd [√*ydd*] 'love' **3** C 3 **4** iv 38

ydd 'beloved' **4** vii 46, 48 **5** i 13 etc.

ydy G 'scratched, scraped' **5** vi 18 [Arab. *waḍâ*]

ydy G 'banished, drove out' **6** vi 51 **16** v 18 vi 47
Ugar. V no. 7 *ll.* 5ff. [‖ *grš*]

yd' G 'knew' **3** A 25 C 24 **6** iii 8 etc.

yd' G 'sweated' **3** D 31 [Arab. *waḍa'a* 'flowed' = Eth.
waza'a 'sweated']

yh **1** iii 7 [truncated or verbal form]

yw name given to Yam **1** iv 14

yḥd 'single' **14** 96

yḥr a venomous lizard *Ugar.* V no. 7 *l.* 73 [Arab.
waḥratu]

yṭp short for *yṭpn* **18** iv 7, 16

yṭpn name of Anat's accomplice **18** iv 6 **19** 214

yẓà, also *yṣà* G 'went forth' **12** i 14, 19 [see p. 30 n. 3]

yld G 'bore, gave birth to' pass. 'was born' **5** v 22
15 ii 23 **17** ii 14 **23** 52 etc. Š 'begat' **23** 65

yly G 'followed, replaced' **15** v 21 N 'treated as a
friend, helped' **12** ii 57 [Arab. *walâ(y)*]

yly 'follower, companion' **12** ii 52

ym [√*ywm*] pl. *ymm* and *ymt* 'day' **4** vi 24 vii 55
6 ii 26 **14** 106 **17** i 33 *Ugar.* V no. 2 rev. *l.* 11
etc.

ym [√*ymm*] 'sea' **2** iii 12 **3** B 43 **4** ii 6 **5** i 16
6 v 19 **23** 30, 33, 63 name of the sea-god 'Yam'
1 iv 15 **2** i 11 iii 7 **4** ii 35 vi 12 etc.

ymàn name of country **4** i 43

ymmt, also *ybmt* 'daughter-in-law' **3** C 9

ymn 'right hand, side' **2** i 39 **4** ii 4 **18** iv 10
23 63 etc.

yn 'wine' **4** iii 43 **6** i 10 **14** 72 **23** 6 etc.

ynq G 'sucked' **15** ii 26 **23** 24

ysd 'foundation' **4** iii 6

ysm 'fair, beautiful' **23** 2 [Arab. *wasîmu*]

ysmsm 'fair, delightful' RS 22.225 *l.* 3 'easy,
comfortable place' **19** 60

ysmsmt 'beauty, delight' **17** ii 42 'easy, comfortable
place' **4** iv 15

ysmt 'beauty, delight' **5** vi 7 **6** ii 20

y'bdr epithet of daughter of Baal **3** C 5 **4** i 19

y'd G 'appointed (a time)' **4** v 69

y'l 'mountain-goat' **6** i 26 **17** vi 22

y'r [√*'ry*] 'razor' **5** vi 18 [cp. Hebr. *ta'ar*]

y'r 'forest' **4** vii 36

yġl 'scrub' **19** 63 [Arab. *waġlu* 'dense tree']

ypy tD 'beautified oneself' **3** B 42 D 89

yp' G impf. *yp'* and *ynp'* with nasalization 'rose up,
sprang up' **2** i 3 **3** D 34, 48 **5** iv 8 **19** 65
[Arab. *yafa'a* 'became adult']

ypt 'cow' or 'fair' (fem.) **10** iii 4 [<*ypnt* (Arab.
yafanatu 'pregnant cow') or √*ypy*]

yṣà, also *yẓà* G 'went forth' **14** 87 **16** i 51 **18** iv 24
19 75 apparently 'put forth' **16** i 53 Š 'brought

forth' **2** iv 2 **17** i 28 **19** 87

yṣb name of Keret's eldest son **15** ii 25 **16** vi 25

yṣbt **17** vi 9

yṣm G 'reviled, cursed' **19** 152 [Arab. *istawḍama*]

yṣq G 'poured, smelted' **3** B 31 **4** i 26 **5** vi 14 **14** 164

yṣr G 'designed, fashioned' **16** ii 87

yqy G 'protected' **2** i 18, 34 [Arab. *waqâ(y)*]

yqġ G 'was awake, attentive' **16** vi 30, 42 [Hebr.
yāqaṣ; Arab. *yaqiẓa*]

yqr 'noble, honourable' *Ugar.* V no. 2 obv. *l.* 2

yr [√*yry*] 'early rain(s)' **14** 93 **19** 40

yrà G 'was afraid' **5** ii 6 **6** vi 30

yrgb place-name **6** vi 57

yrd G 'went, came down' **2** iii 14, 20 **4** viii 7, 8
6 i 63 **14** 36 etc. Š 'made to come down' **14** 77

yrḥ 'moon' **18** iv 9 name of the moon-god 'Yarikh'
15 ii 4 **24** 4 *Ugar.* V no. 1 obv. *l.* 4 etc. 'month'
6 ii 27 **14** 84 **17** ii 43 vi 29 etc.

yry G 'shot' **23** 38

yrq 'pale, yellow gold' **4** iv 11 **14** 53

yrt G 'got possession of' **2** i 19 Gt 'was dispossessed
of' **3** D 44 [Hebr. *yāraš* Niph. 'was dispossessed']

yrt 'heir' **14** 25

yšn G 'fell asleep' **14** 31, 119

yšr 'rightness, legality' **14** 13

ytm 'orphan' **16** vi 49 **17** v 8

ytn G 'gave, gave up' **2** i 18 **3** A 10 **6** vi 10
14 150 etc. 'uttered (voice)' **2** iv 6 **4** v 70
16 i 13 'set, directed (face)' **2** iii 4 **3** D 81
F 12 etc. 'established' **23** 3

ytnt 'gift' **14** 135

ytb G 'sat' **2** i 21 **5** vi 12 **6** i 58 **16** vi 22 **17** v 6
etc. 'stayed' **2** i 19 **5** i 9 **14** 301 Š 'made to
sit' **4** v 109 **6** vi 33

ytq G or L 'was trusting, friendly (with)' *Ugar.* V
no. 7 *l.* 6 [Arab. *wataqa, wâtaqa*]

k, also *km* prep. 'like, as' **3** B 10 E 1, 9 **4** iv 17
6 i 19 **14** 43 etc. 'as when' **16** vi 43 'as it
were' **5** i 17 *Ugar.* V no. 4 *ll.* 7, 8

k, also *km* conj. 'that' **3** E 35 **6** iii 8 **14** 39 **16** i 33
ii 81 etc. 'for, because' **2** iv 29 **3** E 36 **4** iii 21
5 i 4 ii 5 **6** iii 1, 20 **17** ii 14 etc. 'although'
5 i 1, 27 'when, as' **3** B 27 **4** ii 27 v 104 vii 41
17 ii 6 etc. [Hebr. *kî*]

k adv. (usually before postponed verb) 'surely,
indeed' **2** ii 14 iv 27 v 113 vii 53 **17** v 11 **23** 39
[Hebr. *kî* in Gen. xviii 20 Ps. xlix 16 Isa. x 13]

kbd D 'honoured' **3** C 7 **4** iv 26 **17** v 20 etc.

kbd 'liver, inside' **3** B 25 C 13 **5** ii 4 **19** 35, 124 etc.

kbkb, also *kkb* 'star' **3** B 41 C 22 **4** iv 17 **23** 54 etc.

kbrt 'sieve, riddle' **6** v 16

kd 'thus' **1** iv 23 **19** 14 [Arab. *kaḍâ*]

kd 'if' **3** E 11 [Aram. *kdî, kad*]

kd [√*kdd*] 'pitcher' **3** A 16

kdd 'little child' **19** 174 [[k]i-da-di-e 'children'
‖ *ra-ab-bi-e* Uruk. inscr.]

kdrt 'ball(s)' **3** B 9

khn 'priest' **6** vi 55

kḥt 'seat' **2** i 23 iv 13 **4** vi 51 **6** i 58 **16** vi 24
[Hurrian *kišḥi*; ‖ *ksù*]

kkb, also *kbkb* 'star' **10** i 4 [Akk. *kakkabu*]

kknt 'barrel' or the like **6** i 67 [∥ *rḥbt*]

kl [√*kll*] 'all' **3** E 41 F 14 **5** vi 26 **6** i 65 **16** i 45 etc.

klủ G 'shut' **3** B 3 [Hebr. *kālâ* 'restrained, confined etc.']

klảt fem. 'the two, both' of hands **1** iv 10 **3** A 11 **5** i 19 **14** 161 of women **23** 57 [Arab. *kiltâ*, Eth. *keleʾtu*]

klb 'dog' **14** 123 **16** i 2, 15

klbt 'bitch' **3** D 42

kly G 'failed, was finished' **16** iii 14 D 'exhausted' **16** i 26 'made an end of' **2** iv 27 **3** D 36 **5** i 2 **19** 196 'consumed' **6** ii 36 v 24 vi 11

kll D 'completed' **4** v 72

klt [√*kll*] 'totality, all' **14** 69

klt [√*kll*] 'bride' **4** i 16 iv 54

km, also *k* prep. 'like, as' **2** iv 13 **4** v 63, 90 **14** 29 etc. 'as it were' *Ugar.* V no. 7 *l* 73 'as many as' **15** iii 25 [Hebr. *kᵉmô*]

km, also *k* conj. 'because' **16** vi 35 'when' **18** iv 29 'as many as' **15** iii 23 [Hebr. *kᵉmô* 'when' in Gen. xix 15 'as many as' in Zech. x 8]

km adv. 'so' **6** ii 8, 29 [cognate Hebr. *kēn*; cp. *bkm*, *kn*]

kmm a substance used in sacrifice **16** iv 16 [cp. *CTA* 37 7]

kmn a surface area **3** D 82 **4** v 119 viii 25 **17** v 10 etc. [Akk. *kumānu*]

kms tD 'was prostrated' **12** ii 55 [Akk. *kamāsu* 'to kneel']

kmr **19** 12

kmt element in name of deity [see *ẓẓ*; Moabite *kmš*]

kn 'thus' **12** ii 54

kn [√*kwn*] G 'was' **5** iii 6 **14** 15 **17** i 26, 43 L 'established, installed' or 'created' **3** E 44 **4** iv 48 **10** iii 7 Š 'created' **16** v 27

kn 'fixed, stable' **23** 54

knyt fem. 'honoured, noble' **3** E 6 **4** i 16 [Akk. *kanûtu* a title of goddesses]

knkn 'grave' **5** v 13 **19** 147 [from context]

knp 'wing' **10** ii 10 **19** 114

knr 'lyre' **19** 8 *Ugar.* V no. 2 obv. *l.* 4

ks 'cup' **3** A 10 E 42 **4** iii 16 etc.

ks name of mountain associated with El **1** iii 12

ksản 'settle' or the like **12** i 18 [cp. *ksủ*]

ksủ pl. *ksảt* 'chair, throne' **2** iv 7, 12 **3** B 21 **4** vi 52 viii 12 etc.

ksy G 'covered oneself' **5** vi 16 D 'covered, clothed' **10** iii 25

ksl 'loins, back' **3** D 30, 32 **16** vi 50 'bow-string' **3** B 16 **17** vi 11 [Hebr. *kesel* 'loins'; Arab. *kislu* 'bow-string']

ksm 'spelt, emmer' **16** iii 10 **17** i 32 [Hebr. *kussemet*]

ksm 'limit, edge' **5** vi 5 **16** iii 4 [∥ *qṣ*; cp. Akk. *kasāmu* 'to cut down, cut off']

ksp 'silver' **1** iv 21 **3** D 43 **4** v 77 **17** vi 17 etc.

kst [√*ksy*] 'cloak, robe' **19** 36

kp pl. *kpt* 'palm (of hand)' **3** B 10, 13 'tray (of scales)' **24** 35

kpr 'henna' **3** B 2 **7** II 3

kptr name of place associated with Kothar-and-Khasis **3** F 14 *Ugar.* V no. 7 *l.* 46

kpt 'headdress, turban' *Ugar.* V no. 2 obv. *l.* 8 [Akk. *kubsû*]

kr [√*krr*] 'male lamb' **4** vi 47

kry G 'digged' **12** i 23

krkr 'snapped (fingers) in dancing or pleasure' **4** iv 29 [Hebr. *kirkēr* 'danced, capered']

krm 'vineyard' **24** 22

krʿ G 'bowed down' **10** ii 18

krpn 'earthenware pot, flagon' **1** iv 10 **3** A 11 **4** iv 37 **17** vi 6 etc. [Akk. *karpu*, *karpatu*]

krt name of king **14–16** *passim*

kš **22** B 15

kšd G 'attracted' **5** i 16 [Akk. *kašādu* 'to seize, conquer']

kšr **19** 7 [or *k*+*šr*?]

kt [√*kwn*] 'base, pedestal' **4** i 31 [cp. Hebr. *mᵉkônāh*]

ktp 'shoulder' **2** i 42 iv 14 **6** i 14 *Ugar.* V no. 1 obv. *l.* 1?

ktp 'broad-sword' **6** v 2 [∥ *ṣmd*; Arab. *katîfu*]

ktr 'prosperity, good health' **14** 16 [Hebr. *kôšārôt* in Ps. lxviii 7; cp. Syr. *kušrâ*]

ktr name of divine craftsman meaning 'skilful' **2** iv 11 **3** F 18 **4** vii 15 *Ugar.* V no. 2 obv. *l* 5 more fully *ktr-w-ḥss* **2** iv 7 **3** F 21 **4** v 103 **6** vi 51 etc. [cp. Akk. *kešēru* 'to succeed, achieve'; Arab. *katura* 'was much, numerous'; Hebr. *kāšar* and Aram. *kšar* 'succeeded, was profitable' (loan-word from Akk.?)]

ktrm minor deities **2** iii 20

ktrt title of divine midwives **17** ii 26 **24** 5-6, 11 etc.

l, also *lm* and *ln* prep. 'to, into, onto, against' **2** i 23 iv 5 **3** B 12, 17 C 13 D 34 etc. 'to, for' **1** iv 2 **3** B 21 E 11 etc. 'at, in, on, among' **4** v 109 vii 42 **6** i 58 **16** vi 22 **19** 59 **23** 3, 66 'beside' **23** 57 'from' **1** iv 24 **2** i 27 **5** vi 12 **6** i 64 ii 26 **14** 132 **17** i 28 **19** 51 etc. 'of' (in title) **6** i 1 'by' (of numbers) **4** i 44 vii 9 **5** v 20 **14** 92 with infin. **2** i 20 **15** iv 27 [Hebr. *lᵉ* 'from' in Judg. xvii 2 Ps. xl 11 lxviii 21 lxxxiv 12]

l adv. 'not' **2** iv 7, 17 **3** A 14 B 19 C 23 **14** 12 etc.

l adv. 'indeed' **2** iii 17 iv 32 **3** D 81 E 43 **4** vii 50 **5** i 6 etc. [Akk. *lū*; Arab. *la*]

l 'O!' of vocative **2** iv 28 **3** E 37 F 10 **16** iv 11 etc. [Hebr. *lᵉ* in Ezek. xxvii 3 xxxiv 2]

lả [√*lʾy*] G 'was weary' **3** E 26 **4** viii 22 **6** ii 25 [Hebr. *lāʾāh*]

lả [√*lʾy*] G 'was strong, victorious, prevailed' **14** 33 **16** vi 2, 14 *Ugar.* V no. 7 *l.* 68 [Akk. *leʾû*]

lảy 'victory' **24** 44

lản 'strength' *Ugar.* V no. 2 rev. *l.* 9

lỉk G 'sent' **2** i 11 **4** v 103 vii 45 **5** iv 23 etc.

lỉm 'people' **3** B 7 C 9 **5** vi 23 etc. [Hebr. *lᵉʾōm*]

lb, also *lbb* 'heart, mind' **3** B 26 **5** vi 21 **6** ii 6 **12** i 13 etc.

lbủ 'lion' **5** i 14

lbb, also *lb* 'heart' **24** 30

lbn G 'made bricks' **4** iv 61

lbnn 'Lebanon' **4** vi 18 **17** vi 21 **22** B 20

lbnt 'brick' **4** iv 62 v 73 vi 35

lbš G 'put on, wore' **12** ii 47 **19** 206 Š 'clothed' **5** v 23 [cp. *lpš*] *lg* a liquid measure **23** 75

lwả **2** i 46

lḥ [√*lwḥ*] Š 'made into plates' **4** i 26–27

lḥ [√*lwḥ*] pl. *lḥt* 'writing tablet' **2** i 26

lḥ [√*lḥy*] dual *lḥm* pl. *lḥt* 'cheeks, jaws, side-whiskers' **5** vi 19 **17** i 29

lḥk G 'licked' *PRU* II no. 3 *l.* 5

lḥm G 'ate' **4** iv 35 v 110 **5** i 20 **6** vi 42 **16** vi 18 **23** 6 etc. D 'gave to eat' **17** i 3 Š 'gave to eat, fed' **3** A 5 **16** vi 49 **17** ii 30 v 19 *Ugar.* V no. 7 *ll.* 6ff.

lḥm 'food, bread' **4** iv 36 **6** vi 43 **14** 83 **16** iii 14 **23** 6 etc.

lḥmd variant of *mḥmd* **4** v 101

lḥn G 'had understanding, was intelligent' **6** i 48 [Arab. *laḥina*]

lḥn **15** iv 13

lḥšt 'whisper' **3** C 20

lṭpn, also *lẓpn* title of El meaning 'gentle, kindly' **1** iv 13 **4** iv 58 **5** vi 11 etc. [Arab. *laṭîfu*]

lṭš 'burnished, sharpened' **2** i 32

lẓpn, also *lṭpn* title of El **24** 44

lyt [√*lwy*] 'wreath, garland' **6** iv 43 [Hebr. *liwyāh*]

ll name of mountain of divine assembly **2** i 20

llủ 'young beast, kid' **4** vi 43 viii 19 **14** 68 [Akk. *lalû*, *lali'u* 'kid']

llqẓ **19** 146 [or *l+lqẓ*]

lm, also *l* and *ln* prep. 'to' (direction) **15** iv 22 'to' (dative) **14** 102 'at' (time) **19** 210 [Hebr. *lᵉmô*]

lm 'why?' **2** i 24 **4** vii 38 **16** ii 80

lmd D 'taught' **18** i 29

lmd 'disciple' **6** vi 54

ln, also *l* and *lm* prep. 'onto' **2** i 25 'against' **17** i 30 'from' **2** i 27 *Ugar.* V no. 7 *l.* 5 [S.-Arab. *ln* 'from']

ln [√*lw/yn*] G 'passed the night' **17** i 16

lskt **1** iii 8 [or *l+skt*]

lsm G 'ran' **3** C 16 [Akk. *lasāmu*]

lsm 'greyhound' or the like **6** vi 21

lsmt 'speed, alacrity' **22** B 6

lpš 'clothing, garment' **5** vi 16 **6** ii 10 **12** ii 47 [cp. *lbš*]

lṣb 'passage of the throat' **4** iv 28 **17** ii 10 *Ugar.* V no. 1 rev. *l.* 4 [Arab. *liṣbu* 'narrow passage, strait']

lqḥ G 'took' **2** iv 10 **3** A 16 **4** ii 32 **14** 66, 204 **23** 35 etc.

lrgt place-name *Ugar.* V no. 7 *l.* 26 [or *l+rgt*]

lrmn 'pomegranate' **23** 50 [Akk. *lurimtu, lurindu*]

lšn 'tongue' **2** i 33 **5** ii 3 *PRU* II no. 3 *l.* 5

lšn D 'slandered, denounced' **17** vi 51 *Ugar.* V no. 1 obv. *l* 20

lty **20** A 9

ltn name of mythical sea-monster 'Leviathan' **5** i 1

—*m* survival of mimation, possibly for emphasis or variety, after sing. nouns in nominative **16** i 7 **17** vi 35, 39 in genitive **4** vi 6 in accusative **14** 98 after proper names **2** iv 32 **6** vi 48 particularly in vocative **2** i 36 iv 9 **6** v 11 **17** vi 34

—*m* adverbial as in *gm* 'with the voice, aloud' (**4** ii 29 etc.) *ḥṭm* 'with a wand' (**16** vi 8) *kspm* 'in silver' (**14** 205) *ktrm* 'in good health' (**14** 16) *mṭm* 'with a shaft' (**3** B 15) *psltm* 'with a flint' (**5** vi 18) *špšm* 'with the sun' (**14** 118) etc. [Akk. —*am*, —*amma*, —*um*; Hebr. —*ām*, —*ōm*]

—*m* enclitic with no apparent function unless to add emphasis or variety, after sing. nouns in constr. **16** i 10 **24** 26 after dual and pl. nouns in absol. **4** v 113 vi 5–6 in constr. **2** iv 14, 22 **4** viii 9 **6** vi 11 after pronouns **3** D 48 **4** vi 37 **16** i 20 after suffixes **6** vi 10 after prepositions **19** 67 [cp. also *bm, lm, km*] after verbs **2** i 19 iv 28 **3** C 25 **4** vi 13 vii 15 **5** i 6 **23** 6 **24** 18 after infins. absol. **5** i 24 **15** ii 18 **17** vi 38 [cp. Akk.—*ma* in its various usages; for two reasonably certain survivals in Hebr. poetry see Deut. xxxiii 11 (*motnēy+m* 'the loins of his adversaries') and Ps. xxix 6 (*wayyarqîd+m* 'he made Lebanon skip')]

mảd D 'multiplied' **14** 58

mảd 'great quantity, much' **14** 88

mảt crasis of *mh* and *ảt* **14** 38

mỉd 'great quantity, much' **4** v 77 adv. 'greatly, very' **3** B 23

mỉzrt 'loin-cloth' **5** vi 17 **17** i 16 [Arab. *mỉʾzaratu*]

mỉyt, also *myht* 'watery place' **16** iii 4 [Arab. *mâʾiyyu* and *mâhiyyu* 'watery']

mỉnš [√*nš*] 'meeting place' **19** 210

mỉt pl. *mảt* 'hundred' **5** iv 3 **14** 89

mủd 'great quantity, much' **5** iii 17, 22

mbk [√*nbk*] 'source' **2** iii 4 **3** E 14 **4** iv 21 etc. [Hebr. *mibbᵉkēy* and *nibᵉkēy* in Job xxviii 11 xxxviii 16]

mgdl 'tower' **14** 73, 166 **18** i 31

mgn G 'importuned' **4** iii 25 [Arab. *majana* 'was bold, shameless' and Hebr. *māgēn* 'beggar' in Prov. vi 11]

mgn 'bold request' also 'present' given therewith **4** i 22 **16** i 45

mgr (if correctly read) in *lmgr lb* 'of one's own accord' *Ugar.* V no. 1 obv. *l* 12 [Akk. *ina migir libbi*]

mgt [√*ngt*] 'fatling' **16** vi 18 [cp. Arab. *intajatat* 'became fat (ewe)']

md [√*mdd*] 'raiment, robe' **4** ii 6

mdb [√*dwb*] 'ocean, flood, **23** 34 *Ugar.* V no. 3 obv. *l.* 2 [Hebr. *zāb* 'flowed']

mdbr, also *mlbr* 'wilderness' **14** 105 **23** 4, 65

mdgt [√*dgg* or *dgy*] 'dark place' **19** 147 [Arab *dujjatu* 'darkness' and *dâjin* 'dark']

mdd [√*ydd*] 'darling, beloved' **3** D 35 **4** viii 23 **14** 103

mdw [√*dwy*] 'sickness' **16** vi 35

mdl G 'saddled' **4** iv 9 **19** 52 [‖ *ṣmd*]

mdl 'thunderbolt' **3** D 70 **5** v 7 [Akk. *mudulu* 'rod']

mdnt [√*dyn*] 'city, province' **3** B 16 [Aram. *mdittâ*; Arab. *madînatu*]

mdrᶜ 'sown land' **23** 69

mh 'what?' **3** E 36 **6** ii 13 **17** vi 35 **23** 53

mh 'stealthily' **16** vi 6 [Arab. *mah* 'gently']

mh 'water' **3** B 38 D 86 [Arab. *mâhu*]

mhyt, also *mỉyt* 'watery place' **5** vi 5

mhmrt 'miry or watery abyss' **5** i 7 [Hebr. *mahămōrôt*; cp. Arab. *hamara* 'poured down']

mhr 'runner, warrior' **3** B 11, 15 **17** vi 40 **18** iv 26, 27 **22** A 7 [Hebr. *māhēr* 'swift', *māhîr* 'prompt, skilled'; Egyp. *mhr* 'soldier']

mhr '(marriage-) price' **24** 19 *Ugar.* V no. 7 *l.* 74

mzl G 'lagged behind' **14** 99, 100 [Arab. *malaza*]

mzn [√*yzn*] dual 'scales' **24** 34

mzᶜ G or D 'rent' [Arab. *mazaᶜa* 'picked (cotton), mazzaᶜa* 'divided']

mḥ [√*mḥy*] G 'wiped' **3** B 30

mḥmd 'desirable thing, choicest part' **4** v 78 vi 19

mḥrtt 'plough-land' **6** iv 27, 38

mḥ 'marrow, vigour' **16** i 27 **17** i 39 **19** 201

mḥlpt 'tress of hair' **19** 82

mḥnm place-name *PRU* II no. 3 *l.* 4

mḥṣ G 'smote, wounded' **1** iv 27 **2** iv 9 **4** ii 24 **5** i 1 **19** 153, 196 Gt 'smote about one, fought' **3** B 5 D 43

mḥṣ name of weapon **2** i 39

mḥr 'meeting' RS 22.225 *l.* 7 [Akk. *maḫāru* 'to meet']

mḫš G 'struck down, destroyed' **3** D 35 [cognate *mḥṣ*; both ‖ *kly*]

mḫt **16** v 30

mṭ 'staff, shaft' **2** i 9 **3** B 15 **19** 155 **23** 47 [Hebr. *maṭṭeh*]

mṭḫr **2** i 41 [or *mṭ* + *ḫr*]

mṭ'ᵗ [√*nṭ'*] 'plantation(s)' **20** B 7 **22** A 26

mṭr pl. *mṭrt* 'rain' **4** v 68 **5** v 8 **16** iii 6

mṭr G or D 'rained' **6** iii 6 **19** 41

mṭt 'bed' **14** 30 [Hebr. *miṭṭāh*]

mẓȧ G 'found' **12** ii 51 [Hebr. *māṣâ*]

mẓll 'shelter' **3** E 48 **4** i 13

mẓmȧ 'thirsty' **15** i 2 [Arab. *miẓmâ'u* 'burning with thirst'; cp. *ǵmi*]

my 'who?, what?' **5** vi 23 **6** i 6 **16** v 14

my pl. *mym* 'water' **19** 2, 55, 190

mk adv. 'then' **4** vi 31 **14** 107 **17** i 16 [‖ *hn*]

mk [√*mkk*] G 'sank down' **2** iv 17

mk [√*mkk*] 'sunken place' **4** viii 12

mknpt 'span (of wings)' **16** i 9

mknt [√*kwn*] 'place, estate' **14** 11

mks [√*ksy*] 'covering' **4** ii 5

mktr 'skilled work' **4** ii 30

mlȧk 'messenger' **2** i 22 **14** 124

mlȧ D 'filled' **4** i 39 **10** ii 12 iii 9 **14** 114 **16** v 28 **23** 76 N 'was filled' **3** B 25 Št 'was brought to an end, vanquished' **3** D 37 [Syr. *šamlî* 'finished, made an end of']

mlȧ 'full' **10** iii 8

mlbr variant of *mdbr* 'wilderness' **12** i 21

mlg 'wedding gift' **24** 47 [Akk. *mulugu*; M.-Hebr. *mᵉlōg*]

mlḥ adj. 'salted, sharp (knife)' **3** A 7 **4** vi 57 **17** vi 4

mlḥm pl. *mlḥmt* 'bread, loaf' **3** C 12 D 52 **5** ii 23

mlḥš '(snake) charmer' *Ugar.* V no. 7 *ll.* 5ff. [Hebr. *mᵉlaḥēš* in Ps. lviii 6]

mlk G 'was, became king' **2** iii 22 **4** vii 49 **6** i 55 **15** v 20 etc. D 'made king' **6** i 46, 54

mlk 'king' **2** iii 5 **3** E 40 **4** vii 43 **24** 2 etc.

title of deity *Ugar.* V no. 7 *l.* 41

mlk 'kingship' **2** iii 18 iv 10 **3** D 46 **14** 41 etc.

mlkt 'queen' **23** 7

mll G 'rubbed' *Ugar.* V no. 3 obv. *l.* 6

mll in *kmll* **1** iv 11 [or *km* + *ll*]

mm 'cry, clamour' **16** i 34 [‖ *ṣȧt npš*; Akk. *mummu*]

mmᶜ [√*myᶜ*] 'gore' **3** B 14, 35 **18** i 12 [Arab. *mâᶜa* 'flowed']

mmt 'place of death' **5** v 19 **6** ii 20

mn, also *mnm* 'who?' **3** D 34 **5** iv 23 [Aram., Arab. *man*]

mn 'how many?' **16** ii 81 [Syr. *man* 'what?']

mn 'species' **4** i 40 [Hebr. *mîn*]

mn [√*mny*] G 'counted, recited a spell, enchanted' *Ugar.* V no. 7 *l.* 70

mndᶜ [√*ydᶜ*] adv. 'assuredly' **16** ii 86

mnḥ 'gift, tribute' **2** i 38 [Hebr. *minḥāh*]

mnḥl 'sieve' **2** iv 3 [Arab. *munḫulu*]

mnm, also *mn* 'who?' **3** D 48

mnt [√*mny*] 'limb' **6** ii 36 'portion, piece' **17** i 33 ii 21 'formula, incantation' **24** 46 *Ugar.* V no. 7 *passim* [Hebr. *mānāh*, *mᵉnāt* 'portion'; Akk. *minātu* 'limbs', *minûtu* 'number, formula']

mnt **4** vii 56

msd [√*ysd*] pl. *msdt* 'foundation' **4** i 41

mswn **14** 125 **15** i 4

msk G 'mixed' **3** A 17 **5** i 21

msk 'mixture' **3** A 17 **16** ii 78 **19** 224

mslmt **10** iii 22

msm 'opportune moment' **6** i 52 [Arab. *mawsimu*]

mspr 'reciting, narration' **4** v 104 **19** E

msrr a kind of bird **14** 163

mᶜ 'pray, I beseech you' **2** iii 15 **4** i 21 **6** i 12 **16** vi 41 [from context]

mᶜ 'together' **14** 87 [Arab. *maᶜân*]

mᶜd [√*yᶜd*] 'meeting, convocation' **2** i 14

mᶜr in *kmᶜr* **16** iv 6 [or *km* + *ᶜr*]

mǵd [√*ǵyd*] 'provisions' **14** 84 [Hebr. *ṣayid*, *ṣēdāh* 'provisions for a journey']

mǵẓ [√*ǵẓy*] 'gift (to win favour)' **4** i 23 **5** v 24

mǵy G 'proceeded, arrived, came upon' **2** i 30 **3** B 17 **4** ii 22 **5** vi 8 **14** 108 **23** 75 'passed' **17** ii 46 'passed away, died' **16** ii 86 [cognate Arab. *maḍâ(y)*]

mpḥ [√*npḥ*] dual 'bellows' **4** i 24

mṣb [√*nṣb*] 'base' **24** 34

mṣbt dual 'tongs' **4** i 25 [Arab. *ḍabaṭa* 'gripped']

mṣd [√*ṣw/yd*] 'offering of game' **14** 79 *Ugar.* V no. 1 obv *l.* 1 'stronghold, fastness' (or place-name) *Ugar.* V no. 7 *l.* 58

mṣḥ G 'dragged, tugged' **3** E 9 **6** v 4 N 'tugged each other' **6** vi 20 [Arab. *maṣaḥa*]

mṣy G 'drained' **12** ii 29 [Hebr. *māṣāh*]

mṣlt 'fountain' **12** ii 62 [‖ *qr*; cp. Hebr. *mᵉṣūlāh*]

mṣlt [√*ṣll*] dual 'cymbals' **3** A 19 *Ugar.* V no. 2 obv. *l.* 4

mṣprt fem. 'pale, yellow' **23** 25 [Arab. *'aṣfaru*]

mṣṣ 'one draining' **15** ii 27 [Hebr. *māṣaṣ* 'drained']

mṣr **3** E 16

mṣt **12** ii 29

mqm 'place' **14** 54, 127

mqr, also *bqr* [√*qwr*] 'well' **14** 216

mr [√*mrr*] G 'drove away, expelled' **2** iv 19   Š 'banished' *Ugar.* V no. 7 *ll.* 4 ff. [cp. Arab. *marra* 'passed, went away']

mr [√*mrr*] G 'strengthened, fortified, blessed' **15** ii 15 **17** i 25, 36 [Arab. *marîru* 'strong, steady'; Hebr. *mar* in Ezek. iii 14 Eccles. vii 26; ||*brk*]

mr place-name *Ugar.* V no. 7 E *l.* 2

mrả D 'fattened' **4** vii 50

mrủ 'fatling' **1** iv 31   **3** A 8   **4** v 107 etc.

mrg Š 'overlaid' **4** i 33 [Eth. *maraga*]

mrzḥ 'banquet, banqueting hall, guest at feast' *Ugar.* V no. 1 obv. *l.* 15 [Phoen. *mrzḥ*, Palm. *mrzḥ*]

mrḥ 'spear, lance' **6** i 51   **16** i 47 [Hebr. *rōmaḥ*]

mrym [√*rwm*] 'height(s)' **3** D 45, 82   **4** iv 19

mrkbt 'chariot(s)' **14** 56   **20** B 4

mrm [√*rmm*] 'worm(s)' **12** i 11 [Hebr. *rimmāh*]

[*mrǵ*]*b* 'hungry' **15** i 1

mrǵt 'suckling' **4** iii 41 vi 56 [Arab. *raǵata* 'sucked']

mrṣ 'illness' **16** v 15

mrqd 'castanet' **19** 189   *Ugar.* V no. 2 obv. *l.* 4-5 [Hebr. *riqqēd* 'danced']

mrr 'fortified, blessed' **19** 195

mrrt-tǵll-bnr place-name **19** 156

mrt, also *trt* 'new wine' **22** B 18

mšdpt 'citadel' or the like **14** 118 [Arab. *sadafu* 'object seen from afar']

mšḥ G 'wiped, anointed' **10** ii 22

mšḥṭ a slaying weapon **2** i 39

mšknt 'dwelling(s)' **15** iii 19   **17** v 32-33

mšl **2** i 5

mšmš **12** ii 37, 56

mšnqt [√*ynq*] 'wet-nurse' **15** ii 28

mšspdt '(professional) wailer' **19** 172

mšpy 'tower' or the like **16** iv 15 [|| *bnwn*; cp. Hebr. *šᵉpî* 'height']

mšr Š 'started' **3** F 9 [Akk. *mutaššuru* 'to be released, discharged']

mšrr 'hinge' **24** 36 [Akk. *šarāru* 'to oscillate']

mšt *Ugar.* V no. 2 obv. *l.* 9

mt, also *imt* 'truly' *Ugar.* V no. 4 obv. *l.* 9

mt 'man' **3** A 13   **16** i 4   **17** vi 35   **18** i 28   'client' (of god) **17** i 19, 38 etc.   'husband' **23** 40

mt [√*mwt*] G 'died' **5** i 6 v 17 vi 9   **16** i 22 etc.

mt 'dead' **2** iv 32   **6** vi 47   **15** v 14   **19** 91 etc.

mt 'death' **16** vi 1, 13   **17** vi 38   *Ugar.* V no. 7 *l.* 65 name of 'Mot', the god of death **4** vii 46 viii 24   **5** i 7 etc.   also *mt-w-šr* **23** 8

mtḥ 'space, extent, span' **3** D 80 [Syr. *mtaḥ*]

mtn G 'awaited' **16** i 36 [Arab. *matuna* 'was strong, steadfast', *matana* 'remained']

mtn 'muscle, tendon' **17** vi 22   dual 'loins' **12** ii 39

mtn [√*ytn*] 'gift' **1** v 12

mt' G 'carried off' **4** ii 6 [Arab. *mata'a*]

mtq 'sweet' **23** 50

mtrḥt 'betrothed, spouse' **14** 13   **24** 10

mtt 'deadness, mortality' **5** v 17 [Syr. *mîtûtâ*]

mt 'male, boy' **5** v 22 [perhaps Akk. *māšu*, *maššu* 'twin']

mtb [√*ytb*] pl. *mtbt* 'dwelling' **3** E 3   **4** i 14   'seat'

16 v 24   'niche' **23** 19   throne-room' **15** iv 22

mtk G 'grasped' **15** i 1, 2 [cognate Hebr. *māšak* 'dragged' = Arab. *masaka* 'grasped']

mtn [√*tny*] 'repetition' **3** D 75   **4** i 20

mtpd 'layer, stage' **1** iii 20   **3** D 79 [Arab. *matâfîdu* 'lining (of clothes)']

mtpṭ 'rule' **2** iii 18   **6** vi 29

mtt fem. of *mt* 'female, maiden', **14** 143   **17** v 16

nảs G 'reviled' **1** iv 23   **5** iv 26   **17** i 30

nb [√*nbb*] G 'scraped out' **19** 146 [Hebr. *nābab* 'hollowed out']

nb adj. 'coated' or the like **4** i 32 [|| *šmrg*]

nbṭ G 'saw' **4** iii 21 [S.-Arab. name *nbṭ'l*]

nbl 'jar, pitcher' *Ugar.* V no. 3 rev. *l.* 3

nbl pl. *nblảt* 'flame' **4** vi 23 [Akk. *nablu*]

nbt 'honey' **6** iii 7   **14** 72 [Hebr. *nōpet*]

ng [√*ngy*] G 'fled' **14** 131

ngḥ N 'gored, butted each other' **6** vi 17

ngr fem. *ngrt* 'steward, stewardess' **16** iv 4, 5 [Akk. *nāgiru* a palace official]

ngš G 'approached, came upon' **6** ii 21   **23** 68 D 'brought near' *Ugar.* V no. 1 obv. *l.* 19

ngt G (impf. with nasalization) or D 'sought' **1** v 4 **6** ii 6   **12** i 40 [Arab. *najata* 'scrutinized']

nd [√*ndy*] G 'threw, put down' **17** i 4   *Ugar.* V no. 7 *l.* 64   'emitted (a cry)' **10** iii 17 [Akk. *nadû*]

nd [√*ndy*] G 'burst forth, escaped' **4** vi 10, 32 [Syr. *ndâ*; cp. Hebr. *nāzāh*]

nd [√*nwd*] G 'fled' **18** i 26 [Hebr. *nād*]

ndd G 'hastened away' **20** B 2   **21** A 4   **22** A 6 apparently trans. 'chased' **22** B 10 [Hebr. *nādad*; see also *d(w)d*]

ndn *Ugar.* V no. 4 *l.* 18

ndr G 'vowed' **14** 200   **15** iii 23   **22** A 16

ndr 'vow' **15** iii 26

nhmmt 'slumber' **14** i 32 {cp. Hebr. *nām* 'slept'; || *šnt*]

nhqt 'braying' **14** 121

nhr 'river' **3** E **14** F 6   **4** ii 7 iv 21   **14** 6   title of the sea-god Yam **2** i 7 iii 7 iv 4   **3** D 36   **5** i 22 etc.

nzl 'choice food' **14** 69 [Arab. *nuzlu* 'food offered to guests']

nḥ [√*nwḥ*] G 'moaned, bemoaned' **15** i 7 [Hebr. *nûaḥ* in Hab. iii 16; Arab. *nâḥa*]

nḥ [√*nḥy*] G 'resorted to' **12** i 35 [Arab. *naḥâ*]

nḥlt 'inheritance, possession' **3** C 27 F 16   **4** viii 14

nḥš 'serpent' *Ugar* V no. 7 *passim*

nḥt D 'brought down, lowered' **2** iv 11   **23** 37, 40 [Aram. *nḥēt* 'descended']

nḥ [√*nwḥ*] G 'rested, took one's ease' **6** iii 18   **17** ii 13

nḥl 'ravine, torrent' **6** iii 7   *Ugar.* V no. 7 *l.* 68

nḥnpt 'parapet' or the like **16** iv 15 [|| *tkm*]

nḥt [√*nwḥ*] 'resting-place, support, cushion' **3** D 47 **4** i 34   **16** vi 24

nṭṭ G (with strong impf.) or D 'stamped, leapt' **3** D 30 **4** vii 35   **19** 94 [Arab. *naṭṭa*; cp. Hebr. √*nwṭ* Ps. xcix 1]

nyr [√*nwr*] 'lamp, illuminator' **16** i 37   **24** 16, 31

nkyt 'treasury, strong-room' **16** ii 89 [Akk. *bît nākamti* = Hebr. *bêt nᵉkōt*]

nkl-w-ib name of composite deity **24** 1 etc.
17, 32

nkr 'stranger' **14** 102

nkr G 'was a stranger to' *Ugar.* V no. 7 *l.* 62

nmrt 'splendour' *Ugar.* V no. 2 rev. *l.* 8 [Akk. *namurratu*]

ns [√*nws*] G 'fled' **4** iii 5 Gt 'moved to and fro' **2** iv 4 [Hebr. *nās* 'fled'; Arab. *nâsa* 'moved to and fro']

nsk G 'poured' **3** B 40 C 13 D 68 **17** vi 36

nsˁ G 'pulled up, plucked' **2** iii 17 **6** vi 27 **19** 160

nˁl 'sandal' **4** i 37

nˁm 'gracious, charming, pleasant' **5** iii 15 **10** ii 16 **14** 144 **23** 23 *Ugar.* V no. 2 rev. *l.* 12

nˁm 'grace, charm' **14** 145 **16** iii 7 'fair piece' **16** v 29 'pleasant place' **3** C 28 **10** ii 30 iii 32

nˁm 'tunefulness of voice' RS 22.225 *l.* 2 [cp. Ps. lxxxi 3; Arab. √*nˁm*]

nˁm 'minstrel' **3** A 19 **17** vi 32 **23** 17

nˁmy 'pleasantness, pleasure' **5** vi 6 **17** ii 41

nˁmn 'gracious, charming' **14** 40 **17** vi 45 **18** iv 14 **24** 25 'fine' *Ugar.* V no. 3 rev. *l.* 3

nˁr D 'shook' *Ugar.* V no. 7 *l.* 65

nˁr 'boy' *Ugar.* V no. 1 rev. *l.* 3

nġ̌ṣ G 'shook, brandished' **4** vii 41 [cognate *nġṣ*]

nġṣ G 'convulsed, shook' **3** D 31 **4** ii 19 N 'quivered, trembled' **2** iv 17 [Arab. *naġaḍa* 'shook' (trans. and intrans.)]

nġr G 'watched, protected, guarded' **1** v 12 **6** iv 47 **4** viii 14 **23** 68 [Hebr. *nāṣar*; Arab. *naẓara*]

np place-name **3** F 9

npyn 'garment' **4** ii 5 [‖ *mks*, *md*]

npk 'spring, well' **14** 113 [cp. *mbk*]

npl G 'fell' **2** i 9, 15 iv 5 **5** vi 8 **12** ii 37 Gt 'fell' **14** 21

npṣ 'garment' **17** i 34 **19** 206 [Arab. *nifâḍu* 'smock']

npr G 'fled, dispersed' **19** 120 (Arab. *nafara*)

npr 'sparrow' **6** ii 37 [Arab. *naffâru*]

npš 'spirit, breath, life' **6** iii 19 **16** vi 34 **17** i 37 **18** iv 25 'appetite, desire' **5** i 14 **6** ii 17 **17** v 17 'throat' **4** vii 48 **5** i 7 **16** i 35 vi 11 'grave' **2** iii 20

nṣb G 'set up, fixed' **16** i 52 N 'took one's stand' **17** i 27

nṣḥ 'success, triumph' **19** 85 [M.-Hebr. *niṣṣāḥôn*]

nṣr G 'sobbed' **16** vi 5 [Syr. *nṣar* 'chirped, squeaked, grunted']

nqbn 'trapping(s)' or 'strap' **4** iv 11 **19** 54 [Hebr. *nāqab* 'pierced' or *niqpāh* 'rope']

nqd 'shepherd' **6** vi 55

nqmd name of king of Ugarit **4** viii E **6** vi 56

nqpt and *nqpnt* 'revolution, cycle of years' **12** ii 46 **23** 67 [Hebr. *nāqap* in Isa. xxix 1]

nrt [√*nwr*] 'light, lamp' **2** iii 15 **3** E 25 **6** i 8 etc.

nrt [√*nyr*] 'plough-land' **16** iii 10

nš [√*nšy*] G 'forgot' **5** i 26

nšȧ G 'lifted up' **2** i 27 iii 15 **3** D 32 **4** ii 12 **6** i 14 **14** 75 etc. Gt 'raised oneself' **17** v 6 **19** 21

nšb **1** v 6 *Ugar.* V no. 1 obv. *l.* 10

nšg 'sheath, case' **19** 207 [Arab. *nasaja* 'wove, plaited']

nšm pl. 'men, mankind' **3** C 24 **4** vii 51 **6** ii 18

nšq G 'kissed' **17** i 40 **23** 49, 51 D 'kissed' **2** iv 4 **19** 64 **22** B 4

nšr 'eagle' **2** iv 13 **18** iv 17 **19** 114

ntb 'path' **17** vi 43

ntk G 'poured forth' **19** 82 N idem **14** 28

ntn 'giving (voice)' **16** i 4 [elsewhere only √*ytn*]

ntr Š 'made to start up' **22** B 11 [Hebr. *hittîr*]

ntk N 'bit one another' **6** vi 19 [Hebr. *nāšak*]

ntk 'bite' *Ugar.* V no. 7 *passim*

ntq 'weapons' **4** vii 39 [Hebr. *nešeq*]

sȧd G 'served' **3** A 3 **17** v 20, 30 [‖ ˁ*bd*, *šlḥm*]

sȧn 'hem' or similar **6** ii 10

sb [√*sbb*] G 'went round' **5** vi 3 **16** iii 3 **19** 68 'was turned, changed' **4** vi 34 N 'was turned, changed' **4** vi 35

sgr G 'barred, closed' **14** 96 *Ugar.* V no. 7 *l.* 70

sgrt 'closed room' **3** E 20

sd 'council' **20** A 4 [Hebr. *sôd*]

shr **20** B 11

sk [√*skk*] 'covering' **16** ii 93

skn Š 'took care of, supervised, prepared' **4** i 21 [Tell Am. Akk. *sakānu ana*; Hebr. *hiskîn* in Ps. cxxxix 3]

skn 'steward' **17** i 27 [Hebr. *sōkēn*]

sknt 'image, appearance' **4** i 43 [see p. 56 note 7]

smd a product **22** B 19

smkt 'height(s)' **16** i 35 [Arab. *samku*]

snnt 'swallow' **17** ii 27 **24** 41 [Akk. *sinuntu*]

ssw 'horse' **14** 128 **20** B 3

ssn 'grape or fruit cluster' *Ugar.* V no. 7 *l.* 66 [Akk. *sissinnu*]

sˁ [√*sˁy* or *swˁ*] G 'ran' or 'swept' **14** 111 [Arab. *saˁâ(y)* 'ran' or Hebr. *sāˁāh* fem. adj. 'sweeping (wind)' in Ps. lv 9]

sġsġ 'setting, sinking' **24** 3 [Arab. *tasaġsaġa* 'went underground']

sp [√*spp*] 'bowl, basin' **14** 148

spȧ G 'fed, supplied' **17** i 32 N 'was fed, ate' **5** i 5 **6** v 20 **20** B 10 [M.-Hebr. *sāpâ* 'fed (another)']

spù 'feeding' **6** vi 11, 15 **20** B 10

spsg 'glaze' **17** vi 36 [Hittite *zapzaga(y)a*]

spr G 'counted' **4** viii 8 **17** ii 43 vi 29 D 'recited' **23** 57 Š 'made to count' **17** vi 28

spr 'scribe' **6** vi 53 **16** vi E

spr 'number' **14** 90 **24** 45 'message, letter' **1** ii 24

srnm place-name **22** B 18

str G 'hid' **4** vii 48

ˁ*bd* G 'served' **3** A 2

ˁ*bd* 'slave, servant' **2** i 36 **4** iv 59 **5** ii 12 etc.

ˁ*bṣ* G 'hastened, hurried' **3** C 15 D 55 [Imp. Aram. ˁ*bq*]

ˁ*br* G 'crossed, passed' **3** F 7, 8 **22** B 15

ˁ*bš* **22** B 7

ˁ*gl* 'calf' **1** iv 31 **3** D 41 **5** v 4 **15** i 5

ˁ*glt* 'heifer' **5** v 8

ˁ*d* [√ˁ*dy*] prep. 'to, till' **4** v 110 **5** vi 4 **6** vi 47 **14** 64 **19** 176 conj. 'until' **3** B 29 '*d* [√'*dy*?] conj. 'while, as' **5** iv 12 **6** i 9

'*d* [√?] 'time' **12** ii 46 **23** 67 [‖*šnt*]

'*d* 'dais, platform' **16** vi 22 **23** 12 [Arab. '*ûdu*]

'*db*, also '*žb* G 'made, prepared, did' **4** iv 7 viii 17
14 80 **17** v 16 **23** 54, 63 *Ugar.* V no. 7 *l.* 71 etc.
[Hebr. '*āzab* and S.-Arab. '*ḏb* 'restored']

'*db* G 'left, released' **6** i 51 **17** v 27 **18** iv 22, 33
[Hebr. '*āzab*]

'*dbt* 'preparation(s)' **4** vi 38

'*dd* D 'recounted' **5** iv 25 tD 'responded' **4** iii 11
[Arab. '*adda* 'counted']

'*dd* 'herald' **4** vii 46 ['*dd* Zakir inscr. A 12]

'*dy* D 'removed' *Ugar.* V no. 7 *l.* 66 Š 'removed'
16 v 43 [Aram. '*addî*; Hebr. *he*'*ĕdāh*]

'*dm* [√'*wd*] 'again' **15** vi 2

'*dn* 'time' **4** v 68 **12** ii 53 [Akk. *adannu*; Aram.
'*iddānâ*]

'*dn* 'host, multitude' **14** 85, 87 [Arab. '*adânatu*
'numerous party']

'*dr* **4** vii 7 [but see apparatus]

'*dt* [√'*y*'*d*] 'appointed time' **4** vii 16 'assembly'
15 ii 7, 11 'confluence' *Ugar.* V no. 7 *l.* 3

'*dṭ* [√'*dy*] 'scurf, scale' *Ugar* V no. 7 *l.* 66 [Aram.
'*ādîtâ*]

'*žb*, also '*db* G 'made, prepared' **12** ii 27

'*žbt* '(building) wares' **4** v 76 [Hebr. '*izzābônîm*]

'*žr* G 'helped' rescued' **18** i 14

'*wr* 'blind' **14** 99 **19** 167

'*z* [√'*zz*] G 'was strong' or adj. 'strong' **2** iv 17
6 vi 17 *Ugar.* V no. 4 *l.* 18

'*z* 'strength, protection' *Ugar.* V no. 2 rev. *l.* 9

'*ṭr* 'scent' **16** v 45 [Arab. '*aṭaru*]

'*ṭrṭr* a crop **16** iii 11 [‖ *ḥṭt, ksm*]

'*žm* 'bone' **19** 117ff. 'strength, might' **2** iv 5 **12** i 24

'*žm* 'mighty, huge' **3** A 12

'*l*, also '*ln* prep. 'over, upon, because of etc.'
3 A 21 B 10 **4** ii 33 vii 50 **6** v 17 **16** vi 48 **19** 14
etc. 'by, in the presence of' **2** i 21 'into the
presence of' **15** iv 17 **16** i 17 vi 39 'from'
16 vi 9 ['*l* 'from' Ahiram inscr. *l.* 2, Mesha inscr.
l. 14; Hebr. '*al* 'from' in Ps. iv 7 lxxxi 6 Job xxx 2]

'*l*, also '*ln* adv. 'above, on top' **17** ii 9 **19** 208

'*l* [√'*wl*] 'child' **6** iv 43 **19** 197 [Hebr. '*ăwîl* = Arab.
'*ayyilu* 'member of a family']

'*ly* G 'went up' **4** i 24 **6** i 57 **14** 73 **17** i 15 etc.
Š 'brought up' **6** i 15 'offered up' **19** 185
'sent up, discharged' **14** 116 'allowed to mount'
5 v 21 Št 'moved oneself up and down' **23** 31

'*ly* adv. 'on high' **23** 3

'*ly* 'high god' a title of Baal **16** iii 6

'*llmy* **22** B 10

'*llmn* **1** iv 5

'*lm* 'eternity' **2** iv 10 **3** E 39 **5** ii 12 **14** 55 **19** 154
Ugar. V no. 2 obv. *l.* 1

'*ln*, also '*l* prep. 'over, upon' **3** E 41 **6** vi 22

'*ln*, also '*l* adv. 'above, over' **3** D 31 **4** i 38

'*lṣ* G 'was jubilant' **2** i 12

'*m*, also '*mm*, '*mn* 'with' **3** C 21 **5** i 22 v 8 **24** 44, 48
etc. 'like' **6** i 51 **17** vi 28 'to, towards' **2** i 14
3 D 55 E 39 **4** iv 21 **6** vi 12 **24** 16 etc.

'*m* [√'*mm*] pl. 'ancestors' **17** i 28 [Hebr. '*ammîm* in
Gen. xxv 8]

'*md* **7** II 22

'*mm*, also '*m*, '*mn* 'to' **14** 302

'*mm* G or D 'darkened, veiled' **8** 8 [Hebr. *hû*'*am* 'was
dimmed'; Arab. *ǵamma* 'covered, hid']

'*mn*, also '*m*, '*mm* 'with' **3** C 22 **5** v 20 **24** 32

'*ms* G 'loaded, hoisted' **6** i 12 D 'carried, supported'
17 i 31 *Ugar.* V no. 1 obv. *l.* 18

'*ms* G or D 'cemented, constructed' **4** v 73 [Hebr.
'*ōmēs* 'bricklayer' in Neh. iv 11; Arab. *ǵammasa*
'set in cement']

'*mq* 'valley' **3** B 6 **5** vi 21

'*mq* 'deep, wise, strong' **17** vi 45 [Akk. *emqu*]

'*mr* 'straw' **5** vi 14 [Hebr. '*āmîr* 'sheaves', M.-Hebr.
'hay'; Arab. √*ǵmr*]

'*mt* G 'struck' **16** vi 8 [Arab. '*amata*]

'*n* [√'*yn*] G 'eyed, saw, regarded' **3** A 15 B 23 D 83
4 ii 27 vii 53 etc. tD(?) 'eyed each other' **6** vi 16

'*n* [√'*yn*] 'eye' **2** iv 22 **4** ii 12 vii 40 **6** iv 42 **14** 149
etc.

'*n* [√'*yn*] pl. '*nt* 'spring, well, source' **3** D 80 **5** i 17
12 ii 60 **16** iii 4 RS 22.225 *l.* 5

'*n* [√'*ny*] pl. '*nt* 'furrow' **6** iv 25 **16** iii 9 [Hebr.
ma'*ănāh*]

'*ny* G 'answered' **1** iv 13, 16 **2** i 28 iv 7 **5** i 11
16 v 13 etc.

'*ny* G 'was humbled' **16** vi 58 **19** 12

'*nn* 'attendant, lackey' **2** i 35 **3** D 76 **4** iv 59 viii 15
[‖ '*bd*]

'*nn* 'clouds' **10** ii 33

'*nq* **22** B 19

'*nt* the goddess 'Anat' sister of Baal **2** i 40 **3** B 4 etc

'*nt* [√'*ny*] 'now' **19** 154, 161, 168 [Hebr. '*attāh*]

'*s* [√'*ss*] G 'travelled by night' **4** iv 34 [Arab. '*assa*]

'*p* [√'*wp*] G 'flew' **10** ii 11, 23 **18** iv 42 **19** 150
L 'fluttered eyelids at' **4** ii 10

'*p*'*p* 'eyelid' **14** 147, 295

'*pr* pl. '*prt* 'dust' **1** iv 8 **2** iv 5 **3** C 12 **5** vi 15
17 i 29

'*pt* [√'*wp*] 'bird(s)' **22** B 11

'*ṣ* 'tree(s)' **3** C 20 **4** iv 38 vi 18 **23** 66 *Ugar.* V
no. 7 *l.* 64

'*ṣ* [√'*ṣy*] G 'pressed on, strove' **3** C 15 [Hebr. *h*'*ṣh*
'strive' (imper.) (Ben Sira iv 28); Syr. '*ṣâ* 'resisted']

'*ṣr* 'bird' **3** D 45 **6** ii 36 **14** 70 **23** 38

'*q* 'eyeball' or similar **14** 147 [‖ '*p*'*p*]

'*qb* pl. '*qbt* 'heel, hock' **17** vi 23

'*qb* D 'held back, hindered' **18** i 19

'*qltn* 'twisting, wriggling' **3** D 38 **5** i 2

'*qq* 'ravenous beast' **12** i 27 [Arab. '*aqqa* 'rent']

'*qšr* epithet of snake *Ugar.* V no. 7 *passim* [cp.
Hebr. '*iqqēš* 'twisted', *qāšar* 'bound']

'*r* [√'*wr*] G 'roused oneself' **6** vi 31 L 'roused'
4 iv 39 **24** 30

'*r* [√'*yr*] 'he-ass' **4** iv 9 **19** 52

'*r* [√?] 'city' **4** vii 7 **14** 110 **16** v 48 **22** A 4 etc.

'*rb* G 'entered' **3** C 6 **5** ii 3 **14** 26 **17** ii 26 **23** 62
etc. Š 'brought in to, introduced' **14** 204 **15** iv 17
[Akk. *erēbu*; Arab. *ǵaraba* 'departed']

'*rb* 'minister' **23** 7

'*rb* 'setting (of sun)' **15** v 18 **19** 210

'rgz a drug **20** A 8 **24** 43

'rẓ 'terrible, tyrant' **6** i 54 **12** ii 31 [Hebr. *'ārîṣ*]

'rẓ verbal form **12** ii 31

'ry 'bare' **16** ii 91

'rk G 'arranged, prepared' *Ugar.* V no. 1 rev. *l.* 4

'rs N 'was tired' **18** iv 15 [Arab. *'arisa*]

'r'r 'tamarisk' *Ugar.* V no. 7 *l.* 64

'rpt 'cloud' **2** iv 8 **4** v 70 vii 19 **8** 11 **19** 39, 106 [Akk. *urpatu*; cp. Hebr. *'ărāpel*]

'rš 'bed' **14** 98 **16** vi 35 **17** i 39 ii 41

'šy G 'turned' or 'abused' **17** i 30 [Hebr. *'āśāh* 'turned' in Ruth ii 19 1 Sam. xiv 32 Ezek. xxix 20, 'abused, disturbed' in Prov. vi 32 Ezek. xxiii 3, 21; Arab. *'aśâ 'an* 'turned away from', *'aśiya 'alâ(y)* 'wronged']

'šy 'fit, suitable' **17** vi 8 [Arab. *'asîyu*]

'šr D 'prepared a banquet, held a feast for' **3** A 9 **16** i 40 **17** vi 30 [Arab. *'ašara* 'was tenth member of a party'; Eth. *'aššara* 'invited to a feast']

'šrt 'banquet, feast' **16** i 41

'tk D 'stuck, fastened' **3** B 11 [Arab. *'ataka* 'clung, stuck']

'tk name of monster **3** D 41

'tq G 'moved, passed' **6** ii 5 **16** i 2

'tq 'old man' **16** i 5

'ttr the god 'Athtar' **2** iii 12 **6** i 54 **24** 28

'ttrt the goddess 'Athtart' consort of Baal **2** i 40 iv 28 **14** 146 *Ugar.* V no 2. obv. *l.* 2 no 7 *l.* 20 and E as place-name (?) *Ugar.* V no. 7 *l.* 41

ġb 'having an ague' **12** ii 40 [Arab. *ġibbu* 'tertiary fever']

ġb 'cloud' *Ugar.* V no. 3 obv. *l.* 8 [Hebr. *'āb*]

ġdd D 'swelled' **3** B 25 [Arab. *ġuddida* 'was affected with a swelling']

ġz [√*ġzy*] G 'raided' **16** vi 43 [Arab. *ġazâ*]

ġzr 'youth, hero, warrior' **3** A 20 B 22 **4** vii 47 **16** i 46 **17** i 2 etc. [Hebr. *'ēzer* in Ps. lxxxix 20 (if correctly pointed)]

ġẓy G 'winked at, sought favour of, entreated' **4** ii 11 iii 26 [‖ *mgn*; Arab. *ġaḍâ(y)* and *ġaḍḍa* 'lowered, shut (eyes), blinked'; Hebr. *'āṣāh* 'narrowed (eyes)']

ġyr [√*ġwr*] 'lowland, marsh' **3** D 80

ġl 'thicket, reed-bed' **17** vi 23 [Arab. *ġîlu*]

ġly G 'drooped' **19** 31, 160 D 'lowered' **2** i 23 **3** A 1 [root unknown; opposite *nśâ*]

ġll D or L 'plunged' **3** B 13, 27 **19** 156 [Hebr. *'ôlēl* 'thrust in'; Arab. *ġalla* '(was) inserted']

ġll 'thirsty' **12** ii 35 [Arab. *ġalîlu*]

ġll place-name **22** B 19

ġlm 'lad, page' **2** i 13 **3** B 4 **4** ii 29 **14** 19 etc. [Heb. *'elem*]

ġlm G 'hid' **16** i 50 [Hebr. *ne'ĕlam* 'was hidden']

ġlmt 'lass' **14** 204 **24** 7

ġlmt 'concealment, obscurity' **4** vii 54 **8** 7

ġlp 'shell, husk' **19** 19, 204 [Arab. *ġilâfu*]

ġlt [√*ġly*] 'lowering, weakness' **16** vi 32

ġmʾ G 'was thirsty' **4** iv 34 [Hebr. *ṣāmē'* = Arab. *ẓamiʾa*; cp. *mẓmâ*]

ġnb 'grapes' **19** 42 **23** 26 [Hebr. *'ēnāb*; Arab. *'inabu*]

ġnt *Ugar.* V no. 2 obv. *l.* 11

ġṣr G 'confined, bounded' **4** viii 4 [Hebr. *'āṣar* 'restrained']

ġr 'rock, cliff' **2** i 20 **3** B 5 C 26 **4** v 77 vii 5, 32, 37 etc. [Hebr. *ṣûr* = Aram. *ṭûrâ*]

ġr 'skin' **5** vi 17 **19** 173 [Hebr. *'ôr*]

ġr [√*ġwr*] G 'sank down' **2** iv 6 [Arab. *ġâra*].

ġr [√*ġyr*] Gt 'was jealous' **24** 28 [Arab. *ġâra*]

ġr [√*ġyr*] 'rival' **16** vi 31, 44

ġrmn 'vengeance, punishment' **3** B 11 [Arab. *ġarima* 'payed a debt']

ġrt I iii 9 **10** ii 30

ġš **10** i 8 [truncated?]

p 'then, so' **4** iv 59 **5** i 14, 19, 26 **14** 142 **17** i 6 **19** 154 etc. [Old Aram. *p*; Arab. *fa*]

p 'mouth' **4** viii 18 **10** iii 10 (?) **16** v 46 **19** 9, 75 **23** 62

pḍlt 'parched ground' or the like **19** 61 [‖ *âklt*]

pȧm pl. *pȧmt* 'time, occurrence' **23** 20 [Hebr. *pa'am*]

pȧt 'edge' **12** i 35 **14** 193 **23** 68 [Hebr. *pē'āh*; Aram. *pâtâ*]

pȧd 'heart, kindness' **4** ii 10 **5** vi 12 **6** iii 4 **16** iv 10 etc. [Arab. *fu'âdu*]

pȧt dual *ptm* 'brow, temple' **6** vi 38 **16** vi 8 **17** ii 9 [Hebr. *pē'āh*; Aram. *pâtâ*]

pbl name of king of Udm **14** 119 etc.

pd [√*pdd*] G 'crushed, crumbled' **5** i 5 [Arab. *fatta*]

pd 'lock of hair' **19** 80 [Arab. *fawdu*]

pdr 'town' **4** vii 8 **14** 111 **16** vi 7 [‖ *'r*]

pdr name or title of Baal **3** A 25

pdry name of one of Baal's daughters **3** A 23 C 3 **4** i 17 etc.

pẓ 'gold' **2** i 19 [Hebr. *paz*; Aram. *pizzâ*]

ph [√*phy* or *pwh*] G 'saw, perceived' **2** i 22 **3** A 14 D 29 **19** 62 etc. 'experienced' **6** v 12 'considered' **15** iii 28 'was percipient' **16** iv 2 [cp. Syr. *phâ* 'was distracted, occupied with' or Arab. *bâha* 'understood']

pḥl 'he-ass' **4** iv 5 **19** 53 'foal' *Ugar.* V no. 7 *l.* 1 [Akk. *puḥâlu* = Arab. *faḥlu* 'stallion']

pḥlt 'mare' *Ugar.* V no. 7 *l.* 1

pḥm 'coal' **4** ii 9 **23** 39

pḥd 'young beast(s)' **17** v 17 [Akk. *puḥâdu* 'lamb, kid']

pḥyr 'entirety' **14** 25 [‖ *tm*]

pḥr 'assembly' **2** i 14 **4** iii 14 **15** iii 15 **23** 57 'meeting, union' RS 22.225 *l.* 6 [Akk. *puḥru*]

pṭr G 'departed, escaped' **16** vi 8

pẓġ G 'gashed', **19** 173 [Hebr. *pāṣa'*, Aram. *pṣa'* 'split']

pl [√*pll*] G 'was cracked' or noun 'cracked ground' **6** iv 25 [Arab. *falla* 'was notched' or *fallu* 'waterless desert']

plg N 'was divided' *Ugar.* V no. 7 *l.* 69

plg 'channel, water-course' *Ugar.* V no. 7 *l.* 69

plṭ D 'delivered, saved' **18** i 13

ply N 'was separated, distinguished' *Ugar.* V no. 3 obv. *l.* 2

plk 'whorl of spindle' **4** ii 3

pltt 'wallowing' **5** vi 15 [Hebr. *hitpallēš* 'wallowed']

pn '(beware) lest' *Ugar.* V no. 1 obv. *l.* 12

pn [√*pny*] G 'turned oneself' RS 22.225 *l.* 5

pnm pl. 'face, presence, front' **2** iii 4, 16 **3** A 6 D 31,

86 **4** v 84 **16** i 52 etc.

pnm adv. '(in) front' **4** iv 17 'inside, within' **16** vi 5

pnt 'vertebra, joint' **2** iv 17 **3** D 31 **19** 95 [Hebr. *pinnāh* 'corner, pinnacle']

pslt 'flint' **5** vi 18 [Hebr. *pāsal* 'hewed']

pʻ [√*pʻy*] G 'cried, bleated' **19** 13 [Syr. *pʻâ*]

pʻn 'foot' **2** i 30 **3** C 16 F 18 **4** iv 25, 29 v 83 etc. [Akk. *pēnu* 'leg'; Hebr. *paʻam* 'foot']

pʻr G 'proclaimed' **1** iv 15 **2** iv 11 **12** i 28 [Hebr. *pāʻar* 'opened (the mouth)']

pǵt name of Daniel's daughter **19** 34 etc. also apparently 'girl' **15** iii 7

pq [√*pyq*] G 'was supplied with' **4** vi 56 'found, obtained' **14** 12 Gt 'supplied oneself with' **1** v 27 Š 'supplied (another) with' **4** vi 48 [Hebr. *pāq* 'obtained', *hēpîq* 'supplied']

pqd G 'commanded' **16** vi 14

pqq Ugar. V no. 1 rev. *l.* 5

pr [√*pwr*] G 'broke, violated' **15** iii 30 N 'was shattered' **2** i 12 [Hebr. *hēpîr* 'broke']

pr [√*pry*] 'fruit' **5** ii 5

prbḫt personal name **24** 49

prsḥ 'collapsed' **2** iv 22 [Akk. *pulasuḫu, purasuḫu* 'to collapse']

prst **22** A 15

prʻ 'first-fruits' **17** v 37 **22** B 24 [Arab. *faraʻu* 'firstling']

prʻ 'shoot' **19** 18 [Akk. *pirʻu*; Arab. *farʻu*]

prʻt 'princess' **8** 9 [Hebr. *peraʻ* 'prince'; Arab. *farʻu* 'chief']

prṣ chink, breach' **23** 70

prq G 'parted, opened' **4** iv 28 [Arab. *faraqa*]

pršd **4** i 36

prt [√*prr*] 'cow' **5** v 18

pšʻ 'transgression, rebellion' **17** vi 43

pt [√*pty*] D 'enticed, seduced' **23** 39

pt **24** 9 [truncated?]

ptḥ G 'opened' **4** vii 17 **15** iv 5 **16** vi 11 **23** 70

ptḥ 'opening, doorway' Ugar. V no. 7 *l.* 71

ṣảt [√*yṣả*] 'going forth, issue' **3** B 8 **16** i 35

ṣỉn 'sheep' **4** vi 41 **5** iii 22 **6** i 22

ṣb [√*ṣby*] G 'coveted, desired' **17** vi 13 [Syr. *ṣbâ*]

ṣbṭ 'concealment, darkening' **15** v 19 **16** i 36 **19** 209 [Arab. *ʼaḍbaʼa* 'concealed']

ṣbủ 'army, host' **14** 86 pl. 'soldiers' **3** B 22

ṣbrt 'band, company' **3** E 45 **4** ii 25 [M.-Hebr. *ṣibbûr*]

ṣd [√*ṣw*/*yd*] G 'chased, hunted' **12** i 34 **17** vi 40 **23** 16 'scoured' **5** vi 26 **6** ii 15 Ugar. V no. 2 obv. *l.* 12

ṣd 'hunt, chase, game' **17** v 37 **18** i 27 **22** B 11 Ugar. V no. 1 obv. *l.* 1

ṣdynm (for *ṣdnym*) 'Sidonians' **14** 199

ṣdq 'rightness, lawfulness' **14** 12

ṣhl G 'shone' **17** ii 9

ṣḥ [√*ṣwḥ*] G 'cried out (to), called, invited' **1** iv 2 **3** D 33 E 44 **4** v 75 etc. [Hebr. *ṣāwaḥ*]

ṣḥq, also *ẓḥq* G 'laughed' **4** iv 28 v 87 vii 21 **6** iii 16 etc.

ṣḥq 'laughter' **3** B 25

ṣhr 'yellow, tawny' **6** v 4

ṣhr **12** ii 44

ṣhrr 'glowed, turned brown' **4** viii 22 **6** ii 24 **23** 41 [Arab. *ṣaḥara* 'boiled (milk), struck the brain of (sun)', *iṣḥârra* 'dried up, assumed a tawny colour', *ṣaḥrâʼu* 'burning desert']

ṣhrr 'glowing, blazing' **8** 10

ṣyt Ugar. V no. 3 obv. *l.* 10 [truncated?]

ṣly D 'prayed' **19** 39 [Aram. *ṣallî*]

ṣmd G 'bound, yoked' **4** iv 5 **19** 53 **20** B 3 **23** 10

ṣmd 'mace, club' or similar weapon **2** iv 11 **6** v 3 [Hebr. *ṣemed* 'yoke']

ṣml name of female eagle **19** 135

ṣmt D 'silenced, vanquished' **2** iv 9 **3** B 8 D 41 **12** ii 35

ṣmt 'silence, stillness' **18** iv 38

ṣʻ 'bowl' **3** B 32 **5** i 21 **15** v 7 [Aram. *ṣaʻâ*]

ṣʻd G 'advanced' **10** iii 8 **23** 30 [Hebr. *ṣāʻad*]

ṣǵr 'small, young' **15** iii 16 **22** B 4 **24** 50

ṣǵrt 'youth' **10** iii 27

ṣp [√*ṣpy*] 'gaze, glance' **14** 149

ṣpn name of Baal's mountain **3** A 22 **5** i 11 **6** i 16 **16** i 7 etc. of Baal himself **19** 84

ṣpr G 'whistled' **14** 123 [Arab. *ṣafara*]

ṣṣ [√?] Š 'pecked' **3** D 45 [from context]

ṣq [√*ṣwq*] Š 'constrained' **6** ii 10

ṣr [√*ṣwr*] G 'besieged' **14** 133

ṣr 'Tyre' **14** 198

ṣrk G 'lacked, failed' **19** 43 [Aram. *ṣrak*]

ṣrr 'radiance, sheen' **16** i 5 [Akk. *ṣarāru* 'to flash (star)']

ṣrrt 'recess(es)' **3** A 21 **4** v 117 **6** i 16 [cp. Arab. *ṣirâru* 'height not reached by water'; Akk. *ṣurru* 'heart, interior']

ṣrrt 'door-pivot, lintel' **16** i 43 [Akk. *ṣerru*; cp. Hebr. *ṣîr*, Aram. *ṣîrtâ*]

ṣrt [√*ṣrr*] 'emnity; foe(s)' **2** iv 9 **3** D 34

ṣt 'cloak' **17** i 14 [|| *mỉzrt*; cp. Akk. (*a*)*ṣîtu* a garment]

qbảt **6** vi 39

qbẓ for *qbṭ* G 'mixed' Ugar. V no. 4 *l.* 13 [Arab. *qabaṭa*]

qblbl 'lace(s)' **4** i 37 [Arab. *qibâlu*]

qbʻt 'goblet' **19** 216

qbṣ 'gathering, assembly' **15** iii 4, 15

qbr G 'buried' **6** i 17 **19** 111

qbr 'grave' **16** ii 87 **19** 150

qbt [√*yqb*] 'vat' **6** iv 42 [Hebr. *yeqeb*]

qdm D 'went before, advanced' **15** iv 23

qdm 'before, in front of' **3** D 85 **4** vii 40 'east' Ugar. V no. 7 *l.* 62 'east wind' **12** i 8

qdmy 'easterner' **14** 34

qdqd 'head, crown' **2** iv 21 **3** E 32 **4** vii 4 etc.

qdš 'holy' **3** A 13 **4** vii 29 **16** i 7

qdš 'holiness' as title of Athirat **16** i 11, 22 *bn qdš* 'holy ones' or 'sons of Athirat' **2** i 21, 38 **17** i 4 'holy place, sanctuary' **3** C 27 **14** 197 **17** i 27 **23** 65

qdš name of Athirat's servant **4** iv 16 more fully *qdš-*(*w*)*-ảmrr* **3** F 11 **4** iv 8, 13

qṭr 'smoke, vapour, spirit' **17** i 28 **18** iv 26

qẓ [√*qyẓ*] 'summer(-fruit)' **19** 18, 41 **20** A 5 **24** 2

qẓb G 'cut up, off' **5** ii 24 [Arab. *qaḍaba*; cp. Hebr. *qāṣab*]

ql [√*qwl*] 'voice, sound, message' **3** A 20 E 18 **4** v 70 vii 29 **14** 121 *Ugar.* V no. 7 *ll.* 2ff.

ql [√*qyl*] G 'fell, fell down' **2** iii 6 iv 23 **3** C 7 **6** vi 21 **16** vi 57 **19** 3, 109 etc. Š 'brought down, felled' **4** vi 41 **16** vi 32 **23** 10 [Akk. *qâlu* 'fell'; Arab. *'aqâla* 'cancelled (a debt)']

qlṣ G or D 'despised, abased' **4** iii 12 [|| *wpt*; cp. Hebr. *qillēs*]

qlṣ 'contempt' **3** E 36 **18** i 17

qlt [√*qyl*] 'abasement, humiliation' **6** v 12

qlt [√*qll*] 'disgrace' **4** iii 15

qm [√*qwm*] G 'stood, rose up' **2** i 21, 31 **3** A 4 **4** iii 13 **10** ii 17 D 'caused to rise' **22** B 5

qm 'adversary' **10** ii 25

qmm **19** 9

qmṣ G 'curled up' **14** 35 'skipped' **4** vi 43 **22** B 14 [M.-Hebr. *qamṣûṣ* 'squatting'; Arab. *qamaṣa* 'leapt, sprang']

qn 'reed, stalk' **17** vi 23 'windpipe' **4** viii 20 'humeral bone' **5** vi 20 [Hebr. *qāneh*; Aram. *qanyâ*]

qn **17** vi 9

qny G 'acquired, got, possessed' **14** 57 **19** 220 'framed, forged' **17** vi 41

qny 'creator' **10** iii 6

qnyt 'creatress' or 'mistress' **4** i 23 iii 26 etc.

qnṣ Gt 'crouched, stooped, travailed' **23** 51, 58 [cognate *qmṣ*; cp. Eth. *qanaṣa* 'leapt']

q'l place-name **3** F 8

q'l **22** B 16

q't 'shout, cry' **24** 48 [Syr. *q'âtâ*]

qṣ [√*qṣṣ* or *qṣy*] G 'carved, cut up' **3** A 8 *Ugar.* V no. 1 obv. *l.* 2

qṣ 'end, edge' **6** ii 11 **16** iii 3 [Arab. *qaṣâ* 'was remote']

qṣm 'locust' **3** B 10 [Arab. *qamaṣu*]

qṣ't 'arrow(s)' **10** ii 7 **17** v 13 **18** iv 13 **19** 15 [Hebr. *m'quṣṣā'* 'angular' and Arab. *miqṣa'u* 'sharp']

qṣr 'short' **16** vi 34

qr [√*qwr*] 'source, well' **12** ii 61 **16** i 27

qr 'rumbling sound' **14** 120 [Arab. *qarqara* 'cooed, rumbled, grumbled']

qr [√*qrr*] G 'hissed' **17** vi 14 [Arab. *qarra*]

qrả G 'called, called upon, invited' **4** vii 47 **5** i 23 **21** A 10 **23** 1, 23 etc.

qrb G 'approached' **4** viii 16 **14** 37 **15** iii 20 **16** ii 79 etc. D 'brought near, introduced' **24** 27 Š 'brought near' **16** i 44

qrb 'midst' **4** iv 22 v 76, 124 vii 13 **17** i 26 etc. 'private parts' **11** 1

qrd 'hero, warrior' **3** C 11 **5** ii 11 etc. [Akk. *qarrādu, qurādu*]

qry G 'met' **3** B 4 [Hebr. *qārāh* 'met'; Arab. *qarâ(w)* 'sought, followed']

qry G or D 'offered, presented' **3** C 11 D 66 **19** 191 [|| *š'ly*; Arab. *qarâ(y)*, Eth. *'aqāraya*]

qryt, also *qrt* dual *qrytm* 'city' **3** B 7 **14** 81 [Aram. *qirytâ*]

qr-mym place-name **19** 151

qrn pl. *qrnt* 'horn' **10** ii 21 **12** i 30 ii 40 **17** vi 22 **18** iv 10

qr' 'stick' *Ugar.* V no. 1 obv. *l.* 8 [Arab. *qara'a* 'struck with a stick']

qrṣ G 'gnawed' **12** i 11 'pinched' **16** v 29

qrš 'massif' **2** iii 5 **3** E 16 etc. [M.-Hebr. *qāraš* 'became hard, solid, frozen']

qrt, also *qryt* dual *qrtm* 'city' **3** B 20 **4** viii 11 **14** 117 **19** 164 **23** 3 [Phoen. *qrt*]

qrt-ảblm place-name **18** iv 8 **19** 163

qš 'chalice' **3** E 41 **4** iv 45 [|| *ks*]

qšt 'bow' **3** B 16 **10** ii 6 **12** ii 33 **17** v 2 **19** 4 etc.

qt 'handle' **4** i 42 [Aram. *qattâ*]

qt [√*qtt*] G 'dragged out' **2** iv 27 [Arab. *qatta* 'dragged, pulled out']

qtqt [√*qtt*] 'tore out' *Ugar.* V no. 1 obv. *l.* 5

rìmt 'coral(s)' **3** C 1

rìš pl. *rảšm, rašt, rìšt* 'head, top' **2** i 6, 23, 27 **3** D 39 **5** vi 15 **6** i 60 etc.

rù [√*r'y*] 'appearance' **3** A 12

rùm 'wild ox' **4** i 44 **5** i 17 **6** vi 18 etc.

rb [√*rbb* or *rby*] G 'is, was great' **4** v 65

rb [√*rbb*] 'great' **3** D 36 **4** ii 33 **6** v 2 **14** 134 etc. 'chief' **6** vi 54

rb, also *rbb* 'shower of rain' **3** C 4 **4** i 18 **5** v 11 [Hebr. *r'bîbîm*]

rbb, also *rb* 'shower of rain' **3** B 39 D 88 **19** 44

rbbt, also *rbt* 'myriad(s)' **4** i 29

rb' D 'took as fourth' **14** 17 Š 'made fourfold' **17** v 3, 12-13

rb' 'fourth' **4** vi 26 **14** 106 **17** i 9 etc.

rb't 'quarter' **19** 83

rbt [√*rbb*] 'lady' **3** E 48 **4** i 14 **16** i 36 **23** 54

rbt, also *rbbt* 'myriad(s)' **4** i 29

rgbt *Ugar.* V no. 4 *l.* 18

rgm G 'said, told, recited' **2** i 16, 45 **3** C 8, 17 D 76 **4** v 74 **16** i 20, 31 etc. [Akk. *ragāmu* 'to cry, call']

rgm 'tale, word, speech' **2** i 42 **3** C 17 D 75 **4** vi 3 **19** 75 etc. 'roaring' **15** v 13 vi 7

rdyk **1** ii 4 [truncated?]

rdmn name of deity **3** A 2

rz'y **21** A 5

rḥ [√*rwḥ*] 'wind' **5** v 7 **18** iv 25, 36

rḥ [√*rwḥ*] 'scent' **3** B 2 [Hebr. *rêaḥ*]

rḥb 'broad, wide' **16** i 9

rḥbt 'tun, cask' or the like **4** vi 53 **6** i 66 **15** iv 16

rḥd **4** iii 8

rḥm dual 'mill-stones' **6** ii 34 v 15 [Hebr. *rēḥayim*]

rḥm 'was kind, merciful' **16** i 33

rḥm 'girl, damsel' **6** ii 27

rḥmy title of Anat **15** ii 6 **23** 13, 16, 28

rḥṣ G 'washed, washed oneself' **2** iii 20 **3** B 32 **14** 63 **16** vi 10 **17** i 34 Gt 'washed oneself' **14** 62 **19** 203

rḥq G 'was distant, withdrew' **4** vii 5 **14** 132 Š 'removed' **3** D 84

rḥq 'distant, afar off' **1** iv 3 **3** D 78 **4** vii 33

rḥt 'palm of hand' **4** viii 6 **5** v 14 [Arab. *râḥatu*]

rḥnt(t) **4** v 67

rḫp D 'hovered, soared' **18** iv 21, 31 **19** 32 *Ugar.* V no. 2 obv. *l.* 8

rẓ [√*rwẓ*] G 'ran' **6** i 50

rkb G 'rode, mounted' **2** iv 8 **3** B 40 **14** 74

rks G 'bound' **1** v 10 *PRU* II no. 3 *l.* 9

rm [√*rwm*] G 'was high, rose' **15** iii 13 **16** ii 88 **23** 32 L 'raised, erected' **2** iii 10 **4** v 114 vi 17

rm 'high, exalted' **8** 9 *Ugar.* V no. 2 obv. *l.* 7

rm [√*rmy*] Š 'threw down' **17** vi 15 [Aram. *'armî*]

rs [√*rss*] 'breaking, crushing' **5** i 4

r'y 'shepherd' **21** A 6 **22** B 27 *Ugar.* V no. 2 obv *l.* 3

r't Ugar. V no. 3 obv. *l.* 4

rġb G 'was hungry' **4** iv 33 **7** I 10

rġn G 'turned green' *Ugar.* V no. 7 *l.* 61 [Hebr. *ra'ănān* 'green']

rp [√*rpy*] tD 'made oneself slack, drooped' **5** i 4

rpủ G apparently 'became a shade' **14** 7 'healed' *Ugar.* V no. 1 rev. *l.* 3

rpù the deity 'Rapiu' (=Baal) **17–19** passim (in title of Daniel) **22** B 8 *Ugar.* V no. 2 obv *l.* 1

rpủm 'shades' **6** vi 45 **15** iii 14 **20–22** passim

rṣ [√*rṣy*] G 'was pleased, consented' **16** i 45

rq 'thin plate' **4** vi 34 [Arab. *raqqaqa* 'flattened (metals)']

rqṣ Gt 'danced' **2** iv 13 [Arab. *raqaṣa*]

rš [√*ršš*] G 'crushed, shattered' **14** 10, 22

ršp the deity 'Resheph' **14** 19 **15** ii 6 *Ugar.* V no 7 *l.* 31

rt 'shabbiness, dirt' **16** v 29 **17** i 34 [Arab. *ratta* 'was shabby, soiled']

rtủ 'curdled milk' **1** iv 9 [Arab. *ratî'atu*]

rtt 'net' **4** ii 32 [Hebr. *rešet*]

šủb G 'drew (water)' **6** i 66 **12** ii 60 **14** 113 **16** i 51

šủl G 'asked' **14** 38

šủr Gt 'was left' **18** iv 15

šỉ [√*š'y*] 'desolate place, waste land' **1** v 26 [Hebr. *šā'āh* 'was ruined, deserted']

šỉy 'desolate' **12** i 22

šỉy **18** iv 23

šỉr 'flesh' **6** ii 35 RS 22.225 *l.* 3

šb [√*šby*] G 'took captive' *PRU* II no. 3 *l.* 8 Gt 'was taken captive' **3** D 37

šb [√*šyb*] 'old man' **3** B 16 [Hebr. *śāb*]

šbḫ, also *špḫ* 'progeny, family' **14** 290

šby 'captive' **2** iv 29

šblt 'ear of corn' **19** 18, 69

šbn place-name **6** vi 53

šb' 'seven' **3** B 2 D 39 E 19 **5** i 20 **6** v 8 **14** 8 etc. 'seventh' **4** vi 32 **14** 108

šb' D 'did for seventh time' **16** v 20 'took as seventh' **14** 20

šb' G 'was satisfied, sated' **3** B 19 **6** i 9 **17** i 32 **23** 64 D 'satisfied' **4** vii 51

šb'd 'seven times' **23** 12, 14 [*šb'* + *ỉd*]

šb'm 'seventy' **4** vi 46 **5** v 20 **6** i 18 **12** ii 49 etc.

šb'r [√*b'r*] 'torch' **4** iv 16

šbš D 'attracted, wheedled' *Ugar* V no. 4 *l.* 6 [Aram. *šabbēš*]

šbt [√*šyb*] 'grey hair' **3** E 10 **4** v 66 [Hebr. *śêbāh*]

šgr deity of cattle **5** iii 16 [Hebr. *šeger* 'offspring of cattle']

šd a surface area **3** D 82 **4** v 118 **17** v 10 etc. [Akk. *šiddu*]

šd [√*šdy*] 'field' **3** C 14 **5** vi 7, 28 **6** ii 17, 34 **14** 104, 111 **19** 210 etc.

šd [√*šdy*] G 'poured' **6** iv 42 Gt 'was poured' **6** iv 49 [Aram. *šdâ*]

šdmt 'vine-terrace' **2** i 43 **23** 10

šdt **2** iii 11

šḥw reduplicated t-form 'prostrated oneself' **2** i 15 **3** C 7 **4** iv 26 etc.

šḥl 'shore' **5** v 19 vi 7 **6** ii 20 [Arab. *sâḥilu*]

šḥr 'dawn' **12** i 7 name of god of dawn **23** 52 *Ugar.* V no. 7 *l.* 52

šḥt 'bush, shrub' *Ugar.* V no. 7 *l.* 65 [Hebr. *śîaḥ*]

šḥṭ G 'slew' **18** iv 24

šḥn G 'was feverish' **12** ii 39 [Arab. *saḥana*]

šḥp 'milk, colostrum' **10** iii 26 [Syr. *šḥāpâ*]

škb G 'lay, lay down' **5** v 19 **14** 34 **17** i 5

škllt 'enclosure' **16** ii 90 [Akk. *šuklultu*]

škn G 'settled on, stationed oneself' **14** 104 **16** i 43 Gt 'occupied for oneself' **4** vii 44 **6** iv 26

škr G 'hired' **14** 97 N 'hired oneself out' **14** 98 [Hebr. *śākar*]

škr 'drunkenness' *Ugar.* V no. 1 obv. *l.* 4

škrn 'drunkenness' **17** i 31

šlw G 'reposed, rested' **14** 149

šlḥ G 'sent, put forth, bestowed' **2** iii 24 **15** iv 24 **17** vi 18, 28 **24** 21

šlḥ 'spear' **14** 20

šlyṭ 'master, tyrant' **3** D 39 **5** i 3 [Hebr. *šālaṭ*]

šlm 'peace' **23** 7, 26

šlm 'peace-offering' **3** B 32 C 13 **14** 130

šlm name of god of dusk **23** 52 *Ugar.* V no. 7 *l.* 52

šm pl. *šmt* 'name' **1** iv 14 **2** iv 11, 28 **23** 18 etc.

šmủl 'left hand, side' **2** i 40 **23** 64

šmḫ **5** ii 25 *Ugar.* V no. 4 *l.* 16 [variant of *šmḫ*?]

šmḫ G 'rejoiced' **3** E 29 **4** ii 28 **6** i 39 **16** i 14 etc.

šmḫt 'joy' **3** B 26

šmym 'heavenly beings' **19** 186

šmk place-name **10** ii 9

šmm 'heavens' **3** A 13 C 21, 23 E 26 **5** i 4 **14** 76 etc.

šmn 'oil' **3** B 31, 39 **6** iii 6 **16** iii 16 etc.

šmn adj. 'fat' **15** iv 15

šm' G 'heard, obeyed' **2** iii 17 **4** v 121 **5** v 17 **6** i 44 etc. Gt 'hearkened' **16** vi 29, 42

šmt [<*šmnt*] 'fat' **19** 110 ff.

šmt 'cornaline' or other precious stone **23** 21 [also in non-mythological texts]

šn [√*šny*] G 'changed (place), departed' **3** D 77 [Syr. *šnâ*]

šn [√*šnn*] pl. *šnt* 'tooth' **19** 9 'ivory' **19** 189

šn **12** ii 42

šnủ G 'hated' **4** iii 17

šnù 'enemy' **4** vii 36

šnw G 'shone' RS 22.225 *l.* 1 [Arab. *sanâ*]

šnm element in name of composite deity *tkmn-w-šnm* (q.v.)

šnn G 'sharpened (tongue)' **16** i 13 ii 97

šns D 'tied, bound' **3** B 12 [Hebr. *šinnēs*]

šnt pl. *šnm*, *šnt* 'year' **4** iv 24 vi 43 **6** v 8, 9 **12** ii 45 **16** vi 58 etc. [Hebr. pl. *šānîm*, *šānôt*]

šnt [√*yšn*] 'sleep' **14** 33 **19** 151

š'r 'barley' **19** 51 [Hebr. *śe°ōrāh*]

š'tqt name of female demon **16** vi 1 [lit. 'she has removed']

šph, also *šbh* 'progeny, family' **14** 24, 144 **16** i 10 [Hebr. *mišpāhāh*]

špk G 'poured out, spilled' **7** II 7 **18** iv 23

špl G 'was low' **23** 32

špm **1** ii 11 **23** 4

špr Ugar. V no. 2 obv. *l.* 10

špš 'sun' **3** B 8 **14** 107 **15** v 18 **24** 3 name of sun-goddess **2** iii 15 **3** E 25 **6** i 9 vi 22, 44 *Ugar.* V no. 7 *passim*, etc. [cp. Hebr. *šemeš*]

špt 'lip' **5** ii 2 **19** 75 **22** B 4 **23** 49 **24** 46

šqy G 'gave to drink' **3** A 9 **17** i 11 **19** 215 Š 'gave to drink' **17** ii 30 v 19

šql Gt 'started, betook oneself' **3** B 18 **6** vi 41 **17** ii 25 *Ugar.* V no. 1 obv. *l.* 17 no. 7 *l.* 68 [Syr. *'eštqel*]

šr [√*šyr*] G 'sang' **3** A 18 C 2 **17** vi 31 **24** 1 etc.

šr [√*šry*] G 'let loose' **4** v 71 'encamped' **14** 110 [Aram. *šrâ*]

šr [√*šrr*] 'navel(-string)' *Ugar.* V no. 1 rev. *l.* 5

šr [√*šrr*] 'prince' **12** ii 51 **23** 22

šr element in divine name *mt-w-šr* **23** 8

šrg G 'lied' **17** vi 34 [Arab. *saraja*]

šryn 'Sirion' **4** vi 19, 21

šrk **15** v 17 [or *šr+k*]

šr' 'watering' **19** 45 [Hebr. *śe°îrîm* 'rain-drops' in Deut. xxxii 2; dial. Arab. (Transjordan) *ša'râ* 'watering by rain']

šrp G 'burnt' **6** ii 33 v 14

šrr 'assured, sure' **2** iv 33 **19** 85 [Syr. *šar(r)îr*]

šrr 'in secret' **16** vi 7 [Arab. *sirran*]

šrš 'root, scion' **17** i 20 **19** 159

ššrt **5** v 3

št 'bottom' **3** B 5 [Hebr. *šāt* 'foundation'; Hebr. *šēt*=Arab. *situ, istu* 'seat, buttocks']

št [√*šyt*] G 'set, put' **2** iv 27 **3** C 12 D 69, 85 **4** ii 8 iii 14 iv 5, 14 v 123 **5** v 5 **6** i 15 etc.

št [√*šty*] G 'drank' **4** iii 16, 40 **5** i 25 **6** i 10 **19** 219 **23** 6 etc.

št 'Lady' as title of Anat **18** iv 27 **19** 215 **23** 61 [Arab. *sittu*]

štk G **12** ii 59 Gt **12** ii 58 [or from *š(y)t*?]

tầnt [√*'ny*] also *tûnt* 'groaning, sighing' **3** C 21

tỉdm 'rouge' **19** 204

tỉntt 'womankind' **17** vi 40 [cp. *ảtt*]

tûnt [√*'ny*] also *tầnt* 'groaning, sighing' **1** iii 14

tb' G 'departed' **2** i 13 iii 8 **4** iv 19 **5** i 9 **14** 14, 300 etc. [Arab. *taba'a* 'followed']

tbth 'couch' **4** i 30 [Akk. *tapšāhu*]

tgh [√*ngh*] 'lighting up, shining' **16** i 37

tgr **1** iv 12

tdmm 'lewd behaviour' **4** iii 22

tdrq 'fast approach' **3** D 83 **4** ii 15 **17** v 11 [Arab. *daraqa* 'hurried on']

thw 'waste' **5** i 15 [Hebr. *tōhû*]

thm, also *thmt* 'ocean' **23** 30 *Ugar.* V no 7 *l.* 1

thmt, also *thm* 'ocean' **3** C 22 **4** iv 22 **17** vi 12 **19** 45 *Ugar.* V no. 7 *l.* 3 [Akk. *ti'āmtu*; or plur.]

thm [√?] 'message, decree' **2** i 17 **3** C 10 **4** iv 41 **5** i 12 **14** 125 etc. [Syr. *thûmâ* 'boundary; precept'; cp. Arab. *hummatu* 'divine decree']

tht 'beneath, under' **2** iv 7 **3** B 9 D 80 **6** vi 45 **17** v 6 **19** 109

tk [√*twk*] 'within' **2** i 14 **3** C 26 **4** iii 13 v 117 **15** iii 14 etc. 'before' **3** D 85 'towards' **2** i 20 **3** F 13 **4** viii 11 **5** v 12 etc.

tkm **12** i 20

tl [√*tly*] 'quiver, holder' **16** i 52

tl [√*tll*] 'hill' **4** viii 4

tlỉyt [√*l'y*] 'victory' **3** C 28 **10** iii 29 **19** 84 *Ugar.* V no. 3 obv. *l.* 3

tlm 'furrow, ridge' **16** iii 11

tlm **19** 7

tl' 'gnawing creature' **2** iv 4 [Hebr. *tôlā'* 'worm']

tlš name of maidservant of Yarikh **12** i 14

tm [√*tmm*] G 'came to an end' **23** 67

tm [√*tmm*] 'entirety' **14** 24

tmd 'continually' **19** 153

tmn 'form' **2** iv 18, 26 [Hebr. *te°mûnāh*]

tnmy **1** iv 9

tnn 'dragon' **3** D 37 **6** vi 50 **16** v 31 *PRU* II no. 3 *l.* 8

tsm [√*ysm*] 'beauty' **14** 146

t'dt [√*'wd*] 'embassy' **2** i 22ff. [abstract for concrete; cp. Hebr. *te°ûdāh* 'testimony']

t'lt [√*'ly*] 'high estate' **4** ii 4

t'rt [√*'ry*] 'glove' (for falconry) **18** iv 18 'scabbard' **19** 207 [Hebr. *ta'ar* 'sheath']

tğ [√*tğy*] G 'journeyed afar' **4** iv 33 [Hebr. *tā'āh* 'wandered']

tğzyt [√*ğzy*] 'oblation (to gain favour)' **6** vi 44

tp [√*tpp*] 'tambourine' RS 22.225 *l.* 2 *Ugar.* V no. 2 obv. *l.* 4

tph [√*nph*] 'apple' **20** B 11

tq' G 'applauded' **24** 49

tr [√*trr*] G 'shook, trembled' **4** v 83 vii 31 **10** ii 11, 28 **16** iii 2 [Akk. *tarāru*; Arab. *tatartara*]

tr [√*trr*] G 'drove away' **6** vi 52 [Arab. *tarra*]

tr **16** ii 74, 77 [verbal form?]

trbṣ(t) 'stable(s)' **14** 56, 141

trh G 'brought a bride-price, betrothed, married' **14** 14 **23** 64 **24** 18

trh 'married man' **14** 100

trẓẓ **16** i 49

trmmt [√*rwm*] 'contribution, offering' **6** vi 43 [Hebr. *te°rûmāh*]

tr' **12** ii 43

trğzz name of mountain **4** viii 2

trt, also *mrt* 'new wine' **5** iv 20 **17** vi 7 *Ugar.* V no. 1 obv. *l.* 4 [Hebr. *tîrôš*]

tšyt 'triumph, success' **3** B 27 [Hebr. *tûšîyāh*]

tš'm 'ninety' **4** vii 12

ttl place-name **24** 14 *Ugar.* V no. 7 *l.* 15

tảr, also *t'r* G 'set (the table), arranged' **3** B 37 D 'caused (the table) to be set' **2** iii 16, 21

tảt 'ewe' **6** ii 7, 29 [Old Aram. *š*ʾ*t*; Imp. Aram. *tʾt*ʾ]

tỉgt, also *tỉqt* 'roaring, bellowing' **14** 120 [Hebr. *šeʾāgāh*]

tỉṭ 'mud' **17** i 34 [Arab. *taʾṭatu*]

tỉqt, also *tỉgt* 'roaring, bellowing' **14** 223

tỉr 'kinsman' (?) **18** i 25 [Arab. *taʾara* 'sought blood revenge']

tb [√*twb*] G 'turned' **4** vii 8 RS 22.225 *l.* 7 'returned' **4** vi 2 **6** vi 12 'did again' **4** v 104 **19** E **23** 29, 56 'gave reply' **3** D 65 **4** iii 10 **19** 181 **20** B 8 'paid attention' **3** E 7 **17** vi 42 **18** iv 16 Š 'sent, brought back' **14** 136 *Ugar.* V no. 1 rev. *l.* 2

tbr G 'broke' **2** i 7, 13 iii 18 **3** D 30 **16** i 54 etc.

tbrn 'breach' **4** viii 19 **6** ii 23

tbš **22** B 6

tbt [√*ytb*] 'dwelling, seat' **3** F 15 **4** viii 13 **5** iii 2 **6** vi 28 **14** 23

td, also *žd*, *zd* 'breast, teat' **3** A 6 **4** vi 56 **12** i 11 [Hebr. *šad*=Arab. *tadyu*]

tdt 'sixth' **4** vi 29 **14** 84, 107 **17** i 12 [Arab. *sâdisu*]

tdt D 'did for sixth time' **16** v 19 'took as sixth' **14** 19

twy D 'entertained' **16** vi 44 [Arab. *tawwâ(y)* 'detained', ʾ*atwâ(y)* 'entertained']

tkḫ G 'was hot (sexual)' **11** 1 **24** 4 'burnt up (sky)' **5** i 4 [from context]

tkl G 'was bereaved of' *Ugar.* V no. 7 *l.* 61 [Hebr. *šākōl*]

tkl 'bereavement' **23** 8

tkm 'shoulder' **14** 64, 75 **16** iv 14 **22** B 5

tkm G 'carried on the shoulder' **19** 50

tkmn-w-šnm composite deity *Ugar.* V no. 1 obv. *l.* 18

tkt 'ship' **4** v 69 [Egyp. *tkty*]

tlb 'flute' *Ugar.* V no. 2 obv. *l.* 4 [Akk. *šulpu*]

tlḫn pl. *tlḫnm*, *tlḫnt* 'table' **3** B 21 **4** i 39 iii 15 iv 36 **22** B 16 *Ugar.* V no. 1 obv. *l.* 6

tlḫ 'dowry' **24** 47 [Hebr. *šillûḫîm*]

tlt 'three' **3** D 80 **4** iii 17 **14** 55, 89, 95 etc. 'thrice' **14** 206 'three times' *Ugar.* V no. 7 *l.* 71 'third' (adj.) **4** vi 26 **14** 106 etc. 'third' (fraction) **15** ii 7

tlt D 'did for third time' **16** v 9 'harrowed' or similar **5** vi 20 'took as third' **14** 16

tm 'there' **2** iv 4 **14** 199 **22** B 4 **23** 66 [Hebr. *šām*=Arab. *tamma*]

tmk place-name **22** B 17

tmm **5** iii 13, 27

tmn 'eight' **3** E 34 **5** v 9 **12** ii 50 **17** v 2 **23** 19, 67 etc.

tmn Gt 'obtained eight' **15** ii 24

tmnym 'eighty' **4** vii 11 **5** v 21 **12** ii 50 **15** iv 7

tmq name of deity **22** B 8

tn 'scarlet' **10** iii 25 **23** 22 [Hebr. *šānî*]

tn masc. 'two' **3** D 79 **4** ii 6 iii 17 **14** 94 etc. 'double, twice' **14** 205

tn fem. *tnt* 'second' **4** vi 24 **14** 15, 106 **16** vi **22** etc. 'another' **14** 101

tny G 'repeated' **2** i 16 iv 8 **3** C 9, 19 F 22 **14** 27 etc. 'set aside' **15** iii 29 [cp. Arab. *tanâ(y)* 'deterred', ʾ*istatnâ(y)* 'excluded, set aside']

tnm 'twice' **18** iv 22 **19** 224

tnn D 'did twice, repeated' **16** v 8 [Hebr. *šinnēn* in Deut. vi 7]

tnn 'professional soldier, guard' **14** 91 **23** 7, 26 [Akk. (Alalakh) *s/šananu*]

tʿ 'noble, prince' title of Keret **14** 200 etc. [Hebr. *šôaʿ*]

tʿy 'master, supervisor' **4** viii E **6** vi 56 [Akk. *šuʾu* 'lord, master'; Hebr. *šāʿāh* 'gazed']

tʿr, also *tʾr* G 'set (the table), arranged' **3** A 4 B 20, 21, 36 **24** 35 [Eth. *šaraʿa*]

tǵr pl. *tǵrt* 'gate' **3** B 3 **16** i 52 ii 89 **17** v 6 'breach, entry' RS 22.225 *ll.* 6, 7 [Hebr. *šaʿar*]

tǵr 'gate-keeper' *Ugar.* V no. 1 obv. *l.* 11

tpd G or D 'placed, superimposed' **4** iv 29 **6** iii 15 [Arab. *taffada* 'lined (clothes)']

tpṭ, also *tpẓ* G 'judged' **16** vi 34 **17** v 8

tpṭ 'cause, case' **16** vi 34 **17** v 8

tpṭ 'judge' title of Yam **2** i 7 etc. of Baal **3** E 40

tpẓ, also *tpṭ* G 'judged' *Ugar.* V no. 2 obv *l.* 3

tṣr **20** B 11

tqb 'ash' or other tree **17** vi 20

tql 'shekel' **14** 29 **19** 83

tr [√*twr*] 'bull' **1** iv 31 **12** i 31 **15** v 13 **17** vi 23 as title of El **1** iv 12 **2** i 16 **3** E 7 **4** i 4 etc. 'duke, baron' **15** iv 6

trm G 'consumed food' **2** i 21 **16** vi 12, 18 [|| *lḥm*]

trm 'meal' **18** iv 19

trmg name of mountain **4** viii 3

trml 'onyx' or other precious stone **14** 148

trmn place-name **6** vi 57

trp *PRU* II no. 3 *l.* 4

trr 'well-watered' **14** 109 **15** iv 20 *Ugar.* V no. 7 *l.* 64 [Arab. *tarra* 'gave plentiful water']

trry **16** iv 16

tš [√*tšy* or *tšš*] G 'plundered, extorted' **16** vi 48 [Hebr. *šāsāh* or *šāsas*]

tt fem. of *tn* 'two' **16** ii 114

ttmnt name of Keret's youngest daughter **16** i 29

ttʿ G 'feared, dreaded' **5** ii 7 **6** vi 30 [Hebr. *šātaʿ* in Isa. xli 10, 23]

tt [√*tdt*] 'six' **4** vii 9

ttm [√*tdt*] 'sixty' **4** vii 9

Verbal forms of uncertain root:

1 v 19 *tšqb*

5 iii 5 *tkl*

5 iii 5 *tʿtd*

5 iv 19 *tttn*

6 v 23 *dḫẓ*[ ]

10 iii 28 *yrk*

11 3 *ynbd*

12 ii 57 *tttpq*

12 ii 58 *ttkn*

15 i 3 *tttkr*

16 ii 88, 96 *tnqt*

17 v 35 *yqb*

19 83 *ttp*[ ]

23 14 *ṭb*[ ]

23 37 *ymnn*

24 47-48 *yttqt*

Ugar. V no. 7 *l.* 66 *ysynh*

BIBLICAL AND OTHER REFERENCES

HEBREW BIBLE

Genesis
i 3-4 30
i 21 7
i 26 9
ii 6, 10ff. . . . 53
iii 22 . . . 9, 95
iii 24 . . 42, 127
iv 1 83
iv 10 77
iv 11-12 . . . 114
v 29 105
vi 2-4 . . . 109
vii 11 62
viii 22 . . . 45
xi 3 60
xiv 19 . . . 121
xviii 20 . . . 148
xix 1-11 . . . 104
xix 15 . . . 149
xxi 6 105
xxiv 11 . . . 85
xxiv 67 . . . 87
xxv 8 . . . 154
xxv 22 . . . 83
xxvii 28 . . 48, 66, 77
xxx 16 84
xxxi 40 . . . 116
xxxiv 12 . . . 128
xxxvii 34 . . . 115
xxxvii 35 . . . 74
xxxviii 18 . . . 119
xl 13 46
xli 25ff. . . . 18
xli 26 . . . 115
xli 35 . . . 84
xli 47, 54ff. . . 18
xlii 25 . . . 84
xlv 2 94
xlix 11 . . 58, 144
xlix 15 . . . 98
l 10 26

Exodus
i 5 63
i 15 27
iii 2 42
iii 8 77
iii 15 . . . 119
v 7 60
viii 15 . . . 93
x 1 122
xi 7 113
xii 11 . . . 119

xiii 9 44
xv 11 99
xv 15 92
xv 16 . . . 53, 110
xv 17 . . 39, 49, 55, 66
xv 18 . . . 45, 75
xxii 15 . . . 125
xxii 15-16 . . . 128
xxiii 19 . . . 123
xxvi 15ff. . . . 53
xxix 5 72
xxxii 20 . . 6, 19, 77
xxxiv 26 . . . 123

Leviticus
xxiv 11 6

Numbers
xvi 29 . . . 94, 109
xx 26 72
xxii 31 . . . 42
xxiii 10 . . . 109
xxvii 4 . . . 103
xxxv 17 . . . 85
xxxv 33 . . . 114

Deuteronomy
iii 9 63
vi 7 160
x 18 101
xii 2-3 . . . 49
xii 6, 11, 17 . . 81
xiv 1 120
xiv 21 . . . 123
xv 17 83
xx 7 84
xxi 1-9 . . . 119
xxi 16 92
xxi 19 . . . 107
xxiv 5 84
xxviii 28 . . . 119
xxxii 2 . . . 159
xxxii 3 . . . 123
xxxii 6 . . . 54
xxxii 8 . . . 86
xxxii 10 . . . 68
xxxii 13 . . . 65
xxxii 14 . . . 58
xxxii 32 . . . 123
xxxii 37 . . . 78
xxxii 39 . . . 112
xxxiii 2 . . . 64
xxxiii 11 . . . 150
xxxiii 17 . . . 80
xxxiii 20 . . . 68

xxxiii 25 . . . 144
xxxiii 29 . . . 143

Joshua
v 13 42
ix 14 84
xiii 4 10
xxiv 26 . . . 141

Judges
iv 19 121
v 4 . . . . 53, 65
v 4-5 64
v 25 . . . 39, 121
v 26 . . . 93, 148
vi 5 85
vii 12 85
ix 5 63
xvi 16 . . . 101
xvii 2 . . . 149
xvii 5 . . . 104
xix 22-26 . . . 104

1 Samuel
i 4 104
i 22 119
ii 5 84
ii 10 98
iii 1ff. . . . 103
iv 13 83
iv 21 78
ix 11 85
xiv 32 . . . 155
xvi 18 . . . 75
xxi 9 . . . 104
xxiii 1 . . . 54

2 Samuel
i 21 . . . 115, 119
i 24 39
vi 17 83
vii 2 61
vii 3 111
vii 7 61
vii 13 . . . 38, 39
vii 14 94
ix 3 86
xiv 25 . . . 75
xviii 18 . . . 103
xxi 1 . . . 114
xxi 17 . . . 23
xxi 5 66
xxii 5-6 . . . 66
xxii 7 53
xxii 8 65

xxii 9 143	xxii 18 47
xxii 14 60	xxii 21 72
xxii 39 117	xxiii 9 92
xxiii 1 46	xxv 8 19
xxiii 2–5 23	xxvii 1 . . . 7, 50
xxiv 16 42	xxxviii 16 147
	xxix 1 153

1 Kings

i 1–39 23	xxxii 6 76
ii 9 52	xxxiii 13 . . . 39, 65
ii 36, 42 78	xxxiii 22 54
v, vi 14	xxxviii 17 66
viii 27–30 14	xl 12 84
ix 16 129	xl 29, 31 75
xi 30 115	xli 10, 23 . . . 69, 160
xvii 1 . . . 77, 115	xliii 6 . . . 41, 76
xvii 14 98	xlvi 11 112
xviii 24 110	xlvii 1 73
xviii 25–29 . . . 13	xlvii 8–9 123
xviii 28 . . . 73, 120	li 9 . . . . 7, 69
xviii 29 100	li 10 8
xviii 42 41	li 18 104
xxi 19 44	lii 7 61
xxii 10 107	lvii 8 125
xxii 19 42	lvii 20 44
xxii 37 73	lviii 11 66
	lxiii 15 146
	lxvi 11 124

2 Kings

i 2 50	*Jeremiah*
iv 42 115	ii 6 78
v 7 . . . 109, 112	ii 27 49
viii 1 115	iv 13 84
ix 24 44	iv 29 119
x 1 63	viii 23 95
xv 5 . . . . 23, 66	ix 17–18 120
xxiii 12 84	ix 20 62
xxiii 34 4	x 13 60
xxiv 17 4	x 25 80
	xii 4 114
	xii 9 114

Isaiah

i 17 101	xv 7–8 123
ii 10, 19 65	xvi 6 . . . 73, 120
iii 3 122	xix 13 84
iii 7 146	xlvi 21 64
v 1 128	xlviii 18 73
v 14 . . . 66, 68	xlviii 37 73
v 24 68	l 27 92
v 25 79	
vi 1 ff. . . . 14, 42	*Ezekiel*
vii 14 . . . 87, 128	i 24 145
ix 5 . . . 53, 104	iii 14 152
ix 19 124	vii 7 64
x 2 102	viii 16–17 96
x 13 148	xiv 14, 20 26
xi 2ff. . . . 23	xvii 3, 7 94
xi 10 103	xvii 23 107
xiv 9 92	xxi 11 . . . 50, 117
xiv 12 29	xxiii 3, 21 155
xiv 13 . . . 40, 70, 76	xxvi 16 73
xv 2 73	xxvii 3 149
xvi 8 42	xxvii 30 73

xxviii 2 53	
xxviii 3 26	
xxix 4 69	
xxix 5 . . . 6, 19, 77	
xxix 20 . . . 104, 155	
xxx 8 7	
xxxii 14 77	
xxxiv 2 149	
xlvii 1 ff. . . . 53	

Hosea

ii 23–24 49
vii 5 90
viii 1 114
xi 6 80
xi 8 . . . 41, 76
xiii 8 68
xiv 5 79

Joel

ii 8 82
ii 11 60
iv 18 . . . 53, 77

Amos

i 1 81
i 3ff. . . . 79, 97
ii 9 119
iv 13 65
v 10, 12, 15 107
v 11 102
v 26 56
vi 11 68
viii 10 73
ix 9 79

Jonah

ii 3 66
ii 7 66

Micah

i 3 65
i 10 141
i 16 73
vii 8 70

Nahum

iii 15–17 85

Habakkuk

ii 5 . . . 66, 68
iii 8 7
iii 9 47
iii 10 115
iii 14 47
iii 17 . . 42, 69, 98

Zephaniah

i 5 84

Haggai
ii 22 38

Zechariah
ix 9 . . . . 59, 115
ix 13 112
x 1 84
x 8 149
x 9 77
xiii 6 44
xiv 8 53

Psalms
ii 6ff. 23
ii 7 94
ii 12 43
iv 7 154
vi 7 83
vii 11 98
viii 3 43
viii 4 126
ix 8 65
xi 4 14
xiii 5 70
xvi 7 101
xvi 9 48
xvi 10 66
xvii 3 103
xvii 15 . . . . 44, 103
xviii 5-6 66
xviii 7 53
xviii 8 65
xviii 9 143
xviii 14 60
xviii 39 117
xix 2-5 49
xx 3, 7 14
xxi 5 109
xxiv 7, 9 41
xxvii 4 14
xxix 1 58
xxix 2 86
xxix 3 50
xxix 6 . . . . 63, 150
xxix 10 65
xxx 2 70
xxx 10 66
xxxiii 11 119
xxxiii 19 76
xxxv 25-26 70
xxxvi 7 . . . . 49, 109
xl 3 . . . . 66, 135
xl 11 149
xli 4 101
xlii 2 68
xlii 4 78
xlii 8 49
xliii 3-4 14
xlv 3ff. 23
xlv 7 38
xlvi 7 60

xlviii 3 8
xlviii 11 98
xlix 15 . . . . 68, 80
xlix 16 148
lv 9 . . . . 85, 153
lvii 3 . . . . 144, 42
lvii 5 41
lviii 6 158
lviii 11 49
lxi 5 114
lxiii 12 102
lxiv 4 44
lxv 5 18
lxv 6 95
lxv 9 66
lxv 12 67
lxvi 6 3
lxviii 5 49
lxviii 7 . . . . 31, 143
lxviii 8-9 64
lxviii 9 . . . . 53, 65
lxviii 17 65
lxviii 18-19 64
lxviii 21 149
lxviii 23 . . . . 7, 50
lxviii 31 92
lxviii 35 98
lxxii 23
lxxii 10 42
lxxiii 5 75
lxxiii 9 69
lxxiv 13 . . . . 7, 44, 50
lxxiv 13-14 79
lxxiv 14 . . . . 6, 7, 19
lxxiv 15 7
lxxiv 15-17 7
lxxvii 19 65
lxxviii 54 49
lxxx 6 74
lxxx 11 109
lxxxi 3 153
lxxxi 6 154
lxxxi 17 66
lxxxii 1 91
lxxxii 2-4 102
lxxxii 6-7 . . . . 94, 95, 123
lxxxii 7 . . . . 73, 109
lxxxiv 2-5 14
lxxxiv 3 77
lxxxiv 12 149
lxxxvi 9 37
lxxxvi 16 83
lxxxviii 5 66
lxxxviii 7-8 66
lxxxviii 10 83
lxxxix 2 128
lxxxix 7 58
lxxxix 11 7
lxxxix 12ff. 7
lxxxix 20 155
lxxxix 20ff. 23

lxxxix 23 50
lxxxix 26 148
lxxxix 27f. 94
lxxxix 28 92
lxxxix 34 92
xcii 10 43
xciii 3 79
xciii 3-4 7
xciii 4 50
xcv 3 . . . . 54, 66
xcvi 5 72
xcvii 4 65
xcix 1 . . . . 65, 152
ci 1 128
ciii 5 66
civ 6 73
civ 14-15 98
civ 15 105
civ 24-26 7
cv 22 60
cx 23
cx 1 62
cx 5-6 79
cxiv 5 83
cxiv 5-6 65
cxv 2 78
cxvi 3 66
cxvi 16 69
cxxiv 3, 6 68
cxxv 3 123
cxxix 3 73
cxxxii 14 39
cxxxv 7 72
cxxxv 17 104
cxxxvi 13 124
cxxxix 3 153
cxxxix 4 116
cxxxix 7 78
cxxxix 18 109
cxl 11 68
cxli 7 67
cxliii 3 68
cxliii 12 43
cxlv 13 43
cxlv 16 66
cxlvi 4 112
cxlvi 10 75
cxlvii 8 98

Job
i 6 58
ii 1 58
iii 8 7
iv 19 68
v 1 . . . . 100, 110
v 7 82
v 10 98
v 21 143
vi 5 85
vi 18 68
vii 12 7

viii 12 . . . 114
ix 13 . . . 7
x 1 . . . 75, 112
xvii 14 . . . 101
xviii 13–14 . . . 68
xviii 16 . . . 119
xviii 20 . . . 65
xix 25 . . . 77
xx 17 . . . 77
xx 20 . . . 143
xxii 7–9 . . . 102
xxiv 19 . . . 66
xxvi 5 . . . 66
xxvi 7ff. . . . 7
xxvi 10–11 . . . 66
xxvi 12 . . . 7
xxvi 13 . . . 7
xxviii 1 . . . 83
xxviii 9 . . . 93
xxviii 11 . . . 53, 150
xxviii 13 . . . 49
xxix 12–13 . . . 101
xxx 2 . . . 154
xxxi 16–17 . . . 102
xxxii 9 . . . 60
xxxiii 6 . . . 68, 100
xxxiii 22 . . . 66
xxxvii 3 . . . 61
xxxvii 4 . . . 111
xxxvii 11 . . . 46
xxxvii 15 . . . 46
xxxviii 7 . . . 58
xxxviii 13 . . . 65
xxxviii 16 . . . 150
xxxviii 16–17 . . . 53
xxxviii 27 . . . 66
xxxviii 35 . . . 49
xxxix 2 . . . 106
xxxix 30 . . . 114
xl 24–26 . . . 69
xl 25ff. . . . 7
xl 28 . . . 69, 83
xl 31 . . . 69

Proverbs
i 5 . . . 109
i 9 . . . 78
i 12 . . . 66
v 9 . . . 102
vi 11 . . . 150
vi 16ff. . . . 58
vi 32 . . . 155
ix 5 . . . 123, 143
xiii 23 . . . 84
xiv 32 . . . 114
xvi 21 . . . 125
xviii 22 . . . 82
xxi 9 . . . 84
xxiii 5 . . . 117

xxiii 31 . . . 78
xxiii 32 . . . 80
xxiv 21 . . . 53
xxv 24 . . . 84
xxviii 12 . . . 40
xxx 10 . . . 110
xxx 15ff. . . . 97

Ruth
ii 19 . . . 154
iii 16 . . . 74, 83
iv 11, 13 . . . 87

Song of Songs
iv 9 . . . 111
vi 1 . . . 78
vii 5, 6 . . . 86
viii 6 . . . 80

Ecclesiastes
iii 13 . . . 86
vi 12 . . . 109
vii 26 . . . 152
xii 4 . . . 106

Lamentations
ii 10 . . . 41
ii 11 . . . 114
iii 55 . . . 66
iv 20 . . . 23

Esther
i 20 . . . 123

Daniel
iii 33 . . . 43
iv 31 . . . 43
vii 9 . . . 53
viii 5 . . . 44

Nehemiah
iv 11 . . . 145

1 Chronicles
viii 33 . . . 77
viii 36 . . . 80
xxi 27, 30 . . . 42
xxv 7 . . . 81

2 Chronicles
ii–iv . . . 14
xi 23 . . . 39
xxx 10 . . . 64
xxxi 3 . . . 104

APOCRYPHA

Ben Sira
iv 10 . . . 101
iv 28 . . . 154

xxxv 13–14 . . . 102
xliii 17 . . . 85

1 Maccabees
vi 34 . . . 58

NEW TESTAMENT

Matt. xxiv 28 . . . 114
Mark v 9 . . . 9
Mark vi 8 . . . 119
Luke xi 20 . . . 93
1 Cor. xv 26, 54 . . . 19
Revel. xiii 1 . . . 50

OTHER REFERENCES

Old Testament Pseudepigrapha
1 Enoch xxvi 2 . . . 53

Mishna
Sanhedrin iv 3 . . . 107
Aboth ii 7 . . . 58
Kelim xvi 7 . . . 120

Inscriptions
Ahiram . . . 38, 154
Eshmunazar . . 4, 65, 119
Gezer . . . 84
Hadad . . . 104, 121
Karatepe . . 69, 76, 92
Mesha . . . 149, 154
Pyrgi . . . 70
Sefire . . . 115, 119
Uruk . . . 148
Yehaumilk . . . 82
Yehimilk . . . 82
Zakir . . . 154
Zenjirli . . . 142 (bis)

Akkadian
Adapa . . . 117
Code of Hammurabi . 23, 101
Descent of Ishtar . 66, 127
Enuma Elish . . 6, 91
Gilgamesh 17, 25, 73, 84, 88, 100

Hittite
Elkunirsa . . . 11, 63

Greek
Odyssey . 25, 27, 56, 83

Quran
Sura xviii 59–63 . . . 53
Sura cix 4 . . . 85

ADDENDA

M. Dietrich, O. Loretz, J. Sanmartin, *Die keilalpha-betischen Texte aus Ugarit*, Teil 1, *Transkription* (Neukirchen-Vluyn 1976).

This important new edition of the Ugaritic texts based on a re-examination of the tablets in Paris, Aleppo and Damascus reached me after the present edition was in the printer's hands. The texts *CTA* **1–25** are numbered 1.1–1.25 and the other mytho-logical texts as follows:

CTA **26**	1.62		RS 22.225		1.96
27	1.45		Ugar. V no. 1		1.114
28	1.63		no. 2		1.108
PRU II no. 1	1.82		no. 3		1.101
no. 2	2.3		no. 4		1.133
no. 3	1.83		no. 5		1.113
PRU V no. 1	1.92		no. 6		1.124
no. 2	1.95		no. 7		1.100
no. 3	1.88		no. 8		1.107

The following readings, restorations and comments on scribal errors are particularly noteworthy (I do not include places where a reading recorded in my apparatus is supported in preference to one in my text nor minor disagreements about the marking of letters as certain or uncertain or the disposition of word-dividers.):

2 iii

2 [- - - - - - kpt]r.*lr*ḫq [.ỉ]l[m.ḫkpt.lrḫq]
3 [ỉlnym.ṫn.mṫpdm.tḥt.ʿnt.ảrṣ.ṫlṫ.mtḥ.ġyrm] (cp. **3** D 78–80 **1** iii 18–21)
9 *bt.k*[.ṣrrt.ṣ]pn (cp. **4** v 117)
10 . . . . . [ḥklm.ảlp.šd.ảḥd.]*bt*
11 [rbt.]k*mn*[.]ḥk[l] . . . . . (cp. **4** v 118–119)
20 *bn šnq* for *bn*[p]*šny*

1 iv

13 *lṭpn* with *p* written under *n*

2 i

10 ảb.*šnm* 'father of years'
15–16: see at 31
31 *qmm*.åṫr.ảmr 'they advanced (and) spoke'

3

A 1 ảl.*tġl* t[
11 *krpmm* corrected to *krpnm*
26 ỉm.klt (27) [kny]t.*w* (cp. **4** i 16)
B 25 *tddd* corrected to *tġdd*
31 *dt* error for *bt*
D 37 ỉštm.[-]-*h*
52 *ġrdm* corrected to *qrdm*
72 ảr - - bảrṣ
E 8: double line thereafter

18 y[ʿ]*n*.ỉ[l]
32 ảšhlk not ảšplk
52: missing *ca.* 15*ll.*

4

iv 41 ḥkmt
v 67 *dt*
89 *ytn*
127 is perhaps the last line
vi 8 *bhtm* not *bbhtm*
20 *hn.*[l]*bnn*
54: there is no sign of a final [ym], though there is space
vii 33 *rtq*[
38 *t* of *hdt* written over erasure
viii 13: only one divider after ḫḫ
30 *lbn*: letter erased after *n*

5

i 22 *kl* for *k*[n]
vi 4: *k* erased at end
11: letter erased at end

6

i 50 *yrq* rather than *yrẓ*
66 [- - -]ḫṧ.ảbn
67 [- - - -]*n.*ảbn (i.e. no reference to drawing water)
ii 7 *l*ʿ*glh*: the ʿ is written over another letter
36: second *y* erased at end
v 4 ṣġrm.*ymṣḫ* (i.e. no reference to henchmen of Mot)
5 py[ʿl.]b*l
22 ảḥd.bảḫk.šqn
23 hn. - ảḥẓ (or - nḥẓ).y[- -]l
24 ʿnt.ảkly[
vi 32 *bqlh.ytḫ* (or *yty*)[

14

7 ʿ*rwt* 'was laid bare'
16 *mtltt*: the *m* is written over erased *t*
20 ḥ erased at end
24 *bklhn*
27 ʿ*gmm* 'cries of grief': the ʿ is written over erased *p*
33 *tlủản* error for *tlủnn*
56 and parallel passages: *bt rbṣ*
58 *šrm* 'princes'
59 w[yṫ]b
99: two letters erased at end
112 *ḥtbt*: the final *t* is written over erased *h*
113 *bqr* error for *mqr*
175 [mg̈]*ủ* error for [mg̈]*d*
199 *ṣd*[y]*nm*
212 *brnn*: the *b* is erased and corrected to *g* (cp. 215)
213 *sʿt* (cp. 214) erased and first two letters of *šrnả* (error for *šrnn*) substituted

215 *grnm* error for *grnt*
217: two letters erased at end
244/5 [ìd]*w* error for [ìd]*k*

15

i   1 *rg̊b* for [*mrg̊*]*b*
    4 *mswnh* marked very doubtful
ii 8 *šr* for ʿ[*š*]*r*
v 17 [*k*]*rt*
   21 *wy*[ʿ]*ny*
vi 9: *ca.* 40 *ll.* missing

16

i 14 *nšmḫ*
   17 *àt* error for *àp*
   27 *mḫ* error for *my* 'waters'
   29 *bt* followed by two dividers
   30 *dån* . . . . . *lyttb*
   31 *åḫr.àl.*trgm.*làḫtk*
   32 ʿ*w*[-]*ṣlt* (or *llt*).*dm*
   43 *lk.šr.*ʿ*l*
v 32]*ytn*nh (i.e. no reference to dragon)
vi 6: two letters erased at end
   8 *hr* corrected to *pṭr*; *km* for *pṭm*
   32 *šg̊lt* corrected to *šqlt*

17

i 12 *ym* written twice then the first erased
   16 *mìzrth* with *h* crushed in
   17 *àbyn àt*
ii 41 m*ddt* . . . . . *hrt*
   44 *yrḫ.yrḫ* ṭn *yṣ̊ì*
v 30 *ḥ* erased at end
vi 12   ] - *yg̊*ʿ*p* for *mḫ g̊*ʿ*t*
   18 *wtn.qštk.*ʿ*m*
   19 [*btlt.*]ʿ*n*[*t.*]*qṣ̊*ʿ*tk*
   32 *n*ʿ*mn*
   35 *mm* error for *mt*

18

i 27   ]*lt.lk.tlk*
iv 4 *lkl*
   19 *b* erased at beginning of *wbn*
   26 *ùàp* error for *bàp*

19

   8 *ùṣb*ʿ*h* (error for *ùṣb*ʿ*th*).*kḫrṣ*
   11 *gpph* (error for *gprh*).*šr*
   12 *kmrm*
   17 *bmt* - *ḫmṣṣr* -
   18 *yḥ* for *yb*[*l*]
   66 *tìspp* corrected to *tìspk*
   86 *dnål.mdh* (or m*bh*) - -
   87 *rìš.rq*-t*ḫt*-ʿ*nt* yql.1.*tš*--.hwt.[*š*]*ṣàt krḫ*.*npšhm*
   88 *kìtl.brlt.*km[.qṭr.*båph*]
   93 *ìttl* corrected to *kìtl*
   113 *lyṣå* with letter erased under *y*
   115 *tg̊ln* error for *tqln*
   146 *yb* (error for *ybky*).*lyqẓ*
   172 *p*[*z*]*g̊* erased at end
   176 *š* erased at end

201 *npš.hy.mḫ*
203 *d.ttql.bym*
204 w.ṭk*m*
223 *ybl*
224 ends at second *tšqy*

23

14 *g̊zrm g.ṭb.gd* with *m* replacing a previous *ṭb*
    which has been erased
15 *dg̊ṭt*[.*dg̊*]ṭ*t*
51 *tqt*[*nṣn.w*] (cp. 58)
55 *mtqt*[m.mtqtm.klrmnm] (cp. 50 and the very
    long line 14)
57 *lṣlmm*[.]*wyšr* ʿ. . . for (at) the images, and the
    assembly shall sing'
62 *wy*ʿ*rb*

24

3 *bsrr špš*
5 *tld bkṭrt.ḫ* - [- - - *k*] (6) *trt*
15 *hll*[.*snn*]*wt*
29 *b*[*t.å*] (30) *bh*

1

v 20   ].*mbkm*

7

I obv. 5 *lṣbìm* h
II obv. 1 [*bt*]*lt*[.ʿ*nt*
   9 [- -]*yṣq šm*[*n*

8

14 *brt*[(i.e. no reference to lightning)

10

i 2 *hẓm*
iii 10 *blt* corrected to *btlt*
   11 *nḫt* error for *àḫt*
   23 *tḫbq.å*[*rḫ*
   24 *tḫbq.àrḫ*[
   26 *y*ʿ*l.šrh*
   27 - *bšḫp*
   28 *bg̊r* with *b* written over erased *tk*

12

i 33 *bn* corrected to *pn*
   36 *nn* corrected to *wn*
   37 ʿ*qmm* corrected to ʿ*qqm*
ii 5-6: cp. i 40–41
   22–23: cp. i 40–41
   54–56 are complete
   55 *k* (not *p*) erased at end
   56: for *dṣ* read *b*ʿ*l*
   57 *ìttk* error for *ìšttk* (cp. 58)

20

A 3 *km* (or *wm*) *tmtm*
   4 *b.kqrb*
   7   ]*pm*

22

A 18 *nzt* error for *nḥt*
B 7 *brkn* error for *ybrkn*
   10 *ḫḫ* for *y*
   19 *sm d*
   20 *ṭṣ* error for *ṭl*
   23 *tš* erased at end
   25 *bṣq*

PRU II no. 3

   3 [tṣ]*ủn*
   4 *ʿrp* (error for *tʿrp*; cp. 6)
   6 *tʿrp*
   8 *tản* error for *tnn*
   10 *lbnt*
   11 *tbʿn.ṣṣt*
   14 *tḥm*

RS 22.225

   1 *ʿnn* error for *ʿnt*

Ugaritica V

o. 1 obv.   5 *km*.klb
            8 (*bqr*)
           11 *ktp*: the *p* is written over an erased letter
           12 *pn* (error for *hn*).*lm*.*rlb* (error for *klb*)
           14 *ỉl*.wl
           21 *ỉl*.*k*m mt
   rev.   2 *tttb*.[*ả*]ḥd*h*
            3 *km*.*trpả*.ḥn *nʿr*
o. 2 obv.   2 [*ỉl*.]
            6 *gtr* error for *gtrt*
            9 [*bšm*]*m rm* (error for *rmm*)
           10 ḫ]*mr*
           15   ] - *ršp*
   rev.   7 *bžmrh*: the *h* is written over an erased *ỉ*
           8–9 *r*[p]*ỉ*
o. 3 obv.   7 *bt*
   rev.   2   ]*lẓr*.*ủr*[
o. 4 obv.   2 *npšm*
            4 *thwt*
            6: before *šbšt* a letter is erased
           13 *tmn*

   18 *bảbn*
No. 7 19 *ʿt* error for *ʿm*
   65 *ynʿrảh* error for *ynʿrnh*
   68 *h*⟨m⟩*t*
   73 *tn*.*km*. ⟨mhry. ⟩

Further Bibliography:

L. Badre and others, 'Notes ougaritiques I Keret', *Syria* 53 (1976), 95–125

W. Beyerlin (ed.), *Religionsgeschichtliches Textbuch zum Alten Testament* (Göttingen 1975) (selections)

C. M. Bowra, *Heroic Poetry* (London 1966) (omitted from bibliogr. sect. 7)

J. Clear, *Ugaritic Texts in Translation* (N.E. Dept., Univ. of Washington, Seattle 1976)

P. C. Craigie (ed.), *Ugaritic Studies 1972–1976* (Reprint of the 'Newsletter for Ugaritic Studies' nos. 1–10) (Calgary, Alberta 1976)

R. C. Culley (ed.), 'Oral tradition and Old Testament Studies', *Semeia* 5 (1976) (see also Culley's earlier book *Oral Formulaic Language in the Biblical Psalms* [Toronto 1967])

J. Heler, 'Die Entymythisierung des ugaritischen Pantheons im A.T.', *Theol. Lit.* 101 (1976) cols. 2–10

I. Jacobs, 'Elements of Near-Eastern mythology in Rabbinic Aggadah', *J. Jew St.* 27 (1977), 1–11

E. Lipiński in *Orient. Lov. Per.* 3 (1972), 106–109 [on *CTA* **13**] (omitted from bibliogr. sect. 5h)

J. C. De Moor 'Rāpi'ūma-Rephaim', *ZAW* 88 (1976), 323–345

R. A. Oden, 'The persistence of Canaanite religion', *Bibl. Arch.* 39 (1976), 31–36

W. E. G. Watson, 'Puzzling passages in the Aqhat taleʾ, *UF* 8 (forthcoming)

W. R. Watters, *Formula Criticism and the Poetry of the Old Testament* (Berlin 1976)

R. E. Whitaker, *A Formulaic Analysis of Ugaritic Poetry*, Unpublished Dissertation of Harvard University (I owe this reference to Mr Kenneth Aitken)

TABLE OF UGARITIC SIGNS

Column I gives the order in which letters appear in Ugaritic abecedaries (see *CTA* **186**: *PRU* II nos. 184, 185; Dietrich and others, *Die keilalph. Texte* nos. 5.4 and 5.6).

Sign no. 30 is not used in the mythological texts.

1	*à*		12	*k*	
(28)	*i*		14	*l*	
(29)	*ù*		15	*m*	
2	*b*		17	*n*	
3	*g*		19	*s*	
5	*d*		(30)	*ś*	
(16)	*ž*		20	*ʿ*	
6	*h*		(26)	*ġ*	
7	*w*		21	*p*	
8	*z*		22	*ṣ*	
9	*ḥ*		23	*q*	
(4)	*ḫ*		24	*r*	
10	*ṭ*		(13)	*š*	
(18)	*ẓ*		27	*t*	
11	*y*		(25)	*ṯ*	